Architecture as Civil Commitment

Architecture as Civil Commitment analyses the many ways in which Lucio Costa shaped the discourse of Brazilian modern architecture, tracing the roots, developments, and counter-marches of a singular form of engagement that programmatically chose to act by cultural means rather than by political ones.

Split into five chapters, the book addresses specific case-studies of Costa's professional activity, pointing towards his multiple roles in the Brazilian federal government and focusing on passages of his work that are much less known outside of Brazil, such as his role inside Estado Novo bureaucracy, his leadership at SPHAN, and his participation in UNESCO's headquarters project, all the way to the design of Brasilia.

Digging deep into the original documents, the book crafts a powerful historical reconstruction that gives the international readership a detailed picture of one of the most fascinating architects of the 20th century, in all his contradictory geniality. It is an ideal read for those interested in Brazilian modernism, students and scholars of architectural and urban planning history, socio-cultural and political history, and visual arts.

Gaia Piccarolo is Adjunct Professor of History of Contemporary Architecture and Landscape at the Politecnico di Milano and member of the editorial staff of the architectural magazine *Lotus International*. She received her PhD in History of Architecture and Urban Planning from Politecnico di Torino in 2010, with a thesis on Lucio Costa's public charges during the Vargas Era. She curated several exhibitions and published extensively on contemporary architecture and urban planning, with special reference to Brazilian modernism and the circulation of ideas and models between Europe and the Americas. Her research has been presented in Europe, the United States, Canada, and Brazil in the framework of international seminars and conferences.

Studies in Architecture Series
Series Editor:
Eamonn Canniffe, Manchester School of Architecture, Manchester Metropolitan University, UK

The discipline of architecture is undergoing subtle transformation as design awareness permeates our visually dominated culture. Technological change, the search for sustainability and debates around the value of place and meaning of the architectural gesture are aspects which will affect the cities we inhabit. This series seeks to address such topics, both theoretically and in practice, through the publication of high quality original research, written and visual.

Other titles in this series

Global Perspectives on Critical Architecture
Praxis Reloaded
Edited by Gevork Hartoonian

Healing Spaces, Modern Architecture, and the Body
Sarah Schrank and Didem Ekici

Douglas Snelling
Pan-Pacific Modern Design and Architecture
Davina Jackson

On Discomfort
Moments in a Modern History of Architectural Culture
Edited by Andrew Leach and David Ellison

On Surface and Place
Between Architecture, Textiles and Photography
Peter Carlin

Architecture, Death and Nationhood
Monumental Cemeteries of Nineteenth-Century Italy
Hannah Malone

Reconstruction and the Synthesis of the Arts in France, 1944–1962
Nicola Pezolet

For more information about this series, please visit: www.routledge.com/architecture/series/ASHSER-1324

Architecture as Civil Commitment
Lucio Costa's Modernist Project for Brazil

Gaia Piccarolo

LONDON AND NEW YORK

First published 2020
by Routledge
2 Park Square, Milton Park, Abingdon, Oxon OX14 4RN

and by Routledge
52 Vanderbilt Avenue, New York, NY 10017

Routledge is an imprint of the Taylor & Francis Group, an informa business

© 2020 Gaia Piccarolo

The right of Gaia Piccarolo to be identified as author of this work has been asserted by her in accordance with sections 77 and 78 of the Copyright, Designs and Patents Act 1988.

All rights reserved. No part of this book may be reprinted or reproduced or utilised in any form or by any electronic, mechanical, or other means, now known or hereafter invented, including photocopying and recording, or in any information storage or retrieval system, without permission in writing from the publishers.

Trademark notice: Product or corporate names may be trademarks or registered trademarks, and are used only for identification and explanation without intent to infringe.

British Library Cataloguing-in-Publication Data
A catalogue record for this book is available from the British Library

Library of Congress Cataloging-in-Publication Data
A catalog record has been requested for this book

ISBN: 978-1-409-45462-5 (hbk)
ISBN: 978-1-315-56772-3 (ebk)

Typeset in Sabon
by Swales & Willis, Exeter, Devon, UK

 Printed in the United Kingdom
by Henry Ling Limited

Contents

List of figures vii
Foreword by Fernando Luiz Lara xi
Acknowledgements xiv
Abbreviations xvi

Introduction 1

1 The start of a militant career: the direction of the School of Fine Arts 8

   The young director of the School of Fine Arts 8
   A discreet revolution 13
   The Salão dos tenentes 19
   Report of a failure 23

2 Reasons for the new architecture: Gustavo Capanema's *grands travaux* 34

   A history to reconsider 34
   The great public assignments and Capanema's "dossier" 39
   New architecture, between theory and practice 44
   Le Corbusier and the appel à l'Autorité *49*
   Negotiations and lost opportunities 52

3 A programme for national architecture: the years of the Estado Novo 66

   Struggles and compromises 66
   Toward a State architecture 70
   A genealogy of modern Brazilian architecture 78
   A rising intellectualisation 86
   Modernism and national heritage 88

4 A strategy of mediation: between the CIAM and the SPHAN   96

Shaping national heritage 96
Dealing with historical pre-existence 100
The colonial roots of Brazilian architecture 105
Baroque and national personality 110
Brazilian houses 116

5 Shaping the true Machine Age: art, city, landscape   129

Parisian experiences 129
Art and the emancipation of the masses 134
In search of a new monumentality 139
A maquisard in urban planning 144
Landscape and urbanism 151
A new humanism 160

Bibliography   175
Index   203

Figures

1.1 Lucio Costa, drawing for the competition "Bancos e portões," launched by José Mariano Filho, 1922–1923. Casa de Lucio Costa   10
1.2 Interview with Lucio Costa as director of the National School of Fine Arts, *O Globo*, December 1930   14
1.3 Publication of the Instituto Paulista de Architectos against the designation of modern professors at the National School of Fine Arts, 1931   18
1.4 Lucio Costa, drawing of the second version of Casa Fontes, Rio de Janeiro. Perspective view of the interior, early 1930s. Casa de Lucio Costa   22
1.5 Lucio Costa, Frank Lloyd Wright, and Gregori Warchavchik at the inauguration of the Casa Modernista Exhibit in Rio de Janeiro, 1931. Casa de Lucio Costa   27
2.1 View of the Casa Schwartz, by Lucio Costa and Gregori Warchavchik, Rio de Janeiro, 1932–1933. Casa de Lucio Costa   36
2.2 Lucio Costa and team, first project for the Ministry of Education and Public Health in Rio de Janeiro. Perspective view from the main entrance, 1936. Arquivo Central do IPHAN – Seção Rio de Janeiro   45
2.3 Lucio Costa and team, first project for the Ministry of Education and Public Health in Rio de Janeiro. Perspective view from the auditorium, 1936. Arquivo Central do IPHAN – Seção Rio de Janeiro   46
2.4 Lucio Costa, notes and sketches explaining the advantages of modern architectural technique, in reply to the Inspector de Engenharia Sanitária Domingos da Silva Cunha, September 1936. CPDOC, Fundação Getúlio Vargas   48
2.5 Lucio Costa and team, preliminary version of the final project for the Ministry of Education and Public Health in Rio de Janeiro. Perspective view, 1936. Arquivo Central do IPHAN – Seção Rio de Janeiro   54
2.6 View of the main entrance of the Ministry of Education and Public Health, with the mural cladding in *azulejos* realised according to the drawings by Cândido Portinari. © *L'Architecture d'Aujourd'hui*   55

viii *Figures*

2.7	Le Corbusier, perspective aerial view of the project for the University Campus in Rio de Janeiro, 1936. From Le Corbusier and Pierre Jeanneret, *Œuvre complète*, vol. 3. 1934–1938. © Fondation Le Corbusier/SIAE, 2019	56
2.8	Lucio Costa and team, perspective aerial view of the project for the University Campus in Rio de Janeiro, 1936. From Lucio Costa, *Registro de uma vivência*, 1995. Casa de Lucio Costa	57
3.1	Lucio Costa, draft of the letter to Le Corbusier of 24 October 1937. Casa de Lucio Costa	67
3.2	Model of the Ministry of Education and Public Health at the Exposição do Estado Novo, 1938. CPDOC, Fundação Getúlio Vargas	71
3.3	Lucio Costa, competition project for the Brazilian pavilion at the New York World's Fair. Plan of the mezzanine and perspective views of the interior, 1938. Casa de Lucio Costa	73
3.4	Lucio Costa, competition project for the Brazilian pavilion at the New York World's Fair. Sections and perspective view of the patio, 1938. Casa de Lucio Costa	74
3.5	Oscar Niemeyer, competition project for the Brazilian pavilion at the New York World's Fair. Façades, 1938. Casa de Lucio Costa	74
3.6	Oscar Niemeyer, competition project for the Brazilian pavilion at the New York World's Fair. Perspective views, 1938. Casa de Lucio Costa	75
3.7	Lucio Costa and Oscar Niemeyer, view of the Brazilian pavilion at the New York World's Fair, 1939. Casa de Lucio Costa	76
3.8	Colonnade of the Ministry of Education and Public Health. From *The Architectural Forum*'s special issue on Brazil, November 1947	80
3.9	Getúlio Vargas, Gustavo Capanema, and others in front of the sculpture *Mulher reclinada* by Celso Antônio at the inauguration of the Ministry of Education and Public Health, 1945. Casa de Lucio Costa	81
3.10	The Ministry of Education and Public Health after its completion, ca 1945. Casa de Lucio Costa	84
4.1	Portrait of Lucio Costa in a newspaper article of 1965. In the background, a photo of the façade of Aleijadinho's portal of São Francisco de Assis in Ouro Preto. Casa de Lucio Costa	97
4.2	Lucio Costa's Museum of São Miguel das Missões after its completion with the ruins of the 18th-century church in the background. Arquivo Central do IPHAN – Seção Rio de Janeiro	102
4.3	Oscar Niemeyer's Grand Hotel in Ouro Preto, view of the main façade. From *The Architectural Forum*'s special issue on Brazil, November 1947	105
4.4	Lucio Costa, sketches from the text "A arquitetura dos Jesuítas no Brasil," illustrating the stylistic evolution of the altarpieces from the late 16th to the 18th century. *Revista do Patrimônio*	

	Histórico e Artístico Nacional, no. 5 (1941). Arquivo Central do IPHAN – Seção Rio de Janeiro	108
4.5	Church of Nossa Senhora do Rosário and Church of São Francisco de Assis in Ouro Preto (top left); Church of São Francisco de Assis in Pampulha (top right and bottom). From *L'Architecture d'Aujourd'hui*'s special issue on Brazil, August, 1952. © *L'Architecture d'Aujourd'hui*	112
4.6	Lucio Costa, drawings for the Casa Saavedra, Petrópolis. Perspective views of the exterior, 1942. Casa de Lucio Costa	117
4.7	Lucio Costa, drawings for the Casa Saavedra, Petrópolis. Plan and perspective views of the annexes, 1942. Casa de Lucio Costa	118
4.8	View of Lucio Costa's Park Hotel São Clemente, Nova Friburgo. From *L'Architecture d'Aujourd'hui*'s special issue on Brazil, September 1947. © *L'Architecture d'Aujourd'hui*	120
4.9	View of Lucio Costa's Parque Guinle residential complex, Rio de Janeiro. Casa de Lucio Costa	121
4.10	View of the *muxarabi* in the patio of Lucio Costa's Casa Costa-Moreira Penna, Rio de Janeiro. Casa de Lucio Costa	122
5.1	Lucio Costa, preliminary project for the Maison du Brésil, Paris. Plan of the ground floor and perspective view, 1952. Casa de Lucio Costa	134
5.2	Lucio Costa, illustrations for the text "Considerações sobre arte contemporânea," 1952. Casa de Lucio Costa	137
5.3	Lucio Costa, sketch of the Church of Nossa Senhora de Copacabana, Rio de Janeiro. Perspective view of the interior. Casa de Lucio Costa	141
5.4	Lucio Costa, sketches of the altar for the International Eucharistic Congress, Rio de Janeiro. Plans, section and perspective view, 1954–1955. Casa de Lucio Costa	142
5.5	Lucio Costa, studies for the monument to Prince Henry the Navigator in Sagres, Portugal, 1954. Arquivo Central do IPHAN – Seção Rio de Janeiro	143
5.6	Aerial view of Brasilia's monumental axis during the construction. Casa de Lucio Costa	146
5.7	Lucio Costa, study for Brasilia's Plano Piloto. Perspective view of the Three Powers Square, 1957. Back of the envelope with non-identified text draft. Casa de Lucio Costa	148
5.8	Lucio Costa, studies for Brasilia's Plano Piloto. Design process, 1957. Casa de Lucio Costa	149
5.9	Aerial view of Brasilia's Plano Piloto from Lake Paranoá, with the Palácio da Alvorada in the foreground. gta Archiv/ETH Zurich, Sigfried Giedion	153
5.10	Lucio Costa, original sketches for Brasilia's Plano Piloto competition. Plan layout and perspective view of the *superquadra* conception, 1957. Casa de Lucio Costa	155
5.11	View of Brasilia's system of embankments. gta Archiv/ETH Zurich, Sigfried Giedion	156

5.12 Lucio Costa, sketches of the "Plano Piloto para a urbanização da baixada compreendida entre a Barra da Tijuca, o Pontal de Sernambetiba e Jacarepaguá." Territorial sections, 1969. Casa de Lucio Costa 160
5.13 Portrait of Lucio Costa in Brasilia during the construction, 1957. Casa de Lucio Costa 165

Foreword

We are what we narrate.

Scholars learned it from Homi Bhabha almost three decades ago (*Nation and Narration*, 1990) and the general public had to wait until the success of *Sapiens* by Yuval Harari in 2015 to understand that we, *Homo Sapiens*, not only have sophisticated languages, but indeed live inside the fictions created by our ability to narrate. We are what we narrate, and some of us have more abilities or more opportunities to craft and/or transform narratives that shape our lives. Lucio Costa was one of these. Gaia Piccarolo's book analyzes in great detail the many ways in which Costa shaped the discourse of Brazilian modern architecture, from his brief leadership as director of Rio de Janeiro's National School of Fine Arts in the early 1930s, to his fundamental role in the construction of the Ministry of Education building, the coronation of Oscar Niemeyer, the organization of SPHAN, all the way to the design of Brasilia.

In fact, Piccarolo's book is the most detailed account of such endeavor that I have ever read. Digging deep into messy archives to find the original documents, she has crafted a powerful historical reconstruction that is posed to redefine how we look at Lucio Costa for decades ahead. As she writes in the Introduction, it is appalling that "despite the many noteworthy historiographic contributions carried out by several generations of (mostly) Brazilian scholars, the research immediately met the stubborn persistence of a series of canonical interpretations." The genius of Costa was precisely his ability to shape the narratives and hide some uncomfortable pieces of it. The fact that Brazilian scholars have not yet deconstructed Costa enough (myself included) speaks to the power of such a spell. Costa's *oeuvre*, as Piccarolo shows very well in multiple passages, was "affected by multiple contradictions and ambiguities, which continue to challenge our every attempt to outline its discursive synthesis in a satisfactory way."

That said, it is interesting that Piccarolo chose the idea of "Civil Commitment" for the subtitle of her book. Costa's career is indistinguishable from his multiple roles in the Brazilian federal government: the National School of Fine Arts, the Ministry of Education and Health, SPHAN (Serviço do Patrimônio Histórico e Artístico Nacional), and Brasilia, which imply a deep commitment to public service. However, the idea of *civitas* goes beyond the public, bringing with it its Roman root of a top-down approach. Civilization here should be understood as something to be forced on its subjects, not something that would give the public a voice. Costa's successful narrative was based on stitching together modernism and colonial architectures, a template for Brazilian identity created by modernist intellectuals and embraced by the Vargas regime to be imposed on the whole nation. Recent scholarship has unveiled a much more nuanced and critical interpretation of the relationship between modernization and colonization. Led by Arturo Escobar and Walter Mignolo,[1] the modernity/coloniality project demonstrates that these concepts are two sides of the same coin. There is no modernization without colonization. The idea that ways of life and values of the one group should be imposed on another group is integral to both. We learned to abhor colonialism and aspire for modernization without the understanding that one necessarily implies the other. The discussion, in the last chapter, of Brasilia as a tamed landscape brings the reader back to the civilizing mission of young Lucio Costa, now embedded with a good dose of monumentality.

Gaia Piccarolo's rigorous analysis of primary sources allow us to untangle the colonialism imbedded in Lucio Costa's modernization narrative, opening space for a much-needed reinterpretation of this important duality. I have no doubt that in time we will understand more and more the modern/colonial relationship as defined by Escobar, and less and less as defined by Lucio Costa. It is interesting to note that such decolonial deconstruction of the Latin-American modernist canon is being led by young female scholars. This book by Piccarolo now joins the powerful critique of Fabiola López Durán in *Eugenics in the Garden*;[2] Lisa Blackmore in *Spectacular Modernity*;[3] and the artistic works of Lais Myrra, such as *Dois Pesos Duas Medidas* at the 2016 Bienal de São Paulo, or *Estudo de Caso* at the 2018 Gwangju Biennale. In *Estudo de Caso* a full-scale column of the Alvorada Palace rests on a full-scale column of Fazenda Columbandê. The modern Brazil is only made possible by the persistence of the colonial Brazil, and it is about time that we address such an intricate relationship.

Piccarolo's book also demonstrates that Lucio Costa was not alone in crafting his ideal evolutionary line of authentic Brazilian architecture. Architectural scholarship has focused on Costa's relationship with his fellow architects and it is refreshing to see the centrality of Gustavo Capanema, Rodrigo Mello Franco de Andrade, and Carlos Drummond de Andrade in the work of Costa. Together they designed a well-revised national mythography that served their professional and political aspirations well. When discussing how Lucio Costa dismissed the Universidade do Distrito Federal as proposed by Anísio Teixeira, Piccarolo shows that once again Costa and his colleagues were brushing with authoritarianism by refusing to support a progressive educational project. Here I feel like I should remind the readers that, back in 1936, Mário de Andrade had a different project for the SPHAN – more rooted in vernacular expressions and cultural ethnography. The Costa project, more elitist and interventionist, still serves as a reference for Brazilian historic preservation despite decades of efforts to make it more popular. Or, as Gilberto Gil told me in an interview in 2010 after seven years as minister of Culture – "the IPHAN never embraced the processes of popularization that were central to his leadership and became the most difficult part of his cabinet experience."[4]

Another important contribution of Gaia Piccarolo's book to our field of architectural history is to illuminate the events around Lucio Costa's participation in the design of UNESCO's headquarters. While some attention had been given lately to

Niemeyer's central role in the UN Headquarters in New York City, Costa's role in UNESCO's project has been completely ignored by Brazilian and North Atlantic scholarship alike. The story is always the same – participants end up excluded from the scholarly analysis soon after the building's completion, despite having played a major role. We see that happening to women, we see that happening to non-Europeans. The irony here is that Costa helped his own disappearance, allowing us to speculate that he colonized himself. There is an urgent need for decolonizing the histories of modern architectures (the plural is used here on purpose) and this book is a significant step in this direction.

Gaia Piccarolo is very clever to avoid the overexposed debates of the MoMA show of 1943 and the Brasilia competition of 1957, focusing instead on passages of Costa's work that are much less known outside of Brazil, such as his leadership at SPHAN, his role inside Estado Novo bureaucracy, and his participation in UNESCO's headquarters project. By doing so she gives the international readership a detailed picture of one of the most fascinating architects of the 20th century, in all his contradictory geniality.

Fernando Luiz Lara
Professor of Architecture, University of Texas at Austin

Notes

1 Walter D. Mignolo and Arturo Escobar, eds, *Globalization and the Decolonial Option*, 1st edn (London: Routledge, 2013).
2 Fabiola López-Durán, *Eugenics in the Garden: Transatlantic Architecture and the Crafting of Modernity* (Austin, TX: University of Texas Press, 2018).
3 Lisa Blackmore, *Spectacular Modernity: Dictatorship, Space, and Visuality in Venezuela, 1948–1958*, 1st edn (Pittsburgh, PA: University of Pittsburgh Press, 2017).
4 Gilberto Gil, interview with Brazil Center faculty affiliates, Austin, Texas, 7 November 2010.

Acknowledgements

First of all, I would like to thank Maria Elisa Costa, whose intelligence, energy, and passion in sharing her knowledge of her father's life and work gave me a measure of the greatness of the man, as well as of the architect. I am equally grateful to José Pessôa, for his invaluable guidance in identifying the sources and for sharing, with great patience and availability, his profound knowledge of Costa's work. My gratitude also goes to Fernando Luiz Lara, with whom, after our first meeting during an unforgettable visit to Pampulha, I began a fruitful collaboration on the basis of our common Latin-American interests, and to whom I am grateful for having accepted to write with his usual enthusiasm the Foreword to this book. I also owe a heartfelt thanks to Giuliana Ricci, for the constant guidance at the beginning of my academic career and for encouraging me to follow my study interests, without which I never would have dared to face such a demanding research subject. I also thank Carolina Di Biase, for having given me the opportunity to publish part of the findings of the research in Italy and for having followed me along this journey, and the entire teaching body of the doctoral programme in the History of Architecture and Urban Planning of the Politecnico di Torino – in particular, Alessandro De Magistris, Carlo Olmo, and Sergio Pace, for the fundamental critical support and comments with which they participated in the research developments during my PhD course. A special thanks goes to all those with whom I have shared my interest in Brazilian architecture over the years, through travel, conferences, university courses, and long conversations, above all. Among these: Daniele Pisani, Martino Tattara, Giovanna D'Amia, Giovanna Rosso Del Brenna, and Giaime Botti. Stimulating exchanges and thought-provoking experiences came from a large number of scholars, whom I had the fortune to meet during my study trips; among these, special recognition goes to Roberto Segre, whom I had the privilege of meeting before his tragic and sudden passing, and Kenneth Frampton, whose personal interest in my research was an unfailing motivational source. Also, among the many experts of Costa's work and of Brazilian and Latin-American architecture: Carlos Eduardo Dias Comas, Jorge Francisco Liernur, Carlos Alberto Ferreira Martins, Lauro Cavalcanti, Farés el-Dahdah, Margareth da Silva Pereira, Alberto Xavier, Matheus Gorovitz, Otavio Leonídio Ribeiro, José Lira, Marcelo Suzuki, Marcos José Carrilho, Ana Tostões, André Tavares, Josep Maria Montaner, Fernando Álvarez, Patrício Del Real, Helen Gyger, Ana Esteban Maluenda, Daniele Vitale, and many others.

Special thanks go to all those who have made this work possible, allowing me to consult archives and libraries, and making the iconographic material available to

Acknowledgements xv

me. I give warm thanks to Julieta Sobral, Bernardo Krivochein, and Clara Mellac (Casa de Lucio Costa), Murilo Lellis (Biblioteca Noronha Santos, IPHAN), Hilário Pereira, Maria José Soares, and Andressa Furtado da Silva de Aguiar (Arquivo Central do IPHAN-Seção Rio de Janeiro), Arnaud Dercelles and Delphine Studer (Fondation Le Corbusier), Renan Marinho de Castro (Centro de Pesquisa e Documentação de História Contemporânea do Brasil, Fundação Getúlio Vargas), Daniel Weiss and Muriel Pérez (gta Archiv, ETH Zürich), for the patient archival support even from a distance; and to Elisabeth Martins, João Claudio Parucher, and Claudio Muniz (Núcleo de Pesquisa e Documentação, UFRJ), Paulo Mauro and Carlos Warchavchik (Arquivo Gregori Warhcavchik), and to the research group *Lucio Costa: obras completas* (UniRitter, Porto Alegre), Ana Paula Canez and Marcos Almeida in particular, with whom I shared the pleasure of visiting many of Lucio Costa's built works. I also thank the staff of the Museu Dom João VI (Escola de Belas Artes, UFRJ), of the Fundação Casa de Rui Barbosa, of the Biblioteca Paulo Santos, of the Biblioteca e Centro de Documentação of the MASP, of the archive and library of the Museu Nacional de Belas Artes and of the FAU-USP, of the Biblioteca Lucio Costa (UFRJ), of the Biblioteca Central da PUC-Rio, of the library of the IAB-RJ (Instituto de Arquitetos do Brasil, departamento do Rio de Janeiro), of the Fundação Oscar Niemeyer, of the Avery Library (Columbia University), of the Collegi d'Arquitectes de Catalunya, of the libraries of the Politecnico di Milano and of the Politecnico di Torino, and of the Fondazione Einaudi in Turin and Feltrinelli in Milan.

I also thank the staff of Ashgate and of Routledge, in particular Valerie Rose, Aoife McGrath, Emily Collyer, Grace Harrison, Sophie Robinson, and Adam Guppy, for their patience and care in following the long and difficult gestation process of this book, Teodora H. Ott for the competent and patient English translation of the original manuscript, and Dan Shutt for his careful and respectful editing.

Finally, proper thanks are due to all the people who have supported me in various ways over the years, sharing the many joys and sorrows of research. To my friends and fellow companions in adventure, to my doctoral colleagues, but above all to my parents, Daniela Giglio and Stefano Piccarolo, and to Consuelo Giglio and Nina Bassoli, without whose affection, encouragement, and practical help this work would not have been possible.

Abbreviations

ACI-RJ	Arquivo Central do IPHAN (Instituto do Patrimônio Histórico e Artístico Nacional), Seção Rio de Janeiro
AGW	Arquivo Gregori Warchavchik, São Paulo
BPS	Biblioteca Paulo Santos, Rio de Janeiro
CLC	Casa de Lucio Costa, Rio de Janeiro
CPDOC	Centro de Pesquisa e Documentação de História Contemporânea do Brasil, Fundação Getúlio Vargas, Rio de Janeiro
ENBA	Escola Nacional de Belas Artes
FAU-USP	Faculdade de Arquitetura e Urbanismo da Universidade de São Paulo
FAU-UFRJ	Faculdade de Arquitetura e Urbanismo da Universidade Federal do Rio de Janeiro
FCRB	Fundação Casa de Rui Barbosa, Rio de Janeiro
FLC	Fondation Le Corbusier, Paris
GTA	gta Archiv, Institut für Geschichte und Theorie der Architektur, Eidgenössischen Technischen Hochschule, Zürich
MASP	Centro de Pesquisa, Biblioteca e Centro de Documentação, Museu de Arte de São Paulo
MDJ VI	Museu Dom João VI, Escola de Belas Artes, Universidade Federal do Rio de Janeiro
MNBA	Arquivo Histórico, Museu Nacional de Belas Artes, Rio de Janeiro
SPHAN	Serviço do Patrimônio Histórico e Artístico Nacional
UDF	Universidade do Distrito Federal

Introduction

My first approach to the figure of Lucio Costa dates back to about a decade ago, when – as part of my PhD at the Politecnico di Torino – I proposed a thesis that focused on better understanding the central role he held in the peculiar course of Brazil toward modernity.[1] The fascination that the creative season of Brazilian modernism exerted – and continues to exert – on my generation, and acknowledging that its existence was only possible thanks to the presence of a semi-authoritarian political system, raised questions that were worth investigating further and that required – it seemed to me – to be "viewed from afar," to use an expression by Claude Lévi-Strauss.[2] Apart for a limited series of works or events to which his international notoriety is due – Brasilia in particular – I was mostly surprised by the relatively limited interest that his figure seems to have inspired in recent non-Brazilian historiography; a phenomenon that I had tended to blame on the almost exclusive protagonism of Oscar Niemeyer in the field. Furthermore, despite the many noteworthy historiographic contributions carried out by several generations of (mostly) Brazilian scholars, the research immediately met the stubborn persistence of a series of canonical interpretations. My impression was that the more I tried to dismantle each of these interpretations, one by one, the more the canonical narrative proved to be inflexible and resist any real sign of caving in. Therefore, a considerable margin of misunderstanding remained at the bottom of the issues. Things were certainly not made simpler by the fact that almost all these interpretations were to be attributed directly to Costa himself, and by the fact that his authority was surrounded by an aura of deep and unconditional admiration in Brazil. My answer to this seemingly unsolvable puzzle was therefore to start from scratch, so to speak, aiming to confront the enormous amount of existing literature on his account with pure and simple documental data, and trying to resist the temptation of relying on already-established hypotheses. In doing so, I was actually paying my debt to a more recent research tradition that – albeit some previous symptoms – had begun to take shape after the architect's passing at the venerable age of ninety-six, at the turn of "his" century.[3]

Hence, during these first decisive years of research I carried out a delicate operation of encircling the study object from the available documental material, given that Costa's private archive was still – apart for small fragments – in a quite inaccessible phase of reorganisation. However, the situation was practically overturned in a few years' time. Access to the material of the Casa de Lucio Costa[4] allowed me to verify, in time, the hypotheses formulated up until then and extend the research to the entire professional activity of the architect, revealing the exceptional continuity of his vocation in seeing architecture as a privileged instrument of social re-foundation.

From the militant commitment of the early 1930s to the mediation strategies of the Vargas Estado Novo years, to the international opportunities of the 1950s and the increasingly prophetic tone of the last decades, his belief in architecture as a cultural horizon that was inextricably linked to a civic engagement seems to have accompanied him throughout the troubled events of the century and across the ups and downs of his long professional career. This career seems to have had incorporated more professional roles in one – militant architect and urban planner, theorist and scholar, heritage official, ideologist and "spiritual father" of an entire generation – but was also affected by multiple contradictions and ambiguities, which continue to challenge our every attempt to outline its discursive synthesis in a satisfactory way.

It is precisely around Costa's mission of civilisation through architecture that this book takes shape, tracing the roots, the developments, and the counter-marches of a singular form of engagement that programmatically chose to act by cultural means rather than by political ones – as will instead be the case of other important figures of Brazilian modernism, especially in the generations that immediately followed. At the same time, Costa was aware of the fact that in order to ensure a margin of success for his cultural project he was required to negotiate a scope of action within a broader political project, which became a favourable ground for assigning architecture a key role in the nation building process pursued by the Vargas government at the beginning of the 1930s. This explains how he found important promotional channels of his professional ascent in the recurring presence of intellectual figures that were well integrated in the administrative life of the government. Beyond the modest image that historiography insists on attributing him,[5] Costa was deeply aware of his value, committed to carving himself a role, right from the start, in the genealogy of Brazilian architecture he would personally outline.

Costa's relationship with public clients – who were his privileged interlocutors in many of the most significant events of his professional career – becomes one of the fundamental interpretive keys to understand the relevance and newness of his exceptional but fundamentally discontinuous biographical outline. This was in fact marked by a number of great institutional assignments – some of the most emblematic examples of (not only Brazilian) 20th-century architecture – but also by a series of failures, professional defeats, and "lost opportunities," which indicate that his interaction with the institutional structures must not have always been too peaceful. The analysis of the processes underlying the temporary alliance between modernist intelligentsia and the State during the crucial years of the country's modernisation process is a common thread that runs through the entire book, pointing both at the opportunities and the conflicts generated by this same alliance. The Corbusian idea of the indoctrination of a more or less enlightened Authority was applied by Costa – who was an intransigent defender of the autonomy of architecture, although he was always ready to put his technical and intellectual skills at the service of the "good cause of modern architecture" – with an idealistic attitude, projecting it onto an even more utopian horizon.

Determined to claim – along with many others belonging to his generation – the intellectual hegemony of the progressive elite he belonged to at a local level, while also emancipating Brazil from the imperialist model of cultural production on an international one, Costa appears to have been divided between an evident desire for self-legitimisation and a lacking personal propensity to compromise, which brought him to a constant internal conflict between occupying a "front line" and acting more discreetly from "behind the scenes." From unexpected role-reversals to committed militancies and "voluntary reticence and reclusion,"[6] he moved with lucid intelligence, confidently acting even outside the rigid prescriptions of codes and hierarchies, between the different roles that he found himself to cover on each occasion. Without ever losing his grip on reality, in this way he succeeded in orienting interpretations and decisions in the matter of architecture, perhaps more than any other, pushing the solicitations from the international architectural debate to react with the ideological need of the country – an after-effect of the pact between the modernist cultural project and the nation building one – and accompanying the establishment of Brazil on the international scene.

The book thus traces the elaboration process of the fortunate cultural strategies through which Costa built a theoretical framework capable of bridging the gap between past and present, legitimising the "new tradition" of modern architecture as a new alleged expression of the "authentic evolutionary line" of Brazilian national architecture. In this way of seeing things, from a certain moment onwards he will see the work of Niemeyer – a skilful creator of forms and images capable of prefiguring what Brazil aspired to become – not only as an architecture that was truly an art of the State, but as a possible antidote to the increasing aridity of modernism and as a healthy symptom of a new expressive freedom, founded on an unconditional trust in the emancipating power of art.

The militancy for the "new architecture" and the commitment to the protection of a heritage increasingly threatened by modernisation – and carefully traced back to idealised parameters that were coherent with the re-elaboration of Brazil's colonial past – appear as two inseparable components of a broader and more ambitious project; one that was set against the fluctuating political events developing in the country, and that pursued the civilising potential of architecture with "illuministic" faith: the construction of a modern Brazil, endowed with its own artistic and cultural identity. The unbridgeable distance between the "negative Brazil" – comprising the actual structural conditions of the country – and the desired horizon of a "definitive Brazil" will come to show, with tragic evidence, the utopian traits of the modernist project in the discrepancies between the plan for the new capital and its realisation in an actual constructed city, which would in a number of ways be far from the democratic idea of the "Versailles of the people" that Costa had first imagined.

One of the most problematic and yet also most interesting issues in dealing with the figure of Lucio Costa lies in an underlying ambiguity: between his unshakeable faith in the project as a tool for building the future – as well as the present and the past – and the awareness of its limits and its somewhat coercive nature. This was an awareness that was accompanied by a nostalgic and conservative attitude, capable of giving his more private and "intimate" design production – less subjected to the didactic intentions of public, representative, and monumental works – the natural and inconspicuous character of those things that have been around forever.

Costa himself confronted this issue by resorting to the dialectical tension that characterises his thought process, which aimed at combining in great pacifying syntheses the different ideological incentives involved in it and the different souls of his multiple personality. Thus, a particular form of self-discipline and "civil" responsibility seems to have laid at the basis of the deterministic optimism of many of his theoretical positions – bordering dogmatism, at times – from which emerged an unchallenged faith in the power and domain of reason. His deterministic reading of the historical process as a strive toward inevitable progress – fully expressed in his "theory of convergent results" formulated in the early 1950s[7] – can be explained in this view of the matter. The long wave of positivist thinking of which Costa sowed the intellectual heritage – projecting it to the end of the century – was not separable from the option of the modern architect for a militant criticism, which was instrumental to evolution and progress and, therefore, was in line with history's malleability, as history was explicitly placed at the service of its use and functioning in the present.

Costa seems to have remained faithful to the modernist lesson even during the years of profound critical re-evaluation by some of the same modern masters.[8] And yet, the receptive humanism that distinguishes him and his inclusive design attitude – devoid of formalistic emphases and aimed at the practical and psychological need of the user – in some ways brought him closer to the "new guard" emerging within the CIAM in the post-war period. All this casts a new light – of extreme importance in reconsidering his position in the delicate international balances of the time – on the meetings, overlaps, and circularities of the "elective affinities" that emerge if we observe his network of relations and his many European and American interlocutors, including (besides, of course, Le Corbusier) personalities such as Walter Gropius, Sigfried Giedion, and José Luis Sert, but also Alison and Peter Smithson, Georges Candilis, Ernesto Nathan Rogers, etc.

While his built architectural work did not cross national borders – and most of his efforts had in fact been directed toward Brazil – Costa nevertheless appears fully integrated in the world scene of architectural culture, coming to hold an unquestionable position of authority in the 1950s. Retracing his professional biography (he was born in Toulon in 1902 and died in Rio de Janeiro in 1998) is an operation that can be compared to viewing the 20th century through one of its infinite and arbitrary section lines. The resulting image is composite and heterogeneous. Although it is not exhaustive in any measure, it does give us a significant sample of themes emerging from the more-or-less known events that the narration deals with, case by case: from the modernisation and identity building processes of a post-colonial country to the winding road toward the assimilation and simultaneous revision of European-based modernism; from the exchange of ideas and models between Europe and the Americas to the delicate definition of the role of the professional and intellectual and his relation with political powers; from the not-always-linear articulation of practice and theory within the modernist architectural discourse to the transformation of the same rhetoric and spirit of architectural and urban culture in the post-war period; from the development of disciplinary tools for protection and restoration outside of the contexts in which their "official" history was traced to the emergence of a new landscape sensibility.

The book is divided into five chapters, each identifying different thematic issues corresponding to different chronologies of Costa's professional activity.

The first chapter focuses on the years 1930 and 1931, marked by his first important public engagement within the New Republic (Nova República) of Getúlio Vargas: the direction of the National School of Fine Arts of Rio de Janeiro. The affair, brief but considered fundamental to the process of artistic renewal of the country, is here addressed by extending the analysis to the premise of Costa's own formation in the same institution and to the future scenarios that it later gave access to. The institutional clash that was inherent in Costa's direction of the school – in which, in addition to the establishment of modern artistic expressions and updated educational methods, the political balances and power-plays between the old and new forces of the country were at stake – defines it as a crucial stage in his professional formation. Despite his twenty-eight years of age, Costa in fact showed great decision-making autonomy, ethical intransigence, and ability to act as an authoritative cultural animator. The experience, although destined to fail at least in terms of the didactic programme, would give Costa the intellectual stimulation – also thanks to a choral group of actors linked to the modernist movement – and the concrete opportunity to steer his already consolidated professional career toward a strong modernist militancy, finally coming to identify his persona as a reference figure in the broader movement of artistic and architectural renewal.

The second chapter addresses the years between 1935 and 1937, during which he undertook the two prestigious public assignments from Gustavo Capanema, minister of Education at the time, destined to mark a turning point in his career: the new seat for the Ministry of Education and Public Health, and the campus of the Universidade do Brasil, both in Rio. However, the context within which these two assignments were concretised is tackled starting from events that the canonical narrative seems to have deliberately disregarded, like the professional collaborations with Gregori Warchavchik and with Carlos Leão, and the brief interlude of the Universidade do Distrito Federal. The entire process – from the allocation of the assignments to the first design phase – was marked by a strong militancy for the "new architecture" and by an intransigent commitment to the Corbusian orthodoxy, which would lead to Le Corbusier's personal involvement in 1936. The specific role played by Costa in these events is set against a background of often conflicting relations between the different cultural proposals, but also among the contributions of a series of personalities, including Capanema, his head of cabinet Carlos Drummond de Andrade, and a group of remarkably talented architects like Oscar Niemeyer, Affonso Eduardo Reidy, Jorge Moreira, Carlos Leão, etc. The parable of these intensely productive years – which were the result of unrepeatable circumstances and a considerable theoretical-demonstrative inspiration – ends with an unexpected change of tone, marking Costa's temporary loss of faith in a possible constructive partnership with the State at the dawn of the establishment of the Estado Novo.

Chapters 3 and 4 investigate the redefinition of Costa's role during the years of the Estado Novo (from 1937 to 1945), in the context of the somewhat ambiguous position he held in relation to the authoritarian politics of the Vargas government and against the backdrop of the changed international balances. Despite his personal distance from the ideological positions of the Estado Novo, Costa would not shy away from the cause of modern architecture, which in his vision was strictly linked to the one of a modern Brazil. From this moment on, his efforts would focus on the systematisation of a discourse able to filter the spirit and themes of the international debate through the ideological needs of Vargas' Brazil, both in terms of the construction of the new and in terms of the "invention of tradition." Aware of the potential of a narrative discourse that could articulate modernity and tradition in order to satisfy both national and identity issues as well as the pressure of global competition, Costa strenuously supported the image of Brazil's free-form modernism as the one destined to express the emotional and symbolic values that modern architecture was striving for. In an ambiguous balance between an attitude of resistance and one of compromise, he would contribute to strengthening the connections between modern architecture and State, identifying buildings such as the New York World's Fair pavilion of 1939 and the seat for the Ministry of Education and Public Health as icons of the modernisation and civilisation processes of Brazil, therefore contributing to outline the ideal genealogy of modern Brazilian architecture. Meanwhile, he also developed a mature expressive language in his design production – especially in a series of private residences – in which a regionalist approach came to mark his definitive break from the ghost of historicism. The constant reference to the CIAM – from 1937 on – goes together with Costa's involvement in the activity of the Serviço do Patrimônio Histórico e Artístico Nacional (SPHAN). Chapter 4 addresses specific case-studies of his commitment in the cause of national heritage in order to exemplify Costa's influence on the ideological and operational line of the institution. On the one side, the first mission in Rio Grande do Sul and the active participation to the project of the Grande Hotel in Ouro Preto are illustrative of Costa's approach toward historical preexistence. On the other, the scientific opinions together with the essays he produced as part of the editorial corpus of the SPHAN represent a parallel theoretical effort, defining a concept of "tradition" that could serve as a guideline in the selection of what was to be safeguarded and as a narrative in support of the "new architecture." In this sense, Costa would propose a double synchronic interpretation of history, associating the principles of the modern movement to the intrinsic rationality of local vernacular architecture, and identifying Niemeyer and Aleijadinho as interpreters of the local Baroque genius.

Finally, Chapter 5 glances at the years following the so-called "Vargas Era." Starting from the late 1940s to the early 1950s, Costa seems to have been committed to expanding his network of professional relations and to consolidating – not without reservations and failures – the authoritative position he had acquired, in a process that culminated in his winning the competition for the design of the new Brazilian capital. As his interlocutors and "audience" began to cross national borders, the opportunity arose for him to give a final shape – after many years away from the "front line" – to the representative and symbolic face of the nation. The European experiences of the early 1950s – the participation in the Panel of Five in charge of evaluating the project of the UNESCO headquarters in Paris, the draft for the preliminary project of the Maison du Brésil in Paris's university district, and the participation in the International Conference of Artists promoted by UNESCO in Venice in 1952 – laid the foundations for a new creative phase, centred around a series of closely interconnected themes: the synthesis of the arts, a new monumentality, the social role of the architect, and art as an instrument of emancipation of the masses. These ideas would be channelled – to a greater or lesser extent – into the most important enterprise of not only Costa's professional activity, but of the entire urban and architectural history of modern Brazil: the city of Brasilia. The plan for the new capital – which inaugurated a commitment in the urban field that would be pursued in the years to come – came full circle, finally sealing the pact between architecture and

State, the one he had successfully experimented with during the Vargas years and was now ready to define under the democratic government of Juscelino Kubitschek. The military regime that would be established only a few years after its inauguration would come to cast a dramatic light on the plan's original utopian intentions, and the actual construction of the city would, in many respects, "get out of hand" and escape from the author's control. Nevertheless, the civilising effort running through Costa's entire life and activity was finally concretised with greater strength and evidence precisely in Brasilia. It is here that Costa's "new humanism" is expressed most significantly, projecting the utopia of an inclusive settlement model into the solitude of the Planalto Central – a model that was built on the scale of a "definitive Brazil" and was based on the highest values of civil cohabitation.

Notes

1 The thesis, entitled "L'architettura come impegno civile. Lucio Costa nel Brasile di Vargas (1930–1945)" and disserted in 2010, resulted in a few publications, including Gaia Piccarolo, *Un progetto di mediazione. Lucio Costa fra tutela del patrimonio e nuova architettura* (Santarcangelo di Romagna: Maggioli, 2014), which explores the connection of Costa's activity as an exponent of architectural modernism with his role as government official of artistic and historical heritage preservation.
2 Claude Lévi-Strauss, *The View from Afar* (Chicago: University of Chicago Press, 1985).
3 After the pioneering critical interpretations that arose in the 1980s and 1990s following the military dictatorship (among which it is essential to mention, for its innovative hypothesis on the relations between the modernist cultural project and the State, Carlos Alberto Ferreira Martins's master thesis, "Arquitetura e Estado no Brasil. Elementos para uma investigação sobre a constituição do discurso moderno no Brasil: a obra de Lucio Costa 1924–1952," Universidade de São Paulo, 1987), a new line of studies began to develop, based on a methodological system that was true to documental data, opening the way to a more objective reconsideration of Costa's contribution. After the death of the architect in 1998, a particularly intense critical season was inaugurated. This season culminated with an explosion of commemorations on the occasion of the centenary of the architect's birth (2002), against the backdrop of a renewed retrospective interest in modernism's legacy and based on a critical foundation that was generally more willing to highlight any contradictory aspects, albeit in the context of Costa's mythicisation as a spiritual father of the heroic "modern generation." Lacking the space for a greater in-depth historiographical analysis, we refer to the Bibliography at the end of the volume.
4 Access to Costa's archive is possible thanks to the long process of reorganisation, conservation, and digitalisation that was undertaken by his daughter Maria Elisa. Today, the archive can be consulted online, at the address www.casadeluciocosta.org.
5 In 1950, Costa writes of himself: "As for my much lauded modesty, it is more apparent than real, since it includes nothing but an innate critical sense and shameless self-indulgence." Costa to an unidentified editor, Rio de Janeiro, 18 November 1950. CLC, VI A 01-03290.
6 Guilherme Wisnik, *Lucio Costa* (São Paulo: Cosac & Naify, 2001), 9.
7 Costa, "L'architecte et la societé contemporaine," in *L'artiste dans la société contemporaine (conférence internationale des artistes, Venise, 22–28 septembre 1952). Témoignages recueillis par l'UNESCO* (Paris: UNESCO, 1954), 88–99.
8 Costa's fascination for Le Corbusier's lesson was destined to leave a deep mark on his entire human and professional development, despite the fact that his relationship with the Swiss-French master did experience misunderstandings and disagreements. We should not underestimate Le Corbusier's reference model in Costa's desire to present himself as the best interpreter of his own biography – a desire that he would continue to pursue up until the project of his autobiography *Registro de uma vivência*, published a few years before his death (São Paulo: Empresa das Artes, 1995).

1 The start of a militant career
The direction of the School of Fine Arts

The young director of the School of Fine Arts

Addressing the very beginning of the establishment of the militant project pursued from the early 1930s by Lucio Costa leads us to first consider the episode that, in some way, was the main detonator of the same project, while also addressing the context of a professional career that seems framed – at least initially – in the traditional educational upbringing of a young and gifted architect belonging to the Carioca upper bourgeoisie.

In particular, we refer to the direction of the National School of Fine Arts, unanimously recognised – often without detailed historical reconstruction – as the first act of Costa's militant career, frequently called into question by historiography as a fundamental turning point in the process aiming to introduce modern architecture onto Brazilian soil.[1]

It is precisely the importance of this episode that today determines – in light of new interpretative keys – the need to once again question the sources and re-evaluate the role of this first prestigious public appointment, placing it within the broader context of Costa's relations with the political and institutional realities. In order to do so, it is first necessary to take a step back and outline the conditions in which the specific official duty was shaped.

As is well known, Costa's academic training at the same National School of Fine Arts and the first phase of his professional activity have come to raise the issue in the years (especially while the architect was still alive) of the difficulty of containing his eclectic and traditionalist production within the frame of his consolidated image as an authoritative member and "ideologist" of Brazilian modernism. Although this production has long since been redeemed from historiographical silence, it is astonishing to see how few inquiries have been made into this delicate transition from the late 1920s and early 1930s, a transition that cannot be solely explained, as it has up until now, in terms of a sudden "conversion" to the modernist creed, but that rather seems to have been rooted in the solicitations, acquaintances, and opportunities given by a series of important professional occasions.

Costa enrolled in the School of Fine Arts in 1917, at the age of fifteen. His family had in fact just returned to settle in Rio de Janeiro after having lived for several years in Europe, where he was born and where his schooling had taken place.[2]

Once he had completed the three years of the *Curso geral*, in the first months of 1922 he enrolled in the *Curso especial* of Architecture, receiving his *engenheiro-architecto* (engineer-architect) diploma in 1926.[3] From about the third year of his academic record, Costa steadily dedicated himself to professional activities and was promptly noticed by his professors, obtaining a number of job opportunities within the same academic environment. After a design experience at the Rebecchi architecture firm,[4] one of the largest and most successful professional studios in Rio de Janeiro at the time, Costa was invited by the then-professor of "Composição elementar de arquitetura," Archimedes Memória, to work at the prestigious Escriptorio Technico Heitor de Mello, a studio that Memória had recently come into possession of – together with Francisque Cuchet – after the death of Heitor de Mello. His collaboration with the studio continued for at least two years, allowing Costa to take part in a series of relevant projects, including the neo-colonial restructuring of the old arsenal, which was transformed into the Pavilhão das Grandes Indústrias on the occasion of the Independence Centenary International Exposition of Brazil, taking place in Rio de Janeiro in 1922.[5]

While Costa's disposition toward renovation only happened once in contact with the modernist environment, his training developed under the aegis of the academic culture and the neo-colonial movement leading the Brazilian and general Latin-American debate in those years.[6] Costa presumably left Memória's studio with the arrival of the first assignments from academic figures, among which were the home-atelier for painter Rodolfo Chambelland and the renovation of a colonial residence for the then-director of the School, João Baptista da Costa. It was in this moment that he started the collaboration with his colleague Fernando Valentim, with whom he won the great silver medal at the Exposição Geral of the School of Fine Arts in 1924.[7] The projects presented by the two students – who were described as the authors of the more interesting projects on display on the pages of the newspaper *A Noite*[8] – fit in completely with the eclectic style of the time. In addition to a neo-medieval castle for Baron Smith de Vasconcellos in Itaipava, two small neo-colonial-style cottages (similar to the popular models disseminated by a series of widespread periodical publications),[9] and the luxurious cottage for Arnaldo Guinle, the two architects also presented the residence for Chambelland and the project for a Solar Brasileiro (Figure 1.1), which Costa submitted on the occasion of the 1923 competition launched by the Instituto Brasileiro de Arquitetos, upon the initiative of José Mariano Filho, president of the Sociedade Brasileira de Belas Artes and the main promoter of the traditionalist cause.[10]

The relations with Mariano Filho – a central figure in the local artistic debate who was engaged in an intense campaign to promote the neo-colonial movement – held an important role in Costa's professional development. Mariano Filho introduced the young architect to the study of traditional Brazilian architecture, representing – in light of his future commitment in the field of heritage – a surprising element of continuity among the different phases of his professional career. This first impact with the remains of colonial architecture proved to be revealing and symptomatic, since it came to fuel an interest in the legacy of the past that – from a nostalgic Ruskinian approach, combined with a somewhat free design re-appropriation – would lead to a more realistic desire to assess issues in terms of preservation, and – in his more mature design activity – to a surprising ability to re-actualise traditional architectural solutions. Among the initiatives sponsored by Mariano Filho – many of which aimed at collecting research material for his private residence, the neo-colonial Solar Monjope – there was Costa's expedition to the colonial town of Diamantina, in Minas Gerais, in May of 1924, an event that

10 *The start of a militant career*

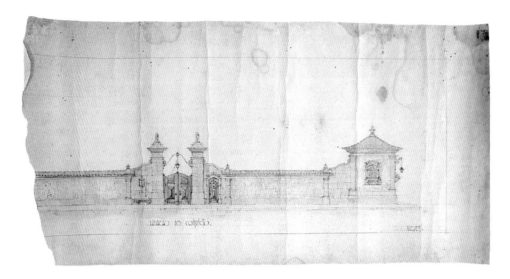

Figure 1.1 Lucio Costa, drawing for the competition "Bancos e portões," launched by José Mariano Filho, 1922–1923. Casa de Lucio Costa.

took place in a period of great interest for national historical and artistic heritage, shared by figures linked to the modernist movement, such as Tarsila do Amaral and Oswald de Andrade.[11] During his stay in Diamantina – with visits to Sabará, Ouro Preto, and Mariana – Costa carefully observed the constructive and decorative details of colonial architecture, of which he began to appreciate the sober simplicity, constructive reality, and proportional beauty, comparing (and contrasting) it – in an interview he released upon his return from the expedition – to the artificiality of the neo-colonial style.[12] According to Mariano Filho, the project Costa later presented for the design competition of the Brazilian Pavilion at the Exposition of Philadelphia (which was also never carried out) represents one of the greatest "spiritual" compromises on the part of the young Costa – who would win, again – with the traditionalist movement.[13]

The years 1926 and 1927 – despite a number of trips to Europe and to the historic cities of Minas Gerais after his graduation[14] – proved to be very productive, with the construction of various residences in collaboration with Fernando Valentim and the participation in a series of public open competitions. In the competition for the Argentine embassy, in particular, Costa achieved double recognition with two projects that were clearly influenced by his recent travels, presenting styles that were, respectively, "Hispanic, imbued with neo-colonial spirit" and "Florentine."[15] In an interview he released for the occasion, the architect openly showed for the first time that he acknowledged some of the avant-garde architectural developments in Europe, although describing them as transitional phenomena in some ways comparable to that of Art Nouveau.[16] Although this project also only remained on paper, it seems to some way represent Costa's definitive recognition in the professional world. In fact, his involvement – together with a small number of local professionals – in the survey launched by the newspaper O *Paíz* on the adequacy of skyscrapers within the context of Rio de Janeiro came only a few months later.[17]

In 1929, year in which Costa claimed to have been slightly scandalised by a conference held by Le Corbusier at the School of Fine Arts,[18] he was commissioned by Manuel Bandeira – a figure that together with Rodrigo Mello Franco de Andrade would play a fundamental role in his appointment to the position of school director the following year – to write his first relevant theoretical essay, "O Aleijadinho e a arquitetura tradicional," from which he would partially distance himself in the following years.[19]

Therefore, during the years of global financial crisis, on the doorstep of the crucial political events that agitated Brazil at the end of the decade, Costa benefited from an undoubtedly relevant position in the disciplinary debate, not only as an architect – with the support of influential clients – but also as a theoretical and intellectual reference. In the aftermath of the Revolution of 1930, his authority was confirmed by various important public engagements; not only was he a member of the commission in charge of evaluating the plan for the capital drawn up by the French urban planner Donat Alfred Agache,[20] but he was also in charge of directing the major renovation of the neo-classical Itamaraty Palace, headquarters of the Ministry of Foreign Affairs, a position he would be forced to give up once appointed school director.

It is in this context – in line with the growing awareness of the partial isolation of Brazil's artistic and architectural scene – that he had the opportunity to bring a significant renewal within the newly formed institutional reality, through the elaboration of an educational reform for the main academic institution in the country. One of the cultural initiatives that was promoted by the provisional government taking office after the Revolution headed by Getúlio Vargas, and by the new Ministry of Education and Public Health in particular,[21] was in fact Costa's appointment to the direction of the National School of Fine Arts.[22]

Strangely, up until now, nobody seems to have questioned the choice of Francisco Campos, minister of Education of the provisional government, to assign the position to Costa, who was only twenty-eight years old at the time; this is even more peculiar if we consider that the school's regulations foresaw that the director was to be selected among the school's own board of professors. Costa himself, on several occasions, defined his election as an act of coercion, attributing his initial positive reception by part of the Congregação – a board consisting of a selected group of professors, responsible for the cultural and academic life of the institution – to the good relations he had established with the academic body during his formative years, as well as to the "fear of the red flag of the revolutionary government."[23]

Sources seem to agree on crediting Costa's nomination to the head of the cabinet of the time, Rodrigo Mello Franco de Andrade, who seemed to have contacted the architect without actually ever having met him in person beforehand, apparently finding him initially unwilling to accept the assignment. Costa's own words regarding this delicate matter are particularly effective.

> I never expected to become director of the E.B.A. I did not know Mr. Francisco Campos, and his invitation caught me by surprise. Called upon by the then head of the cabinet, Dr. Rodrigo de M. F. de Andrade, whom I also had not had the pleasure of knowing, I was surprised by the information regarding the government's intentions. I pointed out my difficulty in accepting

the prestigious invitation for various reasons, as well as the uselessness of changing the director without radically changing not only the organisation but the actual direction of the academic offer in the architecture course and in the painting and sculpture courses as well. Dr. Rodrigo Mello Franco answered that this was the precise intention of the government, the reason for which he had called me and, moreover, for which I would find complete support from the Ministry.[24]

Mello Franco de Andrade himself confirmed this version on more than one occasion.

Dr. Mariano Filho credits me with favours and benefits that are granted to Mr. Lucio Costa, when the truth is that I never had the opportunity to be useful to this distinguished architect in any way. If, in fact, in 1930, as head of the Ministry of Education, I suggested the name of Lucio Costa to Dr. Francisco Campos for the position of director of the School of Fine Arts, I had not received any request in his favour, neither from him nor from any other person. I must add that, at the time, I did not even know him personally: my proposal was based exclusively on the admiration that his work as an architect had always inspired in me.[25]

By comparing various reports, we are able to claim that Mello Franco de Andrade's decision seemed to have pulled together around it a group of intellectuals that was rather compact and favourable in regards to a general spirit of renewal; while Paulo Santos[26] nominated Manuel Bandeira – *traits d'union* between the modernists of São Paulo and the Carioca cultural circle, and commissioner of the 1929 text on Aleijadinho – Mariano Filho, in declining the "glory of the assignment" against the assumptions put forth by the "artistic circles,"[27] claimed that the nomination was caused by the intercession of the "an unidentified group of Futurist scholars."[28] In a letter dated 26 June 1936 to Le Corbusier, Costa credits his election to the "intervention of the refined spirits of Manuel Bandeira and Rodrigo Mello Franco de Andrade," inviting the interlocutor to remember their names.[29] The question remains though: why was Costa identified by this group of intellectuals, who were well integrated in the administrative circles of the new government, as the person best suited to realise its aspirations? Unfortunately, even in the recent reorganisation of the architect's personal archive, no documents have emerged that could help us definitively answer this question, leaving the issue open to various hypotheses. Given the conditions, it is clear that the decisive factor in his appointment was not due to his avant-garde stance, which seems more like a consequence of his commitment to the academic reform and his close contact with figures that were up-to-date on the international artistic debates. Yet, Costa's statement quoted above leads us to believe that there already were good reasons for associating his election to the prospect of a radical change in the academic system and in its cultural orientation.

Given this picture, the visibility gained by Costa in the professional world – and the relevance of a series of influential clients in the political one[30] – seems to have played an important role in his candidacy, especially since he had already received a number of important public assignments.

It is probable that, unlike the members of the School's board of professors – from which, according to the existing legislation, the new director should have been chosen – Costa was identified as a figure that could shake up the closed and anachronistic academic environment from the inside – mediating between the different political forces at hand, as well as between the different sides of the debate – better than anybody coming from outside of the same academic world could. What emerges from the speech that Francisco Campos gave on the occasion of his establishment as minister of Education is how the new government's policies, even in the field of education, were aimed toward a "soft" renewal – in terms of continuity rather than a complete break with the past – and were based on an underlying compromise: "reorganising the study programmes in order to better respond to the different tendencies; the harmony of our cultural system will result from their new combination."[31]

A discreet revolution

On 29 December 1930, less than a month after his establishment as school director, Costa traced a brief outline of the orientation he intended to bring to the academic reform on the pages of O Globo (Figure 1.2). It was the first time that he explicitly declared his intention to "refresh" the system – perhaps also due to the advice of the same intellectuals who had supported his nomination – in relation to modernist experiences, which had been considered "precarious" until then.

> It is necessary that our painters, sculptors, and architects make an effort to hear – without *parti-pris* – this movement coming from overseas, and understand this profoundly serious moment we are living and that will mark the "primitive" phase of a great era. The important thing is to penetrate its spirit, its profound sense, and not force anything; it is important for the movement to come from the inside-out and not from the outside-in, since false modernism is a thousand times worse than any academicism.[32]

Costa's inaugural speech therefore addressed the need for greater architectural authenticity – a position he had already held on previous occasions as well – distancing himself from the traditionalist discourse, and willing to promote an ideal continuity between past and present, in terms of structural sincerity and adaptation of taste to ongoing transformations. Upon closer inspection, his position seems to have been in line with the theories that had emerged from the IV Pan-American Congress of Architects held in Rio only a few months earlier.[33] It is not unlikely that this event of great mobilisation (not only at a national level) within the artistic and architectural world – in which Costa actively participated as a member of the organising committee[34] – presented itself as the perfect opportunity to directly meet some of the leading members of architectural modernism. Among these, it is worth mentioning the Russian architect Gregori Warchavchik[35] and the Paulista architect Flávio de Carvalho, who, in addition to presenting congressional reports, also exhibited their architectural work at the Pan-American Exposition held on this occasion. As reported by the press, the Congress was carried out in a climate of open conflict between those who declared themselves favourable to the assimilation of the modern language and its theories of aesthetic and social renovation, and those who, contrarily, defended an idea of modernity that was based on adapting alleged local traditions

O novo director da Escola de Bellas Artes e as directrizes — de uma reforma

Um programma em breve entrevista com o architecto — Lucio Costa —

O ESTYLO "COLONIAL" E O "SALON"

O GLOBO, no seu programma de bem informar o publico, procurou ouvir a palavra do novo director da Escola Nacional de Bellas Artes que, pela primeira vez, tem a dirigil-a um architecto.

Fomos encontrar o Sr. Lucio Costa no seu gabinete de trabalho:

— Suas impressões com relação á Escola e o seu programma, isto é, as suas intenções?

— Embora julgue imprescindivel uma reforma em toda Escola, aliás como é do pensamento do governo, vamos falar um pouco sobre as necessidades do curso de Architectura. Acho que o curso de architectura necessita uma transformação radical. Não só o curso em si, mas os programmas das respectivas cadeiras e principalmente a orientação geral do ensino. A actual é absolutamente falha. A divergencia entre a architectura e a estructura, a construcção propriamente dita tem tomado proporções simplesmente alarmantes. Em todas as grandes épocas as fórmas estheticas e estructuraes se identificaram. Nos verdadeiros estylos, architectura e construcção coincidem. E quanto mais perfeita a coincidencia, mais puro o estylo. O Parthenon, Reims, Sta. Sophia, tudo construcção, tudo honesto, as columnas supportam, os arcos trabalham. Nada mente. Nós fazemos exactamente o contrario. Se a estructura pede cinco, a architectura pede cincoenta. Procedemos da seguinte maneira, feito o arcabouço, simples, real, em concreto armado, tratar de escondel-o por todos os meios e modos. Simulam-se arcos e contrafortes, penduram-se columnas, atarracham-se vigas de madeira ás lages de concreto. Pedra fica muito caro? Não tem importancia, o pó de pedra apparelhado com as regras da estereotomia resolve o problema. Fazemos scenographia, estylo, *archeologia*, fazemos casas hespanholas de terceira mão, miniaturas de castellos medievaes, falsos coloniaes, tudo, menos architectura.

E, em poucas palavras, o architecto Lucio Costa traçou o programma.

— A reforma visará apparelhar a Escola de um curso technico scientifico tanto quanto possivel perfeito, e orientar o ensino artistico no sentido de uma perfeita harmonia com a construcção. Os classicos serão estudados como disciplina; os estylos como orientação critica e não para applicação directa.

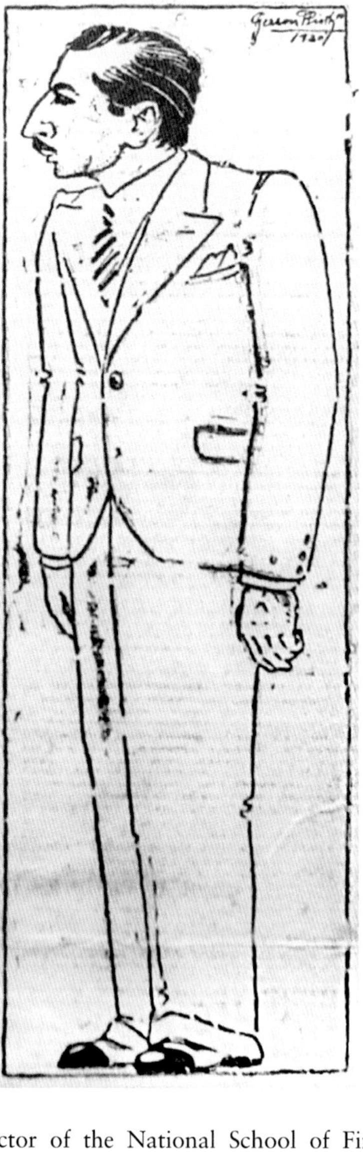

Figure 1.2 Interview with Lucio Costa as director of the National School of Fine Arts, *O Globo*, December 1930.

to modern contemporary life. In addition to a shared aspiration toward modernity, this reveals profound incompatibilities regarding the ways in which modernity was understood, ultimately resolved in favour of more conservative views.

On the other hand, we must remember how at the end of the 1920s Rio de Janeiro was hosting a considerable number of cultural events and conferences of prominent figures from overseas, which contributed to push the local debate toward a mild and progressive update and renewal. While the echo of the famous 1922 Semana de Arte Moderna (Modern Art Week) in São Paulo[36] – the first great exhibit of modernist avant-gardism at a national level – reached all the way to the capital (as Tarsila do Amaral's first 1930 personal exhibition proves), the German cultural entrepreneur Theodor Heuberger began intensely disseminating and promoting European modern art already in the mid-1920s. Le Corbusier himself, as anticipated earlier, held his famous lectures in December of 1929, precisely within the context of the School of Fine Arts, although his ideas had already long been subject of debate among Brazilian architects.[37] It is therefore understandable how, upon Costa's return from Europe, all these stimuli could have brought him to open up toward the various experiments that had been taking place on the international scene. Gerson Pinheiro significantly commented on his proposal by saying that the fear of having the School of Fine Arts transform itself "into a centre of propaganda of the so called traditional-regionalist movement" – as Costa's appointment to the direction of the school seemed to suggest – died out once the young director had proven to be "completely integrated in the contemporary movement."[38]

In his new role as director, Costa immediately showed great independence, relying on the complete trust of the minister, the head of the cabinet, and the latter's technical consultant, Lino de Sá Pereira. Moreover, careful observation of the sources shows how the cultural line of the revolutionary government did leave a mark on Costa's academic reform. In order to better evaluate the affinities between the government's rhetoric and the one adopted by the new school director, all we need is to compare the already quoted inaugural speech by minister Campos and Costa's academic programmatic communication in his interview in *O Globo*: while Campos – giving voice to the frustrations accumulated during the crisis of the Old Republic – praised the institutional renewal and the reaction of the new vital forces of the country to the "calcification and ankylosis" affecting "all major aspects of Brazilian life" like a "malignant infiltration,"[39] Costa, on the other hand, used similar terms in describing the previous annual *Salões*.

> Year after year, one gets the impression that we see the same paintings, same statues, same models, even their collocation barely varies. Despite the abuse of colour (many believe that strong colours are synonymous with modernity), we perceive an absolute lack of life, [...] an irreversible sense of ricketiness and paralysis. The isolation in which most of our artists live, with respect to everything happening in the world, is unbelievable. It almost looks like we live in some remote island of the Pacific; our newest creations barely correspond to the first attempts of the impressionists.[40]

In addition to the dissatisfaction with the monotony of the previous exhibitions – that would, however, bear the fruit of the 1931 "Salão Lucio Costa" – the new director made his intention of radically transforming the architecture course and its

16 *The start of a militant career*

academic programmes quite clear in his interview, steering the educational programmes toward a "perfect harmony with actual construction," toward a study of the "classics [...] as a discipline" and the styles "as critical guidelines."

The decree that was passed on 11 April 1931 – containing the general provisions for the reorganisation of the University of Rio de Janeiro and for the reformulation of the educational system of various institutes, including the National School of Fine Arts (which merged with the university system from that moment on) – seemed to have effectively realised these programmatic intentions. The most direct source to the heart of the contents and implementation methods of the reform are the actual assembly records of the Congregação. Although they were called together only twice in the nine months of Costa's school direction, the records of these assemblies witness quite clearly the progressive exacerbation given by the ease with which the young director made use of the authority that was given him in daily administrative management. In fact, it stretched to the limit of the responsibilities of the same Congregação, whose competences concerning precisely the academic orientation of the institution were reduced to a merely symbolic function.

The first assembly convened on 22 April 1931, immediately after the decree's approval, and aimed at electing the School representatives for the University Board, as well as the members of the Technical and Administrative Board. The inaugural speech by professor Gastão Bahiana summarises the ambiguity behind the academic body's reception of the new director: Bahiana expresses satisfaction for the "more rational and efficient organisation" introduced by the decree; however, in addition to highlighting his disappointment over the Congregação's failure in developing the reform, he also tends to downsize the subversive contents of Costa's measures, arguing that they essentially are the same objectives that the school's professors had been fighting for – unsuccessfully – for years.

> [E]liminating secondary education courses; splitting up other courses; introducing courses in urban planning, landscape architecture, decorative composition, and minor art technology; great development of technical training; compulsory practical activities; better and more serious exams, preceded by multiple tests; the independence of the School's annual final exhibition; and a general organisation that should be identical to that of the other higher education institutions, from admission requests to professor and teaching staff recruitment.[41]

After the tribute to minister Francisco Campos and his technical assistants, and after welcoming the new director – of which he recognises the value but also the complete disassociation from the "teaching" practice – Bahiana's speech confers Costa the merit of having known how to "accurately interpret and assert the points of view [...] that were vainly supported" by the Congregação, despite having impressed "the priceless scent of originality to his educational purpose."

The innovations introduced by Costa's reform were effectively significant and should be compared both with the system active under the previous direction of José Corrêa Lima and with the previous reform attempts by part of the Congregação, especially the one made in 1924, which was never approved and saw the separation of the architecture course from that of fine arts.[42] The most relevant feature of the 1931 reform was, in fact, precisely the autonomous structuring of the two courses. By eliminating the previous subdivision between *Curso geral* and subsequent specialisation, the reform put an end to a type of educational programme that had been substantially structured on an academic model. The provision also met the need for greater specialisation, a need that the professional world had been expressing for a long time; not only were the courses in architecture, painting, and sculpture intended for different professional categories, but, in the case of the architecture course, the title achieved at the end of the studies went from being that of *architecto-engenheiro* to *architecto*.

Other new measures brought in by the reform included a raise in the minimum age of enrolment, an enhancement of the admission exam, and the introduction of compulsory field studies to visit and observe architectural heritage directly on site. As for the actual didactic programme of the architecture course, the difference between the previous system and the new one introduced by the decree was actually significant; the most evident update concerned the enhancement of the examinations related to the study of construction techniques and materials, which were only three in the previous *Curso especial* and were now instead distributed over the entire five-year length of the course. Other new features of the didactic programmes were the larger amount of time dedicated to architecture theory and the introduction of subjects like "urban planning, urban composition and construction," "topography, landscape architecture," "physics applied to construction," "applied arts, technology and decorative composition."

However, a series of elements was persistent with the system of the time, including the division of the architecture composition course in *Gráu minimo* (third year), *Gráu médio* (fourth year), and *Gráu máximo* (fifth year), and the relevance assigned to the future architects' mastery in the field of classical architectural elements and historical styles, in addition to their mastery of design tools and artistic composition. The introduction of a specialisation course in "Brazilian studies" seems to represent – apart from a concession to ex-mentor José Mariano Filho (school director from 1926 to 1927) – a choice aimed at satisfying the common desire of seeing the study of national art introduced into the academic offer, an inclination that also emerged on the occasion of the IV Pan-American Congress of Architects.

However, the most controversial action of Costa's administration remains his choice of splitting up the practical courses into the so-called "parallel courses," the classes of which were assigned to professors of different artistic orientation, giving students the possibility of choosing among them according to their own personal inclinations. Already in the first assembly, professors of clear modernist tendencies – the Russian Gregori Warchavchik and the Belgian Alexandre Buddeus for architectural composition, the German Leo Putz[43] for painting, and the Brazilian Celso Antônio for sculpture – were officially appointed to head the parallel courses, a piece of news that was promptly released by the main national newspapers, triggering reactions of violent opposition[44] (Figure 1.3). Warchavchik, who was officially appointed on 23 May 1931 – right after the Casa Modernista Exhibit organised by the same Russian architect in São Paulo – to "hold an architecture course (*Gráu minimo*) of the current school year with a monthly salary of one *conto de réis*,"[45] provides an interesting interpretation of Costa's cultural policy.

> He will bring together, in this artistic laboratory he directs, the two opposite currents: the modern and the traditional or "classical." Subjected to both these influences, students will no longer be stiffened among the mummified ideas of old artistic

O Ingresso de Professores Futuristas na Escola Nacional de Bellas Artes

Officio dirigido ao Snr. Ministro da
Educação e Saúde Publica

PELO

Instituto Paulista de Architectos

SÃO PAULO
1931

Typographia Camargo
Rua General Couto de Magalhães, 58
São Paulo

Figure 1.3 Publication of the Instituto Paulista de Architectos against the designation of modern professors at the National School of Fine Arts, 1931.

expressions, but they will have the chance to disclose and "air" their artistic sense enough to be able to judge what is most appropriate for their time, for the materials they have at hand, for the current condition of man on the planet ...[46]

Warchavchik's words describe, perhaps a bit too schematically, the substance of the "discreet" revolution that was put in place by Lucio Costa, welcomed with the same enthusiasm by other important figures belonging to the São Paulo modernist environment. The same Mário de Andrade claimed, once the experience was over, that Costa's "ironic ability" consisted precisely in "not taking anyone away from his place" while, at the same time, employing "professors of evident professional respectability" who were able of showing an alternative way to the "antiquated aesthetics of mummies."[47] It is not easy to establish the extent to which adopting this cultural mediation strategy was owed to Campos' administration guidelines, to which Geraldo Ferraz referred to as a "conciliation regime." On the other hand, there is no doubt that the didactic methods adopted by the new professors, the circulation of new publications,[48] and the gradual modification of the activity and exercise themes were issues that effectively contributed to breaking from traditional educational methods and opening the doors to a season of great renewal of the dominant cultural models. Costa himself made no secret of his personal artistic preferences: on the occasion of the Caminhoã award, he drew attention to the project ranked second, "the architecture of which is advocated by the direction board";[49] the project was developed by Affonso Eduardo Reidy, who would become assistant to Warchavchik's course from that moment on. By encouraging a generation of young architecture students – including Reidy, Jorge Moreira, Oscar Niemeyer, Roberto Burle Marx, Alcides da Rocha Miranda, Ernani Vasconcellos, Milton Roberto, Hélio Uchoa, etc. – to assimilate the modern language, Costa's direction will fuel a climate of tension within the academic institution, destined to quickly become uncontrollable.

The Salão dos tenentes

Costa acted autonomously and freely even in the organisation of the 38ª Exhibition of the School of Fine Arts, also known as Salão dos tenentes.[50] It is not by chance that one of the transitional rules of the 1931 decree established that the Exhibition of the same year was "exclusive responsibility of the school director and of a commission established by him."[51] Thus having swept away the authority of the Conselho Nacional de Belas Artes – the body responsible for the Exhibition's organisation up until then[52] – Costa called upon some of the main names related to the modernist movement to join him on the Exhibition's commission board: Manuel Bandeira, painters Anita Malfatti and Cândido Portinari, and sculptor Celso Antônio, who had already been appointed professor of one of the sculpture courses. In subsequent interviews Costa would remember how the first meetings for the organisation of the Exhibition were held in São Paulo at the pavilion-museum of Olívia Guedes Penteado, one of the main personalities belonging to the Paulista intelligentsia of the time, in the presence of some of the animators of the Semana de Arte Moderna, among which were Mário de Andrade and Paulo Prado.[53]

20 The start of a militant career

According to Manuel Bandeira's testimony, the merit of the initiative should be solely attributed to the young director's far-sightedness.

> Lucio Costa has understood, from the very beginning, that in matter of good artistic direction, São Paulo represents almost all of Brazil [...]. Choosing Anita Malfatti as member of the admissions committee has completed the happy idea of the director of the School of Fine Arts. Not only did Anita bring her personal contribution – five paintings from different periods – but she also managed, with the help of Mr. And Mrs. Warchavchik, to bring together a group of paintings that, alone, would have saved the Exhibition. This way, the Carioca audience has had the chance to experience the strength of Brecheret, Gobbis, Warchavchik, and Anita herself for the first time.[54]

The Carioca audience had actually already had the chance on several occasions – among which was the exhibition set up for the Pan-American Congress of Architects, the aforementioned initiatives brought by patron Theodor Heuberger, but also the 1st Salão dos Artistas Brasileiros (Brazilian Artist Exhibition) of 1929 organised by Celso Kelly in the Biblioteca Nacional – to directly come in contact with the work of the artistic and architectural avant-garde. However, up until then, these were works that had been excluded from the annual exhibitions of the School of Fine Arts.

With a committee that was clearly set in its decision to support the work of the avant-garde and was completely alienated from the consolidated institutional approach, Costa was quick to resort to an intelligent mediation strategy that was able to legitimise the operation in the eyes of the academic body. The strategy he developed consisted in bringing together, side-by-side, works of art belonging to different artistic lines, so as to let them speak for themselves and therefore without – at least apparently – displeasing anybody in particular. As a brief note held in the archives of the School of Fine Arts states:

> The organising committee of the 38ª Exposição Geral de Belas Artes informs the artists that the rumours on the exclusively modern character of the 1931 Exhibition are completely unfounded. The 38ª Exposição will be, as the previous ones, an event open to all movements, including the avant-garde ones that were kept away from official juries and prizes up until today. Given the general character of these exhibitions, it is clear that the members of this year's organising committee will adopt a method that is independent from their artistic preferences, admitting only the good within each artistic movement.[55]

In accordance with the general guidelines of the reform, Costa proposed an apparently peaceful principle of reconciliation between the different artistic tendencies, intended to offer a complete outline and a – so to speak – reflection of the actual artistic situation of the country, avoiding evident open alignments with anybody. In response to the criticism that rose against the exhibition's regulation, Costa insisted on the coherency of its organisation, the object of which – despite the programme being divided into a "general section" and a "modern" one – was not the polarisation of the debate in "two distinct artistic movements," but rather the desire to convey the "most legitimate artistic expressions of our time."[56] The same Manuel Bandeira deployed rhetorical weapons in the initiative's defence.

It seems as though the noble attempt of the Director of the School of Fine Arts will be successful in achieving – this year in which the exhibition's organisation has been discretionally entrusted to him – what it always should have: an annual balance of the artistic realities in our country, a meeting point for all the trends, good, bad, terrible, or bearable. A moment of fraternisation above and beyond any alignment that does not exclude moments of criticism, discussions, and even open confrontations if you will. This is life and this is fair play. Ideally, nothing should be excluded, however ugly it may seem; but it is a solution that cannot be considered for the simple reason of lack of space.[57]

The utopian strategy of the parallel courses was therefore literally reiterated in the organisation of the Salão, in the belief that – by virtue of the direct confrontation – part of the audience would have been driven to open their eyes in the face of the tangible manifestations of the renewal underway.

The graphic design for the cover of Lucia Gouvêa Vieira's volume on the exhibition,[58] designed by Costa in the 1980s, effectively expresses this strategy of mediation: a diagonal line separates two equal and opposite triangles – painted with the colours of the Brazilian flag – that together form a rectangle on which appears the writing *Salão 31*. In a note inside his autobiographical volume *Registro de uma vivência*, Costa associates the colours of the flag to a double symbolic component: "Order and progress, perfect integration: conservative and progressive,"[59] highlighting one of the staples of Costa's approach, namely his search for a synthesis capable of bringing together terms that are apparently irreconcilable.

A survey of the press reveals the various reactions to the "inclusive" strategy adopted by Costa, without denying the success of the exhibition in general, especially when compared to the static repetition of the previous annual exhibitions; while Mário de Andrade and Gregori Warchavchik, respectively, saw it as an "admirable competition principle"[60] and a triumph of the "value" method,[61] José Mariano Filho regarded the exhibition as a source that brought nothing but discontent to both "Greeks and Trojans,"[62] creating the premises for a probable failure of Costa's administration.

Although the absence of an actual jury, as well as of a limit to the number of works for each artist, favoured the display of a much richer number of artworks than the previous years – despite many "academic" artists voluntarily refusing to exhibit their works – it is clear that the particular composition of the committee played a significant role in the selection of the exhibited artworks. A note sent by Costa to the painter Di Cavalcanti, urging him to send more paintings, is unequivocal proof of the fact that there was a clear artistic tendency within the committee, of which the modern section was a more or less accurate reflection. A humorous sketch with which Costa decorated the note to Di Cavalcanti significantly represents – aside from a room full of the artist's work – a native man holding a Brazilian flag wrapped around the cartouche of the institution, the hems of which are held by two winged putti, alluding to the coexistence of classical and "anthropophagic" themes.[63] However, it is the actual design of the artwork display (conceived by Costa himself) that mostly expressed the clashing contrast between "old" and "new," rigorously at the expense of the former. Not only were the pieces grouped according to their alignment to one of the two artistic movements – leaving the catalogue in charge of

22 The start of a militant career

classifying them in the traditional subdivision of painting, sculpture, and architecture[64] – but the two "sections" of the exhibition were subject to different treatments. Costa would remember, not without some pride, how the modern section presented simple jute-covered panels, with "paintings displayed individually, instead of bunched up together, one above the other, like in previous exhibitions" – an arrangement that was instead maintained for the display of the "academic" section.[65]

The Exhibition, inaugurated on 1 September 1931, remained open until the 29th of the same month, right after Costa's official resignation. On the same day of the inauguration, news of the request of the removal of Francisco Campos from the position of minister of Education, due to a number of political issues, was released. President Getúlio Vargas, contrary to expectations,[66] was not present at the inauguration ceremony.

Among those exhibiting their work in the architecture section were Affonso Eduardo Reidy and Gerson Pompeu Pinheiro, Flávio de Carvalho, Gregori Warchavchik, Costa, and Marcelo Roberto. Both in the catalogue and in the archive documents,[67] Costa's four projects are listed with the sole initials of the clients, which makes their identification rather difficult. In any case, these are four residential projects, two for himself and two – judging by the initials they bear – for Cesário Coelho Duarte and Pedro Paulo Paes de Carvalho, for whom the architect also worked on other occasions. One of the two houses labelled with L.C. can be maybe identified as the one built in Correias around 1928 for his father-in-law, Modesto Guimarães, where Costa had settled with his family. What is even more surprising is the absence of the project for the house of Ernesto Gomes Fontes, the second version of which is usually dated at 1930 and is usually referred to by Costa as a "first proposal of contemporary tendencies"[68] (Figure 1.4).

Figure 1.4 Lucio Costa, drawing of the second version of Casa Fontes, Rio de Janeiro. Perspective view of the interior, early 1930s. Casa de Lucio Costa.

In any case, the young director found himself at the centre of a heated debate – further fuelled by his sudden resignation – not because of the few projects he presented, but because of the audacity and effectiveness of his work as creator and coordinator of the exhibition. Manuel Bandeira claimed that, once the exhibition was inaugurated, the interest aroused by it was due to "precisely all the scandal that was expected from it and that was never delivered."[69] Cândido Portinari saw the exhibition as a faithful reflection of the artistic climate of the time – "a foreigner wishing to learn about the state of the arts in Brazil," he claimed, "could do so thanks to the Salão 38, or better yet, thanks to the Salão Lucio Costa"[70] – while other press referred to the exhibition as the first actual revolutionary operation of the Vargas administration, depicting the school director as its heroic animator.

> Salão no. 38 – so interesting and intelligent that is doesn't even seem like an actual official exhibition – rehabilitates Brazilian culture. Lucio Costa has given an apt and canny lesson to our people: he has taught us what a true fine arts Exhibition should be like. And I think it would not be incorrect to say that the current director of the School of Fine Arts, with his initiative, did more for the revolutionary spirit in Brazil than if he had taken up arms and fought in the trenches of Itararé.[71]

Report of a failure

The 1931 Exhibition helped exacerbate the professors' hostility toward Costa's academic administration, undermining a situation that had become increasingly more delicate. At the same time, a series of factors external to the academic and disciplinary issues also came to irreversibly weaken Costa's institutional position: Rodrigo Mello Franco de Andrade's resignation from Campos's head-of-cabinet position – caused by the deteriorating relations between the two[72] – in fact deprived the young director of his main supporter, in a moment of political instability that saw Campos's same position threatened as well.[73]

The fuse of this explosion was provided by a protest that took shape starting from a quarrel between the students and professor Gastão Bahiana regarding the educational reform. The protest was organised and managed by the representatives of the Diretório Academico, Luíz Nunes de Souza and Jorge Machado Moreira. On 24 August, they announced a peaceful strike and an interruption of all educational activities, becoming spokesmen of the requests made by the student body – namely, Bahiana's removal from the faculty, and the tenure of the School director.[74] In this phase, the minister, urged by the student representatives, renewed his support for Costa – who, as he said, "is doing a good job and deserves the government's trust and credit" – and expressed his will to keep him in the position of director with "full decision-making independence."[75] It is at this point that the Congregação took action, determined to exploit the general unrest to start up their scheme to oust Costa. They called for an emergency meeting – the second meeting ever held under Costa's administration – which took place on 26 August. On this occasion, Rodolfo Chambelland, as member of the Technical and Administrative Board, approached Costa in these terms:

I feel obliged to inform H. E. and the illustrious Congregação of the considerations I deem necessary to justify the current behaviour of the T. and Adm. [Technical and Administrative] Board regarding the impossibility of applying the legal provisions concerning hired professors, who carry out their duties without making their programmes explicit, as required by tenured professors [...]. H. E. forgets that these provisions are the result of his own free will, and cannot be maintained if they are not kept within the regulation system that governs the School, therefore attributing them to the deliberative power of the Board, which H. E. seeks to deny.[76]

By attributing the responsibility for the recent turmoil to the director's management of the School's daily administration, Bahiana settled the issue in peremptory terms: "either H. E. continues to act as director without the assistance of the T. and Adm. Board or the National School of Fine Arts will take back full possession of the powers conferred to it by law." Subsequently, Raul Pederneiras appealed to article 27 of the decree dated 11 April 1931 – which, among other things, regulated the appointment of the directors of all federal university institutes, providing that the choice be made from a list of three candidates belonging to the same institution's professors – to prove the illegitimacy of Costa's position, since he did not in fact take part in the School's board of professors. The same Perderneiras, in the previous Congregação assembly of 22 April, had proposed to give him professorship *honoris causa*, so as to meet the conditions of the active legislation – a professorship that Costa had refused. Costa commented the affair, in a statement that was published only a few days after his resignation:

On that occasion, I had the opportunity to remind the aforementioned professor that I had accepted the School's direction with the intention of moralising it; therefore, I was shocked at his proposal, since I considered the profession of teaching a very serious investiture and not a pretext to accommodate the given situations. I also added, to make things clear to the professors, that I had asked the minister, upon the coming reform, if it might be necessary to include some specific provision, among the many transitional ones, on my case; H. E. replied that it would have been useless, since it was clear that the law applied only to cases in which the post was left empty and could not be applied retroactively.[77]

The tones of the assembly then grew even more intense. While Costa criticised the teaching staff for not having disputed the legitimacy of his appointment as director from the beginning – rather than offering him "professorship as a gift" – the Congregação retaliated with the argument that the prolonged state of uncertainty caused by the situation – and by the new director not having called other meetings – had consequently prevented the possibility of any clarification in these regards. The meeting finally ended with the unanimous request to proceed with the nomination of three candidates for the election of a new director, from which Costa was therefore automatically excluded. His attempts to defend the legitimacy of his position on the University Board, which achieved no positive result, highlight how little Costa had tried to consolidate his institutional relations, worsening his condition of isolation.[78] In a memorandum compiled by Rodolfo Chambelland (acting as provisional director) and transcribed in the proceedings of the Congregação's assembly, chaired by the new director Archimedes Memória on 21 September 1931,[79] Costa's directorship was violently indicted: the irresponsible management of the previous months was reprimanded as a period during which the director had approved "measures of the utmost importance, autonomously," administering the financial resources of the institution to his liking, reducing the Congregação to a "dead body," and encouraging the rebellious behaviour of students and professors. Costa was even accused of concealing the note in which the Dean informed him of the minister's claim that he, Costa, was in no position to benefit from "any extraordinary investiture," thus proving how he suddenly found himself without any institutional support. It was during the University Board meeting of 10 September – in a particularly violent and conflictual atmosphere – that Costa presented his resignation, as Chambelland reported.

> As the members of the honourable Board will remember, all professors of the University have suffered, to a greater or lesser extent, Mr. Lucio Costa's tirades and accusations. Naturally and understandably, most of them were directed toward the professors of the School of Fine Arts, old mentors of the architect. L. C. has therefore taken his leave, making the strangest statements, like that of judging himself as the only person destined to save the School's future. This statement deserved the following lapidary comment from Prof. Gastão Gomes of the University of Minas: "Then you must be the Messiah…" Immediately afterwards, upon Costa's provocative question of why they did not discharge him, Dr. Candido de Oliveira Filho responded: "You are already automatically discharged." Upon further questions, with the same defiant tone, on why the University Board did not discharge him, Prof. Leonel Gonzaga replied: "Because the Board hoped that you would understand that you should present your own resignation." Mr. Lucio Costa ended the meeting by presenting his resignation, declaring himself dismissed, and immediately abandoning the assembly.[80]

In his reply to the provocations, in a sharp article published in the *Correio da Manhã* on 19 September 1931, Costa attributed the Congregação's inertness to its intention of taking advantage of the delicate political stance of minister Campos, who effectively resigned a few days after the nomination of the three candidates.[81] Two days after the troubled assembly, Rodrigo Mello Franco de Andrade sent a letter of solidarity to the ex-director, who was taking refuge in his residence in Correias. In this letter, he compliments Costa for the "complete and fruitful reform" that he had been able to achieve in his few months of administration and for that year's Exhibition, increasing the "public esteem and recognition" that he already benefited from. In praising the "exceptional gifts" that Costa showed in the direction of the institution entrusted to him, Mello Franco de Andrade expresses his disappointment in how his resignation was due to the "most futile and unfounded pretext," bitterly ending the letter by saying that the provisional government had lost "the only one in office holding an authentic revolutionary spirit."[82] Rodrigo Mello Franco de Andrade and Manuel Bandeira took to the former director's defence on a public platform as well, participating in the lively debate around the chaotic administrative situation of the School of Fine Arts.[83]

26 *The start of a militant career*

In fact, after Costa's resignation, the student movement became more aggressive, threatening to strike indefinitely if their request to have the director reinstated – or to appoint somebody from outside of the faculty, able to complete Costa's reform – was not accepted.[84] The nomination on 17 September 1931 of Archimedes Memória to the position of director helped exacerbate the student protest, given the students' demand to preserve the professors that had been nominated by the now ex-director. Claiming to be "guided by a shared ideal" and to support "the orientation of the architect Lucio Costa," the student representatives sent a letter to Gregori Warchavchik – who had expressed the intention of leaving the School after Costa's resignation as a gesture of solidarity – to convince him to continue issuing the "remarkable teachings" that they could "no longer live without."[85] The telegrams with which the new director requested the programmes of the courses and released the date of the beginning of the academic activities testify how the Russian architect had not communicated his resignation,[86] by December of 1931 at least (although years later Memória would claim that after Costa's resignation only Alexandre Buddeus and Celso Antônio continued with their normal academic activities for some time).[87] On 15 December, Francisco Campos, reconfirmed as minister, issued a provision stating that the academic courses had been reopened, entrusting the Dean with the task of appointing six members (external to the Congregação) to assist director Memória. Not satisfied, the students attempted to forcibly cause the director's resignation; what they achieved was having the reorganisation of the educational offer entrusted to the government officials who had collaborated in the compilation of the reform in 1931, therefore putting an end to a strike that had lasted for more than four months.

These months of strike had a deep impact on its participants, who were propelled in a fervent and passionate climate of debate and daily exchange with some of the figures destined to become the protagonists of the international artistic and architectural scene in the years to follow. Even Frank Lloyd Wright – who visited Rio de Janeiro as jury member of the Columbus Memorial Lighthouse Competition – took an active part in the debates, supporting the student protest in a series of conferences in which he looked forward to the establishment of an educational system based on the "advanced thought of the world." Wright himself enthusiastically described his stay in Rio:

> Well, the Bellas Artes "strike" began to turn on the heat. I don't remember where or how many times I spoke, or how many newspaper articles I wrote for *El Globo* and *El Manha* [*O Globo* and *Correio da Manhã*], the leading newspapers of Brazil.
>
> The boys would come after me and I would go, and Herbert Moses would "interpret" – if that is what he did. He became fiery eloquent – I suspect he frequently put more into me than I had put into him. I met the "modern" professors the boys wanted. They were good architects and excellent men.[88]

Among these "excellent men" there was of course Lucio Costa, who – while maintaining a certain distance from the events concerning the school – had the opportunity to personally meet the American architect on the occasion of the inauguration of the Casa Modernista Exhibit that was organised in Rio de Janeiro by Gregori Warchavchik[89] (Figure 1.5).

Figure 1.5 Lucio Costa, Frank Lloyd Wright, and Gregori Warchavchik at the inauguration of the Casa Modernista Exhibit in Rio de Janeiro, 1931. Casa de Lucio Costa.

28 The start of a militant career

At this point we may try making an assessment of the brief but intense Costian administration. If we consider that, after this interlude, the disconnection between academic and professional world continued to repeat itself – with the exception of the short-lived attempt of the Universidade do Distrito Federal – we can only conclude that the impact on the educational system was basically inconsistent. Costa himself ruthlessly evaluated his contribution from the educational and organisational point of view.

> On a practical level, my contribution was a negative one, since I upset something that already existed, good or bad – I am referring to the academic reality, not the Exhibition. Something organised did exist and was destroyed, without leaving anything in return. Because now, there is neither one thing nor the other left. Still today. The educational system has remained disorganised and lacks a clear orientation.[90]

Yet, the results of that experience should be measured in relation to some of the promising professional careers that were fuelled by it, thanks to which a group of former students actively took part in a critical experimental phase on the theme of modern language assimilation. This atmosphere of "holy war" – referring to the widespread use of military and religious terminology – fuelled by the heated tones of the debate, determined the conditions for a partially distorted historiographical reception that tends to exaggerate the ideological issues, transmitting an image of the "rebels" as prophets of a just cause and an image of the academics as enemies against which this war should be fought. However, locating this affair within its effective nature of institutional conflict seems to be the most accurate thing to do. Besides the establishment of updated artistic expressions and educational methods, what was really at stake were in fact the political balances of the institution, with the country's representatives of the old and new generations engaged in, respectively, safeguarding and conquering their positions of power and authority.

In this contextual frame, the public image of the former director emerged as a strong one, laying the foundations for his identification as a reference point for all architects and artists in favour of a renewal. Despite its failure, the experience of the School direction undoubtedly represented – even from a biographical point of view – a crucial step in steering Costa's vocation toward the militant tones of the following years, seemingly fuelled by the sense of responsibility toward future generations that he developed in these months. We find much regarding this process in a letter written by Costa to Le Corbusier in 1936.

> In the meantime, an actual upheaval was taking place: from the "traditionalist" that I was – in the equivocal sense of the word – little by little, I was able to overcome the repulsion that your books inspired in me; and suddenly, like a revelation, the thrilling beauty of your appeal clouded my mind. In a "state of grace" and with the intransigent faith of a neophyte, I took it upon myself to "save" the young students of the School: nine months later – which is quite normal since I was effectively expelled – they threw me out, covering me with insults.[91]

On October 1932, Gregori Warchavchik wrote Sigfried Giedion and informed him of his experience at Rio's School of Fine Arts, adding Costa's name – already his associate at the time – at the top of a list of potential candidates for the Brazilian CIRPAC group.[92] Using the rhetoric of the resistance to a nemesis shared with the CIAM, the Russian architect claimed to have won the battle on moral grounds, by virtue of the fact that "these young students have talent and will grow on their own, now that" – in Corbusian terms – "their eyes are open."[93] It was the first time that Costa was seen and acknowledged, on the international scene, as a "leading figure" of Brazilian modernism.

Notes

1 Literature on the specific episode of the National School of Fine Arts is limited. In addition to the doctoral thesis of Helena Uzeda (2006), which constituted an essential reference to understand the cultural strategies and the ENBA educational system prior to Costa's direction, we also make special mention of: Maria Lucia Bressan Pinheiro, "Lucio Costa e a Escola Nacional de Belas Artes," in *Livro de resumos e anais do 6° Seminário Docomomo Brasil*. Niterói: UFF, 2005; Paulo Santos, "A reforma da Escola de Belas Artes e do Salão," in Alberto Xavier, ed., *Depoimento de uma geração: arquitetura moderna brasileira* (São Paulo: Cosac & Naify, 2003), 60–63; and Luis E. Carranza, Fernando Luiz Lara, *Modern Architecture in Latin America: Art, Technology, and Utopia* (Austin, TX: University of Texas Press, 2014), 61–63.
2 Lucio Marçal Ferreira Ribeiro de Lima Costa was born on 27 February 1902 in Toulon, France. His father, Joaquim Ribeiro da Costa, was a naval engineer from Salvador; his mother, Alina Gonçalves Ferreira, was born in Amazonas. In 1910, the Costa family moved from Rio de Janeiro to Newcastle upon Tyne (England), where Costa attended the Royal Grammar School. Afterwards, they spent several years – up to 1916 – in other European locations, including Montreaux (Switzerland), where Costa completed his primary education at the Collège National. Upon his return to Rio – and prompted by his father – Costa enrolled in the *Curso geral* of the National School of Fine Arts, where he developed his passion for architecture, finally enrolling in the *Curso especial de architectura* between 1921 and 1922.
3 In the "Livros de matrículas no Curso geral," kept in the Museu Dom João VI, the date of Costa's habilitation with the *Pequena medalha de ouro* is 5 May 1926. The dates of Costa's official diploma qualification – as usually reported by himself and by historiography in general (1922–1924) – are therefore inaccurate. See "Livros de matrículas no Curso geral, n. 1, 1916–1921. Ad vocem Lucio da Costa, 80". MDJ VI.
4 This could refer to the studio of Raphael Rebecchi, a large professional studio that won several public competitions in those years. See Paulo Santos, *Quátro séculos de arquitetura* (Barra do Piraí: Fundação Educacional Rosemar Pimentel, 1977).
5 See "Universidade do Brasil, Faculdade Nacional de Arquitetura. Cópia autêntica da Ata da sessão da Congregação do dia 17 de março de 1954," 17 March 1954. CLC, IV A 01-00320.
6 See Aracy Amaral, ed., *Arquitetura neocolonial: América Latina, Caribe, Estados Unidos* (São Paulo: Fundação Memorial da América Latina, 1994).
7 *Catalogo da XXXI Exposição Geral de Bellas Artes* (Rio de Janeiro: Typ. Revista dos Tribunaes, R. do Carmo 55, 1924).
8 "O nosso salão de 1924. É modesta a secção de architectura; os estudos coloniaes e seus derivados," *A Noite*, 4 September 1924.
9 *A casa*, *Architectura no Brasil*, *Mi casita* and, shortly after, *Arquitetura e Urbanismo*.
10 See "Bellas-Artes. Instituto Brasileiro de Architectos – O concurso de architectura tradicional," *O Jornal*, 10 February 1924. Costa's participation in the competition was encouraged by the same Mariano Filho (see Mariano Filho to Costa, September 6, 1923. CLC, VI A 02-01378) following the architect's double victory of a competition on the theme of *Bancos e Portões*: see "Architectura Colonial. O concurso José Mariano Filho," *Ilustração Brasileira*, March 1923. This first contact gave way to a collaboration that continued until 1930. The young architect's first interview happened in correlation

with the competition for a Solar Brasileiro, in which Costa was awarded second place: "A alma dos nossos lares. Porque é erronea a orientação da architectura do Rio: falanos um verdadeiro e commovido artista," *A Noite*, 19 March 1924. Here, in line with his mentor's positions, Costa indicates past colonial models as the source from which to draw the search for a complete artistic expression of the "Brazilian home."

11 As is known, the trips made in 1924 by Mário and Oswald de Andrade, Tarsila do Amaral, Blaise Cendrars, and others, would be fundamental to the development of the Pau-Brasil movement and of the Antropophagic Manifesto of the same de Andrade.
12 "Um architecto de sentimento nacional. Lucio Costa e a sua excursão artistica pelas velhas cidade de Minas. Considerações sobre nosso gôsto e estilo," *A Noite*, 18 June 1924.
13 José Mariano Filho, "Mas, que capadócio," *Diário da Noite*, 11 September 1931c.
14 The main stages of his trip can be reconstructed through the letters sent to his family members. In September of 1926, Costa departed from Salvador de Bahia; in October he travelled to Lisbon, and then made his way to Le Havre and Paris; in November, he was in Italy, where he visited Florence, Rome, Turin, Milan, Verona, Padua, and Venice. In Minas Gerais, he visited Caraça, Sabará, Mariana, Ouro Preto, and Diamantina.
15 Marcelo Puppi, *Por uma história não moderna da arquitetura brasileira. Questões de historiografia* (Campinas: Pontes Editores, 1998), 93.
16 "O palácio da Eimbaxada Argentina. Fala a 'O Jornal' o sr. Lucio Costa, vencedor do concurso de projectos estabelecido pelo governo argentino," *O Jornal*, 28 April 1928.
17 "O arranha-céo e o Rio de Janeiro. 'O Paiz,' em proseguimento da sua 'enquête,' ouve os architectos constructores Preston & Curtis e Lucio Costa," *O Paíz*, 1 July 1928. Also see Gaia Piccarolo, "Un dibattito: il grattacielo e Rio de Janeiro. Intervista a Lucio Costa," *Le culture della tecnica*, no. 20 (2009): 74–99.
18 Costa to Le Corbusier, 26 June 1936. FLC, I3-3-16.
19 Costa, "O Aleijadinho e a arquitetura tradicional," *O Jornal*, 1929, special issue on Minas Gerais, in Alberto Xavier, ed. *Lúcio Costa: sôbre arquitetura* (Porto Alegre: Editora UniRitter, 2007, 1st edn 1962), 12–16.
20 See Alfred Agache, *La remodelation d'une capitale. Aménagement – Extension – Embellissement* (Paris: Société Coopérative d'Architectes, 1932).
21 The Ministry was established with Decree n. 19.402 of 14 November 1930. On 24 October, the coup d'état with which the armed movement – led by the states of Minas Gerais, Paraíba, and Rio Grande do Sul – had ended, caused the deposition of the President of the Republic, Washington Luís, and prevented the appointment of the President-elect Júlio Prestes. On 3 November, Getúlio Vargas took command of the provisional government, officially ending the so-called "Old Republic." For more information on the cultural repercussions of the new political scene, see Antônio Cândido, "A Revolução de 1930 e a cultura," *Novos Estudos*, no. 4 (April 1984): 27–36.
22 Although lacking official documentation attesting to Costa's appointment, the date of 8 December 1930, indicated by Xavier (or of 12 December, indicated by Santos) proves to be coherent. The Vargas government took office at the beginning of November and Costa's first statement to the press as director dates to 29 December. Bressan Pinheiro claimed that Costa would have taken over the position of director a few months before the outbreak of the Revolution; this interpretation is based on the presence of Costa's signature on the official proceedings of the Congregação assembly of September 1930; however, it does not consider the fact that these were signed by the director in charge at the time of their re-reading, which took place during the following meeting. See "Acta da Sessão da Congregação da Escola Nacional de Belas Artes, efetuada em 12 de setembro de 1930. Presidência do Prof. José A. Corrêa Lima, Director." MDJ VI, 6158.
23 Costa, "A direção da Escola de Belas Artes," *Correio da Manhã*, 19 September 1931.
24 Costa, "A direção da Escola de Belas Artes." See also Costa, *Registro de uma vivência* (São Paulo: Empresa das Artes, 1995), 438.
25 Mello Franco de Andrade to the director of *Diário de Notícias*, 9 November 1937. ACI-RJ, LC-TT02(02).
26 Santos, *Quátro séculos de arquitetura*; id., *Presênça de Lucio Costa na arquitetura contemporânea do Brasil, Conferência*, Rio de Janeiro 1960. Typescript, BPS.

27 José Mariano Filho, "Escola nacional de arte futurista," *O Jornal*, 22 July 1931b.
28 José Mariano Filho, "A desnacionalização da Escola de Belas Artes," *O Jornal*, 1 August 1931a.
29 Costa to Le Corbusier, 26 June 1936.
30 Including João Daudt de Oliveira, who appears to have been in direct contact with minister Francisco Campos and for whom Costa had built two residences in Rio de Janeiro between 1927 and 1928, together with Fernando Valentim.
31 Inauguration speech by Francisco Campos for his appointment as minister of Education and Health (18 November 1930). CPDOC, GC pi Campos, F.
32 "O novo director da Escola de Bellas Artes e as directrizes de uma reforma. Um programa em breve entrevista com o architecto Lucio Costa. O estylo 'colonial' e o 'Salon'," *O Globo*, 29 December 1930.
33 The Congress took place from 19 to 29 June 1930 at the School of Fine Arts. The reported information refers to the press articles of the time that are preserved at the Biblioteca Paulo Santos.
34 According to Paulo Santos, Lucio Costa and Fernando Valentim had been among the collaborators that created the *décor* for the Theatro Municipal on the occasion of the Congress's inauguration.
35 Costa claims that his first encounter with the work of Warchavchik had taken place in 1928, through an article in the magazine *Para Todos*. He could be referring to "A architectura moderna na cidade de São Paulo. Dois aspectos da residencia Warchavchik recentemente construida," *Para Todos* X, no. 501 (21 July 1928): 35. About Warchavchik, see Geraldo Ferraz, *Warchavchik e a introdução da nova arquitetura no Brasil: 1925 a 1940* (São Paulo: MASP, 1965); José Lira, *Warchavchik. Fraturas da vanguarda* (São Paulo: Cosac & Naify, 2011). A collection of his theoretical texts can be found in Warchavchik, *Arquitetura do século XX e outros escritos*, ed. Carlos Martins (São Paulo: Cosac & Naify, 2006).
36 See Aracy Amaral, *Artes plásticas na Semana de 22* (São Paulo: Perspectiva, 1970a); Ronaldo Brito, *A Semana de 22: o trauma do moderno*, in Sérgio Tolipana et al., eds, *Sete ensaios sobre modernismo* (Rio de Janeiro: Funarte, 1983): 13–18.
37 Le Corbusier's name is mentioned in the press even before 1929; according to Paulo Santos, the magazine *L'Esprit Nouveau* had been in circulation already for some time in the same academic environment.
38 Gerson Pinheiro, "O ensino da architectura no Brasil," *Jornal do Brasil* [1931], BPS, "Recortes de jornais 1930–1961 72 L. Costa Luc."
39 Inauguration speech by Francisco Campos …
40 "O novo director da Escola de Bellas Artes …"
41 "Acta da Sessão da Congregação da Escola Nacional de Bellas Artes realizada em 22 de Abril de 1931. Presidencia do Snr. Architecto Lucio Costa, Director." MDJ VI, 6158.
42 See Helena Cunha de Uzeda, "Ensino acadêmico e modernidade. O curso de arquitetura da Escola Nacional de Belas Artes 1890–1930," PhD dissertation, UFRJ, 2006. For the measures that were introduced by the reform, we directly refer to the text of the decree (Decree n. 19.852, 11 April 1931).
43 The person responsible for indicating the name of Leo Putz seems to have been Manuel Bandeira, friend of the painter. See Lucia Gouvêa Vieira, *Salão de 1931: marco da revelação da arte moderna em nivél nacional* (Rio de Janeiro: Funarte-Instituto Nacional de Artes Plásticas, 1984), 65.
44 The press of the time clearly records the heated contrast between the different sides of the debate. The Instituto Paulista de Architectos was among the most critical and oppositional, issuing a public appeal to the minister of Education against the director's initiative of involving foreign professors in the main artistic institution of the nation. *O ingresso de professores futuristas na Escola Nacional de Bellas Artes. Officio dirigido ao Snr. Ministro da Educação e Saúde Publica pelo Instituto Paulista de Architectos* (São Paulo: Typographia Camargo, 1931).
45 Costa to Warchavchik, 23 May 1931. MASP, "Pasta Lucio Costa."
46 "A nomeação para professores da Escola Nacional de Bellas Artes, de dois artistas modernos," *Diário da Noite*, 22 April 1931.

The start of a militant career

47 Mário de Andrade, "Escola de Belas Artes," *Diário Nacional*, 4 October 1931a.
48 Paulo Santos claims that Alexander Buddeus was responsible for the circulation of the German magazines *Form* and *Modern Bauformen*. Paulo Santos, "A reforma da Escola de Belas Artes e do Salão."
49 See Paulo Santos, "A reforma da escola de Belas Artes e do Salão," 62.
50 Tenentism (*tenentismo*) was a political philosophy of junior army officers who contributed significantly to the Revolution of 1930.
51 Decree n. 19.852, 11 April 1931, art. 247.
52 See Elmer Corrêa Barbosa, "Lúcio Costa. A revolução nas artes plásticas," *Jornal do Brasil*, caderno B, 6 January 1981.
53 Gouvêa Vieira, *Salão de 1931*.
54 Manuel Bandeira, "O 'Salão dos tenentes'," *Diário Nacional*, 5 September 1931b.
55 "O Salão. A comissão organisadora da 38ª Exposição Geral de Belas Artes…" MNBA, AIEN85, "Exposição Geral da ENBA – 1931."
56 Costa, "A inexplicabilidade de uns tantos dispositivos…" [1931]. CLC, IV A 01-03707.
57 Cit. in Costa, "Impotência espalhafatosa," *Diário da Noite*, 9 September 1931.
58 Gouvêa Vieira, *Salão de 1931*. See Costa, study sketch for the volume cover, CLC, III E 03-02424.
59 Costa, *Registro*, 49.
60 Mário de Andrade, "Escola de Belas Artes."
61 "A reforma da Escola de Bellas Artes e o Salão official deste anno," *Diário da Noite*, 26 August 1931.
62 José Mariano Filho, "Uma a Deus, outra ao Diabo," *Diário da Noite*, 8 September 1931d.
63 Costa, *Registro*, 71 (original: CLC, VI A 01-01354).
64 *XVIII Exposição Geral de Bellas Artes 1931*, Escola Nacional de Bellas Artes, n.p., n.d. Printed catalogue. CLC, IV A 01-03713.
65 Costa, *Registro*, 71.
66 See the draft for the invitation to the inauguration of the 1931 Salão, addressed to President Getúlio Vargas. MNBA, AIEN85, "Exposição Geral da ENBA – 1931."
67 See "Cadernos de recibos de entrega e devolução das obras expostas na XXXVIII Exposição Geral de Belas Artes de 1931." MNBA, AIEN85, "Exposição Geral da ENBA – 1931."
68 Costa, *Registro*, 60. The two versions of the Casa Fontes – an assignment that Costa will abandon due to the client's preference for the first solution – are presented by Costa as emblematic of the transition from an eclectic-academic language to a modern one.
69 Bandeira, "O 'Salão dos tenentes'."
70 Cândido Portinari, n.t., *Boletim de Ariel*, November 1931. ACI-RJ, LC-TT01.
71 Peregrino Junior, "O Salão nº 38," *O Cruzeiro* III, no. 45, 12 September 1931. The decisive moment of the 1930 Revolution took place in Itararé, a municipality of the State of São Paulo.
72 Costa himself alludes to this situation in an interview several years later: "Rodrigo disagreed with Francisco Campos, minister of Education, and left the direction of the cabinet. From that moment on, Campos began to feel unsupported and lost interest in my proposals. That was when the professors began to demand the direction." "Destruí algo que existía," interview by Hajfa Y. Sabbag, *AU, arquitetura e urbanismo* II, no. 5 (April 1986): 18–21: 19.
73 With the fragile balance of national politics between revolutions in the background (the 1930 Revolution and the 1932 Constitutionalist Revolution of São Paulo), Campos was in danger of losing his position as minister, one he would definitely abandon in September 1932. See Simon Schwartzman, Helena Bomeny, Vanda Ribeiro Costa, *Tempos de Capanema* (Rio de Janeiro-São Paulo: Paz e Terra-Edusp, 1984).
74 The episode is discussed in detail in the press of the time. See the various extracts on the matter in BPS, "Recortes de jornais 1930–1961"; 72 L. Costa Luc.
75 "Na Escola de Bellas Artes. A greve dos estudantes e sua solidariedade ao director. Declarações do Directorio Academico," unidentified newspaper [1931]. BPS, "Recortes de jornais 1930–1961; 72 L. Costa Luc."

76 "Acta da Sessão da Congregação da Escola Nacional de Bellas Artes realizada em 26 de agosto de 1931. [Presidencia do Snr.] Architecto Lucio Costa, Director." MDJ VI, 6159.
77 Costa, "A direção da Escola de Belas Artes."
78 Costa made particular reference to the note of the previous director, in which it is made clear that the nomination of the three candidates was not necessary if the director position was not vacant. What emerges from the director's communication – transcribed in the proceedings of the Congregação assembly of 21 September 1931 – is how Costa seemed to have taken little or no part in the University Board meetings.
79 See "Acta da Sessão da Congregação da Escola Nacional de Bellas Artes realizada em 21 de Setembro de 1931. Presidencia do Prof. Archimedes Memória, Director." MDJ VI, 6159.
80 "Acta [...] 21 de Setembro de 1931."
81 "Thus, while it 'waited patiently,' as stated by Mr. Chambelland, the Congregação followed the political situation of the State of Minas with an interest that was impossible to fake; while Mr. Francisco Campos's position became gradually more precise, in a curious synchronism, the ease of certain professors increased, until finally – once the Congregação got together – they sent the University Board the famous brief asking for the application of the provision in art. 27 of the Statute." Costa, "A direção da Escola de Belas Artes."
82 Mello Franco de Andrade to Costa, 12 September 1931. CLC, VI A 02-03215.
83 See, among others, Rodrigo Mello Franco de Andrade, "O caso da Escola de Belas Artes," *O Jornal*, 18 September 1931; Manuel Bandeira, "A Revolução e as Belas Artes," *Para Todos* (26 September 1931a).
84 Much press of the time was consulted for the reconstruction of these events. Most of the consulted materials are preserved at the MASP archive ("Pasta Lucio Costa" and "Dossiêr Gregori Warchavchik") and at the Gregori Warchavchik archive, periodical section.
85 1º Segretario do Directorio Academico da Escola Nacional de Bellas Artes to Gregori Warchavchik, 14 September 1931. MASP, "Dossiêr Gregori Warchavchik."
86 Telegrams by Memória to Warchavchik (26 November, 16 December, 21 December 1931). AGW, correspondence section.
87 "Universidade do Brasil, Faculdade Nacional de Arquitetura. Cópia autêntica da Ata da sessão da Congregação do dia 17 de março de 1954."
88 Frank Lloyd Wright, *An Autobiography* (London: Faber and Faber Limited, 1965), 448–449.
89 The inauguration of the residence for William Nordschild, in Copacabana, took place on 22 October 1931, and saw the participation of many modernist artists and intellectuals (Celso Antônio, Cândido Portinari, Manuel Bandeira, Herbert Moses, Jorge Machado Moreira, Paulo Prado, Prudente de Morais Neto, and Sérgio Buarque de Holanda).
90 Costa, "Destruí algo que existia."
91 Costa to Le Corbusier, 26 June 1936.
92 There are two versions of this letter: the draft copy dated 26 June 1932 (Warchavchik to Giedion, 26 June 1932. AGW, correspondence section), and the copy that was actually received, dated 7 October 1932 (Warchavchik to Giedion, 7 October 1932. GTA, 42-K-1932-Warchavchik). In a letter dated about two years later, the names indicating the potential members of the CIRPAC change: while Costa (to whom Warchvachik dedicates a special mention, referring extensively to the events related to his direction of the school), Gerson Pinheiro, and Affonso Eduardo Reidy appear in both, the names of Emílio Baumgart, Jayme da Silva Telles, Flávio de Carvalho, and Rino Levi – mentioned in the first letter – are replaced by those of Warchavchik's ex-students Alcides da Rocha Miranda, João Lourenço da Silva, and the German Alexandre Altberg. Warchavchik to Giedion, 27 July 1934. AGW, correspondence section. Note that Warchavchik had been the CIAM representative for Latin America since 1930, first involved at the prompting of Le Corbusier after the visit to the house in Rua Santa Cruz, in São Paulo.
93 Warchavchik to Giedion, 7 October 1932.

2 Reasons for the new architecture
Gustavo Capanema's *grands travaux*

"When the normal state of things is 'organised disease,' and error is law, departing from the norm imposes itself, and only illegality becomes fruitful."

—Lucio Costa

A history to reconsider

Costa's experience as director of the National School of Fine Arts was followed by a delicate moment in his professional career, one that would, however, be marked by a turning point in the mid-1930s, with the attainment of his most prestigious assignments – up until then at least. The exceptional nature of the episode of the Ministry of Education and Health[1] – destined to have enormous repercussions – has contributed reading the years between 1931 and 1935 as a gestation period of things to come; retrospectively, this period was attributed a precise meaning in the context of Costa's biographic parable, to which many have assigned an almost mythical sense of predestination.

In his autobiography,[2] Costa essentially dismisses this moment of his professional life with obscure references to a sort of "second training," in order to ideally connect the "grand projects" for minister Gustavo Capanema of the mid-1930s (the Ministry in particular) with the previous school reform attempt. The available sources, however, allow us to clarify certain aspects of this canonical narrative, defining the circumstances that shaped the premises for two major projects in the late months of 1935 – the one for the headquarters of the Ministry of Education and the one for the campus of the Universidade do Brasil – and their connection to lesser-known assignments such as his brief engagement in the project for the Universidade do Distrito Federal.

We must not forget that the University Campus of Rio de Janeiro – an integral part of an ambitious project aimed at establishing the Universidade do Brasil – was the most urgent issue on minister Capanema's agenda in those years. The chronological overlap of the two projects allows us to follow the development, step by step, of the difficult relationship between a group of architects guided by Costa and a public contracting authority that was strong in its political programme but divided among many different cultural proposals. The unfortunate gestation of the project for the Cidade Universitaria (University Campus) – to which a series of studies in the 1980s finally gave proper consideration[3] – came to determine the moment in which we can identify the first emergence of conflict between the architects and their clients, revealing the fragile balance on which their relationship was founded.[4] The position held by Costa in these events is perhaps the most symptomatic of this problematic entanglement. By attributing himself the role of mediator – both technical and intellectual – between the members of the institutional power and the different project groups he was called to coordinate, Costa would continue his efforts in claiming the intellectual hegemony of the progressive elite he belonged to, even during the controversial transition to the dictatorial regime of the Estado Novo.

In the aftermath of his experience at the School of Fine Arts, Costa started a professional collaboration with Gregori Warchavchik, although destined to a short life.[5] The Warchavchik & Lucio Costa construction company – which was founded back in June 1932[6] – lasted no more than a year-and-a-half because of the logistical difficulty given by the distance between Rio and São Paulo, among other things. However, regardless of its brief life, its importance is evident. It is thanks to Warchavchik that Costa had the chance to challenge himself with his first actually constructed modernist projects; moreover, he did so alongside one of the few active professionals on the national territory that, at the beginning of the 1930s, already boasted a respectable curriculum of modernist work, in addition to holding relations with CIAM and a great promotional platform from which he could spread the modernist lesson. Although Costa would later tend to attribute to himself the paternity of the more famous projects of this period – like the Casa Schwartz (Figure 2.1) and the Vila Operária da Gambôa – the "manner" of the first modernist houses built by the Russian architect between São Paulo and Rio de Janeiro at the end of the 1920s is quite recognisable. Yet, the rigid volumetric quality of Warchavchik's earlier work – like the Paulista houses of Rua Itápolis or Rua da Bahia – seems to become more complex, favouring a horizontal development and, in some cases, a rearrangement of the plan around a patio. Some of the projects of this period were never developed, like the Marimbás nautical club – a successful interpretation of the International Style thanks to its rounded and "nautical" volumes – and the residential building for Maria Gallo, which perhaps represents Costa's first experiment in multi-storey buildings. On the other side, the renovation of the residence for Paulo Bittencourt[7] in Largo do Boticário – a suggestive colonial courtyard in Rio de Janeiro – is a particularly mature example of contemporary architectural language inserted within the setting of a pre-existing historical one.

The company's work found a prestigious showcase opportunity at the first Salão de Arquitetura Tropical held in Rio de Janeiro in 1933. The cover of the catalogue – containing a text by Walter Gropius and the CIAM statute – presents Alexandre Altberg as curator, Frank Lloyd Wright as honorary president, João Lourenço da Silva, Alcides da Rocha Miranda, and Ademar Portugal as members of the organising committee, and finally Lucio Costa, Gregori Warchavchik, and Emílio Baumgart as *precursores* ("pioneers").[8] However, the incompatibilities destined to break the professional partnership between the two would emerge shortly after: in addition to the difficulties given by Warchavchik's frequent trips between São Paulo and Rio – aggravated by the outbreak of the Constitutionalist Revolution in 1932 – what also seems to have weighed in on the final breakup of the two partners was Costa's substantial divergence in the design approach – one that he shared with one of the collaborators of the company, Carlos de Azevedo Leão.

Figure 2.1 View of the Casa Schwartz, by Lucio Costa and Gregori Warchavchik, Rio de Janeiro, 1932–1933. Casa de Lucio Costa.

That "stylised modernism" that sometimes surfaced did not seem – to Carlos Leão and myself – adequate for the true "Corbusian" principles to which we referred; a discrepancy that manifested itself on the matter of the "decorative" furniture of Casa Schwartz – sofas and folding chairs with the same chrome structure – when impeccable series of chairs for various functions designed by Le Corbusier, Charlotte Perriand, and Pierre Jeanneret already existed.[9]

The aspiration toward a greater intransigence in the interpretation of the modern lesson – and Le Corbusier's in particular – finally contributed to the dissolution of the company Warchavchik & Lucio Costa, while also sealing a new professional collaboration in the meantime. It is likely that the same Carlos Leão, who was cultured and up-to-date even in European matters, may have played an important role in bringing Costa closer to "Corbusian" principles.[10] It was in fact in these years that the fascination for Le Corbusier took a central position in Costa's theoretical horizon. By choosing the term *chômage* (unemployment) to describe these years, Costa attributed them the meaning of a "new apprenticeship" – one that was necessary to better approach the work of the masters. It was an experience that, time and time again, would be presented as an epiphany before a doctrine that manifested itself to Costa's conscience for the first time with the full power of an indisputable truth. Therefore, we can say that the Corbusian militancy that would mark the years to come found its roots in a failure.

Not many traces remain of Costa's collaboration with Leão, especially since the actual lack of commissions – which Costa blamed on the general refusal to "design in style" but which was probably partly due to the aftermath of the economic depression of 1929 – seems to have drastically limited the company's production. To date, there is only one documented project that can be attributed to the Costa-Leão firm with certainty, namely, the one presented in May 1935 at the design competition for the new headquarters of the Club de Engenharia, a twenty-storey-high tower in the middle of Rio de Janeiro's Avenida Central.[11] Thanks to its façade with continuous horizontal windows, culminating in an oversized glass volume, the building flaunts a rationalist expressive language and in some way represents the crowning moment of a period destined to see almost all of Costa's projects remain only on paper. The names and titles that Costa would associate to the projects belonging to this phase of his professional career in his autobiography *Registro de uma vivência* – "Casas sem dono," "Projeto rejeitado," "Projetos esquecidos" (houses without owners, rejected project, fogotten projects)[12] – highlight the frustration of a prolonged period of non-activity. However, Costa and Leão's firm, despite the lack of commissions, must have been considered one of the most promising laboratories of architectural renovation by the young architects that were eager to open up to new languages in the mid-1930s, as evidenced by the fact that Oscar Niemeyer began his career as an architect precisely in their studio.[13] These were also the years in which a group of undeveloped projects and lost competitions, undertaken by Costa on his own, took place; among these we find the 1934 project presented at the competition for the Cidade Operária de Monlevade, in Minas Gerais.[14] In this case, Costa was explicit in his references to Auguste Perret (in the reinforced-concrete church), and to Le Corbusier (in the *pilotis*-supported houses, clearly inspired by Maison Loucheur);[15] it was also here that Costa proposed, seemingly for the first time, an integration of the traditional *barro armado com madeira*[16] technique and modern prefabrication construction processes. The same Casas sem dono – conceived as design exercises on an abstract lot of standard dimensions – represented an attempt to calibrate rigorously modernist modalities – which, in addition to Le Corbusier, also looked at the fluid spatiality of Mies's houses – for spatial layouts that fit the local conditions.

Costa's solid position as a reference for a specific artistic and professional community is confirmed by his involvement, alongside other important names, with the board of professors of the Instituto de Arte of the Universidade do Distrito Federal. His collaboration with this university – established in 1935 on the initiative of the Bahian educator Anísio Teixeira – in addition to representing one of the greater gaps that still exist in his biography, also seems to have placed him in the difficult conditions of a compromise, highlighting the existence of conflicts between the modernist intelligentsia and the cultural project of the Vargas government. In July of 1935 – the same year in which Gustavo Capanema appointed a board of experts to "set a model of higher degree education for the country"[17] with the establishment of the Universidade do Brasil – the Universidade do Distrito Federal launched a programme centred on high-level cultural education and on a liberal and democratic ideology. The initiative – destined to a short life in the repressive context of the Estado Novo – brought together, for the first time, intellectuals like Gilberto Freyre, Prudente de Morais Neto, Cândido Portinari, Sérgio Buarque de Holanda, Mário de Andrade, and Celso Antônio, some of whom would find themselves collaborating again at the SPHAN a few years later. The libertarian nature of the institution's ideology and its independence from the government's political agenda exposed it to the hostility of the same Capanema, who saw a threat to his centralised control of the masses.

Although the fragmentary nature of the sources does not allow us to exactly trace how Celso Kelly nominated Costa among the professors of the Instituto de Arte, his name appears on the list of professors assigned to the architecture course, together with the name of his then-collaborator, Carlos Leão.[18] In a document preserved in Costa's archive, we seem to be able to identify the draft of an educational programme related to the improvement of the architecture course of the Universidade do Distrito Federal. The text of this draft is particularly premonitory: it proves that the synthesis between the affiliation with Le Corbusier's lesson and the interpretation of local specific characters – the "lesson of the past" and the lesson of the *mestres de obra* (master builders) – was in fact already perfectly defined in its main aspects.[19]

It is, however, in the essay "Razões da nova arquitetura" – which was published on the *Revista da Directoria de Engenharia* – PDF in 1936 and elaborated in a period of time between 1933 and 1935,[20] and therefore was probably directly linked to the experience at Universidade do Distrito Federal and used as a basis for the educational programme of the Instituto de Arte – that the considerations made in the previous years came together in a first systematic way. In "Razões," a true theoretical manifesto, the reference to the earlier "Acerca da arquitetura moderna" by Gregori Warchavchik,[21] which is undoubtedly present, seems minor when compared to the evident independent reexamination of the modernist lesson – of Le Corbusier in particular – and to the theoretical breadth that certainly qualifies the text, despite a few rhetorical excesses. However, the fundamentally original aspect of the text should perhaps be found in the broader interpretation of functionalist theories, embracing social, economic, productive, and taste transformations, and forming a sort of *Kunstwollen* that Costa defines with the term "plastic expression": an unmistakable sign of the development of a new "style," the expressions of which included the entire artistic domain, and the roots of which were to be found in Latin and Mediterranean traditions. These are theoretical foundations that were concisely translated in the programme held in the abovementioned document, drawing abundantly from the lexical baggage developed in "Razões."

These promising premises, however, would not lead to any practical effect, since Costa's commitment with the Universidade do Distrito Federal found an abrupt interruption only a few months after its start. In the draft of his resignation letter (undated), addressed to the director of the university, Costa limits himself – in justifying his choice – to calling upon greater forces.

Since it is not possible – for reasons beyond my control – for me to continue [to serve] in this University, I indicate as my possible substitute – in both the actual course and the investigative Committee – my assistant, Mr. Carlos de Azevedo Leão, who will certainly contribute to a successful beginning, development, and completion of all work.[22]

This document reveals two important facts. The first is that Costa never had the chance to settle into the educational activities by the time of his resignation, which would justify his omission of any reference to the Universidade do Distrito Federal when – in refusing the "Organização Social das Cidades" course offered to him in 1954 by the director of the Faculdade Nacional de Arquitetura, upon Paulo Santos's request – he would claim to be affected "as I was in '31 [...] by a congenital lack of vocation in teaching."[23] The second is that the reasons behind Costa's resignation should not be aligned with the ones that inspired the many spontaneous resignations that followed the so-called Intentona Comunista of November 1935, since a political and ideological stance would certainly have been made explicit in his letter to the director. In fact, many professors explained the reasons for their withdrawal, in their resignation letters, as an act of solidarity toward Anísio Teixeira, who had been dismissed from his position of director of the Departamento Municipal de Educação as a reactionary measure following the military uprising that had taken place.[24] Therefore, it seems more likely to assume – given the violent campaign led by minister Capanema against the Universidade do Distrito Federal – that Costa's collaboration with this university was substantially incompatible with his chances of getting the two biggest public assignments of his career, including the project for the seat of Universidade do Brasil – two assignments that took place toward the end of 1935.

The great public assignments and Capanema's "dossier"

The design competition for the new seat of the Ministry of Education and Public Health, which was supposed to occupy an entire *quadra* of the Esplanada do Castelo in Rio de Janeiro,[25] was announced by Capanema in April 1935. Despite the fact that Costa's project was never disclosed and never emerged from any archives, his participation is proven by his signature on the document with which all competitors, on 18 May 1935, asked the minister to extend the deadline for the submission of the final project.[26]

The records of the jury meetings – a jury composed of a professor of the School of Fine Arts (Adolfo Morales de los Rios), a member of the Instituto Central de Arquitetos, a member of the Escola Politécnica, the superintendent of Serviço de Obras (Eduardo Souza Aguiar), and the same Capanema as president – should be read together with two letters kept in the personal archive of Capanema's head of cabinet, poet Carlos Drummond de Andrade.[27] In these two letters, Rodrigo Mello Franco de Andrade contacts Drummond as an intermediary for an unidentified architect – referred to as "talented and trustworthy" – who had already been consulted by Mello Franco and Manuel Bandeira for a technical opinion on the competition projects. The author's unusual care in not revealing the architect's identity, even in the context of a confidential communication, leads us to imagine that the mysterious expert advisor could be the same promising theorist of modern architecture that Rodrigo Mello Franco de Andrade and Manuel Bandeira had already mentioned to Francisco Campos as a favourite candidate for the direction of the National School of Fine Arts. The assumption would be coherent with a typical trait of Costa's attitude – determined to take action beyond individual interests, in view of a common fight for a presumed "truth," but also interested in obtaining a scope of action for himself and for his protégés – and with the specific circumstances of his following assignment, alongside the other modern competitors.

The first meeting of the jury, during which the envelopes were opened, took place on 17 June 1935.[28] On 23 June, Mello Franco de Andrade sent the first letter to Drummond, reporting the projects chosen by the expert advisor, referred to as "our friend": the first project is indicated with the pseudonym J.Q.L. and seems to be – "despite the poor presentation" (another element that seems to refer to Costa) – "the most interesting and intelligently conceived," with the adequate "public building character" and appropriately "detached from the neighbouring buildings by means of the garden." Following this first one are the Chanaan, Popoff, X.X., Alpha, and Minerva projects. The short descriptions show that the Chanaan and X.X. projects (possible pseudonyms for Reidy and Moreira-Vasconcellos)[29] were raised on *pilotis*: an element that was appreciated for the garden area it created beneath the building, but that was also deemed unnecessary. The Alpha project (by Gerson Pompeu Pinheiro) was instead criticised for presenting an internal area. Finally, although the Minerva project (Rafael Galvão and Mário Fertin) – preferred by Mello Franco – was reprimanded for its lack of unity, the harshest judgement was delivered to the Pax project (by Archimedes Memória, who would later win the competition) and the rest of the ones presented.

> Our friend considers the other projects completely inadequate. Among these, he carefully examined the project under the pseudonym "Pax," if I am not mistaken, which presents ornamentations in the Marajoara style. Mr. Souza Aguiar seems to be greatly inclined to classify it first, despite it being in fact one of the most undesirable projects, both for its extremely bad taste in composition and for the serious technical defects it suffers from. In this regard, we should note that the building presents six or more internal areas simply because the architect didn't try to solve, or was not able to solve in another manner, issues that "J.Q.L." and "Chanaan" instead solved intelligently.[30]

The jury's second meeting on 5 July approved the motion to eliminate all projects that did not comply with the competition's regulation regarding the distance limit of at most ten metres from the street.[31] This decision automatically led to the elimination of thirty-three projects, among which were the first four indicated by Bandeira and Mello Franco's trusted architect. In this regard, the second letter from Mello Franco to Drummond de Andrade significantly expresses the contrast between two opposite models of urban settlement: following the Plan Agache with traditional closed blocks, on the one hand (which was subjected to a municipal regulation that allowed a physical margin that was even smaller than the one required by Souza Aguiar); and following the functionalist city advocated by the modernists, on the other (which featured the elimination of the *rue corridor* and a free arrangement of buildings within the site). In the letter, Mello Franco de Andrade, presumably following the instructions of the unknown person mentioned above, expresses his favour for the second urban settlement modality.

> Considering that the competition notice does not make reference to the issue of the alignment of the building's side elevations – and since the building cannot occupy the entire area of the lot intended for it – it will always be preferable to push back all building elevations instead of creating closed internal areas, according to the deplorable taste of the project that holds the favours of Mr. Souza Aguiar.
>
> On the other hand, nowadays, a building like the one for the Ministry of Education does not require having a front façade that contrasts with the side ones: the first polished and impressive, while the others modest and simple. The main one will stand out from the others because of the respective main entrance, which must draw more attention.[32]

Further on – when claiming that "nobody seems to take the Prefecture regulation requirements seriously" and hoping that an intercession by part of the minister could be sufficient – he suggests a few expedients to bypass the obstacle.

> And if Mr. Souza Aguiar should insist on this rigorously formalist position, the following arguments by part of Capanema should suffice against his point of view: the competition notice does not determine which street the main façade of the Ministry should face on. Therefore, taking the project signed "J.Q.L." as an example, we could consider the façade that falls within the limits as the main one. If we consider instead the project with the pseudonym "Chanaan," we see that it is equipped with an awning that extends toward the limit imposed by the competition notice, and therefore should be measured from that point (as the same Prefecture regulation foresees).

The next-to-last jury meeting, held on 8 July 1935, determined Archimedes Memória's "Pax" project as first classified, while second and third place respectively went to Rafael Galvão-Mário Fertin's and Gerson Pompeu Pinheiro's projects.[33] In September of the same year, a controversial article on the jury's choices appeared in the *Revista da Directoria de Engenharia – PDF*,[34] disclosing the projects by Affonso Eduardo Reidy and by Jorge Machado Moreira and Ernani Vasconcellos (which were both disqualified). The article complains about the poor visibility given to the disqualified projects and criticises the ones presenting one or more "closed internal areas," recommending the solution of a framed structure, "allowing for the standardisation of the structural elements and flexibility in the use of space." Finally, the article sends out a veiled criticism of Memória's project – which was officially declared the winning project in the final jury meeting on 1 October[35] – because of its "false grandeur, so frequent in exhibition pavilions."

At this point, it is necessary to turn our attention to the events regarding the University Campus, since they developed simultaneously with the Ministry's and are therefore inextricably intertwined with them. In July 1935, Capanema's decision to entrust the campus project to the Italian architect Marcello Piacentini – who was about to inaugurate the new campus of Rome University at the time – fuelled a heated response by part of the national professional world, given that they saw it as a missed opportunity for Brazilian architects and engineers.[36] The arrival of the Italian architect – who stayed in Rio for a few days in August 1935, mainly to study the project's location – was therefore preceded by a series of protests, addressed to the minister, by part of various professional entities; first, the Conselho Regional de Engenheiros e Arquitetos do Rio de Janeiro (CREA), who appealed to the legislation that saw foreigners excluded from the exercise of liberal professions in the country.[37] CREA's opinion was echoed by the Club de Engenharia and the Syndicato Nacional de Engenheiros, whereas the only voice falling outside of the chorus was that of the Instituto Central de Arquitetos, declaring itself in favour of assigning the general project to Piacentini, but also suggesting that each of the individual buildings should be commissioned to Brazilian architects. It is the Syndicato Nacional de Engenheiros that finally proposed, as a possible alternative to an international competition, the establishment of a committee of Brazilian technicians, chosen on the basis of the proposals of each of the professional entities in question, consequently reducing Piacentini's role to that of a consultant. Between 8 and 17 August 1935, the Syndicato Nacional dos Engenheiros, the Clube de Engenharia, and the Instituto Central de Arquitetos expressed their preferences for possible committee members. The first and third group indicated, among others, the name of Lucio Costa, who also appeared on the list of names pointed out by the Diretório Acadêmico of the School of Fine Arts on its own initiative. The first document (dating back to 13 January)[38] attesting Costa's involvement in the activity of the committee – which also included Affonso Eduardo Reidy, Angelo Brunhs, Firmino Fernandes Saldanha, and Paulo Fragoso – quite clearly determines that the collaboration had been defined for some months already. It is therefore plausible that the two assignments – the one for the Ministry and the one for the University Campus – had come to shape themselves in a very tight and shared timeframe, which can be placed around the last months of 1935.

As is well known, Capanema would not be indifferent to the press's reaction to the outcome of the competition for the new Ministry headquarters, and especially would not be indifferent – in light of the correspondence between Drummond de Andrade and Mello Franco de Andrade – to the firm opposition of the head of the cabinet's advisors. The same Costa, in the following letter to Le Corbusier, provides valuable information on the matter.

> In September 1935, I was called to the Ministry of Education. Minister Capanema has Carlos Drummond De Andrade as head of the cabinet: a poet – namely, someone who, like Bandeira, has a profound understanding of the meaning of "true" reality and knows how to transmit it (do not infer from this that, here, poets spring up like mushrooms; on the contrary, there are three or four of them on 8,522,000 km^2). It seems that, having learned of my experience at the School, he intervened in my favour with the minister, who – disappointed by the result of the competition that he had promoted for the construction of a building in which his ministry was to be established (the project that finally classified in first place is simply idiotic) – assigned me and five other architects, the names of which you already know (first letter by Monteiro), with the task of drafting a new project.[39]

It is therefore through the mediation of a group of intellectuals that had previously supported Costa's nomination to the direction of the School of Fine Arts in 1930 that Capanema decided to entrust him with the draft of the new project, saving him, as Costa himself asserts, from a slow and relentless return to anonymity.[40] As we know, Costa would then decide to also involve, in different ways, Carlos Leão, Jorge Moreira, Oscar Niemeyer, Affonso Eduardo Reidy, and Ernani Vasconcellos.[41]

It is from this moment that official dates and unofficial ones begin to diverge; therefore, the cross-reference of information from different sources becomes a fundamental process. What we can piece together is a chronicle of Capanema's effort to dress up the informal agreements taken with Costa in seemingly official apparel, producing documents that should have appeared – in the midst of the administrative process documenting the phases of the project – in a credible chronological order. For starters, on 5 November 1935, Capanema obtained authorisation not to comply with the municipal regulation in the specific matter,[42] justifying the issue to Vargas as a necessary measure to eliminate obstacles to the "construction of a beautiful architectural piece." At the beginning of January, the minister received a contract proposal in which the group in charge of the Ministry project specified the required financial conditions.[43] At the same time – taking advantage of the competition provision that established how the government was not obliged to "hire the competition-winning architects for the execution of the project"[44] – Capanema proceeded to pay the awarded projects before definitively archiving them. On 17 November, a law was approved to authorise the establishment of a special account at the Banco do Brasil, dedicated to the construction of the seat of the Ministry of Education and Public Health. The law provided that the project should not be subject to the disposition that bound large public building commissions to competition regulations. Two months later, in March 1936, the minister asked some professionals to express their technical opinion on Archimedes Memória's project, which was unanimously criticised for its poor functionality. Finally, the minister sent Costa – making reference to "previous agreements on the matter" – an official employment letter, dated 25 March 1936.[45]

In this regard, it is interesting to quote a letter sent by Costa to Carlos Drummond de Andrade a few days after receiving the official assignment.

> Carlos,
>
> Today I met with Dr. Capanema. He showed me the respectable "dossier" with which he intends to document and present the adventure of the new Ministry headquarters to president Vargas;[46] explaining the choice of my name with the fact that I was the only one – among all architects – that was appointed by more than one trade association during the consultation regarding the works for the future University Campus. In case it was necessary to explain – even if only verbally – the reason why I extended the invitation to the others, here it is: these are the authors of the best projects that were submitted during the competition, disqualified by the jury on the grounds of not meeting the alleged municipal requests.[47]

Even before Costa's appointment was made official, the *Correio da Manhã* accused Capanema of "working for disqualified contestants" and made fun of the inexperienced young architects charged with carrying out the building project.[48]

44 *Reasons for the new architecture*

Archimedes Memória also had an understandable reaction: reviving the grudge he still held for the misadventures that took place five years earlier, he directly addressed the Brazilian President.

> Once we developed the preliminary projects and having passed the second phase of the competition, we had the satisfaction of seeing our project ranked first. In the meantime, we have just learned, to our great surprise, that the minister of Education – having procured, without competition, various projects to architect Lucio Costa, among which the future *Palacio* of the Ministry – has just authorised the payment of the important sum of *cem contos de reis* for the project, according to information that has come to my knowledge. And the surprise grows even bigger when we consider that there is no justification for this act in common morality, since we know that architect Lucio Costa was disqualified during the first phase of the competition. And what we have just reported becomes, at the present moment, even graver if we consider that this architect, among other things, is associated with Gregori Warchavchik, a Russian Jew of suspicious tendencies, invited by the same Lucio Costa to hold a course at the National School of Fine Arts, where both are accountable for the constant agitations the school has found itself to deal with.[49]

In the rest of the letter – which did not seem to particularly worry Getúlio Vargas – Memória disparagingly refers to the minister's head of cabinet as a "patron and intransigent defender" of the "followers of the modernist movement."

Although the process was effectively managed by Carlos Drummond de Andrade at an institutional level, Costa emerges from documental sources as an active participant, unlike what seems to have happened – at least according to the testimonies of the ones involved – in his appointment to the direction of the School of Fine Arts.

By virtue of the friendship that bound him to the group of intellectuals that were well integrated in administrative areas of the Vargas government, and the common battle they had been invested in since the early 1930s, it is plausible that Costa's presence behind the scenes could have directly taken advantage of the disappointment for the winning project and of the dissatisfaction of the other architects that were disqualified from the competition. Such an interpretation would undermine the image of modesty with which Costa has been depicted up to this moment. What emerges is the image of a professional determined to claim intellectual hegemony of the progressive elite he belonged to, quickly understanding the high potential of a public project like the Ministry's, able to weld together his project of architectural renewal to the broader project of modernising the image of the nation.

New architecture, between theory and practice

During the following months and for the rest of 1936, sources show Costa in the position of main operations manager, spokesman for both project groups, and advisor to all players involved.

Reasons for the new architecture 45

The first project for the new Ministry headquarters was delivered to Capanema on 15 May 1936, complete with drawings and descriptive report. The connection between this first proposal and the competition projects presented by Affonso Eduardo Reidy and by Moreira-Vasconcellos (from which it borrowed the "U-shaped" planimetric layout) is evident, with the exception of the position of the auditorium, set against the outer wall instead of the one facing the courtyard, where the entrance and terraced garden were placed. The project assimilated Reidy's proportions but forwent the busy volumetric articulation given by the asymmetrical wings and the different heights of the volumes in question. On the other hand, it maintained the rigid axis system of the Moreira-Vasconcellos project, while the curvilinear canopy of the Centrosoyuz – a main reference for all three projects – perhaps inspired the curvature of the external auditorium wall. Le Corbusier's lesson was applied quite slavishly,[50] filtered by the recent academic training of the involved designers and by a didactic tone in general, coherent with the priorities that seemed to guide Costa in this moment of his professional career, where each design opportunity – especially in the case of a public building – offered itself as a vehicle to implement his own militant project. In a letter Costa would write to Oscar Niemeyer many years later, we read that this first project – jokingly called "Mummy" by Le Corbusier[51] (Figures 2.2, 2.3) – is largely attributable to Costa, according to all members of the group involved.[52] Costa is, however, the author of both the descriptive report and the reports (which include interesting "Corbusian" sketches) that were formulated after technicians and professionals sent by Capanema assessed the draft of the project during the month of June.

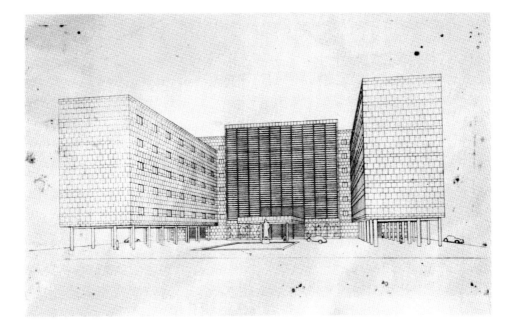

Figure 2.2 Lucio Costa and team, first project for the Ministry of Education and Public Health in Rio de Janeiro. Perspective view from the main entrance, 1936. Arquivo Central do IPHAN – Seção Rio de Janeiro.

46 *Reasons for the new architecture*

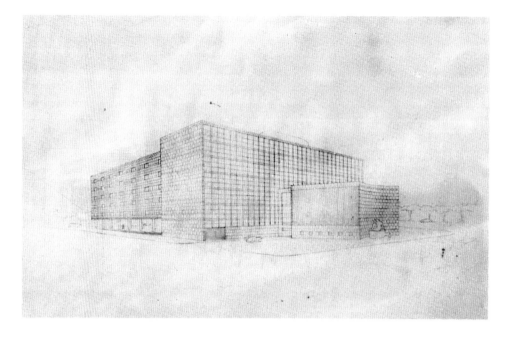

Figure 2.3 Lucio Costa and team, first project for the Ministry of Education and Public Health in Rio de Janeiro. Perspective view from the auditorium, 1936. Arquivo Central do IPHAN – Seção Rio de Janeiro.

Certain passages of "Razões da nova arquitetura" – which had only recently been published – are mentioned, when not directly quoted, in various sections of the descriptive report. Costa seemed fundamentally interested in showing the conceptual rigour with which the modern principle of independence between frame structure and cladding was applied to the project, "accepting all the consequences" of its use (*pilotis*, displacement of the supports toward the interior, freedom of plans and façades, continuous ceilings, etc.) for the benefit of the "flexibility" required by the programme. He was also interested in showing how, in addition to the "rational principles of the new construction technique," the project followed the "permanent principles of proportion, rhythm, and symmetry that are common to all true architecture."

> This way, we effortlessly achieved a building with strict lines, with a sober and dignified appearance; not in a "specific style" – which could be arguable – but "with style," in the most positive sense of the term. Wall paintings in the conference and waiting rooms, bas-reliefs in the main entrance, and two large granite figures on the north and south façades will naturally come to earn their positions; this way, the Ministry entrusted with the artistic destiny of the country will provide – with the construction of its headquarters – an example to follow; restoring, after more than a century of disorientation, a right direction to architecture – faithful, in its spirit, to traditional principles.[53]

This conclusion is similar to that of "Razões," where inevitable formal variation is countered with the permanence of the "fundamental laws" at the base of the Mediterranean tradition, a tradition of which "new architecture" represented, for Costa, an unexpected renaissance. The same theoretical inspiration drove Costa's response to the opinion of the Inspector de Engenharia Sanitária Domingos da Silva Cunha; here, Costa defended his design choices with a series of sketches and short texts (sometimes with a highly polemical tone) aimed at informing his interlocutor of certain fundamental principles of "modern technique" (eliminating the *rue corridor*, the functional and aesthetic benefit of having free columns in internal hallways, resorting to the use of *brise-soleil*, etc.), using sarcastic remarks against Domingos da Silva Cunha's criticism regarding the aesthetic qualities of the project[54] (Figure 2.4).

On 18 July, the superintendent of the Serviço de Obras sent the minister a summary of the main observations made by various professionals in assessing the project, proposing a series of measures to solve the main identified issues.[55] However, in many cases, these requests completely undermined the more programmatic design choices: proposing to eliminate the *pilotis*, to replace the continuous glass walls with masonry walls with windows, to extend the wings toward the auditorium in order to achieve an "H-shaped" plan arrangement (more easily extensible), and – finally – to replace the *brise-soleil* with another solar shading system. Costa, however, remained inflexible, accepting only a few insignificant changes to the general distribution but rejecting all proposals that would distort the nature of the project.[56]

As for the University Campus, it seems that the operational phase only began in May 1936,[57] slightly after the Ministry's, which at that date was already at the end of the project's first phase. In fact, that same month saw the "five-man committee" deliver a contract proposal, which divided the project into two phases – one referring to the urban and general campus design, and one referring to the actual architectural design of each building – each to be drawn up on the basis of the committee's established programmes (the so-called Comissão do Plano da Universidade).[58] In particular, the work would have been followed by the so-called Escritório do Plano, formed of professor committee representatives and presided by Inácio Azevedo do Amaral and Ernesto de Souza Campos.

It is no coincidence that the *Revista da Directoria de Engenharia – PDF* published, that same month, an article in which Costa stresses the need to equip the Universidade do Brasil with a general plan that would avoid the formal disarticulation given by the previous separate and autonomous project designs of the ministerial offices in Esplanada do Castelo. He therefore invites the minister to maintain the clarity, patience, and courage proven up until that moment, in order to "frame the contructions of today within a general plan that guarantees the normal development of the enterprise tomorrow."[59] On 26 June 1936, Costa informed Le Corbusier of having unofficially anticipated to Capanema the idea that would be presented officially shortly after: that of locating the University Campus on the water, on the Lagôa Rodrigo de Freitas, disregarding the long-discussed choice of the site near Quinta da Bôa Vista (between January and April of the same year, in particular), as proven by the press of the time.[60] Thrilled by an idea that – according to the letter – seemed to shape itself into a solution "of great lyrical potential" worthy of the Swiss-French master, he later reported Capanema's incredulous reaction, commenting on how "very pure ideas" have the power to "scandalise everybody."[61] Nevertheless, he was

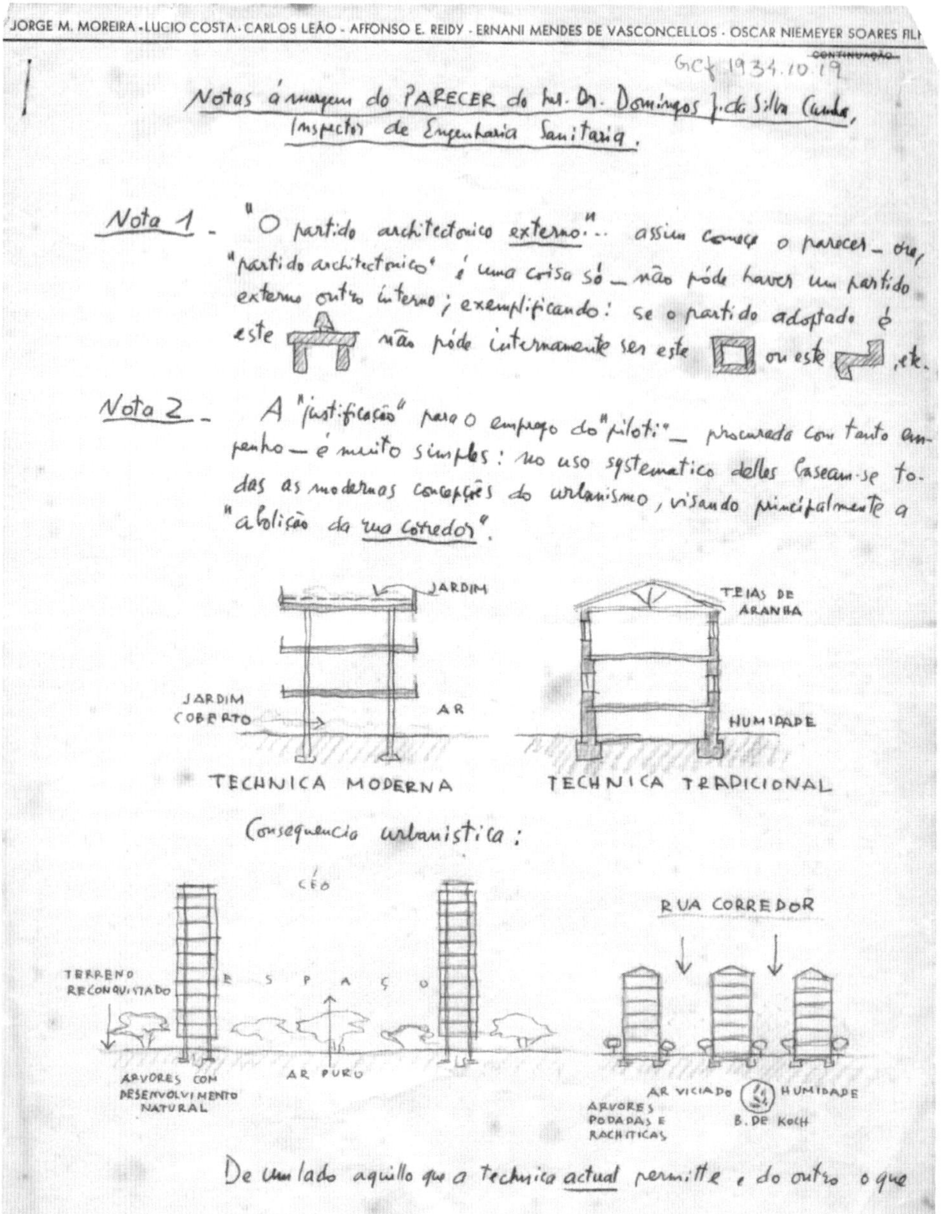

JORGE M. MOREIRA · LUCIO COSTA · CARLOS LEÃO · AFFONSO E. REIDY · ERNANI MENDES DE VASCONCELLOS · OSCAR NIEMEYER SOARES FILH

CONTINUAÇÃO

GCf 1934.10.19

Notas á margem do PARECER do sr. Dr. Domingos J. da Silva Cunha, Inspector de Engenharia Sanitaria.

Nota 1. "O partido architectonico externo"... assim começa o parecer – ora, "partido architectonico" é uma coisa só – não póde haver um partido externo outro interno; exemplificando: se o partido adoptado é este não póde internamente ser este ou este, etc.

Nota 2. A "justificação" para o emprego do "piloti" – procurada com tanto empenho – é muito simples: no uso systematico delles baseam-se todas as modernas concepções do urbanismo, visando principalmente a "abolição da rua corredor".

Consequencia urbanistica:

De um lado aquillo que a technica actual permitte, e do outro o que

II 43

Figure 2.4 Lucio Costa, notes and sketches explaining the advantages of modern architectural technique, in reply to the Inspector de Engenharia Sanitária Domingos da Silva Cunha, September 1936. CPDOC, Fundação Getúlio Vargas.

confident that his patient work of persuasion could, in a very Corbusian way, achieve good results in the minister's "lucid intelligence." A few days later, on 30 June 1936, Costa officially presented the project (the drawings of which we have no trace of) to the professor committee, presided by Campos and Amaral. On 14 August 1936, they wrote the following account.

> In this session, architect Lucio Costa spent much time illustrating the plan he developed together with the other architects of the committee. It provides for the development of the Universidade do Brasil on the Lagôa Rodrigo de Freitas without a relative embankment; that is, on the water. All university buildings would be suspended on pillars, and would be of the same "standard" height with hanging gardens; while each building would be connected to the others by means of bridges. The hanging gardens would communicate thanks to a large aerial avenue that, starting from rua Humaytá, would run through the entire lake university complex. In a project conceived in this manner – said the architect – there can be no objection to the construction of the university buildings on pillars – of which he [the architect] has determined the number and unit load – explaining that this process would also facilitate circulation within the study centre.[62]

Citing reasons of mostly technical nature, the committee – who had sent a briefing to Capanema in May inviting him to solicit a "closer and more immediate cooperation of the architects and engineers"[63] with respect to the guidelines previously established with Piacentini – finally rejected the project, pointing out that the choice of the area (selected by the committee after extensive investigation) had already been approved by Capanema.[64] Therefore, the profound incompatibility of the approaches, ideas, and design references became immediate evidence of the conflict between the committees, which would nevertheless continue to work in a disjointed manner – an incompatibility that was further aggravated by Costa's unwillingness to compromise and, most of all, by the direct involvement of Le Corbusier, which would take place shortly after.

Le Corbusier and the *appel à l'Autorité*

The idea of involving Le Corbusier in the *grands travaux* of the Capanema administration[65] dates back, according to Costa, to a year before his arrival.

> [Capanema] was making his way toward the construction of the "University Campus" [...] and, informing me of the invitation sent by him to Piacentini, he asked me what I thought of it. "It is a pity," I desolately replied. I then proceeded to explain the situation of architecture in the face of the new times, the plastic possibilities that would derive from it, the impasse given by the *status-sociale* and your call to authority, ending my plea with these words: "there are hundreds of Piacentinis, everywhere and all the time – it takes centuries to find one Le Corbusier!"[66]

It is interesting to note how Costa, from the beginning, considered the possibility of an involvement by part of Le Corbusier in the wake of the theses Le Corbusier had formulated shortly before in *La Ville Radieuse*, dedicated to an ideal "Authority," in the hopes that this authority would accept a challenge launched by the architect-urban planner (no matter the political alignment it belonged to).[67]

The first moves toward getting Le Corbusier involved – something that Costa not only proposed but in which he invested all his energies – are documented in a letter sent by the Swiss-French master, on 21 March 1936, to the Brazilian engineer Alberto Monteiro de Carvalho, who was an initial mediator.[68] As the same Costa would report years later:

> Hence the impetus and vigour of my actions in considering it essential to involve him [Le Corbusier] in the case of the Ministry, even hoping to involve Monteiro de Carvalho during the first contacts – this thanks to Carlos Leão, acquaintance of an engineer from the Monteiro & Aranha studio. I did so much in this effort that the minister – Dr. Capanema, as I used to address him – ended up taking me to Catete to personally intercede for the cause.[69]

It is therefore understandable how Monteiro, in the letter to Le Corbusier, makes mostly reference to Leão, professor of the Universidade do Distrito Federal and collaborator of Lucio Costa, defining the latter as "the most creative of the young Brazilian architects." Both are indicated as supporters of the initiative, on behalf of the larger group of professionals to whom the Ministry project had been entrusted, whereas the other members of the committee for the University Campus – apart for Reidy, who belonged to both project groups – are never mentioned.

> The two (Lucio Costa and Carlos Leão), as well as a group of modernists "à la Le Corbusier" (among which are Affonso Reidy, Jorge Moreira, Oscar Niemeyer, Ernani Vasconcellos, etc.), claim that the minister could invite you to hold a two- or three-month-long course at the School of Fine Arts; and also, once you are here, he will probably ask your opinion about the University Campus, making it easier to ensure at least your direction of the project, drawing on the collaboration of the young Brazilians.[70]

As a result, there is obvious ambiguity regarding the actual contribution that was asked of Le Corbusier, fuelling a series of misunderstandings and different historiographic interpretations. In fact, in response to the architect's enthusiastic reaction – "the important thing," Le Corbusier seems to have claimed, "would be my possible participation in the construction of the new Ministry of Education"[71] – Monteiro reiterated the possibility of his taking part in the University Campus committee, underlining how the Brazilian architects were already busy with the Ministry project, therefore openly suggesting that what was required of him was a consultation of an already-existing project and not a project *ex novo*. Regardless, in the first letter addressed to Le Corbusier, Costa points out that the required consultancy – although originally defined (on the occasion of Piacentini's first invitation) as only in regards to the University Campus – would have interested both projects. As evidence of the ambiguity connected to this delicate mediation process, Capanema would ask Vargas, in a letter dated 2 June 1936, to authorise him to request the joined consultancy of both Le Corbusier and Piacentini (with the same identical remuneration), presenting the proposal as a demand that was expressly made to him by the "five-man committee."[72]

In turning to Le Corbusier, Costa reveals that he was moved, at least in part, by ideological reasons as well, clearly unaware of his interlocutor's previous attempts to gain Mussolini's favour.[73]

> I insisted once again with minister Capanema for him to invite you all the same – but it was useless: there is the Italian embassy, and Piacentini did the best he could; Brazil sells its meat and coffee to the Duce's puppets in Africa, etc. Time went by... reactionaries all over the place. Then, about one month ago, the minister put together a committee of five architects in order to develop – on the basis of the chosen land property and of the closing programme – the plans for the future University Campus, always with the idea of having Piacentini back to ask him for advice. As part of that committee, I took the opportunity to charge again, and this time with good results: the minister has authorised us to contact you to see under which conditions you might be willing to come to Rio for a cycle of conferences to illustrate your opinion of the Ministry's project – of which I am sending a copy – and the general or particular way in which, according to your principles, the masterplan of the University Campus should be defined.[74]

Costa immediately became the main interlocutor, holding a correspondence even on behalf of the other involved architects and, during Le Corbusier's stay, he systematically operated as a mediator and spokesperson for the work in progress. His role as a point of reference extended to the University Campus once he was nominated president of the five-man committee by his own collaborators;[75] in turn, he appointed Jorge Machado Moreira, Oscar Niemeyer, and José de Souza Reis to assist him in this full-time commitment. During the official meetings with the contracting authorities, Costa and Le Corbusier were those charged with presenting (and defending) the project to Campos and Amaral,[76] who would complain about the incompatibility of the proposals with the technical and financial needs of the project and of the programme – in addition to complaining about the "different work development" compared to the productive months under Piacentini between August 1935 and March 1936. One of the sore points was undoubtedly the separation of vehicular from pedestrian traffic through the creation of suspended overpasses that, according to Campos and Amaral, in addition to being costly and superfluous, were also the product of a sterile doctrinaire approach, highlighting the unbridgeable divergences that would sentence the project to fail shortly after.

A marginal but significant episode – connected to the conferences held by Le Corbusier at the Instituto Nacional de Música between 31 July and 14 August 1936[77] – allows us to understand how Costa saw his role in the midst of this experience. Among the original documents referring to the conferences are two short notes that shed light on the equal relationship he held with Le Corbusier. As *connoisseur* of the audience to which the conferences were directed, Costa proposed himself as a trusted interlocutor able to suggest the most effective ways to convey specific messages, indicating, for example, to "not talk too much about the sun: we have too much of it and do not know what else to do with it."[78] The core of these notes touches the very heart of Le Corbusier's proposal, hoping to overturn the condition of man's enslavement to machines and addressing the issue of the collaboration between professionals and public administrations. Not by chance, Le Corbusier opened his conference cycle with a tribute to Pereira Passos, the *grand prestidigitateur*, the mayor who had turned Rio de Janeiro into "a miracle, an admirable spectacle"; by mentioning King Louis XIV, Napoleon, and Haussmann, he states that "everything today depends on the grandiosity of vision of the leaders";[79] in case the public opinion were not to be ready, the "Authority" should have the duty of being a precursor, paving the way for the newest proposals formulated by the tecnhnicians. Regardless of the role that was played by these small "corrective" measures on certain theoretical nuances of the conferences, the emphasis on the theme of "Authority" – long cherished by Le Corbusier – is an indication of the strategy put in place by Costa to influence the minister, persuading him of the fact that Le Corbusier's principles lent themselves, more than others, to be used in the ambitious projects of his administration, investing the minister with the responsibility of possibly carrying them out. With the presence of Le Corbusier, Costa knew he had the chance of consolidating the positions he had so painstakingly conquered in a context that was still unwilling to welcome innovation and renewal. However, it was also an opportunity for him to place his work within a broader context, finally able to claim a complete integration of his group's work with the European developments in the modern architectural debate. After all, there was much more at stake than the construction of a building or university campus: there was the modernist project's faith in the emancipatory force of architecture, in its potential as a vehicle for social change, in its guiding role in the construction of the future. From this moment, Costa would develop, step by step, a narrative aimed at legitimising the "new architecture" not only as a style of the new times, but also as an official art that was representative of the "public matter" – an image of Brazil that was renewed in its institutions as well as in its cultural base, destined to hold a leading role on the international scene. This set the premises for the temporary but profitable partnership between architecture and State that was destined to mark the "canonical" moment of Brazilian modernism from the Ministry project onwards.

Negotiations and lost opportunities

Immediately after Le Corbusier returned to France, his relationship with the group of architects slowly began to loosen; the correspondence became less frequent in time – although Costa would pursue it, on and off, until Le Corbusier's death – undergoing a completely silent phase during the war. From the end of 1936, in response to Le Corbusier's frustration with his inability to carve himself out a role in at least one of the projects he had collaborated in, there was fervid activity on the part of the Brazilians, intent on measuring themselves with the failure of both proposals devised by the "master."

As for the Ministry, the impossibility of replacing the land in Esplanada do Castelo with that originally indicated by Le Corbusier in Praia de Santa Luzia – together with the inadequacy of the sketch that the illustrious guest devised for the final site in Esplanada do Castelo (forsaking a possible view on Baía de Guanabara by aligning the main part of the building to Avenida Graça Aranha, namely setting the long side of the building in parallel with the long side of the lot) – brought to the recovery of the project that was originally developed by the Brazilians, despite Le Corbusier's doubts on its design.[80] This project was approved by Capanema on

19 October 1936 with the request of some changes, such as a greater number of floors, a less symmetrical composition (as the same Le Corbusier had suggested) through a different design solution for the auditorium volume,[81] the replacement of part of the glass surfaces with opaque or translucent glazing, and better lighting of the service corridors.

We will hold out from repeating the over-mythicised narrative, still reported by authoritative sources, on the "truth" of what really happened. Apart from its legendary quality – given by the ex-post interpretation that was made in light of the Ministry building's international success – the story could essentially be confirmed – although more in the facts than in the critical interpretations, on which we will reflect later. An exchange of letters between Costa and Niemeyer many years later concerning the matter of the paternity of the Ministry's giant *pilotis* – and the private nature of the conversation seems to make the source more reliable than the public statements on which previous reconstructions rely on – seems to confirm that the final solution of the project was due significantly to Niemeyer's contribution. Niemeyer wrote.

> If it weren't for the solution that was finally adopted, the pilotis of the MES would have been only 4m high, according to the project that was being developed [...]. I would like to remind you – without false modesty – how much the solution I proposed has weighed on the history of our collaboration on Le Corbusier's project. I still remember Jorge Moreira complaining, afflicted: "Lucio, we must design everything all over again." But you understood that my idea was better and we developed a new project.[82]

In his reply, Costa recalls the various instances in which he attributed the merit his friend was entitled to, confirming that there wasn't the "slightest trace of disagreement" on this point. He also added a significant clarification.

> The important thing, in this case, is that the original projects – both ours (or "mine," as you prefer to call it) and those proposed by LC – were relatively low because of the exaggerated limits imposed at the time by the proximity to the airport, and were not the highest building structure that was finally adopted. It is evident that he never would have proposed 4-metre *pilotis* for a building of such height – especially if we consider that, in the original design for the land on the sea (despite it being a low and elongated structure), he had already planned for five double-height *pilotis* in the central part of the entrance.[83]

Even the correspondence between Costa and Le Corbusier presents several passages in which Niemeyer's fundamental role in the Brazilian group project is underlined, a project that brought together, in a new synthesis, elements that were drawn from all three previous ones: on 21 November, Le Corbusier asked "that worthy Oscar and his good perspectives,"[84] and on 3 July 1937, Costa confirmed how his collaborator – who suddenly turned into "the *star* of the group" – was mainly responsible for the project.[85] In the final design solution, owing much to the studies of Le Corbusier, the main eleven-floor block of the building was rotated ninety degrees – compared to the previous solution devised by the architect for the site of Esplanada

54 *Reasons for the new architecture*

do Castelo – allowing for the glass façade to look south-east on the Baía de Guanabara, and for the north-west façade to be completely fit with *brise-soleils*. The same block was also brought back and distanced from Rua Pedro Lessa by virtue of the insertion of a low exhibition hall[86] – perpendicular to it, mirroring the auditorium – so that the main volume of the building took over the central part of the lot instead of one of its sides, articulating the public space in a pleasant alternation of covered and uncovered areas (Figure 2.5).[87]

Despite its lucid and rigorous use of Corbusian principles, the project appears to present an intelligent re-elaboration of them, with subtle formal differences denoting remarkable expressive independence. The use of local stone and *azulejos* as coating material (both suggested by Le Corbusier), the curvilinear layout of the auditorium and technical rooms, the bare simplicity of the main building block, the elegant proportions of a building wonderfully inserted in the surrounding urban environment, the richness of the works of art within it, and Roberto Burle Marx's extraordinary landscaping contribution are all elements that – rightfully – make the Ministry the most significant expression of Brazilian modernism's hard-earned maturity. Together with Brasilia, it perhaps represents the most emblematic synthesis of Costa's participation in defining the identity of the nation's official architecture, sublimating any reference to tradition in composed monumentality. Here – more than in the New York pavilion that came shortly after – Niemeyer's creative exuberance is alleviated by the proportional balance and harmony that Costa owed to his solid academic education (Figure 2.6).

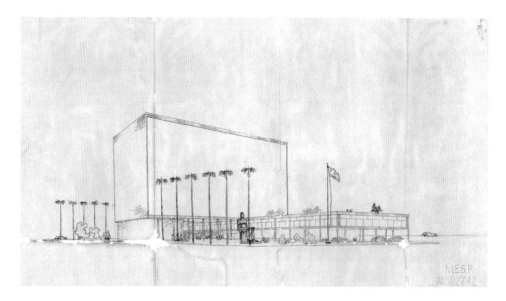

Figure 2.5 Lucio Costa and team, preliminary version of the final project for the Ministry of Education and Public Health in Rio de Janeiro. Perspective view, 1936. Arquivo Central do IPHAN – Seção Rio de Janeiro.

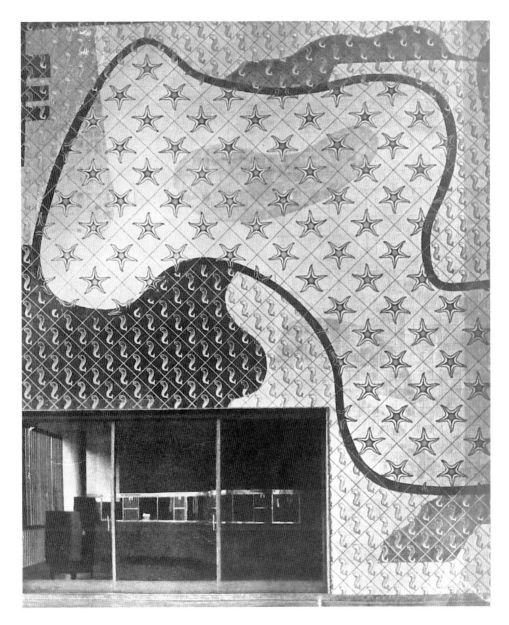

Figure 2.6 View of the main entrance of the Ministry of Education and Public Health, with the mural cladding in *azulejos* realised according to the drawings by Cândido Portinari. © *L'Architecture d'Aujourd'hui*.

Even the development of the University Campus proceeded at a much faster pace immediately after Le Corbusier's departure, if we consider that on 12 October 1936 Capanema submitted a new project to the professor committee[88] – one that was developed in the previous two months by the group presided over by Costa. In fact, Costa specifies in different documents that the project directly derived from Le Corbusier's proposal, despite the fact that the attempt of adapting to the needs expressed by the professor committee had suggested using a completely opposite layout – all this in a way that unequivocally highlights Costa's academic background.[89]

Le Corbusier's project was structured on an orthogonal grid of pathways that connected all the buildings, which were each treated in a substantially independent manner or arranged in groups (Figure 2.7). Costa's project, on the other hand, arranged the various faculties perpendicularly to a 100-metre-long central axis, along a service "spine" that connected to the classrooms, forming a series of patios. The axis ran across the entire site, north to south, marking different moments, different spatial and plastic sensations, which are described in the project report (Figure 2.8).[90] From the entrance portal – recalling elements similar to the ones used by Piacentini and Morpurgo in the campus project[91] – you had access to a square where you could find the monumental auditorium building already envisaged by Le Corbusier – formally reprising one of the two great halls of the Palace of the Soviets – and the pure geometric prism containing the library and rectorate. The two buildings were brought together in a way that Costa describes as a synthesis between the "Oriental-Gothic" spirit of the first and the "Greek-Latin" spirit of the second. The large central avenue began at this point, with the horizontal school buildings developing off its sides. It was followed by an overpass that crossed the train tracks before continuing with more schools, the avenue at this point being characterised by the presence of six rows of imperial palm trees. This element, too, was borrowed by Le Corbusier, who placed them perpendicularly to the axis that ideally connected the separate buildings of the hospital, the so-called Museum of Knowledge of Brazil (a prototype for the Museum of Unlimited

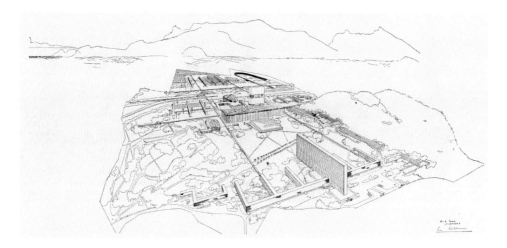

Figure 2.7 Le Corbusier, perspective aerial view of the project for the University Campus in Rio de Janeiro, 1936. From Le Corbusier and Pierre Jeanneret, *Œuvre complète*, vol. 3. 1934–1938. © Fondation Le Corbusier/SIAE, 2019.

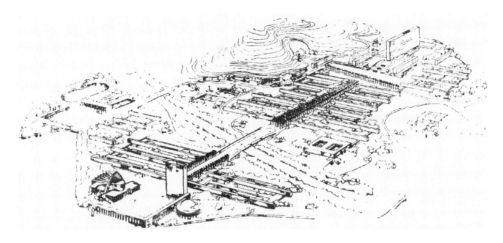

Figure 2.8 Lucio Costa and team, perspective aerial view of the project for the University Campus in Rio de Janeiro, 1936. From Lucio Costa, *Registro de uma vivência*, 1995. Casa de Lucio Costa.

Growth), and the auditorium, on a north-south line equivalent to Costa's. The composition ended with the great mass of the hospital, described in the report as the "last sensation that gradually imposes itself upon stepping through the entrance portal, with the crescendo of a musical motif."[92] It was also arranged on a slightly elevated position, thanks to the orographic quality of the land. The vertical conformation of the building – counterpointing the prism of the rectorate building – and the north-south line running parallel to the main axis of the project are all elements that were substantially borrowed from Le Corbusier's proposal. It is evident that this was the largest-scale project that Costa had faced up to this point, and it is no coincidence that some elements of Brasilia's plan are here recognisable in embryonic form. The compelling perspective views of the project were performed by Niemeyer, who is also the author of the small university club building, the core generator of themes that would later be developed in the New York pavilion and in the Pampulha complex.

The project report lists a series of themes that, once developed in the following years, will form the backbone of Costa's discourse, bringing theoretical depth to the "antropophagous" operation that both projects for Capanema led to in their final versions. Among these, there was the search for a synthesis between contemporary construction technology – "eminently international by nature" – and an "unmistakable local character, whose bare and modest simplicity owes much to the good principles of old familiar constructions" – things that could be achieved through planimetric expedients (patios, open galleries), through the use of finishing materials ("walls of rustic stone, gneiss slabs, *azulejos*, plaster or paint on exposed concrete"), and through appropriate vegetation. The will of creating a "variety of sensations" and favour "plastic sobriety" – while maintaining a "predominance of horizontality" so as to not rival the "tormented landscape of Rio" – clearly suggest the attempt of shaping something of monumental character and with expressive intensity. The emphasis on plastic expression and on the inherent artistic value of architectural works – already essentially present in "Razões" – would be fundamental in Costa's battle against the schematic approach of functionalist rhetoric. In this regard, a specific passage in the text presents a definition of architecture that owes much to Le Corbusier, especially in reference to the emotional content of the *recherche patiente* over space.

> If it only satisfies technical and functional requirements – it is not yet architecture; if it is lost in purely decorative intentions – it is nothing but scenography; but if he who has conceived it – whether popular or learned – stops and hesitates in front of the simple choice of an inter-axis between the pillars or of a relation between the height and width of a compartment; if he dwells in the search of a right balance between full and empty, or in the volumetric composition in the attempt to subordinate it to some sort of law; or if he lingers on the materials and their expressive value; when all this is put together following the strictest technical and functional precepts, but also following that superior intention that selects, coordinates, and directs all this confused and contradictory mass of details in a determined direction, thus transmitting a sense of rhythm, expression, unity, and clarity – namely what grants it a permanent character – this, yes: it is architecture.[93]

On 3 November 1936, Costa informed Carlos Drummond de Andrade of his concern regarding the delay in the remuneration for the project of the University Campus, in a letter that – in addition to confirming the importance of Niemeyer's contribution to the group – represents one of the first signs of his subsidence.

> Carlos, I no longer know what explanation to give to the collaborators: Reis, who has been kidnapped by the "professors"; Jorge, who has only worked one month, is at the mercy of events; and especially Oscar, whose work is truly remarkable – I'll tell you this: without his help we certainly would never have been able to succeed in bringing this adventure to a satisfactory conclusion. He has abandoned projects that paid him well to follow this one, as we agreed – and, in the meantime, more than three months and twenty days have gone by and he still has yet to receive even one *vintem*![94]

In another letter sent to Le Corbusier on 31 December 1936, this state of mind seems to be further exacerbated – in addition to the Swiss-French architect's disappointment in the failure of his proposals and payment delays – by the emergence of an unfavourable situation on both fronts: on the one side, Costa saw the temporary disinterest of Capanema (engaged in the more urgent reform of the Ministry), while also declaring himself pessimistic about the possibility of having the professor committee accept his proposal for the University Campus.

> As I have said: your visit cost me a year of insistence with Capanema, with marches and countermarches – in short, a real "miracle." Now you have proof. The point is that everything that has to do with the government is very complicated here. [...] As far as I am concerned – tired of these fights and struggles that bring nowhere and annoy me – I deserve your friendship. I have done everything possible to be of use. If – in your opinion – things have not always gone the right way, I ask you to forgive me.[95]

Therefore – despite the exceptional intensity of the earlier months – the year ended in pessimism, leading Costa to steer away from the full-time commitment of the Ministry, which he would delegate to younger colleagues only five months after the onset of construction. At the beginning of the new year, on 5 January 1937, the group working on the Ministry presented the preliminary project for a new building to Capanema.[96] On 22 February 1937, the project was developed with a few changes, like the reshaping of the atrium's monumental staircase from a square plan to a circular one, the elimination of the *pilotis* from the service corridors, and other distribution and technical changes. The project was approved, in record time, on 26 February, so as to avert the danger – that the same Costa had expressed well-founded concern for[97] – of not being able to complete the work during Capanema's administration, which would subsequently be extended to unlimited tenure with the establishment of the Estado Novo.

In the meantime, on the front of the University Campus, after having held many meetings between October 1936 and February 1937 (in which Costa repeatedly defended his project from the attack of the professors), on 2 March 1937, the committee unanimously rejected the project, arguing – in contrast with what the designers stated in the report – that it did not respect the programme indications. Moreover, a specific passage of the descriptive report – mentioning the committee's tepid reception of Le Corbusier's project – raised controversy with the University Rector, to which Costa replied by publishing the entire incriminated report in the *Revista da Directoria de Engenharia – PDF*.[98]

On 24 April 1937, while laying the first foundation stone of the new Ministry building, Capanema's celebratory speech presented the new building as a "great architectural monument, the project of which was developed with conscience, perseverance, precision, and accuracy [...] with the dual objective of creating a work of art and a house of work."[99] The key words that summarised the rationalist spirit of the Vargas government public service – "simplicity, speed, economy, precision" – were swiftly associated with the modern architectural image of the new Ministry headquarters. Starting from May 1937, Costa and his collaborators were called to face the most demanding construction site of their professional careers. Its direction was assigned to the superintendent of the Ministry's Serviço de Obras, Eduardo Souza Aguiar, with Emílio Henrique Baumgart as structural engineer.

From the tone of various records, we get the idea of how the disappointment over the rejection of the University Campus project – experienced by Costa as a defeat, to which he would surrender only after having addressed the professor committee for many further clarifications[100] – would prevail on the enthusiasm for the start of the new Ministry construction site. Costa in fact expressed his frustration in a letter he sent to Capanema on 17 July.

> Now that everything seems "settled," I must confess how much it hurts me to see how an elevated and pure idea like that of the University Campus can take shape and develop in this way. When I read the report and verified that everything was nothing but a sham, I wanted to demand an investigation, to protest, to cry out against such injustice and bad faith. But I soon learned that, at best, it would only serve as entertainment for the practiced wickedness of the *medaglioni*. Therefore, Dr. Capanema, do not believe that – by distancing myself – I am accepting the many criticisms that the report contains; nor that I intend to avoid further inconveniencing your work (which would be appreciable, in other

circumstances); simply – as desperate as I felt – I was certain that everything would have been in vain. And the saddest thing is that as long as we continue to persevere, for years and years, in the development of this wrong thing, some drawing table somewhere will be cradling the "real" solution – the right thing.[101]

In the last two years, Costa was subject to a great pressure: on one side, he had taken the responsibility for a series of unpopular choices, in contrast with large part of the public opinion; on the other, he had simultaneously coordinated two different project groups, mostly made up of young first-time professionals, in the development of two grand-scale public projects with considerable repercussions on the public image of an important national political institution. Although we may surmise that Costa had already been developing the need to distance himself from the commitment made with Capanema, it seems no coincidence that his final decision to do so followed the reprise of the collaboration with Piacentini (who would entrust Vittorio Morpurgo in his place). In fact, the minister recontacted him after the "embarrassing situation" resulting from the rejection of the project elaborated by "five of the best Brazilian architects."[102]

The two messages with which Costa communicated – to Capanema and to the head of the cabinet – his temporary withdrawal from the Ministry construction site, are dated 21 September. In the first one, he limits himself to blaming his decision on generic "health issues,"[103] while the confidential tone of the second one gives away the existence of other more profound reasons. By arguing that the "University issue" was not a factor in the development of his decision – if not for having relieved him from feeling as if he had acted as a "deserter" and for having pushed him to not give up his salary "whatever the duration of the impediment had been" – he finally leaks the real reasons behind it.

> Tired and incapable of constant awareness, far from being of help, my presence has only served to hinder a good work progress. You understand me, Carlos; I owe so much to you and to Capanema that I would never interrupt my commitment if there was no serious reason for doing so. Besides, the project has very little of mine; it belongs much more to my friends: it remains in good hands.[104]

It is clear that Costa is questioning his ability to keep control of the situation, perhaps also as a result to the downsizing of his authoritative position in face of the growing independence of his collaborators, Oscar Niemeyer's in particular. The few lines addressed to Carlos Drummond de Andrade from Capanema, following Costa's resignation, clarify the importance that the minister assigned to his role, both in terms of the effective realisation of the project and in terms of the architectural and artistic choices related to it.

> Carlos, tell Lucio the following: 1) I approved the project because he convinced me that I had to approve it; 2) the technical part of the construction site is unimportant; the Serviço de Obras could take care of it; 3) the important part, which still has to be developed, is choosing the solutions with artistic character: the finishing, the paint, sculptures, gardens, etc., and for this reason I cannot dismiss him; I wouldn't take a step without him.[105]

The following month, the architects' committee that had collaborated in the University Campus project was dissolved. Sending a letter to each of its members, the minister thanked them for "the culture, the talent, and the generosity [...] that have been an important contribution to the solution of the problem."[106]

Notes

1 See the Bibliography for an overview of the existing studies on the Ministry. However, we would like to mention here a few specific titles that have been a fundamental reference and that have a particular monographic and documental approach: Cecília Rodrigues dos Santos et al., *Le Corbusier e o Brasil* (São Paulo: Tessela-Projeto, 1987); Maurício Lissovsky and Paulo Sergio Moraes de Sá, *Colunas da educação: a construção do Ministério da Educação e Saúde (1935–1945)* (Rio de Janeiro: Edições do Patrimônio, 1996); Roberto Segre, *Ministério da Educação e Saúde. Ícone urbano da modernidade brasileira (1935–1945)* (São Paulo: Romano Guerra, 2013).
2 Costa, *Registro de uma vivência* (São Paulo: Empresa das Artes, 1995).
3 Donato Mello Jr., "Um campus universitário para a cidade do Rio de Janeiro," *Arquitetura Revista*, no. 2 (1985): 52–72; Matheus Gorovitz, *Os riscos do projeto: contribuição à análise do juízo estético na arquitetura* (Brasília-São Paulo: Edunb-Studio Nobel, 1993); Matheus Gorovitz, "Os riscos da modernidade: um estudo dos projetos de Le Corbusier e Lucio Costa para o campus da Universidade do Brasil," *Projeto Design*, no. 264 (February, 2002): 22–25; Klaus Chaves Alberto, "Três projetos para uma Universidade do Brasil," master thesis, FAU-UFRJ, 2003.
4 We should point out that the background against which the historical narrative and the comparison of the various interpretative hypotheses take place was provided by a series of studies aimed at reconstructing the cultural policies of the Ministry of Education during the "first Vargas Era." We refer, in particular, to the work of Sergio Miceli, Antônio Cândido, Simon Schwartzman, Helena Bomeny, Vanda Ribeiro Costa, Luciano Martins, and to the more recent work of Alexandre Barbalho, Murilo Badaró, and Daryle Williams. See the general Bibliography for more details.
5 For a more in-depth analysis of the firm's design activity, also see Geraldo Ferraz, *Warchavchik e a introdução da nova arquitetura no Brasil: 1925 a 1940* (São Paulo: Museo de Arte de São Paulo, 1965), and José Lira, *Warchavchik. Fraturas da vanguarda* (São Paulo: Cosac & Naify, 2011). The consulted documentation regarding the projects belongs to the private archives of the two architects and to the Coleção Warchavchik at the FAU-USP.
6 "Estrato de Estatutos," *Diário Oficial*, June, 1932. AGW, periodical section. The studio was located in the *A Noite* skyscraper in Rio de Janeiro.
7 Paulo Bittencourt was the director of the *Correio da Manhã* at the time.
8 Alexandre Altberg, ed., *1º Salão de arquitetura tropical inaugurado a 17 de abril de 1933 pelo Exmo. Sr. Ministro Washington Pires*, exhibition catalogue, n.p., n.d.
9 Costa, *Registro*, 72.
10 See Elizabeth D. Harris, *Le Corbusier: riscos brasileiros* (São Paulo: Nobel, 1988). It seems as though Leão's library had been a precious source for the study and research of the architect's friends and collaborators.
11 Costa and Leão had been invited to participate alongside four other professional studios. "Concurso de ante-projecto do novo edificio do Club de Engenharia," *Revista do Club de Engenharia* II, no. 20 (May 1936): 1098–1101.
12 Costa, *Registro*, 84–107.
13 See Costa, Foreword to Stamo Papadaki, *The Work of Oscar Niemeyer* (New York: Reinhold Publishing Corporation, 1950), 1–3.
14 See Costa, "Ante-projeto para a Villa de Monlevade. Memorial descriptivo," *Revista da Directoria de Engenharia – PDF* III, no. 3 (May 1936): 114–128. This competition – in which Costa did not win – was launched in 1934 by the Belgian-Mineiro Iron and Steel Company for a location in the State of Minas Gerais.

15 See Carlos Eduardo Dias Comas, "Lucio Costa e a revolução na arquitetura brasileira 30/39. De lenda(s e) Le Corbusier," *Architextos* II, no. 022.01 (March 2002a).
16 A construction technique consisting of a clay infill and wooden plank armour, similar to *pau a pique*, commonly used in the rural areas of Brazil from the colonial period, as it was lightweight and economic.
17 Speech by Gustavo Capanema for the official appointment of the commission for the University Campus plan, 22 July 1935. CPDOC, GC g 35.07.19, I-3. The Universidade do Brasil was established on 5 July 1935, and the so-called *Comissão do Plano da Universidade* took place on 22 July. See Simon Schwartzman, Helena Bomeny, and Vanda Ribeiro Costa, *Tempos de Capanema* (Rio de Janeiro-São Paulo: Paz e Terra-Edusp, 1984).
18 A small group of documents on the UDF is held at the Gustavo Capanema and Anísio Teixeira funds of the CPDOC. Also see Lectícia J. Braga De Vincenzi, "A fundação da Universidade do Distrito Federal e seu significado para a educação no Brasil," *Forum Educacional* 10, no. 3 (July–September 1986): 16–60. As reported by De Vincenzi, according to the documentation held at the Secretaria do Instituto da Educação, it appears as though the professors of the Instituto de Arte had been Costa and Leão (architecture), Nestor de Figueiredo (urban design), Cândido Portinari (painting), and Fernando Valentim (plastic and industrial arts).
19 Costa, "Curso de aperfeiçoamento para arquitetos" [1935]. CLC, IV A 02-01818.
20 Costa, "Razões da nova arquitetura," *Revista da Directoria de Engenharia – PDF* III, no. 1 (January, 1936): 3–9, reported in Alberto Xavier, ed., *Lúcio Costa: sôbre arquitetura* (Porto Alegre: Editora UniRitter, 2007, 1st edn 1962), 17–41.
21 Warchavchik, "Acerca da arquitetura moderna," *Correio da Manhã*, 1 November 1925, reported in id., *Arquitetura do século XX e outros escritos*, ed. Carlos Martins (São Paulo: Cosac & Naify, 2006), 33–38.
22 Costa to the director of the UDF [1935]. CLC, VI A 01-01202.
23 Costa to Paulo Ewerard Nunes Pires (director of the Faculdade Nacional de Arquitetura), n.d. ACI-RJ, LC-CR(B)04(05). Also see Paulo Santos to Costa, 8 February 1954. ACI-RJ, LC-CR(B)04(03); and Nunes Pires to Costa, 14 January 1954. ACI-RJ, LC-CR(B)04(06).
24 See: Júlio Afranio Peixoto's letter of resignation from the office of rector of the UDF [30 November 1935]. CPDOC, PEB c 35.11.30; Celso Kelly's letter of resignation from the office of director of the Instituto de Arte of the UDF [2 December 1935]. CPDOC, PEB c 35.12.02. Anísio Teixeira's vacant office would later be filled by Francisco Campos, minister of Education during the Costian reform of the National School of Fine Arts, as well as main author of the subsequent 1937 authoritarian Constitution.
25 This was a large area in the urban centre that was not yet occupied. The area resulted from the demolition of the hill of the same name on the occasion of the 1922 Independence Centenary International Exposition, which would host various ministerial headquarters in these same years. See Lauro Cavalcanti, *Moderno e brasileiro. A história de uma nova linguagem na arquitetura (1930–60)* (Rio de Janeiro: Jorge Zahar, 2006).
26 Letter to Gustavo Capanema signed by the participants of the competition, 18 May 1935. ACI-RJ, Administrative Procedure 6870/35 related to the construction of the Ministry of Education and Public Health (henceforth PA 6870/35), vol. IA, 46–47. Roberto Segre speculates that Costa – who may have participated in the competition on his own or together with Carlos Leão – might have destroyed the documentation attesting to his presented project because of his dissatisfaction with it.
27 Mello Franco de Andrade to Drummond de Andrade, June 23 [1935]. FCRB, CDA-CP-0093(35); Mello Franco de Andrade to Drummond de Andrade [1935]. FCRB, CDA-CP-0093(36).
28 "Acta da primeira reunião do jury do concurso para escolha do ante-projeto do edifício do Ministério da Educação e Saúde Pública," 17 June 1935. PA 6870/35, vol. IA, 60–62.

29 See "Concurso de ante-projectos para o Ministério da Educação e Saúde Pública," *Revista da Directoria de Engenharia – PDF* IV, no. 18 (September, 1935): 510–519, in which are published the projects by Reidy and by Moreira-Vasconcellos.
30 Mello Franco de Andrade to Carlos Drummond de Andrade, 23 June [1935].
31 "Acta da segunda reunião do jury do concurso para escolha do ante-projeto do edifício do Ministério da Educação e Saúde Pública," 5 July 1935. PA 6870/35, vol. IA, 65–66.
32 Mello Franco de Andrade to Drummond de Andrade [1935].
33 "Acta da terceira reunião do jury do concurso para escolha do ante-projeto do edifício do Ministério da Educação e Saúde Pública," 8 July 1935. PA 6870/35, vol. IA, 68.
34 "Concurso de ante-projectos para o Ministério da Educação e Saúde Pública."
35 "Acta da reunião de encerramento do concurso para escolha do projeto do edifício do Ministério da Educação e Saúde Pública," 1 October 1935. PA 6870/35, vol. IB, 79–81.
36 Relations between fascist Italy and Vargas's Brazil remained friendly up until Brazil joined the Allies in the war. Piacentini's stay – as well as his project for the University Campus in Rome – found plenty of space in the press of the time, only partially eclipsed by the controversy given by the assignment of the Rio University Campus to a foreign architect.
37 Particular reference was made to Decree n. 23.569 of 11 December 1933, and to the 1934 Constitution. The documents relating to these events, which we will not mention individually for reasons of space, are held in the CPDOC within the Gustavo Capanema archive; they are also partially reported in the aforementioned PA 6870/35, held in the ACI-RJ.
38 Capanema to Costa, 13 January 1936. CPDOC, GC g 35.07.19, II-293.
39 Costa to Le Corbusier, 26 June 1936. FLC, I3-3-16.
40 On his way to New York to follow the project of the Brazilian pavilion for the 1939 New York World's Fair, Costa writes: "Carlos, as I told you before, you will never know the good you did to me when – almost three years ago – you came looking for me. Nobody remembered my existence anymore – not even to insult me." Costa to Drummond de Andrade, 26 March 1938. FCRB, CDA-CP-0477(3/4).
41 We learn from various testimonies that, initially, the involved architects had been Leão, Reidy, and Moreira. This last architect had then asked to also include his collaborator, Vasconcellos, while Niemeyer – who at the time was a draftsman in the studio of Costa and Leão – would have personally insisted on joining the group.
42 The same Secretaria-Geral de Viação, Trabalho e Obras Públicas had recommended making arrangements on this point with the architect in charge of the Directoria de Engenharia, namely Affonso Eduardo Reidy. See Mario Machado to Capanema, 5 November 1935. CPDOC, GC f 34.10.19, I-15.
43 "Proposta para a elaboração do projecto do novo edifício para o Ministério da Educação e Saúde Pública," 8 January 1936. CPDOC, GC f 34.10.19, II-2.
44 Lissovsky and Moraes de Sá, *Colunas da educação*, 5.
45 Capanema to Costa, 25 March 1936. CPDOC, GC f 34.10.19 (PA 6870/35, vol. IB, 197).
46 Cfr. with Gustavo Capanema's reports to Getúlio Vargas, 11 February 1935, and 21 November 1936. PA 6870/35, vol. V, 365–370.
47 Costa to Drummond de Andrade, 3 April 1936. FCRB, CDA-CP-0477(1).
48 See Lissovsky and Moraes de Sá, *Colunas da educação*, 27–29.
49 Memória to Vargas [1936]. CPDOC, GC f 34.10.19, II-57.
50 In the letter sent to Le Corbusier with the copies of the project papers sent in attachment, Costa also felt the need to justify himself beforehand, in case the Swiss-French architect were to find the project to be "too influenced by his own work." Costa to Le Corbusier, 26 June 1936.
51 Costa to Le Corbusier, 3 July 1937. FLC, I3-3-41.
52 Costa to Niemeyer, 23 December 1988. CLC, VI A 02-02671.
53 Costa, "Projecto para o edifício do Ministério da Educação e Saúde Pública a ser construido na Quadra F da Esplanada do Castello; Memorial descriptivo" [15 May 1936]. CPDOC, GC f 34.10.19, II-12.

Reasons for the new architecture

54 Costa, "Notas á margem do parecer do Snr. Dr. Domingos J. da Silva Cunha, Inspector de Engenharia Sanitaria" [September 1936]. CPDOC, GC f 34.10.19, II-42.
55 Examination of the scientific opinions drawn up by the Superintendência de Obras e Transportes, 18 July 1936. PA 6870/35, vol. V, 316–324.
56 Costa, "Esclarecimentos à informação da Superintendência de Obras e Transportes" [September 1936]. PA 6870/35, vol. V, 353–355.
57 Inácio Azevedo do Amaral and Ernesto Souza Campos's report for Gustavo Capanema, 13 May 1936. CPDOC, GC g 35.07.19, II-298-99.
58 Mello Jr., "Um campus universitário para a cidade do Rio de Janeiro," 56.
59 Costa, "Uma questão de oportunidade," *Revista da Directoria de Engenharia – PDF* IV, no. 3 (May 1937), reported in Xavier, ed., *Sôbre arquitetura*, 63–66; 64.
60 See the numerous press clippings held at the Biblioteca Paulo Santos.
61 Costa to Le Corbusier, 26 June 1936. In the letter, Costa describes the project in detail as "something unique in the world and with a lyrical potential worthy of the master, with "immense gardens on the building roofs, screened from the sun by large canopies," and, "in contrast to the sharpness of the architecture, islands where the exuberance of the tropical vegetation could expand without limits – all connected by viaducts, bridges, and the natural outline of the edges of the lake," within the "magnificent setting of the mountains, sky, sun, and water."
62 Inácio Azevedo do Amaral and Ernesto Souza Campos's report for Gustavo Capanema, 14 August 1936. CPDOC, GC g 35.07.19, II-326-34, 12.
63 Amaral and Campos's report for Capanema, Rio de Janeiro, 13 May 1936, 1.
64 As emerges from what he writes to Le Corbusier, Costa considered this area unsuitable for the establishment of the University Campus, especially due to the presence of the railway lines and to the unfortunate landscape situation.
65 We have chosen to dedicate relative prominence to Le Corbusier's stay in Rio de Janeiro in this present work, pointing out the aspects concerning his relationship with the clients and the role played by Costa in the affair. From the first studies by Pietro Maria Bardi (1984) to the already mentioned pioneering volume by Harris, *Le Corbusier: riscos brasileiros*, and by Rodrigues dos Santos, Campos da Silva Pereira, Veriano da Silva Pereira, and Caldeira da Silva, *Le Corbusier e o Brasil*, the literature on the matter has grown with numerous contributions, for which I recommend seeing the general Bibliography.
66 Costa to Le Corbusier, 26 June 1936.
67 Le Corbusier, *La ville radieuse. Éléments d'une doctrine d'urbanisme pour l'équipement de la civilisation machiniste* (Paris: Freal, 1964, 1st edn 1933). A copy of the volume – probably given to the minister by Le Corbusier himself – is held in Capanema's personal archive. Also see Le Corbusier, "L'Autorité devant les taches contemporaines," *L'Architecture d'Aujourd'hui* V, no. 9 (September, 1935): 22–23.
68 Monteiro de Carvalho to Le Corbusier, 21 March 1936, in *Le Corbusier e o Brasil*, 134.
69 Costa, "Ministério, 1987." CLC, III A 41-01167. In this regard, also see Costa, "Relato pessoal," *Módulo* X, no. 40 (September 1975): 23–24.
70 Monteiro de Carvalho to Le Corbusier, 21 March 1936.
71 Le Corbusier to Monteiro de Carvalho, 30 March 1936. FLC, I3-3-1.
72 Capanema to Vargas, 2 June 1936. CPDOC, GC g 35.03.09, IV-10.
73 In this regard, see Giorgio Ciucci, "A Roma con Bottai," *Rassegna* II, no. 3 (July 1980): 66–71; François Chaslin, *Un Corbusier* (Paris: Seuil, 2015); and Xavier de Jarcy, *Le Corbusier, un fascisme français* (Paris: Albin Michel, 2015).
74 Costa to Le Corbusier, 26 June 1936.
75 Capanema to Vargas, July 1936. CPDOC, GC g 35.03.09-A, IV-42.
76 Amaral and Campos's report for Capanema, 14 August 1936.
77 As is well known, the conferences represented above all the official reason for Le Corbusier's remuneration, since national legislation prevented the exercise of the architect profession by part of those who did not hold a Brazilian citizenship. Le Corbusier's intention of publishing the conference proceedings – the drafts of which are held in the Capanema archive – did not result in anything. The conference contents were recently

published in Yannis Tsiomis, ed., *Conférences de Rio. Le Corbusier au Brésil* (Paris: Flammarion, 2006).
78 These refer to two manuscript sheets (FLC, F2-17, 279–280). See Tsiomis, *Conférences de Rio*, 66–68.
79 Tsiomis, *Conférences de Rio*, 51.
80 Le Corbusier had in fact expressed – in accordance with the invitation to diplomacy put forth by Costa before his arrival – some reservations on the excessively symmetrical solution and on the plastic effect that could have been achieved with a different configuration of the auditorium.
81 See the sketches by Capanema on the various possible configurations of the building, held in his personal archive. CPDOC, GC f 35.05.00, II-15.
82 Niemeyer to Costa, 22 December 1988. CLC, VI A 02-02671.
83 Costa to Niemeyer, 23 December 1988.
84 Le Corbusier to Costa, 21 November 1936. FLC, I3-3-29.
85 Costa to Le Corbusier, 3 July 1937. FLC, I3-3-41.
86 The project answered to a specific request by part of Capanema, who had expressed the need of an easy-access space destined to temporary exhibitions on the Ministry's activity. Costa to Capanema, 5 January 1937. PA 6870/35, vol VI/VII, 375–376.
87 For a detailed reconstruction of the different versions of the project, see Segre, *Ícone urbano da modernidade brasileira*.
88 Costa to Le Corbusier, 31 December 1936.
89 See Costa's interview by Matheus Gorovitz, July 1986, kindly made available to me by Gorovitz. Part of the interview is published in *JornAU* I, no. 6 (December 2002–January 2003): 19–24.
90 Costa, "Universidade do Brasil," *Revista da Directoria de Engenharia – PDF* IV, no. 3 (May 1937), henceforth quoted from Xavier, ed., *Sôbre arquitetura*, 67–85.
91 "Progetto per l'Università del Brasile a Rio de Janeiro: arch. Marcello Piacentini, arch. Vittorio Morpurgo," *Architettura*, no. 17 (September 1938): 521–550; Also see: Marcos Tognon, "Arquitetura fascista e Estado Novo: Marcello Piacentini e a tradição monumental no Rio de Janeiro," in Luiz Cesar de Queiroz Ribeiro, and Robert Pechman, eds, *Cidade, povo e nação: gênese do urbanismo moderno* (Rio de Janeiro: Civilização Brasileira, 1996).
92 Costa, "Universidade do Brasil," 84.
93 Costa, "Universidade do Brasil," 80.
94 Costa to Drummond de Andrade, 3 November 1936. CPDOC, GC g 35.03.09, IV-186.
95 Costa to Le Corbusier, 31 December 1936. FLC, I3-3-32.
96 Costa to Capanema, 5 January 1937.
97 Costa to Le Corbusier, 31 December 1936.
98 Costa, "Universidade do Brasil."
99 Lissovsky and Moraes de Sá, *Colunas da educação*, 150.
100 Costa to Capanema, 25 May 1937. CPDOC, GC g 35.03.09, V-214.
101 Costa to Capanema, 17 July 1937. CPDOC, GC g 35.03.09, V-19.
102 Capanema to Vargas, 1 September 1937. CPDOC, GC g 35.03.09, V-240-241.
103 Costa to Capanema, 21 September 1937. CPDOC, GC f 34.10.19, III-16.
104 Costa to Drummond de Andrade, 21 September 1937. CPDOC, GC f 34.10.19, III-15.
105 Capanema to Drummond de Andrade [September 1937]. CPDOC, GC f 34.10.19, III-15 A.
106 Chaves Alberto, *Três projetos para uma Universidade do Brasil*, 121–122.

3 A programme for national architecture

The years of the Estado Novo

Struggles and compromises

The coup d'état that led to the inauguration of the Estado Novo took place on 10 November 1937. It was the closing episode of president Vargas's manoeuvre aimed at boycotting the presidential elections, firmly holding onto power.[1] As recent studies on the Estado Novo period reveal, the premises for the authoritarian fall-back of the government began to form in the aftermath of the proclamation of the new Constitution in 1934. This happened through a series of initiatives aimed at securing certain concessions from Congress (in reaction to the oppositions from both right and left parties), finally proclaiming a new constitutional charter that gave the executive government powers comparable to those of the totalitarian European regimes.[2]

The incompatibility of the ideological positions taking place in this delicate phase of the country's political life risked undermining the collaborative relation between the minister and the members of the modernist intelligentsia. The same Carlos Drummond de Andrade, as we learn from Gustavo Capanema's papers, occasionally confided to the minister that he felt a "vivid intellectual inclination" for political positions more oriented toward the left, while also expressing his disenchantment before the first signs of the resurgence of conservative positions.[3] Drummond's case is emblematic of how personal ties and friendships often vouched for the ambiguous political balances and ideological compromises underlining the institutional roles held by various intellectuals. Costa's position in relation to the reactionary turn of the Vargas government was – in part – similar to that of his poet friend, and in the years to come would not fail to affect his professional affairs. A long letter to Le Corbusier – dated less than a month before the coup, shortly after his voluntary withdrawal from the Ministry construction site – is particularly significant in this matter; in addition to his frustration with the difficult decision-making processes in dealing with public commissions, Costa expresses his discontent over the increasingly anti-democratic turn of the country's politics, although he expresses it in rigorously confidential circumstances. The only hope was entrusted to the utopian "advent" – religious terminology is often used by Costa – of "true machine civilisation," understood as a necessary condition for the development of a democratic society (Figure 3.1).

> He himself [Charles Ofaire][4] admits that we still have to endure, everywhere and for a long time still, the "fascist" reaction; that all this strange nationalist folly and tense energies will end up sinking in mud and in death; and one day,

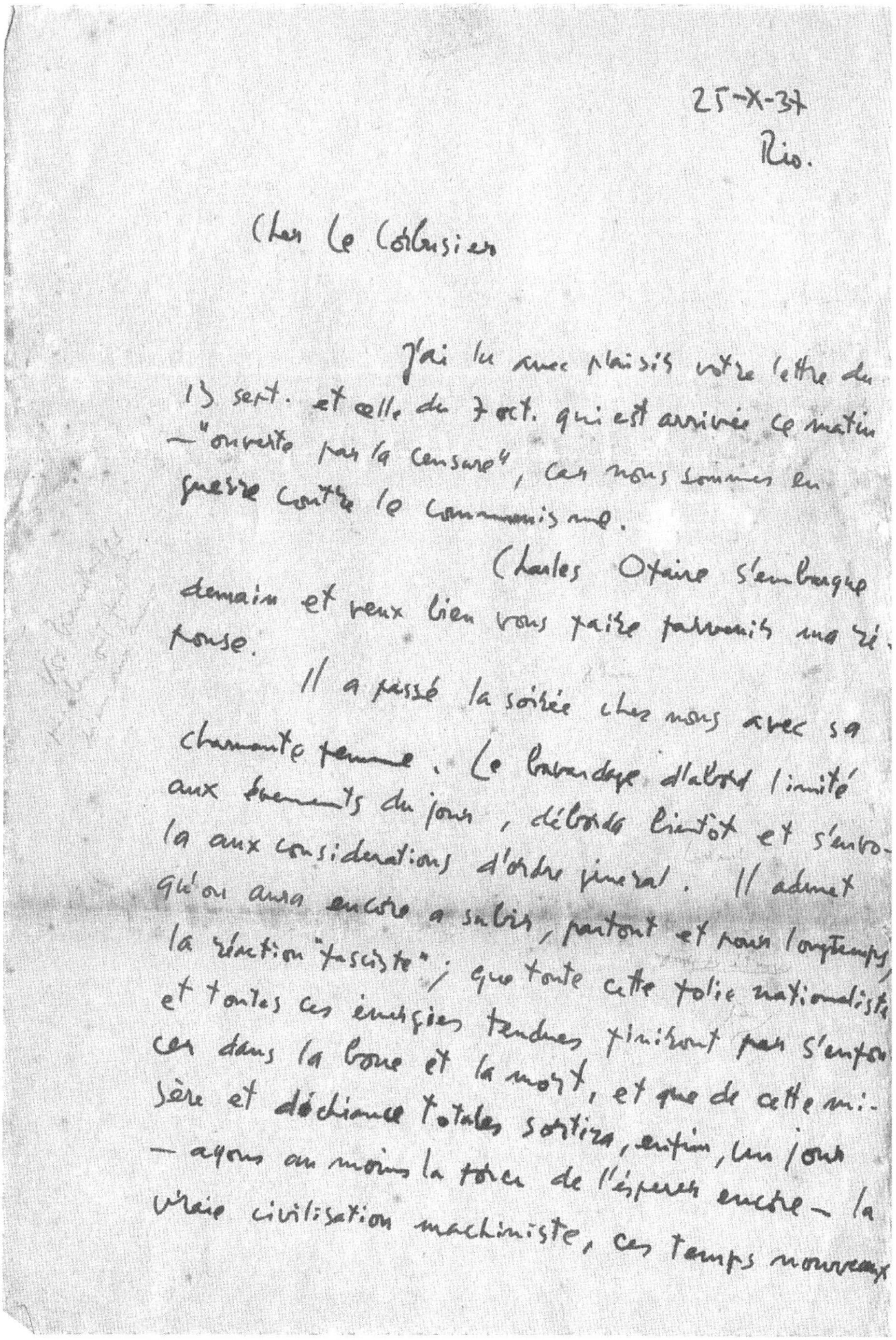

25-X-37
Rio.

Cher Le Corbusier

J'ai lu avec plaisir votre lettre du 13 sept. et celle du 7 oct. qui est arrivée ce matin — "ouverte par la censure", car nous sommes en guerre contre le communisme.

Charles Ofaire s'embarque demain et veut bien vous faire parvenir ma réponse.

Il a passé la soirée chez nous avec sa charmante femme. Le bavardage d'abord limité aux événements du jour, déborda bientôt et s'envola aux considérations d'ordre général. Il admet qu'on aura encore à subir, partout et pour longtemps, la réaction "fasciste"; que toute cette folie nationaliste et toutes ces énergies tendues finiront par s'enfoncer dans la boue et la mort, et que de cette misère et déchéance totales sortira, enfin, un jour — ayons au moins la force de l'espérer encore — la vraie civilisation machiniste, ces temps nouveaux

Figure 3.1 Lucio Costa, draft of the letter to Le Corbusier of 24 October 1937. Casa de Lucio Costa.

> finally, from this complete misery and decline, will emerge – let us hold on to this hope – the true machine civilisation, the new times to which your life and work have been devoted.[5]

The vision of a better future, associated with man's hard-earned emancipation from material needs (the "*struggle* pour la vie"), is however abruptly interrupted by considerations on the present day.

> But let us leave these beautiful visions of Utopia up in the clouds, and let us try to consider this chaotic and distressed 1937, blinded by mistrust, hate, and fear – the best of all possible worlds; and this dear Brazil, which turned overnight into a sort of "Catholic-fascist" Ku Klux Klan, where the police imprison those who have the audacity to think freely – the paradise of my self-indulgence.

It is not difficult to imagine how a growing concern for the fate of the country and personal frustrations could have fed off each other, especially for somebody like Costa, who focused his personal research on combining the idea of a new architecture with that of the expressive possibilities of a higher form of civilisation. The Corbusian idea of the indoctrination of an enlightened Authority seems to have been replaced – at least temporarily – by a deep mistrust in the possible shared objectives of intellectuals and institutions. However, this change of position – aside from his voluntary withdrawal from the Ministry project and from the events regarding the University Campus,[6] he also more frequently refused to take part in public and social events of any kind[7] – would not lead to a complete break from the public clients that a few years earlier had critically changed his career. Instead, it presented the grounds for a gradual redefinition of this collaboration, characterised by a marked presence behind the scenes as opposed to the open militancy of the previous years. Despite having to face sacrifices, compromises, and missed opportunities, Costa did not abandon his militancy in favour of the new architecture. On the contrary, this was the moment in which the premises for a development of an ambitious cultural strategy took place, one aimed at creating a mediation, not without some ambiguity, between the ideological demands of the Vargas regime and the pursuit of a utopian determination set to transform society through architecture; between the "good cause" of modern architecture and the nation building process that had been taking place since the beginning of the century.

Toward the end of 1937, two significant events came to influence Costa's career and narrative: Sigfried Giedion's invitation to enter the CIAM, and the beginning of Costa's collaboration with the Serviço do Patrimônio Histórico e Artístico Nacional (SPHAN). Giedion's invite – which symbolically sanctioned Costa's introduction in the international debate – was drawn up in the context of the V CIAM Congress (Paris, September 1937), at the prompting of Le Corbusier. He had in fact already mentioned his candidacy to Costa, urging him to "use this power" to "fight more effectively [...] against the public opinion or authority."[8] In a letter dated October 1937, Giedion officially calls for Costa to create a Brazilian group of the CIAM, "choosing the best architectural forces" of the country in support of the nucleus of São Paulo, whose activity had been quite irrelevant up until then.[9] However, in thanking Le Corbusier on behalf of the group – which seemed to have been already clearly defined, at least in theory, despite the fact that Giedion had only mentioned the name of Gregori Warchavchik, CIAM delegate for Latin America[10] – Costa proves to be sceptical on the matter.

> I have received Giedion's letter. I do not think it will be easy to finish the job; anyhow, since it is a done deal, I will work at organising a homogeneous group, to pass the torch to some friends. First of all, I will contact dear Warchavchik to find out what he thinks. In any case, we are grateful for this proof of confidence; and, as you say yourself, it truly is a power that can be used.[11]

Although he pointed out his belonging to the CIAM on various occasions, especially after this "official" appointment, Costa would not honour the commitment, nor would he ever take part in the meetings of the organisation. In 1952, once again calling upon his "absolute vocational lack in teaching or training affairs,"[12] the architect refused the invitation to participate in the CIAM's summer school, which was offered him on the occasion of his stay in Venice for his speaker activity at the International Conference of Artists organised by UNESCO. In 1953, in inviting him to attend the 9th CIAM in Paris, Giedion claims to greatly rely on this presence "to tell members of the CIAM council what South America expects from our organization," and in another letter he adds: "I tried in vain to make your acquaintance in Rio and in Paris, but I hope to have this pleasure at our next meeting in Paris."[13] At the end of the 1950s, in commenting the plan for Brasilia in two letters to Costa and Niemeyer, Giedion would express his regret for never having had the opportunity to personally meet the author of the plan for the new capital.[14] The same Costa – in a letter to José Luis Sert, sent on the occasion of the involvement of the five-man committee for the UNESCO headquarters in Paris – presents a peculiar interpretation of his relation with the CIAM, which seemed to be based more on spiritual grounds rather than material ones ("although I am not properly CIAM – only my heart is CIAM").[15]

Roughly at the same time, almost as a counter-reaction to Giedion's invite, Costa started off his collaboration with the Serviço do Patrimônio Histórico e Artístico Nacional (SPHAN), established by Capanema that same year and directed by Rodrigo Mello Franco de Andrade. As a government official of heritage preservation – a role he would hold for almost forty years with only a few formal changes – Costa would benefit from a position that was somewhat less exposed to the ups and downs of political events. Therefore – in addition to being able to count on a fixed salary rather than having to work his way through individual commissions – Costa could now devote himself to his long interest for traditional architecture, as well as guiding the outcome of important decisions in the field of architecture, while also sparing himself the formal compromises that would derive from an explicitly recognised status of leadership.[16]

Coherently with his dual CIAM and SPHAN affiliation, between the end of the 1930s and the early 1940s, Costa's theoretical discourse tended toward a progressive systematisation: the attempt to bring together the opposition between "modern" and "national" became an opportunity for a subtle re-elaboration of international debate topics in light of the country's cultural, political, and architectural climate, a climate that was marked by the merging – within Vargas' centralising and nationalist programme[17] – of the angsts and agitations related to the formation of an identity, which had been concerning the country already since the 1920s. While the Brazilian pavilion project for the 1939 New York World's Fair represents the concretisation of this in architectural terms, the allocation of meaning following the events regarding the Ministry up until its inauguration in 1945 (and afterward, as well) is where its theoretical development took place.

It is perhaps in this "programme" for Brazilian architecture that we should search for Costa's main concession to the politics of the Estado Novo. In ambiguously seeking a balance between an attitude of resistance and one of compromise, Costa would contribute to strengthening the ties between modern architecture and the State, identifying buildings like the Ministry of Education's as icons of Brazil's processes of modernisation and civilisation, while also contributing to outline an ideal genealogy of modern Brazilian architecture.

Toward a State architecture

At the turn of the 1930s, in terms of international relations, the Vargas government seemed to be substantially caught between two fires: on one side, the Axis Powers (Rome especially), with which it held strong cultural and ideological ties but also long-standing economic relations; and the United States of America on the other side, with Nelson Rockefeller newly appointed as head of the International Relations Department and set to open a series of cultural exchanges with "neighbouring South America" (the so-called Good Neighbour Policy) aimed at strengthening the relations with Latin America on strategic and economic levels as well.[18] On 16 June 1941, Vargas officially decided to suspend the neutral position he had held until that moment and "cooperate with the government of the United States if required by the circumstances and in accordance with the rules and conventions that have already been discussed and accepted"[19] – a premise to the official entry in the Second World War alongside the Allies in 1942.

Two important events occurred right before entering the war, and their chronological contiguity was quite relevant to the double political and cultural engagements of the government: the Exposição do Estado Novo of 1938 and Brazil's participation in the New York World's Fair of 1939. The first event was destined to represent the regime at a national level, while the second – clearly welcomed as an opportunity to establish closer relations with the neighbouring North America – was destined to represent Brazil on the international scene.

The Exposição do Estado Novo – held between August and December 1938 – aimed at displaying a rundown of the governmental activities developed since its establishment in 1930.[20] It is reasonable to ask why Costa did not take part in the exhibition project of the pavilion dedicated to the Ministry of Education, coordinated by Niemeyer.[21] Although this absence could be ascribed to his weakening relations with Capanema, Costa did not lack his own ideological reasons for it as well: the public event was conceived as a culminating moment of the regime's propaganda and an effective vehicle of its authoritarian rhetoric (including, among other things, sections entirely dedicated to anti-Communist propaganda).[22] Architecture seems to have played a leading role in the Exposição. The many public buildings displayed in the various pavilions – among which were the seats of the different Ministries recently emerging in Esplanada do Castelo – showed a lack of stylistic unity much criticised by important people involved in the artistic debate, becoming a focus of much historiography.[23] The coexistence and overlapping of different cultural projects was a peculiar aspect of the Vargas government, at least in the years preceding modernism's final stylistic hegemony. The pavilion of the Ministry of Education, conceived by Gustavo Capanema in every detail,[24] was no exception: the model of the new Ministry seat, in its final fifteen-storey-high version, stood out from the various school buildings in neo-colonial style and a series of great hospital complexes (Figure 3.2). In addition, the section dedicated to the Ministry project also displayed materials related to various ministerial initiatives, represented in a modern and efficient way by Oscar Niemeyer's graceful lines.

Only one year later, in 1939, Costa returned to the scene, on the occasion of the design competition for the Brazilian pavilion of the New York World's Fair (inaugurated on 30 April 1939 in Flushing Meadows Park).[25] Upon the initiative of the Instituto de Arquitetos do Brasil, the competition notice – announced by the Ministry of Labour at the end of 1937 – called for a representation of the country making its way toward modernisation, using a language that was both contemporary and referable to a national character, while also interpreting the design theme given by the Exhibition Committee: "The World of Tomorrow." In compliance with the Exhibit Committee's ban of resorting to historical styles in the foreign pavilion section, the Brazilian government also suspended the obligation (first introduced in 1922) of using the neo-colonial style to represent the country abroad.[26]

Figure 3.2 Model of the Ministry of Education and Public Health at the Exposição do Estado Novo, 1938. CPDOC, Fundação Getúlio Vargas.

72 *A programme for national architecture*

Although none of the submitted projects fully met the jury's expectations, Costa's was awarded first place. It was regarded as a project equipped "with general good harmony, in the wake of the modern spirit, without imposing determined elements of modern construction technology," and especially of a certain "*brasilidade* spirit" (spirit of Brazilianness),[27] which the second-classified project by Niemeyer was considered lacking. Costa himself would decide to involve Niemeyer in the development of a new project, in the awareness – according to what he would claim many years later – that the time had come for Niemeyer's talent to gain recognition at an international level.[28] The two architects flew to New York in March of 1938 to dedicate themselves to the project for the pavilion, in collaboration with Thomas Price and Paul Lester Wiener, respectively in charge of landscape and exhibition design.[29]

After many years with no documented history regarding the competition projects, a number of original drawings of both Costa's and Niemeyer's entries emerged from Costa's archive, enabling us to reconstruct the two projects submitted to the jury in a fairly detailed manner.[30] As the description in *Arquitetura e Urbanismo* reads, the competition's winning project consisted of a "long exhibition room with large windows opening onto a patio, easily accessible from the street."[31] It was a building with a prominent horizontal character and a rigorously symmetrical rectangular plan, except for the external side ramps giving access to the auditorium, whose sculptural volume emerged from the main exhibition building on the opposite side of the entrance. The main volume, suspended on *pilotis*, enclosed a completely permeable inner patio, while the outer façades presented a decorative figurative cycle. The entrance façade, facing south, had a tripartite composition characterised by fixed honeycombed sunshades and preceded by a monumental triangular portico, whose central column culminated in a gigantic Brazilian flag, similar to a ship's mast. A sculptural group – vaguely reminiscent of Jacques Lipchitz's *Prometheus* – was suspended above the column, as if propelled toward the crowd. The entrance hall was equally monumental. Above the opening toward the inner courtyard on the back wall, there was a great map of Brazil. The side walls presented a rhythmic session of colossal-order columns above the *pilotis*, clearly resembling – as Comas states – the ones of the Ministry of Education. The mezzanine, which hosted the exhibits, was accessible via two symmetrical side staircases. A monumental sculpture of a seated man stood tall in the centre.[32] The real heart of the pavilion, however, was the inner patio, where a sculpture representing a reclined woman – similar to the Celso Antônio's *Mulher reclinada*[33] – was put on display in the middle of a lush garden, with a tropical lily pond – the famous *Victoria Regia* that had been "rediscovered" by Roberto Burle Marx in the Berlin-Dahlem Botanical Garden[34] – and other native species. It would have been possible to view the bustling life of the Fair through the *pilotis*, but the continuous façade of the mezzanine – shielded by vertical *treliça* panels,[35] moveable like *brise-soleils* – gave the courtyard an intimate and closed atmosphere, intelligently integrating the different programme requirements and the different "souls" – modern and Brazilian – of the pavilion. It is therefore clear why the jury identified a certain "Brazilianness" in the project, awarding Costa first place. With its landscape arrangement, columned patio, and pictorial cycle on the outer façades, the project effectively displayed a successful synthesis between a subdued modern spirit – which, despite the Corbusian inspiration, traced back to an academic approach, with symmetrical composition and rigorous monumentality – and the attempt to provide a solution to the delicate theme of a national modern style.

A programme for national architecture 73

However, this formal solution differed quite significantly from the definitive one, despite the fact that Costa's project already presented some of its elements (Figures 3.3 and 3.4).

At this point, it becomes necessary to examine Oscar Niemeyer's project, which placed second in the competition. From the few drawings kept in Costa's archive it seems that the plan of the structure was more similar to the final design than Costa's winning project: developed around an open patio, it was based on an approximately L-shaped layout, which was further articulated into protruding elements. The entrance offered a floor-to-ceiling glazed opening, preceded by a covered plaza decorated with a billowing Brazilian flag, onto which looked a great balcony, as an extension of the mezzanine level. The canopy – itself an extension of the building's roof – folded out into a sinuous curve at the entrance, as if welcoming visitors and inviting them to step across the covered entrance plaza and into the more intimate open space of the patio. The curve then extended to the entire perimeter of the pavilion, offering – on the west side – a completely fluid yet opaque façade – shaped by the curve of the road, as in the final design – and opening up onto the patio with a great portico with colossal-order *pilotis* (Figures 3.5 and 3.6).

In general, the two projects present some affinities: both express the pavilion's ephemeral character to the max, focusing on the permeability, lightness, and horizontality of the building volume; according to Costa, the pavilion's size was not to stand out from the ones of the other countries (especially when compared to the heavy mass of the adjoining French one).[36] However, the ways in which the

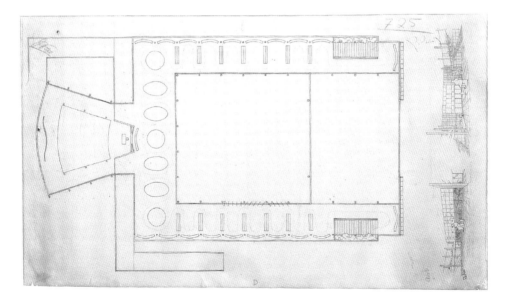

Figure 3.3 Lucio Costa, competition project for the Brazilian pavilion at the New York World's Fair. Plan of the mezzanine and perspective views of the interior, 1938. Casa de Lucio Costa.

74   *A programme for national architecture*

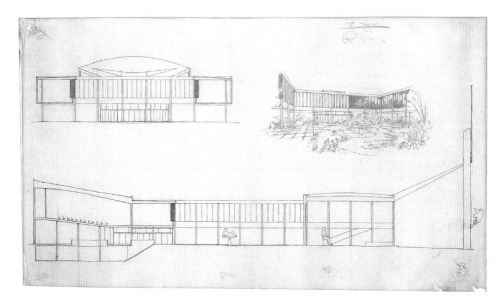

Figure 3.4 Lucio Costa, competition project for the Brazilian pavilion at the New York World's Fair. Sections and perspective view of the patio, 1938. Casa de Lucio Costa.

projects differ are already representative of the unbridgeable gap that would mark the development of the two architects' future production: Costa's aiming to integrate a traditional lexicon with a modern syntax (maintaining recognisable traditional elements); and Niemeyer's aiming to explore the potentials of free form to

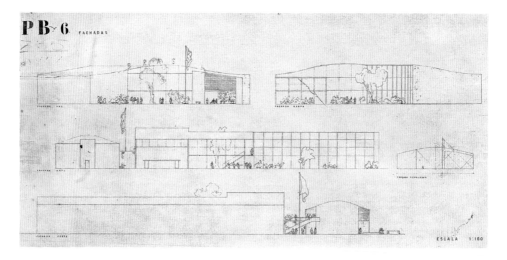

Figure 3.5 Oscar Niemeyer, competition project for the Brazilian pavilion at the New York World's Fair. Façades, 1938. Casa de Lucio Costa.

A programme for national architecture 75

Figure 3.6 Oscar Niemeyer, competition project for the Brazilian pavilion at the New York World's Fair. Perspective views, 1938. Casa de Lucio Costa.

the extreme. It is difficult, and perhaps of little interest, to evaluate which of the two projects is better. Upon careful observation, both present unconvincing elements that seem to have been successfully resolved in the final solution. The definitive design in fact does owe much to both projects, although Costa would later tend to attribute it largely to Niemeyer. Costa's offered a more marked monumental character – of a somewhat more canonical monumentality – that the final project would lose and exchange for a clean spatial and plastic quality; the symmetry of Costa's design would be replaced by the more dynamic L-shaped layout of Niemeyer's; the articulation between the mezzanine and the *pilotis*, already present in Costa's project, would inherit the movement and sinuosity of Niemeyer's wall perimeter, while raising the main building on *pilotis* helped break the monotony of Niemeyer's entirely closed perimeter walls; the *treliça* panels (together with the honeycombed façade) of Costa's proposal would inspire the successful solution of the final design's entrance façade (consisting of a sculptural alveolar diaphragm, halfway between *brise-soleil* and *cobogó*).[37] The final project would also be enriched by a curvilinear ramp, perhaps a synthesis and evolution of Costa's side ramps and Niemeyer's entrance balcony. The patio – which presented an amoeboid-shaped water pool, which was present in both projects – would come to host the *Victoria Regia* proposed by Costa, capable of evoking both the lush Amazonian landscape and the botanical gardens of Rio de Janeiro, city of origin of both architects. Finally, the rigidity and symmetry of Costa's project – left unscathed even by the introduction of the auditorium (which would reappear in a different position in the final project) – would give way to a building that was modern and yet revitalised by the freedom of its plastic expression, by the alternation of full and empty, and by the playful spatiality taking place between the sinuous concrete membranes (in many ways, anticipating the captivating sensuality of Pampulha). In light of this, it is easy to assume that without Niemeyer's involvement, Costa's winning project would not have received as much international attention.[38] More importantly, it would not have been identified as a symptom of the emergence of one of the most interesting local productions at an international level: a knowledgeable interpretation of a certain tropical grace, able to shake up the canonised formulas of the International Style from the inside (Figure 3.7).

In addition to the far-sightedness Costa proved in calling Niemeyer to collaborate with him, he also should be recognised for having understood the importance of this occasion in the conquest of a greater cultural relevance in the international arena. In a series of texts written in connection with the New York World's Fair participation, Costa did not miss the opportunity to give his own interpretation of this issue as well. In aligning his design orientation to the spirit of the CIAM, Costa emphasises – as he did in his report on the University Campus – the "plastic intention" of which the pavilion was, in his opinion, expression.

Figure 3.7 Lucio Costa and Oscar Niemeyer, view of the Brazilian pavilion at the New York World's Fair, 1939. Casa de Lucio Costa.

> We follow the teachings of Le Corbusier. We do not want to exclusively subordinate the modern spirit to matters of technical and functional nature, nor do we want to make "pseudo-modern" scenography, as is fashionable in the USA. Rather, we want the rigorous application of modern technique and a precise fulfilment of the needs required by the programme and context; all guided and monitored, as a whole and in every detail, by the constant desire to create a work of art in the purest sense. Painting and sculpture will find their natural place in this conception of architecture, not as mere ornaments or decorative elements, but provided with independent artistic value that is, at the same time, also an integral part of the composition.[39]

During the attempt at building a discourse in support of the modern-national synthesis that seemed to have been the reason for the success of the pavilion among the international audience, Costa elaborated the theory of a correspondence between Brazilian modern architecture – identified shortly after almost exclusively with Niemeyer's architectural production – and Brazilian colonial Baroque. This theory – although lacking rigorous historical motivations, and influenced by Costa's activity in the Patrimônio (where it would find a fruitful field of application) – was destined to have an extraordinary impact on subsequent historiographical interpretations. In explaining the reasons behind the key design choices (the use of the site's curvilinear layout, in particular), he wrote:

> Benefiting from the beautiful curve of the site was an aspect that presided over the entire layout of the project. It is the central motif that – in more or less marked ways – repeats itself in the canopy, the auditorium, the ramp, the independent partitions of the ground floor, etc., bringing a general grace and elegance to the whole, having it correspond – in the academic language – to the Ionic and not Doric order, as opposed to what happens in most cases of contemporary architecture. This fracture of the rigidity, this ordered movement running from one side to the other of the composition, indeed holds a Baroque quality – in a positive sense of the word – which is very important to us since it represents, in some way, a connection with the traditional spirit of Luso-Brazilian architecture.[40]

The most original features of the pavilion were therefore traced back to the expression of a "national spirit" endowed with "deep roots and a continuing impact."[41] The reference to Luso-Brazilian tradition was consequently sublimated – according to an idealistic cultural reading – in a sort of spiritual dimension, in the instinctive and almost magical re-emergence of a creative spirit tending to express itself through specific formal structures.

At a time when modernism faced a sort of identity crisis – and the themes of the debate shifted toward territories that were less explored by the "heroic" 1920s – Costa's appeal to the value and legitimacy of architecture's "plastic intention" – as a response to the theory of the synthesis of the arts and in relation to the symbolic representation of an individual and collective identity – seemed to answer different subject matters and open up new perspectives. Taking advantage of all the occasions that international attention had focused on Brazil, and taking note of the great potential of a combination that brought together modernity and tradition, Costa began to build – before the onset of the *Brazil Builds* phenomenon[42] – the "official" historiographic image of Brazilian modernism, or at least of a part of it. Starting from this first international showcase, Brazilian architectural production – and Niemeyer's work in particular, on and off – would end up representing the chance to address the issue of free form, opening up new possibilities to modern architecture, and granting official citizenship to Corbusier's Law of the Meander.

A genealogy of modern Brazilian architecture

At the beginning of 1938, construction work on the Ministry was well underway, considering that Superintendent Souza Aguiar wrote Capanema on 18 February informing him that the inauguration could very well take place the same year, if they could only settle with giving up the four extra storeys above the main building block.[43] However, the building would not be inaugurated until 1945. In addition to the inevitable slowdown caused by the war (during which construction continued nevertheless), what seems to have also weighed on matters was the not always constant dedication of its authors. Evidently, Costa's vacant position was not easy to fill, resulting in long periods of adjustment and an unstable development of the construction phases, the direction of which was transferred from the superintendence of the Serviço de Obras to the Departamento de Administração do Serviço Público. The documentation available makes it possible to identify Niemeyer as the minister's main interlocutor during the last defining phases, from the design of the details and furnishings to the outline of the exact arrangement of the sculptures.[44] However, this did not prevent Costa from participating in some important choices. For example, he claimed the merit for suggesting to prepare the foundations for more than the ten floors allowed (a suggestion that was upheld by the engineer Emílio Baumgart), challenging – "as the good Carioca man" he was – the height limits imposed by the site's vicinity to the Santos Dumont airport.[45] In other similar testimonies, the architect reveals how – despite his tendency to delegate the practical management of the site to his collaborators – he did not feel less involved than others in the design choices, and how his participation had been decisive on several occasions, even in defining the actual works of art to be displayed within and outside of the building.[46] His most important contribution at this stage, however, seems to have been his natural vocation as interpreter of the building's significance in theoretical and symbolic terms. During and after the construction period, Costa maintained complete control of the rhetoric through which a series of experiences – culminating in the one of the Ministry – would be read as expressions of modern Brazilian architecture's hard-earned official status.[47]

Attaching itself to the first signs of modernist revision taking place near the end of the war, Costa's discourse around the Ministry project was set to highlight its specific nature as a public work, expression of the highest moral values related to the idea of *civitas*, in addition to its innate value as a work of art and as an architectural monument. Determined to legitimise the new architecture as veritable Art of the State – putting aside the tensions and uncertainties expressed in more confidential circumstances – Costa identified the new ministerial building as the symbol of the country's political and cultural renewal, as well as the symbol of the collaboration between a group of modern architects and an enlightened authority.

> The history of architecture shows us that – in artistically thriving eras – the seat of public institutions has always had the last word, offering itself as an example; instead, in times of decadence, it prudently follows rather than guides. It is therefore natural that in this time of "renewal" of national activities, the Ministry of Education and Public Health – with the construction of its headquarters – seeks to confidently indicate the new direction to follow; setting – in accordance with the results of the International Congresses of Modern Architecture – the model that will serve as an example in the future.[48]

In this view of the matter, we understand the emphasis that was placed on the representative features of the building, like the "construction of a grand *esplanada* for civic-cultural ceremonies," the public entrance's "portico of monumental proportions," the richness and variety of the finishing materials, and its significant artistic apparatus. In response to Capanema's concerns regarding its high costs,[49] Costa calls on the building's nature as a public office, the *status* of which required a certain "nobility of intentions, made explicit by the monumental proportions of the building and the simplicity and good quality of its finish"; he also mentions how such a building was required to be able to resist the erosive test of time (in line with the principles of economy and efficiency so dear to the Vargas government).

> In constructing public buildings holding not only a utilitarian value but also a representative one, one should not "primarily" consider financial factors as much as the necessity of translating the idea of prestige and dignity that is logically associated with the concept of public affairs. [...] Incidentally, with time, the good quality of the finishing materials – in addition to satisfying the need for a dignified appearance – also brings to long-term economy; since the better they are, the more they are durable and capable of preserving their quality appearance – which is of paramount importance when it comes to projects that are undertaken for the needs of more than one generation.[50]

The use of still uncommon construction techniques and materials, together with the importance attributed to works of art, would have (in Costa's opinion) played to the advantage of the project's success – whose "international impact" as a first example of public building in which the "principles of new construction techniques" were used on a monumental scale is proven by the interest of many of the "best foreign technical magazines" – decreeing its grand entrance into the "history of contemporary architecture" (Figure 3.8).

The inauguration ceremony of the Ministry finally occurred in 1945 (Figure 3.9). More specifically, the chosen date for the event was 3 October 1945, since it was the anniversary of the revolution that first brought Vargas to govern the country in 1930. In the spirit of its turbulent beginning, Vargas' first mandate prepared itself for an equally turbulent conclusion, which would in fact be decreed shortly after by a military coup.[51]

As if to seal his special position – with respect to the architects who were present and active until the end of construction, albeit in different degrees – Costa declined – as would happen even more frequently in the years to come – Capanema's official invitation to the inauguration ceremony,[52] entrusting his spirit of participation to a letter.[53] This document seems to present the discursive structure of

Figure 3.8 Colonnade of the Ministry of Education and Public Health. From *The Architectural Forum*'s special issue on Brazil, November 1947.

Figure 3.9 Getúlio Vargas, Gustavo Capanema, and others in front of the sculpture *Mulher reclinada* by Celso Antônio at the inauguration of the Ministry of Education and Public Health, 1945. Casa de Lucio Costa.

a precise historical project, one in which each of the characters – including Costa, who for the first time explicitly pronounced himself in regards to his role in the matter – and each of the mentioned events – linked together according to an inherent necessity – find their place within a virtuous process. As Costa suggests, this process would have led to the development of the legitimate artistic and cultural expression of the new times, and consequently to man's freedom in his reconquered control of his means and resources. He describes the Ministry not only as an "architectural work destined to be featured, from now on, in history of art in general," but also as a fundamental element of this history, "emblem of a new fruitful cycle of the eternal art of building" that embodied for the first time, "with attention to detail and full conceptual purity, the ideas for which the genius of Le Corbusier had fought for a quarter of a century, with the passion, courage, and faith of a true crusader." The theme of a "holy war" to be fought against the resistance to artistic renewal – which had played a big role in the debates of 1931, and which Costa saw as something inseparable from the utopian prediction of a freer and more democratic future – now seemed to align itself with the rhetoric that Capanema had acquired during the years of alliance with the United States[54] – all the more relevant now given the recent outcome of the Second World War.

82 A programme for national architecture

> This is why, in this oasis surrounded by uniform and monotonous-looking barrack blocks, now thrives, unreal in its crystalline clarity, a so beautiful and pure flower; a flower of the spirit, a sure message that the world in which we inescapably move will become, in spite of the sinister predictions of reactionary pastism, not only more human and socially just, but also more beautiful.[55]

The letter goes on to present one of the key issues of the historiographical narrative of Brazilian modernism: why would "such a beautiful and pure flower" have grown in a context that was so "technically and culturally" less evolved than others? What was this unexpected overturning of the "traditional position of dependence," which had always qualified the relationship with Europe and the United States, owed to? Costa answered these questions in an apparently paradoxical way; yet, precisely because of the nature of the argument, his answers were also incontrovertible: it appeared to be a true "miracle," something that was difficult to seize and comprehend, where only a mysterious force could have been at play. The rest of the letter is dedicated to the others who contributed to making the "miracle" possible; the first recognition went to Capanema, who was able to bravely face the "growing tide of criticism" thanks to the support of the "poetic intuition" and the "critical acumen of intellectuals such as Carlos Drummond de Andrade, Manuel Bandeira, and Rodrigo Mello Franco de Andrade." The joint efforts of a group of people and the minister's headstrong will – albeit "in very unfavourable circumstances" – gave the Ministry, according to Costa, a monumental significance in the broader sense of the word, transcending its materiality.

> This way, this monument – in addition to its significance as a work of art – also possesses a moral content: it symbolises the victory of intelligence and honour over obscurantism, malice, and ill faith.[56]

The list of the miracle's authors goes on, calling into question the other two institutional figures that, in different roles and ways, contributed to the success of the project: President Getúlio Vargas and Carlos Drummond de Andrade, head of the president's cabinet, whose complicity was constant throughout the entire affair. As mentioned, Costa did not miss the opportunity to mark the relevance of his own personal contribution as well.

> As for my personal contribution, in this case, it consisted in having known how to extend your invitation to the other architects who developed, together with me, the definitive project (based on the original design by Le Corbusier for another site), and who also developed and completed its construction; but it also consisted mainly in being able to convince you, at the right moment, of the need to obtain the president's authorisation to involve Le Corbusier. The presence of this brilliant man among us was decisive for the current boom of Brazilian architecture. It was thanks to this three-month cohabitation that the exceptional talent of architect Oscar Niemeyer (Oscar de Almeida Soares, as I would rather call him, given my attachment to Lusitanic tradition and since it is his rightful name), inexplicably unexpressed up until then, finally revealed itself completely: not only in the development of the project for this building and for our pavilion at the New York fair (again, with my participation), but above all for his incomparable constructions in Pampulha and other works

A programme for national architecture 83

scattered throughout the country, where he reveals himself not only as our greatest architect, but also as one of the greatest masters of contemporary architecture.

Given the scale of the consequences, it is clear that by limiting his merits to the involvement of Le Corbusier, Costa was actually claiming a crucial role in what he defined the true beginning of modern Brazilian architecture. A few years later, in the so-called "Carta depoimento," he would have the opportunity to further discuss how all the modern works made in the country before then – before the "advent" of Niemeyer that followed the daily exposure to Le Corbusier – were nothing but shy attempts to import a European model, once compared with the fruits of the "authentic seeds planted here by Le Corbusier."[57] This is how he explained the reasons for this miracle; however, it was also an explanation that left the real reasons even more in the dark. The miracle, in fact, could only be explained by once again resorting to the ironclad arguments of a religious creed. Brazilian architecture was a gift by Le Corbusier, yes, but it also was a gift that could only bear its fruit in the fertile land of Brazil, predestined to the new architecture just as Niemeyer was predestined to become the individual expression of a "national personality,"[58] ready to re-emerge at the first sight of a good opportunity.[59]

The letter then continues by presenting a construction of an actual genealogy of Brazilian art and architecture, to which the formation of the new generations should have been entrusted, based on the idea that the success of the Ministry was the right compensation for Costa's failed experience of the National School of Fine Arts. In addressing the minister, Costa illustrates the measures that finally would enable him "to make education keep up with life,"

> given that we cannot understand why the country's official education persists in ignoring the great achievements of contemporary art; or why buildings like this one are merely considered as expressions of a movement that has developed behind its back; a movement that still represents, in some way, the continuation and evolution of the failed reform of 1931.[60]

Among the suggested measures there is the nomination of Cândido Portinari to the direction of the National School of Fine Arts, as he was "a figure that is internationally accepted as the most representative of our artistic production." In order to allow his nomination, Costa suggests first entrusting him a painting course at the School by opening a new position and doubling the course offer, paradoxically reintroducing the same situation he had been protagonist of in 1931. He then continues by indicating the names of Alberto da Veiga Guignard and Jacques Lipchitz for the courses in sculpture and design, respectively. As for the recently inaugurated Faculty of Architecture, Costa proposes to remedy the "recent injury" of the separation between the teaching of architecture and that of plastic arts by introducing "true plastic artists" within the teaching staff, nominating Oscar Niemeyer for the position of architectural composition professor – "regardless of the official competition for the position, given that, as for Mr. Portinari, the international relevance of his work dispenses him from such formalities" – and Roberto Burle Marx for the position of landscape design professor. Apart from its obvious unfeasibility, it was an ambitious long-term project, based on the awareness that the association

Figure 3.10 The Ministry of Education and Public Health after its completion, ca 1945. Casa de Lucio Costa.

between artists and institutions that had made the Ministry project possible could not be taken for granted: "let us get to work, then, Mr. Minister," he urges, "so that the fruit of this shared effort will not be lost in future administrations."

As can be deduced, this historical narrative perfectly coincides, according to this interpretation, with that of Costa's professional one, as if to delineate how his biography was centred on the role of "spiritual guide"[61] of a generation destined to leave its mark: from the 1931 attempt to guide the artistic debate by renewing the academic institutions through the formalisation of those same principles of renewal, which were finally sanctioned years later by their first successful application on a monumental scale (which is to say, with the Ministry).

In a letter from Capanema to Rodrigo Mello Franco de Andrade, dated a few months after the collapse of the Estado Novo, the ex-minister expresses his gratitude to the collaborators of the SPHAN for the services rendered to his administration, taking the opportunity to give a special thanks to Costa.

> I extend a word of thanks, in my name, to each of your collaborators. I know the value of them all, and I feel bound by a cordial feeling of respect to many of them. I mention the name of Lucio Costa, in particular, to ask you to thank him even for the beautiful and generous letter he wrote regarding the inauguration of the building of the Ministry of Education, which I hope one day to publish.[62]

It is not clear why Capanema found it necessary to resort to the mediation of Rodrigo Mello Franco de Andrade, or why he waited two months after having received Costa's letter in the first place. From autobiographical notes that came later, we can assume that he did not appreciate how Costa viewed the influence of modernist intellectuals on his own choices.[63] Yet, the sporadic documented exchanges that occurred in the following years witness a sincere mutual admiration that seems to have remained intact over the years. In a letter sent to Costa on the occasion of his seventieth birthday, Capanema claims to have immediately identified with Costa's ideas and work, recalling how he had unreservedly joined "the cause of the brave innovators, of which you were already, among all of us, the guiding figure, the most prestigious and respected name."[64]

What we can take from the presented reconstruction of these events is that both instances are true and, at the same time, much more complex. Consistently with their respective roles, both had great reasons to believe that a mutual collaboration would have been fruitful. The Ministry is a paradigmatic example of how a temporary and strategic allegiance together with an extraordinary desire for self-affirmation – much more than an actual shared cultural project and a favourable coexistence of two "elected" personalities – were at the actual base of the "miracle" of modern Brazilian architecture. The political and public natures of the building are the key elements in understanding the innovative character of the Ministry. For the first time, modern architecture was put in the condition (for the price of a series of compromises and sacrifices) to represent the solution to a – completely political – search for a new image of the nation-state, earning a leading role in the nation building process that was already well underway.

A rising intellectualisation

The loosening relations with Capanema did not, however, exclude other opportunities for collaboration, albeit of a more theoretical and intellectual nature rather than properly related to project design. Costa himself communicated his availability in resuming contact with the minister after his withdrawal from the Ministry construction site, on the occasion of his trip to New York.

> [S]ince I would be very happy, dr. Capanema, if this short trip to the USA could be useful in any way, I declare myself available for any arrangement, information, and study within my reach – regardless of anything properly concerning the building – as these are issues that already belong to our programme.[65]

Apart for the involvement in the SPHAN, which we will further discuss later on, the only documented assignment received directly from Capanema[66] in the following years was destined to end unsuccessfully. It took place in the context of the reform of secondary education, approved in April 1942, which aimed at establishing secondary school as the key educational institution of the country, with the objective of forming a new "Catholic, male, classically trained, and militarily disciplined" élite to which to entrust the "leadership of the masses."[67]

We should keep in mind that the establishment of the Estado Novo marked a change in the direction of Capanema's politics in the field of public education, creating favourable political circumstances for a more coercive action and focusing on the conveyance of regime values and ideologies. The exacerbation of the conflict regarding the independence of the Universidade do Distrito Federal – just when it was beginning to fully stand and work on its own after an almost three-year effort[68] – is a prime example of this change. Capanema would soon give the institution a hard blow, decreeing its extinction and incorporating most part of its structures in the Universidade do Brasil.[69] What emerges from the different drafts of the decree, and from the minister's observations to President Vargas, is that the final decision was due to the fact that the coexistence of two parallel and, in part, overlapping university institutions worked against the "essential principles" of the Estado Novo, namely "discipline, economy, and efficiency."[70] To make matters worse, the independence of the cultural line of the Universidade do Distrito Federal was seen as incompatible with the ambitious consensus building project that the Estado Novo was pushing through multiple channels, especially through the ones dedicated to the information and education of the citizens. Various intellectuals would publicly protest against the closure of the Universidade do Distrito Federal, arguing that in addition to causing the abrupt interruption of the academic career of more than 500 students, and of the professional career of about fifty Brazilian and foreign professors, its closure also nullified one of the most relevant cultural initiatives of the country. Years later, Costa – who had actively supported the project of the Universidade do Brasil – would merely state that the short life of the project he had briefly taken part in was due to "political issues" and to the fact that "Capanema considered it redundant."[71]

Therefore, in 1942 Costa was called, as a consultant, to help draw up a draft regarding the reorganisation of the drawing course programme in secondary schools.

The text of his programme[72] can be considered a fundamental testimony of his reflections on art, which would fully develop at the beginning of the following decade and collect new contributions up until the last years of his life. The influence of the SPHAN is greatly present, especially in the references to the anonymous and popular art and architecture that – although already topical in his theoretical world before 1937 – took on a significantly relevant role from the beginning of his collaboration with the institution.

Costa identifies three design categories – "technical," "observational," and "creative" – with educational programmes that foresaw a further articulation into three progressive series, respectively. By doing so, he conceived a proposal that – setting itself apart from traditional methods, both in terms of discipline approach and in terms of evaluation – aimed at "saving" the students (as in 1931) from a false notion of art that non-expert professors could instil in them by discouraging their expressive potential with an excessively coercive educational method. However, it was precisely the subversive potential of the proposal that seems to not have been appreciated by the general director of the Departamento Nacional da Educação of the time, Lourenço Filho, called by Capanema to express his opinion on the matter. In his report on Costa's proposal, the director argues that his programme lost sight of the true objective pursued by the law concerning design courses in secondary schools, which should in fact consist in the transmission of precise drawing techniques and not focus exclusively on the personal development of tastes and expressive abilities by part of the students. He then criticises the proposal's tendency to encourage the students' spirit of rebellion, delegitimising the role of the professor and openly expressing itself against the application of normal criteria of evaluation. Therefore, despite recognising the "sincerity" of the proposal's attempt to "regenerate" the teaching format of the discipline – and expressing interest for some of the provided suggestions – he finally came to consider the programme generally unusable because of its incompatibility with the regime's inspiring principles in the field of education.[73]

Costa would have the opportunity to express himself again on the subject of education – and this time specifically university education – on the occasion of the official decision to separate the architecture course from the one in fine arts, which brought to the foundation of the Faculty of Architecture on 31 August 1945. This was the last major initiative of Capanema's administration, occurring on the eve of Vargas' deposition and sealing the ambition for the disciplinary independence that had been sought since Costa's own direction of the National School of Fine Arts. In an article published in September 1945, the architect claims to be in favour of separating the two courses – if not in theory, at least in practice – justifying it as a "preliminary defensive measure against this dangerous misunderstanding" of art by part of the "official professors in artistic disciplines."[74] On the other side, he also declares himself strongly against absorbing the first two years of the architecture course within the engineering course, taking advantage of the opportunity to further clarify the meaning and sense of the architectural discipline.

> While architecture is fundamentally art, it also is fundamentally construction, no less. It therefore logically is construction conceived with plastic intention. An intention that clearly distinguishes it from simple construction [...]. We can consequently also define architecture as construction conceived with a specific

plastic intention, on the basis of a specific time period, a specific context, a specific material, a specific technique, and a specific programme.[75]

Revisiting the speech given by Capanema on the occasion of the inauguration ceremony of the Faculty of Architecture on 6 September 1945 – just one month before the inauguration of the Ministry – we easily understand how the minister had absorbed and adopted Costa's own positions, proving how the influence of his theoretical discourse was slowly catching on and consolidating itself. Calling Le Corbusier into question, Capanema identifies the two "prejudicial and deforming principles" – functionalism for its own sake and a decorative conception of architecture – hurting the purity of "true architecture," which in turn was defined – almost literally paraphrasing Costa's own words – as a fusion of "plastic art and technical construction."[76]

While there is no doubt that the emphasis on architecture's plastic expression was the focal point of a series of previous theoretical elaborations, the different reference framework gave it new meaning: from this moment onwards, this discourse seems to have better consolidated itself with the establishment of Brazilian architecture on the international scene, finding a powerful platform in the *Brazil Builds* exhibition, held at the New York MoMA in 1943.[77] It is no coincidence that Costa's first international essay – published on the pages of *L'Architecture d'Aujourd'hui* in 1952 – addresses the theme of architecture's plastic expression in particular, presenting it as the biggest contribution made by Brazil to the international debate.[78] In the changed context of the mid-1940s, the affirmation of architectural values able to undermine, from the inside, the inadequacy of the International Style, seem to have settled around the contemporary questioning of the more radical issues of the modern movement, partly anticipating some of its main arguments.

Modernism and national heritage

As part of the reform of the Ministry of Education and Public Health – implemented with Law n. 378 of 13 January 1937 – the Vargas government officially established the Serviço do Patrimonio Histórico e Artístico Nacional (SPHAN), "with the aim of promoting – permanently throughout the entire country – the protection, preservation, enrichment, and knowledge of the national historical and artistic heritage."[79]

The heated debate accompanying the establishment of the institution reveals the deep divide between the various cultural stances, based on ideological and aesthetic factors; however, it especially exposes the existence of opposite views on the relation that was to be held with the past and with historical pre-existences. While the first initiatives that introduced a "culture of preservation" at an institutional level had been shaped starting from the 1920s thanks to people often linked to conservative circles – within a general process of national identity building and in the context of a renewed interest for Luso-Brazilian tradition – the management of heritage would finally be resolved in favour of the modernists with the establishment of the SPHAN.[80]

Consistent with the custom of Capanema's administration to involve the progressive intellectual élite in the political and administrative activity of the country, effectively exploiting established personal and professional partnerships, the draft of the preliminary project – which would undergo significant changes before being finalised – was entrusted to Mário de Andrade in March 1936, while the direction of the new public institution was given to Rodrigo Mello Franco de Andrade.

Meanwhile, the SPHAN began to work on a provisional basis. Once the coup d'état had blocked the pending legislative measures, Capanema turned to Vargas to ensure the formalisation of the proposed law, resorting to the executive powers conferred upon the president of the Republic by the new Constitution. On 30 November 1937, twenty days after the establishment of the Estado Novo and the re-establishment of Capanema as minister of Education, Vargas issued the decree intended to manage the "preservation of the national artistic and historical heritage."[81] The legislative foundations regarding heritage preservation in Brazil, partly still valid today, were therefore developed under the new authoritarian government and were the result of what Daryle Williams has defined as a "unilateral executive decision."[82]

The group that Rodrigo Mello Franco de Andrade selected for the enterprise during the first years of the institution is emblematic of the clear hegemony of the modernists. From the very beginning, important personalities of modernist orientation entered the SPHAN. Among these were the same Mário de Andrade, Carlos Drummond de Andrade, Manuel Bandeira, Gilberto Freyre, Joaquim Cardoso, Vinícius de Morais, and Sérgio Buarque de Holanda some of whom had already held public positions in the Vargas government. The group also included a substantial team of modernist architects, like Lucio Costa, Oscar Niemeyer, Carlos Leão, José de Souza Reis, Renato Soeiro, Alcides da Rocha Miranda, etc. This special working environment, with the charismatic leadership of Rodrigo Mello Franco de Andrade,[83] would inevitably come to establish a stimulating platform for research around common themes, fuelled by daily exchanges and constructive debates.

The foundation of the SPHAN under a modernist ideology had a crucial impact on the institution's policies and on the principles behind the conceptual definition and material selection of national heritage, principles that were conceived within an idea of tradition employed to both support and legitimise the aspirations of renewal. Besides their commitment in creating new values, the modernists also proved to be able to support Vargas' project of centralisation through the definition of a national-scale identity reference model. On the one hand, the heritage narrative they came to form turned out to be a formidable tool to fuel what Londres Fonseca has referred to as "the State's project of nation building";[84] on the other hand, the Vargas government provided these same intellectuals with a golden opportunity to implement their cultural project, finding a privileged institutional space – with relatively no strings attached – in the SPHAN. The preference for colonial architecture was a predictable consequence of the deal between modernist project and official nation building process. In fact, not only was colonial artistic and architectural heritage the only significant set of historical traces in a country that had not seen a relevant development of any pre-colonial civilisation, but, moreover, the heritage from places such as Minas Gerais was directly linked, in the collective imagination, to the regional Brazilian Gold Rush and its national "heroes": Tiradentes, leader of the Inconfidência Mineira,[85] and Aleijadinho, undisputed protagonist of Luso-Brazilian Baroque. It is therefore understandable how Luso-Catholicism became the symbol of the national culture,[86] as it was seen – within the SPHAN – as the first evidence of a native artistic expression, whose adaptation process and gradual emancipation from Portuguese models would become the subject of passionate and not-always-impartial studies. According to the same principle, the architectural eclecticism of the *fin de siècle* – historically significant as it was the representative style of the First Brazilian Republic – was often perceived as an imported product that, through the influence of the French Artistic Mission in Brazil and of the National School of Fine Arts, hindered the production of local architecture of Luso-Brazilian tradition.[87] Naturally, this way of seeing things also influenced the practice of restoration, which – despite looking to be updated with respect to the international scene – often ended up simply condoning procedures of reconstruction according to an alleged original status of the monument. In fact, the SPHAN's methodologies and conceptual tools lacked the theoretical support of their European counterparts; therefore, its activity was relegated, at least initially, to an empirical approach to the issue of heritage management, both in terms of protection, and in terms of preservation and restoration. This approach – directly influenced by its protagonists' individual wavering ideologies and aesthetic preferences – lent itself to becoming an instrument for the benefit of an actual cultural supremacy, exercised by a small group of intellectuals and professionals among whom Costa played a major role.

Costa's collaboration with the SPHAN began in November 1937,[88] at the same time as the enactment of the decree intended to regulate heritage protection. It is understandable that Rodrigo Mello Franco de Andrade – director of the newly established institution, as well as long-time friend and supporter of Costa's career on different important occasions – immediately decided to involve him in institutional activities, as it was an extremely delicate moment of his professional career. After all, he was well aware of his interest in colonial architecture and of the authority he held among the intellectual élites that were close to the modernist movement.

Costa expressed ambiguous feelings in regards to his role as an officer of the SPHAN: while he often presented himself as an assistant or as a sort of trusted advisor to Mello Franco de Andrade,[89] he also seemed to refuse his position as a mere civil servant, restricted within the rigid formality of rules and responsibilities. As the militant architect and main ideologist of Brazilian modernism that he was, he would never come consider himself a government employee at the service of the institutions, but – if anything – as an architect and scholar directly engaged in his personal battle for a national architecture, and as a symbolic point of reference within the heritage institution.[90] Although he presented a well-crafted modest disposition,[91] the independence and freedom he had shown in other occasions also qualified his activity in the SPHAN, despite the smaller public exposure his new role entailed. In charge of providing the scientific reports on the assets to be protected, settling theoretical and operative issues, providing advice, compiling historical-critical texts, and expressing opinions in matter of restoration, Costa became a reference point of unquestionable authority, whose personal stances were often crucial in guiding the cultural and methodological approaches of the institution. Lauro Cavalcanti even claims that – starting from his promotion to director of the Divisão de Estudos e Tombamentos in 1946 up until his retirement in 1972 – Costa held the "last word on all operations involving isolated assets, their surroundings, and their protected urban areas; which corresponds to an architectural and urban control of the main Brazilian cities,"[92] although his decision-making power, as José Pessôa states, was still subject to the greater authority of the SPHAN director. In the following chapter, we will try to show how Costa's most original contribution within the SPHAN consisted in the elaboration of a complex mediation strategy between modern architecture and historical heritage: something that would lead him to take somewhat dogmatic and anachronistic positions, but that would also enable him to open up new perspectives for architectural culture, and not solely Brazilian.

Notes

1 See Simon Schwartzman, ed., *Estado Novo, um auto-retrato (Arquivo Gustavo Capanema)* (Brasília: Editora Universidade de Brasília, 1983).
2 The new Constitution was drafted by Francisco Campos, the minister of Education during the years of Costa's direction of the National School of Fine Arts. Known as the *Polaca* (Polish) Constitution because of its many similarities with the authoritarian one active in Poland, it remained in force until 1946.
3 Already in March 1936, on the occasion of a conference held by Alceu Amoroso Lima – literary critic and writer of firm Catholic ideas, also known under the pseudonym of Tristão de Ataíde – and organised by Capanema, Drummond de Andrade entrusted his post back to the minister. See Simon Schwartzman, Helena Bomeny, and Vanda Ribeiro Costa, *Tempos de Capanema* (Rio de Janeiro-São Paulo: Paz e Terra-Edusp 1984).
4 Charles Ofaire, general agent of the *Encyclopédie Française* and long-time friend of Le Corbusier, had been presented to Costa by the same Le Corbusier with a letter announcing his transfer to Rio. Le Corbusier to Costa, 23 January 1937. CLC, VI A 02-01561.
5 Costa to Le Corbusier, 24 October 1937. FLC, I3-3-50. The letter begins with a direct allusion to the escalating political situation: "I read with pleasure your letter of 13 September and your letter of 7 October, which arrived this morning – 'opened by the censorship' because we are at war against communism."
6 While updating Le Corbusier on the affairs regarding the University Campus, Costa expressed his scepticism about the compromises that would gradually be adopted, as well as a veiled criticism toward his less intransigent ex-collaborators. After having, once again, set aside the proposals of Piacentini and Morpurgo, on 26 March 1939, the Serviço de Arquitetura temporarily took office with Oscar Niemeyer, Jorge Moreira, Hélio Uchoa, and Carlos Azevedo Leão serving as president, with the task of developing a new project under the direct control of Campos and Amaral. See, in particular, Costa to Le Corbusier, 14 April 1939. FLC, I3-3-76. The University Campus would be built only in the second half of the 1950s, in a project coordinated by Jorge Moreira and on a different site from that envisaged by Capanema. On this occasion, Costa would ask Moreira to dedicate a forum of Imperial Palms to Le Corbusier in the new campus of the Ilha do Fundão: Costa to Moreira, 1 June 1950. CLC, VI A 01-00744.
7 Ofaire defines him "invisible, as usual." Ofaire to Le Corbusier, 12 February 1938. FLC, I3-3-57.
8 See Le Corbusier to Costa [1937]. ACI-RJ, LC-CR(B)02(06). Also see Le Corbusier to Costa, 7 October 1937. CLC, VI A 02-01562.
9 Giedion to Costa, 2 October 1937. GTA, 42-K-1937-Giedion; CLC, VI A 02-02622.
10 Le Corbusier had instead mentioned the names of Oscar Niemeyer, Carlos Leão, Affonso Eduardo Reidy, and José de Souza Reis, stating that he saw much more potential in the Rio group.
11 Costa to Le Corbusier, 24 October 1937. Note that Costa appears, together with Warchavchik, on the list of the CIRPAC Executive Council of the CIAM, as delegate for Brazil for the year 1937. See Le Corbusier, *The Athens Charter* (New York: Grossman Publishers, 1960), 109.
12 Costa to unknown recipient, n.d. CLC, VI A 01-00710.
13 Giedion to Costa, 18 March 1952 (CLC, VI A 02-03424) and 19 January 1953 (CLC, VI A 02-03026).
14 Giedion to Costa, 4 December 1957. GTA, 43-K-1957-12-04(G).
15 Costa to Sert, 15 November 1952. GTA, 42-JLS-27-93.
16 I partly owe this interpretation to the important work of Carlos Alberto Ferreira Martins, "Arquitetura e Estado no Brasil. Elementos para uma investigação sobre a constituição do

discurso moderno no Brasil: a obra de Lucio Costa 1924–1952," master thesis, Universidade de São Paulo, 1987.
17 See Edward Bradford Burns, *Nationalism in Brazil. A Historical Survey* (New York: Frederick A. Praeger, 1968).
18 See Antonio Pedro Tota, *O amigo americano: Nelson Rockefeller e o Brasil* (São Paulo: Companhia das Letras, 2014).
19 Dispatch of Getúlio Vargas, 16 June 1941. CPDOC, GC i 39.09.06.
20 See Lauro Cavalcanti, *Moderno e brasileiro. A história de uma nova linguagem na arquitetura (1930–60)* (Rio de Janeiro: Jorge Zahar, 2006).
21 A letter of thanks sent by Capanema to Niemeyer after the end of the exhibition leads us to understand that Niemeyer had coordinated a larger workgroup. Capanema to Niemeyer, 30 January 1939. CPDOC, GC b Niemeyer, O.
22 In this regard, see "Exposição anti-comunista." [1938]. CPDOC, GC f 35.05.00, and the general documents on the Exhibition held in the Capanema archives.
23 See, for example, Hugo Segawa, "Arquitetura na Era Vargas: o avesso da unidade pretendida," in José Pessôa, Eduardo Vasconcellos, Elisabete Reis, and Maria Lobo, eds, *Moderno e nacional* (Niterói: EdUFF, 2006), 83–99.
24 The Capanema archives hold his notes and study sketches, showing his careful consideration for the exhibition contents and their arrangement. See, in particular, CPDOC, GC f 35.05.00, II-15.
25 On the New York pavilion and, more generally, on the relations between Brazil and the USA during this crucial moment in time, see: Carlos Eduardo Dias Comas, "Arquitetura moderna, estilo Corbu, pavilhão brasileiro," *AU, arquitetura e urbanismo*, no. 26 (October–November 1989): 92–101; Jorge Francisco Liernur, "*The South American Way*. El 'milagro' brasileño, los Estados Unidos y la Segunda Guerra Mundial (1939–1943)," *Block*, no. 4 (1999): 23–41; Zilah Quezado Deckker, *Brazil Built. The Architecture of the Modern Movement in Brazil* (London/New York: Spon Press, 2001), 54–63; Lauro Cavalcanti, *Architecture, Urbanism, and the Good Neighbor Policy: Brazil and the United States*, in Carlos Brillembourg, ed., *Latin American Architecture 1929–1960. Contemporary Reflections* (New York: Monacelli Press, 2004), 50–59; Carlos Eduardo Dias Comas, "A feira mundial de Nova York de 1939: o pavilhão brasileiro/New York World's Fair of 1939 and the Brazilian pavilion," *ARQtexto*, no. 16 (2010a): 56–97.
26 The competition events were reconstructed in detail by Quezado Deckker on the basis of several articles published on *Arquitetura e Urbanismo*, official journal of the Instituto dos Arquitetos do Brasil.
27 Quezado Deckker, *Brazil Built*, 63, 56.
28 Costa, *Registro de uma vivência* (São Paulo: Empresa das Artes, 1995), 190.
29 For more details on the design process, the construction, and the exhibition programme, see Comas, "A feira mundial de Nova York de 1939: o pavilhão brasileiro."
30 The drawings, some of which were displayed at the Paço Imperial of Rio in 2002, were disclosed and published in the 2010 essay by Comas, "A feira mundial de Nova York de 1939: o pavilhão brasileiro," and then republished in Roberto Segre, *Ministério da Educação e Saúde. Ícone urbano da modernidade brasileira (1935–1945)* (São Paulo: Romano Guerra, 2013). Today, they can be consulted online on the Casa de Lucio Costa website.
31 Quezado Deckker, *Brazil Built*, 56.
32 Possibly recalling one of the versions of the famous *Homem brasileiro* sculpture by Celso Antônio for the Ministry of Education.
33 The sculpture, also present in Niemeyer's competition drawings, would indeed find its place in the pavilion in its final version.
34 Lauro Cavalcanti, Farés el-Dahdah, and Francis Rambert, eds, *Roberto Burle Marx: The Modernity of Landscape* (Barcelona: Actar, 2011).
35 The *treliças* are perforated panels composed of crossed wooden slats; they are used to screen windows, separate spaces, and as railings for balconies and verandas.
36 Costa particularly insists on this issue in various texts dedicated to the pavilion, repeatedly arguing that "an exhibition pavilion must present the characteristics of a temporary construction and never artificially simulate a permanent one," and that "in front of the

A programme for national architecture 93

heavy, higher, and much larger mass of our neighbouring French pavilion," it was necessary to adopt "a different structure, light and open, that would contrast with it instead of being absorbed by it." Costa, "Memória descritiva" [1939]. CLC, III A 46-01344.

37 The *cobogó* is a particular type of perforated brick of Pernambucan origin that is used as a sun-screening system; it recalls the modus operandi of *muxarabis* and its use is characteristic of many masterpieces of Brazilian modernism.
38 It is worth pointing out here how the rhetoric on the international positive reception of the pavilion – which would become a historiographical *leitmotiv* – began straight away with its official album, in which the Commissioner General Armando Vidal reports the flattering comments of magazines such as *The Architectural Forum* and *The Architectural Review*. The fact that in 1952, on the pages of *L'Architecture d'Ajourd'hui*, Giedion would indicate Brazil and Finland as the two emerging countries in the field of contemporary architecture was the direct result of a process that found its catalyst moment precisely in the New York World's Fair.
39 *Pavilhão do Brasil. Feira Mundial de Nova York de 1939* (New York: H. K. Publishing, 1939).
40 *Pavilhão do Brasil. Feira Mundial de Nova York de 1939*.
41 Costa, excerpt from a text on the Brazilian pavilion [1938]. CLC, III A 46-00926.
42 Philip Goodwin, *Brazil Builds: Architecture Old and New 1652–1942* (New York: Museum of Modern Art, 1943). The exhibition catalogue, with photographs by George Everard Kidder Smith, quickly spread through Europe after the war, and was unanimously considered the main dissemination vehicle of Brazilian architecture on the international scene. For a critical reading of the exhibition, see Quezado Deckker, *Brazil Built*.
43 The building, initially designed with ten above-ground floors in compliance with the height limits imposed by its proximity to the Santos Dumont airport, was later raised to fifteen floors.
44 See, in particular, the correspondence between Niemeyer and the minister held in the Capanema archives.
45 Costa, "Relato pessoal," *Módulo* X, no. 40 (September 1975): 23–24, reported in Costa, *Registro*, 135–138. Also see Costa, "1935 – Concurso público. O resultado…" CLC, III A 41-01293.
46 For further information, see Maurício Lissovsky and Paulo Sérgio Moraes de Sá, *Colunas da educação: a construção do Ministério da Educação e Saúde (1935–1945)* (Rio de Janeiro: Edições do Patrimônio, 1996).
47 The wording of the commemorative plaque in the entrance hall of the building was carefully formulated by Costa, who placed his name next-to-last, only above the name of Ernani Vasconcellos: "President of the Republic Getúlio Vargas and Minister of Education and Health Gustavo Capanema, the present building of the Ministry of Education and Public Health was built according to a project by architects Oscar Niemeyer, Affonso Reidy, Jorge Moreira, Carlos Leão, Lucio Costa, and Hernani Vasconcellos, which is based on the original design by Le Corbusier. 1937–1945." "Sendo Presidente da República Getúlio Vargas…" [1945]. CPDOC, GC f 34.10.19, XI-41.
48 Costa, "O novo edifício do Ministério da Educação e Saúde" [ca 1938]. CLC, III A 41-01168.
49 The involvement in the war and the economic inflation would contribute to increasing the controversy on the high costs of the work, as numerous published articles come to show; see, for example, "Mania de grandeza," *A Notícia*, 29 June 1942, in which the Ministry is addressed as the fruit of Capanema's megalomania.
50 Costa to Capanema, 27 October 1939. CPDOC, GC f 34.10.19, V-7.
51 On 29 October 1945, Vargas was deposed by a military movement headed by some of his own generals. General Eurico Caspar Dutra was elected, regularly, in his place.
52 Capanema to Costa, 26 September 1945. ACI-RJ, LC-CR(B)1.
53 Costa to Capanema, 3 October 1945. CPDOC, GC b Costa, L., 1-A.
54 See Gustavo Capanema's speech for the inauguration of the Ministry [October 1945]. CPDOC, GC f 34.10.19, XI-46. Some of the official speeches given by the minister on the occasion of Brazil's entry into the war – the drafts of which are held in his personal archive – are revealing in this regard.

55 Costa to Capanema, 3 October 1945.
56 Costa to Capanema, 3 October 1945.
57 Costa, "Carta depoimento," in Alberto Xavier, ed., *Lúcio Costa: sôbre arquitetura* (Porto Alegre: Editora UniRitter, 2007, 1st edn 1962), 119–128; 124. The letter, originally published in *O Jornal*, 14 March 1948, was written in response to an article in which the critic Geraldo Ferraz had contested the title of "pioneer" that had earlier been attributed to Costa in the magazine *Anteprojeto* by part of the students of the Faculdade Nacional de Arquitetura.
58 This expression, used alternatively to that of "national genius," appears for the first time in the already mentioned "Carta depoimento" and will reappear in many subsequent texts, including the fundamental one intended for an international audience: Costa, "Imprévu et importance de la contribution des architectes brésiliens au développement actuel de l'architecture contemporaine," *L'Architecture d'Aujourd'hui*, no. 42–43 (August 1952): 4–7.
59 I would like to specify here that I attribute the clarification of certain passages of this formulation to the fruitful exchange of ideas held in recent years with Daniele Pisani, as he has addressed the theme of Brazilian architecture's "origin myth" in a series of unpublished texts.
60 Costa to Capanema, 3 October 1945.
61 Costa attributed himself this same title, considering it more appropriate than that of "creator and guide" of contemporary Brazilian architecture awarded to him by Ademar Guimarães, professor of the School of Fine Arts of Bahia, as he found it to be representative of the "somewhat symbolic" role that he claimed to have held in the renewal process of Brazilian architecture. Costa to Ademar Guimarães, 30 May 1957. ACI-RJ, LC-CE03(01A/B).
62 Capanema to Mello Franco de Andrade, 18 December 1945. ACI-RJ, RM-Cn23(6/6.3).
63 Lissovsky and Moraes de Sá, *Colunas da educação*, XVIII.
64 Capanema to Costa, 25 February 1972. CPDOC, GC b Costa, L. 1008. The Costa archive holds several correspondence exchanges that testify to how the good relationship between Costa and Capanema would remain unaltered, even many years later.
65 Costa to Capanema, 25 March 1938. CPDOC, GC f 34.10.19, IV-14.
66 From a letter sent by Costa to Le Corbusier, we understand that in 1939 Capanema had named Costa official delegate of the Brazilian government at the International Congress of Modern Architecture in Washington, DC; in this letter, he says that he intends to focus his speech on the work of the CIAM and of the same Le Corbusier. Costa to Le Corbusier, 14 April 1939. FLC, I3-3-76. However, there are no further traces or documents regarding his speech.
67 Schwartzman, Bomeny, and Ribeiro Costa, *Tempos de Capanema*.
68 Report on the performance of the UDF in 1937. CPDOC, LF f UDF.
69 In this regard, see Lectícia J. Braga De Vincenzi, "A fundação da Universidade do Distrito Federal e seu significado para a educação no Brasil," *Forum Educacional* 10, no. 3 (July–September, 1986): 16–60.
70 See Capanema, "Observações sobre a Universidade do Distrito Federal." CPDOC, GC g 36.09.18, and the various decree drafts held in the archives of the minister.
71 Costa, "Destruí algo que existía," interview by Hajfa Y. Sabbag, *AU, arquitetura e urbanismo* II, no. 5 (April 1986): 18–21; 20.
72 The text – the manuscript of which can be found in the Capanema archives – would appear six years later in the first issue of the magazine *Cultura*, published by the Serviço de Documentação of the Ministry of Education: Costa, "Ensino do desenho," *Cultura* I, no. 1 (September–October 1948): 47–68. Certain documents held in the Capanema archives once more reveal the presence, behind the scenes, of Rodrigo Mello Franco de Andrade and Carlos Drummond de Andrade.
73 Report by Lourenço Filho (director of the Departamento Nacional de Educação) on Lucio Costa's opinion regarding the drawing course programme in the context of the secondary school reform, 10 August 1942. CPDOC, GC g 42.06.11.
74 Costa, "Considerações sobre o ensino da arquitetura," *ENBA, Revista de Arte*, no. 3 (September 1945), reported in Xavier, ed., *Sôbre arquitetura*, 111–117.
75 Costa, "Considerações sobre o ensino da arquitetura," 112–113.

76 Lissovsky and Moraes de Sá, *Colunas da educação*, 205–206.
77 Goodwin, *Brazil Builds*.
78 Costa, "Imprévu et importance …"
79 Law n. 378, 13 January 1937, art. 46.
80 The direct precedent of the SPHAN was the Museu Histórico Nacional, established in 1922. From 1933, the year in which the city of Ouro Preto was listed as national monument, the Museu Histórico Nacional provided itself with an Inspetoria de Monumentos Nacionais, directed by Gustavo Dodt Barroso. The 1934 Constitution expanded the State's power in matters of protection and safeguarding, leading to the proposal of establishing the SPHAN.
81 Decree n. 25 of 30 November 1937.
82 Daryle Williams, *Culture Wars in Brazil. The First Vargas Regime, 1930–1945* (Durham, NC/London: Duke University Press, 2001), 103.
83 Rodrigo Mello Franco de Andrade remained in office as director until 1967. For more information on his contribution to the SPHAN, see in particular *Rodrigo e seus tempos. Rodrigo Mello Franco de Andrade* (Rio de Janeiro: Fundação Nacional Pró-Memória, 1985); and *Rodrigo e o SPHAN; coletâneas de textos sobre o patrimônio cultural* (Rio de Janeiro: MEC-Fundação Nacional Pró-Memória, 1987).
84 Maria Cecília Londres Fonseca, *O patrimônio em processo: trajetória da política federal de preservação no Brasil* (Rio de Janeiro: UFRJ-IPHAN, 1997), 96.
85 The *Inconfidência Mineira* was an independence movement against the Portuguese colonisation that took place at the end of the 18th century.
86 It is no coincidence that during the first years of activity of the SPHAN, the selection of assets to be protected was strongly in favour of 18th-century religious architecture from Minas Gerais: suffice it to say that in 1938, six historical cities – including Ouro Preto, São João del Rey, and Diamantina – were granted protection *en bloc*.
87 In view of this, *fin-de-siècle* architecture was almost completely excluded from the selection; in very rare cases, its protection was justified for its historical interest, which was in contrast with the propensity of including most protected assets in the *Livro de Belas Artes*. The criteria governing the enhancement of heritage assets were completely consistent with the disciplinary composition of the workgroup, which in fact did not initially include even one historian: the construction of the *Patrimônio* to be protected was carried out starting from "a predominantly aesthetic point of view," where what mattered was the artistic value of the concerned assets. See Londres Fonseca, *O patrimônio em processo*, 114.
88 The fundamental reference text on Costa's activity at the SPHAN is José Pessôa, ed., *Lucio Costa: documentos de trabalho* (Rio de Janeiro: Edições do Patrimônio-IPHAN, 1999).
89 Even after his appointment as director of the Divisão de Estudos e Tombamento, Costa points out his intention to continue to act as "assistant-consultant, of irregular but trusted implementation." Pessôa, ed., *Documentos de trabalho*, 89–90.
90 Of particular interest, in this regard, is a letter Costa sent to the director in 1962, in which he claims: "what makes me consider my case different from others is the presumption, possibly groundless, of having already contributed, in the professional sphere, to the realisation of some significant projects of collective interest, for which I have been badly compensated; a circumstance that leads me to accept the money I perceive in the symbolic function I hold here as the deserved compensation from the government." Costa to Mello Franco de Andrade, 28 May 1962. ACI-RJ, LC-CE02(03).
91 See Carlos Drummond de Andrade, "Lúcio Costa na repartição," *Jornal do Brasil*, 4 March 1982, reported in Costa, *Registro*, 435–436. Drummond de Andrade – who shared his daily work in the *repartição* with Costa – describes him as somebody always ready to "take a step back," somebody that seems to "want to hide from everything and everyone, even from the same name of Lucio Costa."
92 Lauro Cavalcanti, *Moderno e brasileiro*, 120.

4 A strategy of mediation
Between the CIAM and the SPHAN

Shaping national heritage

We can place Costa's full intellectual and professional maturity between the late 1930s and early 1940s. Parallel to the development of a design approach increasingly marked by a hybridisation between the modernist vocabulary and a reinterpretation of traditional architecture – fuelled by the experiences carried out, directly or indirectly, in historical contexts and sites within the SPHAN – these were the years in which Costa developed a successful cultural strategy capable of bridging the gap between past and present. This strategy – aimed at tracing the similarities and kinships between anonymous colonial architecture and modern architecture, between the genius of Aleijadinho and that of Niemeyer – would allow him to legitimise "new architecture" as a form of continuity of the "good tradition" of Brazilian architecture.

In order to follow the genesis and evolution of this discourse, it is necessary to look into Costa's activity within the SPHAN from a long-term perspective. The scientific opinions he drafted over the years, the programmatic documents he drew up as director of the Divisão de Estudos e Tombamento, and the correspondence with his SPHAN colleagues allow us to track the models, references, value criteria, methodological approaches, and areas of action that guided the choices regarding conservation and restoration time after time, outlining the laborious process of defining strategies of protection, on both technical and conceptual levels. On the other hand, the writings developed during the study trips and the editorial initiatives promoted by the SPHAN represent the expression, albeit fragmented, of a parallel theoretical commitment aimed at defining the concept of national tradition that served as the selective criterion for heritage and, at the same time, as the discursive support for the legitimisation of the new architecture.[1]

Building an "authentic evolutionary line" of Brazilian architecture in light of which it could have been possible to distil a moral and artistic identity of the nation – rooted in a well-revised national mythography – was an issue that uninterruptedly involved Costa throughout his entire SPHAN career and was an integral part of his identity building programme. As the main argument in support of modern architecture, which Costa interpreted "in illuministic terms" as a "final station of a long process"[2] – borrowing the words dedicated by Manfredo Tafuri to Alexander Dorner – it had substantial repercussions on the conservation practices that were adopted, on the careful selection of the heritage sites, and on the choices regarding restoration. Evading a direct confrontation with the disciplinary baggage

Figure 4.1 Portrait of Lucio Costa in a newspaper article of 1965. In the background, a photo of the façade of Aleijadinho's portal of São Francisco de Assis in Ouro Preto. Casa de Lucio Costa.

that had been developed, most of all, in Europe – which he didn't ignore, nevertheless – and settling on a pragmatism that was instrumental for the immediate effectiveness of the proposed measures, Costa subjected the past and its memory to the same intransigent and meticulous test of "authenticity" – considered as synonymous with artistic quality – to which he subjected the products of his own era. While his ideas on conservation seem to have been drawn from both Athens Charters, the one of 1931 on restoration – namely the general conclusions of the First International Congress of Architects and Technicians of Historic Monuments – and, perhaps to a greater extent, the CIAM one of 1933, he also was engaged in an ambiguous relation with the arguments of functionalist urbanism on the subject of historical heritage – which were largely accepted yet in some ways superseded – and with the dictates of the so-called "scientific restoration" – which were deemed valid as long as they did not contradict the aesthetic judgement, elected as decisive choice criterion.[3] In this sense, the past was a territory that was anything but neutral for Costa; like the present and future, it could be designed or at least freed from its alterations.

The same heritage selection criteria of the institution – which had been keeping up with the shifting value judgements and urban phenomena dimensions – experienced significant changes. Up until the 1950s, for example, these criteria were mainly applied to works and architectures dating back to the periods of the colonisation and of the Empire, between the 18th century and the first half of the 19th. In the following decades, they also came to include numerous urban architectures of the 19th and early 20th centuries, which were threatened – as José Pessôa stressed – by real-estate speculation. In many cases, these were buildings that, according to Costa, exemplified the connection with the anonymous "good tradition" of the Luso-Brazilian builders or were neo-classical and eclectic buildings worthy of note for their historical or artistic importance.[4] However, they also constituted few exceptions, if we consider that – in a discussion held with Paulo Santos in 1972 on the Cinelândia area in Rio de Janeiro – Costa would have the opportunity to declare that the SPHAN's orientation had always been that of "excluding academic eclecticism from its competences as it was considered outside of the legitimate evolutionary line of architecture,"[5] therefore taking a negative stance against the proposed protection bond on the eclectic buildings in the area. In some cases – and in the cases of "display" eclecticism of the early 20th century in particular – demolition was deemed necessary, despite the fact that Costa had proved to be strongly reluctant to the measure.[6] For example, he was personally involved in the removal from Rio's historical centre of the Pavilhão dos Estados – built on the occasion of the 1922 International Exposition – and of the Pavilhão Monroe – the Brazilian pavilion of the 1904 St. Louis Exposition, later reassembled between the pier and the Passeio Público, which was destined to various uses, including that of Senate Building – resorting to arguments like those of "urban health" and "urban outlet" (*desafogo urbano*).[7] According to the same principle, the intention of isolating some monuments in their plastic "purity" seems to have legitimised the partial demolition of the surrounding urban fabric; in consonance with the CIAM Athens Charter, the resulting vacant spaces were destined to become green areas and parking lots: pockets of that much-hoped-for Ville Verte, capable of enhancing the urban landscape and providing new public spaces. In Costa's urban vision, the green areas covered an important role as an integral part of the built environment, as a substitute for architecture to help restore the balance in disjointed urban areas. As he was often critical of the poor quality of contemporary construction works that were insensitive to authentic architectural and urban values, he ultimately entrusted the "redemption" of many parts of the city – disfigured by short-sighted and harmful interventions – to the vegetation and landscape. Ultimately, for Costa, the quality of the urban environment depended chiefly on the intrinsic value of the architecture and on the relation it held with its surrounding natural and artificial landscape, which applied to both historical and contemporary cities. As a consequence, each case was to be assessed individually. As José Pessôa claims, Costa's vision of the city was "never a strictly conservative one, founded on the maintenance of what is still existing, but it is based on a qualifying comparison between old and new, as happens with the relation between the built environment and nature."[8]

However, different rules had to be applied to historical cities from those undergoing a full real-estate development. In the first case of historical contexts, the operation sought to preserve the uniformity of the built environment, even prescribing – in some cases – precise rules for the development of new buildings or completely safeguarding the entire urban area.[9] By turning Ouro Preto into a "laboratory of nationality"[10] and exercising direct control over all interventions concerning the urban fabric, the SPHAN would be able to crystallise the city into an idealised image, codifying a series of rules aimed at ensuring a harmonious integration of the interventions with the colonial remains.[11] On the other hand, in Rio and in other big urban centres (at least during the first ten years of the SPHAN's activity), only isolated buildings or groups of buildings were subject to similar protection. The city was destined to grow directly on top of itself if necessary; and the past was destined to remain relegated to the state of a fragment, increasingly incorporated and crushed by the rapid growth of the city itself.

Although Costa's competences did not directly fall within the Divisão de Conservação e Restauração, he often commented on the restoration of heritage assets, playing an important role in defining the criteria adopted by the SPHAN, not only in choosing which past should have been preserved, but also how it should have been handed over to history. The valorisation of the authenticity of historical evidence – and the propensity to leave the original matter unaltered when possible – guided Costa's approach to restoration; this principle was often associated with the idea that any stylistic reproduction or imitation of the ancient – even if philological – should be fundamentally avoided. The case was different when both the matter and the image of the monument had been, to put it in Costa's terms, "disfigured" by subsequent interventions. These were the circumstances in which he would have allowed a certain kind of stylistic reconstruction, aimed at giving back the building – more or less philologically – its lost integrity, returning it to its alleged "original state."[12] As a result of this approach, which undoubtedly was one of the most controversial points of his vision in the field of restoration, the same principle of authenticity found itself supporting the removal of part of the historical layers of the monument in question. However, this was only an apparent contradiction; whether associated to the physical matter of the monument or to its figurative nature, the principle of authenticity was considered valid exclusively for what fell within the ideal evolutionary line of authentic Brazilian architecture that he himself had traced.

At the same time, once they had achieved the status of legitimate heirs of that evolutionary line, even contemporary architectural pieces could quickly receive an official investiture as an integral part of national heritage, before history itself could issue its impartial judgement. Inaugurated in 1947 with the preventive protection bond on Oscar Niemeyer's church of São Francisco de Assis in Pampulha[13] – and followed by the cases of the Ministry of Education and Public Health,[14] Attilio Corrêa Lima's Estação de Hidroaviões of the Santos Dumont Airport, Affonso Eduardo Reidy and Roberto Burle Marx's Aterro do Flamengo, the cathedral of Brasilia the Catetinho and the same Plano Piloto of the capital city,[15] preceded by two pieces by the same Costa (the São Clemente Park Hotel in Nova Friburgo and the Parque Guinle residential complex in Rio de Janeiro) – the practice of safeguarding Brazilian modernist architecture and monuments rapidly began to consolidate itself. Officially nominating certain modern pieces as national monuments of public interest was a logical corollary of the process aimed at establishing modernism as the "Art of the State." Modernists were therefore preparing themselves to make their entry into history, delivering a careful selection of their architectural production to posterity.

Dealing with historical pre-existence

Historical inheritance was to be handed over to posterity in an idealised guise in order to act as an *exemplum*; however, this was all the more true when it was placed in direct contact with an equally "authentic" modern context.

The first assignment Costa received by the SPHAN at the beginning of the institution's activity in 1937 provided a first opportunity to challenge himself with an archaeological site of great importance, the Jesuit ruins of the Sete Povos das Missões in Rio Grande do Sul, which would result in one of the projects that is perhaps most emblematic of Costa's approach in the late 1930s. After an accurate survey and documentation of the state of the ruins,[16] Costa decided to operate on a double register: preserving what still remained standing and enhancing the lost vitality of the Jesuit settlements, to which he referred with Corbusian terms like "radiant villages"[17] conceived by "admirable urban planners." The suggested measures were simple and based on the principle of minimum intervention: clearing the area occupied by the ancient village of São Miguel (where the ruins of the original 18th-century church still existed), consolidating the ruins, and bringing together all that was found during the excavations of the entire Sete Povos in the same site of São Miguel, in a small museum to hold and display the archaeological findings.[18] Since, according to Costa, the advanced state of destruction did not allow any attempt at reconstruction, he suggested enhancing the "already much erased" traces of the mission's urban structure.

Costa devoted most of his design efforts to the small museum, which he imagined as "a simple refuge for pieces that, all of regular size, would gain much from being assessed in direct contact with the rest of the ruins."[19] Once he had discarded the solution that saw the display of the archaeological findings within the lateral naves of the church, he decided to create a new building to host the museum and the house of the groundskeeper, making use of some of the materials found *in situ* – according to a procedure that he defines with the term *dépose* (anastylosis) but that rather consisted in freely introducing the original fragments within the new design – and positioning the museum at "one of the ends of the ancient square, to serve as a reference point and give a better idea of its size." This resulted in an L-shaped building at the corner of what had once been the square around which the houses were originally arranged; it presented a stone-porticoed pavilion with tile roofing – evoking the "ancient porticoes running along the side of the houses," without actually creating a reproduction – and a small patio building destined for the groundskeeper.

The final building, completed in 1941 under the supervision of Lucas Mayerhofer, is a variant of the solution first devised by Costa: given the increase in number of the archaeological pieces it was to host, Costa's project came to include the addition of a glass diaphragm to help close the exhibition space – set up among plastered white partitions that were perpendicular to the long side of the pavilion – introducing a new level of complexity in the dialogue between the building and the surrounding landscape. Volumetrically defined by its hipped roof in traditional tiles, the museum represented a free re-evocation of the original covered walkway, a solution that was far from a scientific application of the anastylosis method, and from a reconstruction of the site "where it was, as it was," which had already been previously dismissed. Its location in the northwest corner of the ancient square, ideally reconstituting its shape, made it possible to read its original spatial quality. Therefore, the transparency of its shell made it possible to juxtapose and visually integrate the different chronological and archaeological layers of the area, allowing the displayed artefacts to resonate with the church's monumental ruins in the background, enriching them and their perception. Any authentic fragment that could have been reused – capitals, bases, even entire columns and portions of original flooring from the various villages – was freely introduced into the new construction. When the retrieved fragments were not sufficient, similar pieces were reconstructed on the basis of the models and materials of the original ones. The philological intent yielded to the architectural effect and, we could say, to the effectiveness of the intervention in terms of urban design, in the attempt to better narrate, albeit with few measured words, the long-lost past.[20] The subdued tone and essential character of the project – and its aim to harmoniously match the historical pre-existences without, however, risking being confused with them – are the expression of a pioneering behaviour: respectful of the vestiges of the past while at the same time also capable of introducing new values, delivered through contemporary techniques and materials[21] (Figure 4.2).

The year 1938, following the first mission in Rio Grande do Sul, saw the SPHAN deal with another delicate design challenge: the construction of a modern hotel, fully equipped with all comforts, in a lot within the historical site of Ouro Preto, which had been declared a national monument in 1933 and registered in the Livro do Tombo de Belas Artes precisely in 1938. Although Costa was not personally in charge of this project, his contribution turned out to be crucial in guiding the decisions on the matter from behind the scenes, inaugurating a strategy that was destined to repeat itself on many other occasions.[22] The preliminary project, entrusted to Carlos Leão by Rodrigo Mello Franco de Andrade, consisted of an imposing neo-colonial building, conceived in order to "not come into conflict with the typical architecture of Ouro Preto,"[23] as requested by the SPHAN director. Informally called upon to give a scientific opinion on the project that had already been approved during his stay in New York for the work on the Brazilian pavilion, Costa expressed a strong disapproval of the use of stylistic imitation, proposing to engage Niemeyer to draw up a new project for the hotel.[24] Upon returning from New York, Niemeyer therefore elaborated a project with a marked horizontal character and strictly modern lines, with the long side running parallel to the land's contour lines, presenting a façade that was articulated in series of double-height *pilotis* and in a rhythmic succession of duplex room windows (consisting of a glass

Figure 4.2 Lucio Costa's Museum of São Miguel das Missões after its completion with the ruins of the 18th-century church in the background. Arquivo Central do IPHAN – Seção Rio de Janeiro.

diaphragm and sun-screening elements). In an attempt to reduce the impact of the hotel on the urban landscape as much as possible, Niemeyer decided to give the building a flat green roof. The episode was accompanied by a lively debate that – in addition to seeing SPHAN members divided in conflicting and irreconcilable positions[25] – came to engage the public opinion and various artistic and institutional figures, showing once again – as happened for the Ministry of Education – how modernist experiments were distrusted, despite the rhetoric of their rapid and uncontested success. Costa did not fail to defend Niemeyer's project, attracting heavy criticism and personal accusations.[26] A famous letter addressed to Rodrigo Mello Franco de Andrade – in which Costa presents one of the rare theoretical statements directly related to this first phase of the institution – clearly and effectively enucleates the arguments in support of this project. Claiming to take the floor "as an architect appointed by the CIAM to organise the Rio group, and as a technical specialist appointed by the SPHAN to study our ancient architecture," he writes:

> I know from personal experience that reproducing the style of the houses of Ouro Preto is possible, today, only at the price of a great artifice. Even assuming that the special case of this city justifies, exceptionally, the uptake of such methods, what we would achieve at the end of the construction is

> either a perfect imitation – and the inexperienced tourist would risk exchanging, at first sight, an imitation for one of the main monuments of the city – or otherwise, were the attempt to fail, a "neo-colonial" fiction with nothing in common with the true spirit of the old buildings. Now, the project of O.N.S. [Oscar Niemeyer Soares] has at least two things in common with these: beauty and truth. Composed in a calm, direct, and uncompromising way, it resolves a current issue with present-day techniques and in the best possible form, just as the builders of Ouro Preto resolved their own issues in the best possible way.
>
> With its exceptional purity of lines and great plastic balance, it is, effectively, a work of art, and as such it should not shy away from the close presence of other ones, although different, since the good architecture of a given period always fits well beside other ones from any previous periods; whereas a lack of architecture does not fit well with anything.[27]

As an architect engaged in the militant movement for the establishment of the "new architecture," he condemned every form of stylistic reproduction, theorising the insertion of the new within the old based on an idea of historical continuity for which old values could be complemented by new ones, without necessarily resulting in the diminishment of the first. Moreover, Ouro Preto was the ideal place to be elected for the site of an open-air museum holding authentic monuments of the past – and for the future – of the nation. The co-existence of these two temporal dimensions would have helped trigger the feeling of the heritage's irretrievable loss, giving the project an undisputable "official" quality and, at the same time, enhancing the mythical and symbolical dimension of the past in question.

> Just as a latest-model car can circulate through the roads of the monument-city without causing visual damage to anyone – in fact, on the contrary, it would contribute to help perceive the "past" as even more alive – the construction of a modern hotel, of good architecture, would in the same way not affect Ouro Preto at all; not even from the sentimental-touristic point of view, because next to such a light and clear structure – such a young one, if we may call it so – the ancient rooftops piled one above the other, the beautiful portal adornments of São Francisco and Carmo, the solidity of Casa dos Contos, with its corner pillars made of stone from Itacolomy, everything belonging to this small yet dense past [...] will seem much more distant, it will gain at least one hundred years in age.

While it created unexpected connections with the new architectural intervention, the pre-existent fabric also revealed an unbridgeable distance that separated it from the present. In the ruins of São Miguel das Missões and in the static immobility of Villa Rica, the inevitable contrast expressed – not without dignity – the desolation of the loss,[28] and it was precisely in this idealised dimension of the past that the contradictions of this formulation were hidden. The second part of the letter in fact presents a sudden change of tone. Now cautious and confidential, Costa appeals to his long-standing friendship with the interlocutor and – fearing that the negative reactions aroused by Niemeyer's project might compromise the success of the operation – he somewhat dampens the intransigent tone of his previous statements, suggesting that they should not disdain a solution that could attenuate the perception of conflict between ancient and modern.

> Given that yesterday you told me you have prompted O.N.S. to devise an alternative that better meets local Ouro Preto characteristics – a solicitation made upon your own initiative, without any suggestion or interference from my part – I wonder if, keeping the CIAM and SPHAN in sight, in cases as particular as this one and given the similarities often found between modern construction made in metal and reinforced concrete and the traditional one of the *pau a pique*,[29] it could be possible to find a solution that – maintaining the adopted configuration and respecting the current sincerity of the construction and its good architectural principles – could better be adapted to the context and that – without claiming in any way to reproduce the ancient constructions or be confused and exchanged for them – could less accentuate the contrast between past and present; a solution that tries, despite its dimensions, to "appear" as little as possible, to not be relevant, or better yet not say anything (just like certain tall and large people we indeed end up not remembering the presence of), in order that Ouro Preto can quietly continue, alone in its corner, to relive its history.[30]

A certain degree of ambiguity becomes evident here: between the desire to accentuate the contrast between old and new, and the desire to wish for a "silent" operation to help preserve the integrity of the monument-city, destined to "relive its history" forever. In essence, the paradoxical situation that emerged was that of an inverted Plan Voisin, where a limited number of monuments separately found their place within the structure of the historical city, which became a museum where the past could relive in memory, even if for just one moment. Therefore, under his inflexible theoretical line, Costa reveals the progressive development of a design approach that acknowledged the selected and "filtered" elements from Luso-Brazilian architecture (which would reach complete formal maturity in the residences built in those same years in Rio). He consequently suggested employing a subtle strategy of "adaptation" or "acclimatisation" of the new within the pre-existing environment. The difficulty of translating the ambivalence of this positon into concrete architectural solutions would have the predictable effect of an indirect intervention on Niemeyer's project, the "adaptation" process of which would finally end up being led by Costa.[31] The suggested modifications, which were almost entirely accepted in the final version, albeit not without indecision and second thoughts, included substituting the green roof with a traditional one in tiles, replacing the glass diaphragms on the façade with *treliça*-screened openings, and finally choosing pillars with square cross-sections over *pilotis*, in order to better accentuate the similarity between the reinforced concrete structure and the *pau a pique* construction technique (Figure 4.3).

In Costa's vision, the insertion within the historical pre-existing site was resolved by resorting to a "modern adjustment" – which more intransigent champions of modern architecture would later steer away from – that, in some ways, mimicked the surroundings, without, however, foregoing the "sincerity of the construction" and its "good architectural principles." More than relying on codified rules, the operation required a certain sensitivity in emotionally understanding the past, attempting to

Figure 4.3 Oscar Niemeyer's Grand Hotel in Ouro Preto, view of the main façade. From *The Architectural Forum*'s special issue on Brazil, November 1947.

reveal its essence through few measured interventions and renewing its values without, however, replicating its original features. It is the artist – not the historian or philologist – who is able to recognise the work of art and, when necessary, uses his creative inspiration to help make it understandable to a contemporary observer and usable for the spiritual and material needs of his time. It is therefore thanks to an artistic approach that Costa saw it as possible to re-actualise the formal structures and the construction and compositional principles, and bridge the co-existence – if not actually underlining the continuity – between different eras. The adaptation of the new within the old and of the old within the new, the relation between the two, developed on thin ice: suspended between nostalgic evocation, a yearning for modernisation, and a sophisticated hybridisation of regionalist nature.

The colonial roots of Brazilian architecture

The first issue of the *Revista do Serviço do Patrimônio Histórico e Artístico Nacional* – the main vehicle for the dissemination of the institution's research activities under the direction of Rodrigo Mello Franco de Andrade – was published in 1937, at the same time of the expedition to the Sete Povos das Missões. It presents the first of a series of critical studies that Costa dedicated to the investigation of the roots of Luso-Brazilian art and architecture. The essay, entitled "Documentação necessária,"[32] somehow took up the traces of his first study trip to Diamantina in 1924, where he had first identified colonial civil architecture as a rich source for contemporary professional practice, a heritage that had been greatly neglected by a tradition of studies devoted mainly to religious architecture. The explicit objective was that of inaugurating a new and unprecedented field of research, while also delivering a vast repertory of design solutions, developed over the centuries.[33]

In the essay he wrote in 1929, "O Aleijadinho e a arquitetura tradicional," Costa limited himself to reading colonial civil architecture in sentimentalist terms – "robust, strong, solid"[34] – on the basis of the contrast with the strenuous spirit of Aleijadinho's work and with the academic eclecticism of the beginning of the century. Now, in his new essay, his programme was much more ambitious: it was in fact the first stage of a complex investigation – destined to be carried on for decades to come – on the adaptation modalities of Portuguese architecture in the new continent, aimed at capturing the qualities of Brazilian architecture during its formation process and identifying the teachings that could still be valid in his present day, reprising the reflections he had initiated on the roots of the national culture at the beginning of the century.[35]

> Now, in our opinion, popular architecture in Portugal is of greater interest than the "erudite" kind – to use an expression proposed by Mário de Andrade, and lacking other terms, to discriminate the art of the people from the "cultured" one. It is within its own villages – in the virile aspect of their rural buildings, both crude and welcoming at the same time – that the qualities of the race best show themselves. Lacking the affected and often pedantic mannerisms it [architecture] gains when perfected, there, at home and completely at ease, it develops naturally; finding in its accurate proportions and in the absence of "make-up" – so to speak – a perfect plastic health.[36]

Recognising the artistic value of anonymous Luso-Brazilian architecture, as well as its dignity as "architectural work," therefore rested exactly on what had originally excluded it from consideration: its modest origin as fruit of the labour of "old master builders and 'uneducated' stonemasons." The idea of a correspondence between modern principles and the involuntary construction rationality of anonymous architecture – which fuelled a sober aesthetic, free from rigid compositional schemes – was supported by the compliance to alleged constructive, distributive, and formal analogies – analogies that were researched in their evolutionary processes from a deterministic point of view, aimed at extrapolating expressive choices from precise functional needs.

> We thus prove that, already in 1910, the *mestres de obra* were on the right path. Faithful to the good Portuguese tradition of not lying, they naturally applied all the new possibilities of modern construction – such as the almost completely open façades, the very thin iron columns, the balcony decks armed with double T-shaped beams and vaults, and the loose and slender stairs also made of iron – to their crude structures [...] while also non-intentionally searching for a different plastic balance.[37]

A series of sketches that accompany the text schematise the façade's evolution, from the 17th century to the 1930s, as a progressive expansion of the glazed window surface, finally reaching the dimension of a *fenêtre en longueur*; whereas, the simplification process that had led to smooth wall surfaces and simple volumes was presented as the effect of a gradual elimination of elements that had become superfluous, such as ledges and gutters. The service façade of a colonial residence, fitted with an asymmetrical portico and a sinuous staircase toward the garden, is defined as "pure Le Corbusier." The apparently arbitrary connection between the evolution of the traditional Brazilian house and the European experiments of the 1920s does not seem to have constituted a problem for Costa, who probably considered the common Latin and Mediterranean roots – already presented in "Razões da nova arquitetura" – a valid support to such a hypothesis.[38] Even the *barro armado* construction technique, a system commonly used in colonial houses, was compared to the contemporary reinforced concrete frame and indicated as a system that was still valid for small economic houses.

Costa's emphasis on the usefulness of the "lesson" of Luso-Brazilian vernacular architecture for modern architecture – which, moreover, needs to be framed among the general cultural climate of the SPHAN – seems to have found a more direct reference model in Le Corbusier's revaluation of anonymous architecture as a "learning ground" that was alternative to the academies,[39] also finding surprising correspondences – which should perhaps be investigated more in depth – with certain European experiences taking place more or less in the same years.[40] Vernacular architecture, as a direct and involuntary expression of the pre-industrial societies that produced it, was employed as an ideal model for modern architecture since it was considered the product of an organic integration of life and form, of artistic expression and functional needs, and of architecture and society. Seen as a-stylistic and a-historical at the same time, as it was an expression of a live tradition, it was used as an alternative to a cynical and nostalgic view of the past, and as an argument to support and legitimise modernist proposals.

Two years later, Costa's "Notas sobre a evolução do mobiliário luso-brasileiro" presented itself as an ideal continuation of "Documentação necessária." Here, the evolution of Luso-Brazilian furnishing elements is steered so as to connect with the modern furnishings of Le Corbusier, Charlotte Perriand, and Mies van der Rohe. With their "elegance and pure lines,"[41] these modern examples configure themselves as the formal outcome of an update of tradition, in light of new industrial production techniques that restored the original "sober" quality to the Brazilian house. The year 1941 saw the debut of the essay "A arquitetura dos Jesuítas no Brasil,"[42] which prepared for a complete critical reintegration of the work of Aleijadinho. In this text – one of the most ambitious studies conducted by Costa for the SPHAN – the architect compiles an actual classification of Jesuit architecture, identifying stylistic and compositional peculiarities based on temporal and geographic references. His main goal was that of identifying the true beginning of Brazilian artistic expression in certain popular reinterpretations of Portuguese Baroque, which was attributed an "artistically superior" character – not without some coercion – compared to the first models; while, as the essay recites, "the erudite altarpieces of the first phase, with their elegant style and regular and composed appearance [...] seem to effectively derive from Portugal, the same cannot be said for the extremely interesting 17th-century popular version of the same altarpieces," which, "disfiguring the modular relations of the erudite models in their own way, often give rise to new and unexpected plastic relations, full of spontaneity and spirit of invention"[43] (Figure 4.4).

Figure 4.4 Lucio Costa, sketches from the text "A arquitetura dos Jesuítas no Brasil," illustrating the stylistic evolution of the altarpieces from the late 16th to the 18th century. *Revista do Patrimônio Histórico e Artístico Nacional*, no. 5 (1941). Arquivo Central do IPHAN – Seção Rio de Janeiro.

In attempting to identify the stages of the formation and evolution of the typological, architectural, and construction characters of Luso-Brazilian architecture, the research carried out on the Brazilian territory – and the parallel research on the sources – turned out to finally be insufficient, making it necessary to turn to its Portuguese "ancestors." It was in these circumstances that Costa undertook his study missions in Portugal, which – in addition to decisively contributing to the development of a personal theory on the assimilation of Portuguese models within the colony – triggered a series of significant connections between the two countries and laid the foundations for a few figurative bridges across the Atlantic, helping to create relations and exchange opportunities with other European countries as well.

The only document testifying the results from a first 1948 trip[44] – during which Costa travelled across Portugal, north to south, making his way through the inland regions – is a text, later entitled "Introdução à um relatório," that seems to actually declare the mission a failure.[45] Apart for the obvious difficulties of the enterprise, the failure was blamed on the impossibility of finding "logical and coherent affiliation connections" that could allow systematically reconstructing the assimilation of Portuguese architecture in the colony, given the extreme complexity and non-linearity of the phenomenon, which cast a shadow on the architect's belief in the positive methods. The formation process of colonial architecture in fact presented the same "rectifying or disintegrating capricious interferences" that had characterised the same process in Portuguese architecture: they both were a product of the inextricable connections of heterogeneous influences. In theorising the development of Brazilian architecture as independent from its original source, Costa claimed it held "its own personality" and specific characteristics, and therefore could also claim equal legitimacy with respect to the Portuguese one. These considerations were further developed in a presentation he held in Washington shortly after, in 1950, at the International Congress of Luso-Brazilian Studies, entitled "A arquitetura brasileira colonial." As the brief compendium that is published in the proceedings shows, Brazilian architecture is here considered, among the various "legitimate" branches of Portuguese art, as the one branch in which the original reference source reaches its artistic culmination at the end of the Baroque cycle.

> In the overview of Portuguese art, Brazilian colonial architecture should not be considered as a copy of the metropolitan models, but as an equally legitimate and autonomous manifestation of the Portuguese creative genius in other locations. A manifestation determined by the Portuguese origins of artists and craftsmen, enriched by the colonial experience in Africa and in the East, and marked by the same differentiating action of the native environment and from the genuine art – in the erudite and popular sense – of the native artists of the country. This art is so significant that the most original and valuable contribution to Portuguese art in its final Baroque phase is due to the Brazilians of Minas Gerais, in architecture as much as sculpture and ornamental painting.[46]

Costa refers here to the work of Aleijadinho, Mestre Valentim (Valentim da Fonseca e Silva), and Mestre Ataíde (Manuel da Costa Ataíde). In fact, an introduction to Rodrigo José Ferreira Bretas's volume on Antônio Francisco Lisboa was published the following year, the first of a series of theoretical contributions by the architect on the artist between the 1960s and 1970s.[47] Riding the high of his international rediscovery,[48] Costa interpreted the work of Aleijadinho – whose "passionate and often mystical temperament" contrasted with the "elegant and mannered style of the time"[49] – as the crowning moment of an artistic venture that had started centuries earlier in Portugal; therefore, he not only considered it "the highest expression [...] of the Portuguese art of the time," but also "the last valid manifestation of Christian architecture and sculpture in the art history of the world, before the long hiatus preceding the legitimate reformulation of contemporary architecture."[50]

The loss of Costa's notebooks, while the architect was still alive, holding sketches and annotations on his travels in Portugal, and his partly scarce vocation in constructing a systematic theoretical *corpus*, are perhaps to blame for the absence of a complete study on a regular theme running through his entire professional life. Even in the other two texts addressing the issue – probably conceived around the 1980s for his autobiography *Registro de uma vivência* – Costa limited himself to proposing interesting considerations on the regional qualities of Portuguese architecture and on their Brazilian declinations. In "Tradição local,"[51] for example, he postulates the relationship between the *transmontana* house,[52] the native house, and various kinds of colonial residences, based on distributional and functional analogies, like the presence of the two verandas (domestic and social), or the recurrence of specific heating systems, to which he attributes many Portuguese regional formal and construction differences. In "Anotações ao correr da lembrança,"[53] Costa reviews "the architectural treasures" scattered throughout the different regions of Brazil, without expecting to do so in any comprehensive manner – "they are so many that it is impossible to enumerate them in these simple annotations." The complexity of the adaptation and assimilation processes of these "architectural treasures" seems to have discouraged him from entrusting them to a narrative that could differ from the light and informal one of random annotations.

Scrolling through the images that accompany the text – from the Fazenda Columbandê, an example of "rural architecture with porticoes presenting Tuscan columns in the Minho fashion, but completely plastered white in the Estremadura fashion," to the almost entirely glazed and "current-style" elevation of the Misericórdia de Parati – we almost seem to view, at least in part, the multifaceted idea of national tradition that was so painstakingly being elaborated by the SPHAN. In assessing the matter this way, on practical and theoretical levels simultaneously, highlighting the common ground with the architecture of the former colonisers seems to have finally helped decree the belonging of Brazilian artistic production to the history of Western art, allowing it to link up – through a subtle theoretical gap – with the "new tradition" of modern architecture. Costa's contribution to the SPHAN should therefore be identified in this wide-ranging project perhaps more than anywhere else, a project that was certainly steeped in ideological motivations but also, at the same time, focused on emancipating Brazil from the legacy of cultural imperialism.

Baroque and national personality

In the 1954 "Report on Brazil" – ringing from the pages of *The Architectural Review* as a first harsh judgement of Brazilian architecture on the part of international critics – Ernesto Nathan Rogers describes Costa as the one who, "after having been considered for many years as the Allah of Brazilian architects, decided (in a gesture of unheard-of and, perhaps, excessive modesty) to become Oscar's Mohammed, his most devout and generous prophet."[54] In fact, the almost religious tone with which Costa would support the career of his ex-collaborator from a certain point onwards may seem surprising, at least until we understand the reasons behind it. By analysing the arguments in support of the new "star" of Brazilian architecture, we see how Rogers's impression was in fact exact, yet not motivated by modesty and certainly not by naivety. In the gradual development of a theoretical apparatus capable of holding together the two apparently irreconcilable conceptual universes of "modern" and "national," the celebration of Niemeyer's work as the manifestation of a "national genius"[55] inserted itself perfectly, like a keystone. As is also claimed by Jorge Francisco Liernur, associating Niemeyer to Baroque – which first happened in theory, as we have seen, in regards to the Brazilian pavilion in New York – allowed Costa to solve the equation according to which national and modern architecture, *à la* Le Corbusier, were built on a past that found its highest expression in colonial Baroque.[56] In addition to having enormous repercussions on subsequent historiographical interpretations, starting with *Brazil Builds*, this interpretation found a direct response in the SPHAN's celebration of colonial Baroque (Figure 4.5).

The first text in which Costa addressed this specific topic, the already mentioned "A arquitetura dos Jesuítas no Brasil," was published in 1941 on the *Revista do Serviço do Patrimônio Histórico e Artístico Nacional*, alongside an essay by the German scholar Hanna Levy.[57] Her pioneering commitment in the rehabilitation of Baroque in Brazil coincided, not surprisingly, with the moment in which the modernist intelligentsia within the SPHAN was working on the cause of the "invention of [national] tradition," overcoming any concerns regarding Baroque art in order to be able to dedicate itself, as Ítalo Campofiorito suggests, to the cult of national heroes: Mestre Ataíde in painting, Mestre Valentim in sculpture, and Aleijadinho in sculpture and architecture. In this 1941 essay – perhaps influenced by the writings of Eugeni d'Ors[58] – Costa acknowledges Baroque as the outcome of a renewal process of artistic forms: "a new plastic conception, free from previous assumptions and based on logical and sound principles,"[59] and not expression of a phase of decadence (as he instead claimed in "Razões da nova arquitetura)."[60] However, this transition did not take place without leaving some traces, as the terminology in the text seems to express – like "ornamental delirium," "barbarian accent," and "creative vigour." The intensity of the language explodes in the description of the altarpieces of Santo Alexandre in Belem do Pará.

> Despite the lack in scale and size, the plastic boldness and passionate sense of the conception of the pulpits reveal such fervour, such great transport, that an analysis cannot fall within the limitedness of an objective criticism. The impetus with which the shapes break out from the upper wall indeed has a telluric quality to it, recalling Hindu sculptures carved directly from mountainous slopes.[61]

In these works of art, Costa found the traces of a sort of *Kunstwollen* tending to modify and renew, from within, a given original model; as the symptom of a creative vitality, he perceived its potential to possibly redeem society as a whole, apparently presiding over the re-elaboration process of foreign models.

Trois églises édifiées dans l'État du Minas Gerais : 1. Notre-Dame-du-Rosaire à Ouro Preto ; 2. Saint-François à Sao Joao d'El Rei ; 3 et 4. Deux aspects de la chapelle Saint-François-d'Assise à Pampulha (1943), O. Niemeyer, Architecte, Azulejos de C. Portinari.

EDIFICES RELIGIEUX AU BRÉSIL

Figure 4.5 Church of Nossa Senhora do Rosário and Church of São Francisco de Assis in Ouro Preto (top left); Church of São Francisco de Assis in Pampulha (top right and bottom). From *L'Architecture d'Aujourd'hui*'s special issue on Brazil, August, 1952. © *L'Architecture d'Aujourd'hui*.

> These Paulista altarpieces are not mere clumsy copies but, on the contrary, legitimate "re-creations" and therefore can be considered – along with the splendid and original antropomorphic torchères that are part of it, and with the São Miguel communion bench – as some of the most ancient and authentic expressions of "Brazilian" art, as opposed to most of the Luso-Brazilian pieces of the time that should instead be defined as "Portuguese Brazilian."

It is not difficult to see a reference to the Brazilian pavilion of New York, which had subjected the Corbusian (and Miesian) model to a creative *tour de force* that would be completed a few years later in the Pampulha complex – perhaps the culmination of the alleged neo-Baroque style of Niemeyer's work – which, coincidentally, was created not far from the Baroque masterpieces of Minas Gerais. After the international celebration of Pampulha, all the passages that had been set up so far found a new systematisation, developed between the late 1940s and early 1950s.

Already at the time of his letter to Capanema, sent on the occasion of the Ministry's inauguration, Costa had traced the parable of the "epiphanic revelation" of the genius – "inexplicably unexpressed up until then"[62] – of Niemeyer, first triggered by the presence of Le Corbusier and, therefore, from that moment on, also coinciding with Costa's own vision of the parable of Brazilian architecture itself. In this sense, for Costa, supporting Niemeyer meant supporting his own civilising project and giving a face to his own personal contribution to history, which was beyond what an external observer like Rogers could understand. As mentioned in the previous chapter, among the many merits that Costa accredited himself with in this matter, there was that of having created the conditions for Le Corbusier's "daily cohabitation" with "the exceptional talent of architect Oscar Niemeyer," therefore also suggesting the existence of an elective affinity between Niemeyer and Aleijadinho, as they both had interpreted the grace and vigour of Baroque "curves" and, consequently, of the "national genius."

> In particular, it was our own national genius that expressed itself through the elected personality of this artist, in the same way that it already expressed itself in the 18th century – furthermore, in similar circumstances – through the figure of Antônio Francisco Lisboa, Aleijadinho.
>   Both found a fundamental and already defined new plastic vocabulary, but the grace and force, the refinement and crudeness, the measure and passion in their work combined with such ease and genius that the known elements and shapes transfigured themselves, gaining an unmistakable personal style, to the point of being able to claim that, in this sense, there are many more affinities between Oscar's work – like the admirable Pampulha complex – and Aleijadinho's – like his church of São Francisco de Assis in Ouro Preto – than between Oscar's and Warchavchik's; which – in my opinion – is significant.[63]

The architect makes the comparison between Niemeyer and Aleijadinho in more than one of his writings, starting from his first and only attempt at a historiographical synthesis of Brazilian architecture, commissioned in 1951 by the newspaper *Correio da Manhã* and initially published with the title "Muita construção, alguma arquitetura e um milagre."[64] Here, every moment – from the establishment of the French Mission in Rio and the consequent introduction of the academic style, to the "misunderstanding" of the neo-colonial style and the first appearances of imported modernism – seems to have had contributed to the preparation for the "miracle" of contemporary Brazilian architecture, symbolised by the building for the Ministry of Education and Public Health, in its dual nature as monument to modernity and as beginning of a new creative era. The obscure sense of uncertainty that permeates "Razões" seems to have given way to the triumph of a conquered truth; a univocal and "objective" truth with the shape of Niemeyer's fluent architecture and, at the same time, with the clarity of the Ministry's curtain wall, tropicalised by Portinari's *azulejos* and by Burle Marx's landscape design.[65] These considerations soon began to greatly circulate, especially if we consider that one of the passages of this 1951 text was reported the following year on the pages of *L'Architecture d'Aujourd'hui*.

> [D]espite the innate international character of modern architecture – as also was true for Medieval and Renaissance art – current Brazilian art stands out from the general contemporary production and identifies itself, in the eyes of a foreigner, as a manifestation with local character; not only because it renovates certain solutions that are typical of the country, but mostly because it is the same national personality that is expressed through the individuality of the native artistic genius with the materials, techniques, and plastic vocabulary of our times.[66]

It was perhaps no coincidence that only one year later, in 1950 and 1951 respectively, Costa wrote the preface to Stamo Papadaki's monography on Niemeyer,[67] in which he points him out as the only contemporary architect able to take up the Corbusian challenge of an architecture that was – first and foremost – a plastic expression; and the first of a long series of historical-critical contributions dedicated to Aleijadinho, complied as an introduction to the re-edition of the artist's biography edited by Rodrigo José Ferreira Bretas, already mentioned in the previous paragraph. The surprising correlations between the two tend to blur and confuse their characters, creating a set of circumstances that have mysteriously renewed themselves over the centuries, tracing the outline of that "national personality" so often summoned. Isolating the passages on Aleijadinho in which Costa comments on the "extremely graceful curves of the façade," the "movement of the curves and counter-curves," or on the "refinement, grace, and spontaneity" that the artist was able to infuse the inanimate matter with, we could easily almost assume he is describing the New York pavilion or the buildings in Pampulha. Both Niemeyer and Aleijadinho are presented as strong impulsive characters, capable of "mental agility, unexpected reactions, and apparent contradictions," determined to impose their genius even at the cost of clashes and misunderstandings. Thanks to the emphasis on the two artists' desire for self-assertion and on the inscrutable ways of their creative processes, along with the use of a shared lexicon, the entire range of "elective affinities" becomes so well designed that it appears convincing. It is worth quoting the full description of Aleijadinho's design for a new portal for the church of São Francisco in Ouro Preto.

> You can perceive in the present [drawing], in its entirety, one same spirit and one single hand; you can even perceive a certain specificity in relation to

the general sense of the predominant plastic movement of the composition; a detail of fundamental importance since it is not evident in any other portal, consisting of a slightly nervous contraction of the jambs – at a certain height – as if to help boost the length of the portal beyond the frame, taking a rest above it and its angels, and from here, leaping through the friezes and the medallion up to the crown, from which the movement immediately afterwards slowly expands, accompanying the capricious design of the ribbon and making its way among the other accessory elements of the composition, finally coming to rest on the pedestal and finish in the keystone of the flagpole with the three cherubs.[68]

In recognising this solution for the portal as "typical of Baroque dynamic conception," Costa considers it capable of transmitting "such vibrations and energy to make it truly unique," noting, moreover, how this happened in spite of that "extreme finesse and gentleness" that he had first identified, in 1929, as a symptom of the poor affinity of Aleijadinho's work with the true spirit of Brazilian architecture. The rehabilitation of Aleijadinho's image therefore happens through the "revelation" of Niemeyer's, which allowed an interpretive leap that saw aberration transform into grace, and delirium into creative energy.

Importantly, it is again the appeal to the vitality of a national "creative genius" that animated the arguments responding to the criticisms coming from Europe on the decorative tendencies of Brazilian architecture. In the early 1950s, in response to the accusations of formalism and lack of social content that Max Bill had directed to some of Niemeyer's works,[69] Costa replied:

> As for the chapel [São Francisco in Pampulha] – first work in which all is genius and grace: the parabolic curve of the nave, the way in which the apse is illuminated, the connection of the sacristy with the body of the church, the great ascending articulation from the portico to the bell tower, the perfect integration of the *azulejos* within the apse, of the painting in the altarpiece and of the sculpture in the baptistery – as one could have foreseen, it was qualified as Baroque, in the usual denigrating sense; which is absurd, as this time we are dealing with a Baroque style of legitimate and pure native origin, proving that we do not descend from watchmakers but from creators of Baroque churches. After all, it was precisely here, in Minas Gerais, that these were developed with the most grace and invention.[70]

The construction of an image of Brazil as a country capable of an original artistic production – and, in some ways, a pioneering one – was the battle that Costa and many others of his generation were engaged in, fighting the other image of the country that was widespread at the beginning of the century: that of a marginal country, only capable of feeding on second-hand cultural products. The challenge therefore consisted in erasing an inferiority complex from history and reaffirming the country's dignity as a modern nation with a well-defined identity, despite its young age. In this sense, nothing seemed more appropriate than to glorify the values of the architecture that Niemeyer had become interpreter of, with its apparent spontaneity, its extreme ease in assimilating the legacy of the masters, and its sophisticated vitality. A vitality that – filtered by

Eugeni d'Ors's interpretation of Baroque's impetuous, irrational, and expressive spirit – seemed to refer to mysterious correlations with the golden era of the colonial 18th century, when the foundations of the nation-state were laid with the first movements for independence.

Brazilian houses

The Costian narrative slowly developed and refined the attempt to bring apparently irreconcilable polarities together in a new synthesis. Classic and Baroque, static and dynamic, monumental and vernacular, modern and traditional, and national and international: these are only a few of the main contradicting pairings that run through his theoretical research and, partly, his architectural production. The articulation between these categories always had the purpose of defining precise cultural strategies; while anonymous popular architecture proposed the general principles within which to act, thanks to a century-old process of improvement and settling of formal repertoires and construction methods, the work of the main artistic individuals was required to point toward new expressive horizons, taking a hold on the conscience of the masses and, at the very most, pushing the already traced principles to the point of renewing them from within.

Costa chose to hold an ambivalent stance between these two positions. While he seemed to have delegated the task of shaping the official face of modern Brazil to Niemeyer and other young modernists, he did not relinquish the opportunity to give shape – especially around the 1950s – to numerous monumental programmes,[71] finally imposing his participation in the competition for the new capital of the country. At the same time, he developed a very original production in the field of residential architecture, since – given that it was less subjected to the didactic intentions of public works and more representative programmes – it became a privileged field for the experimentation of the "inclusive" vocation that ran through his theoretical vision and that – albeit with a limited number of buildings – marked an extremely rich and complex design period.

The need to combine modern architecture with the search for an ideal "Brazilian house" is one that ran throughout this entire production period. As we have mentioned before, Costa had been trying already since the 1930s to adapt strictly modernist principles to distribution patterns that suited local conditions. This is proved – in the Casas sem dono, in the second version of the Casa Fontes, etc. – by the abundance of open or semi-open spaces such as patios, verandas, and balconies; by the presence of artisanal *redes* (hammocks) and colonial furnishings; by the use of solar screening systems that show an attention to the harsh tropical climate and to ways of living that are not always compatible with the transparency and permeability that are typical of modernism; and by the use of diaphragm elements – panels, curtains, simple pillars or furnishings – helping to specify the vocation of the spaces rather than properly separate them. A relaxed horizontality and a calm and serene spaciousness qualify these first autonomous experiments of rationalist nature, anticipating the evocative atmosphere of ancient colonial dwellings that would characterise the houses of Costa's maturity.

As has been extensively described, after the period of his great public projects for Gustavo Capanema, a fundamental transitional moment of Costa's career coincided, in 1937, with his involvement in the SPHAN. From this moment on, the time spent

A strategy of mediation 117

measuring himself with interventions on historical contexts naturally brought to subtly changing the ways in which his much-sought-after integration of modernity and tradition could have taken shape. The almost liberating role that the SPHAN activity played on Costa's design choices – less and less inhibited in their re-appropriations of tradition and increasingly based on sophisticated and precocious regionalism – sealed the architect's definitive expressive maturity and brought to the development of a completely personal language, far from Niemeyer's structural emphasis and languid graphic gestures, as well as from Le Corbusier's vigorous formal syntheses.

In the Saavedra (Figures 4.6 and 4.7), Hungria Machado, Marinho de Azevedo, and Paes de Carvalho houses – built between 1942 and 1944 around Rio – the theoretical symbiosis between vernacular Luso-Brazilian architecture and new architecture found a concrete realisation in the more frequent use of traditional construction and architectural elements, which seem to have helped smooth out the strict modernist vocabulary of his more radical 1930 projects. These houses were the result of a finally completed process of hybridisation: the walls – almost always plastered – regain their consistency, only dematerialising in correspondence with the diaphragm elements acting as filters to patios and verandas, and therefore usually porous and permeable to help let in air and light. Sloping rooftops in traditional tile replace flat roofs and canopies, while pillars with rectangular cross-sections – similar to those of the *pau a pique* structures – replace the classic *pilotis* with circular cross-sections. Glazed windowed façades

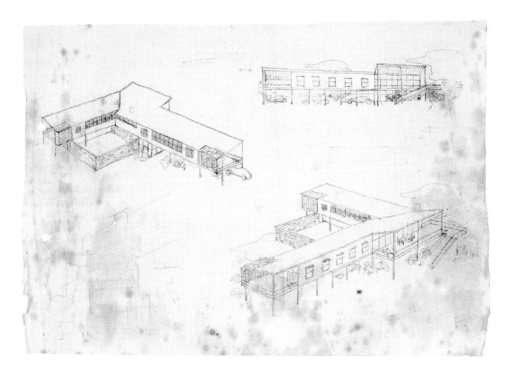

Figure 4.6 Lucio Costa, drawings for the Casa Saavedra, Petrópolis. Perspective views of the exterior, 1942. Casa de Lucio Costa.

118 A strategy of mediation

present a variable geometry of fixtures and typical Venetian blinds; other windows shun uniformity and are characterised by different shapes, opening systems, light-filtering qualities, and their relation with the outside: *muxarabi, gelosías, janelas de rótula*,[72] and *janelas-conversadeiras*[73] are only some of the many motifs of a repertoire belonging to the Iberian chromosomes of the Brazilian people, lending themselves to effectively filter and "tame" the blinding light of the southern hemisphere, as well as preserve a continuity with the traditional lifestyles. In the same way, balconies, *treliças*, eaves, ornamental ceramics and *azulejos*, carved and painted wooden handrails, period furnishings, and entirely frescoed walls – like the one created by Cândido Portinari in Casa Saavedra – also reappear. In the earlier projects of the 1930s, all these elements had been subjected to a process of abstraction or were put in contrast with clean volumes and ribbon windows. Now, they appear completely at ease in the line-up of heterogeneous references that the houses of these more recent years can be assimilated to. The same interior spaces each present different qualities and characters, thanks to the presence of patios, verandas, and *treliças*. This came to generate a complex relation – between the various house environments and between the inside and outside – that, while not denying the modern spatial continuity, tends – as Guilherme Wisnik notices – to explore the intervals and the identity of the individual parts more than the rational coherency of the whole.[74]

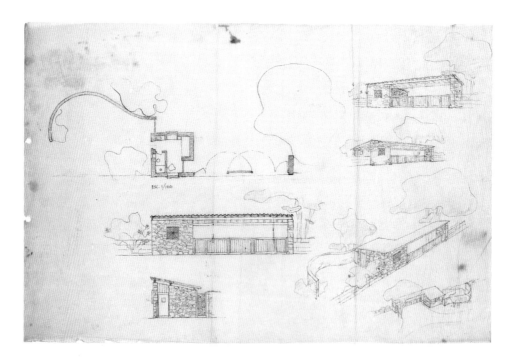

Figure 4.7 Lucio Costa, drawings for the Casa Saavedra, Petrópolis. Plan and perspective views of the annexes, 1942. Casa de Lucio Costa.

A strategy of mediation 119

Far from a nostalgic and reactionary return to the neo-colonial style, this renewed freedom in handling the language of tradition rather marked a definitive break from the ghosts of historicism. The most profound sense of the conquered identification with the technical and expressive means of his age ultimately resided, for Costa, in the possibility of continuity more than in the need for innovation. The selection of what still lent itself to be re-appropriated – and the ways of its transposition and re-actualisation in the present, and combination with other reference models – constituted the territory within which the architect was called to make his choices, with technical awareness, artistic sensibility, and respect of the context, programme, and resources.

The result was an architecture with a marked tectonic character, presenting an articulated and asymmetrical layout in some cases, and a more compact and collected one in others; rigorous in its construction logic and accurate in its details, sober and welcoming, harmonious in its proportions, fitted with refined tactile and chromatic qualities, measured and almost intentionally rigid in its volumetric configuration; an architecture that made extensive use of local materials and modern ones, favouring orthogonal and horizontal dimensions, stretching out into the landscape and aspiring to take root even when suspended,[75] an architecture that shunned a synthetic and comprehensive perception, favouring the dimension of intimate pathways and light variations and direct dialogue with the vegetation. An architecture ultimately conceived to be used, as already hoped for in the 1920s – "in harmony with the temperament of its inhabitants [...] finally, a house that has a soul"[76] – and yet, somehow, also nostalgic and imbued with atmospheres and reminiscences of the past.[77]

The themes and methods that were developed for these houses were further explored, albeit with greater figurative character, in two important projects developed from the early 1940s: the Park Hotel São Clemente in Nova Friburgo, and the residential complex in Parque Guinle in Rio, which was completed only in the mid-1950s.[78] In the case of the small hotel, which was built within a park with careful attention to resources, the integration with the landscape represented an important design inspiration (Figure 4.8).

Taking advantage of a natural slope to help hide the accessory service quarters from sight, Costa laid out a horizontal block – of two storeys and with a wooden frame structure – parallel to the sloping ground, with two smaller blocks on the north side containing the distribution systems. The ground floor, open and permeable, was destined to common areas, while the first floor, partially suspended on *pilotis*, was reserved for the bedrooms. The south-facing side, from where the bedrooms and common areas look out, formally presents the regular rhythm of *pilotis* on the ground floor, characterised by an alternation of full and empty spaces, and one of window surface and verandas. Here, wood stands in for the reinforced concrete, dialoguing with the raw stone of the inner walls and base, and with the large windows overlooking the park. The south-facing glazed façade outlines a zig-zag path between the outer row of *pilotis*, creating a sort of invitation to the veranda and exemplifying the separation between load-bearing elements and elements that are supported. Here, Costa seems to have wanted to prove how modern spatiality could be devised with the exclusive use of traditional materials.[79]

In the three residential buildings in the Parque Guinle[80] – the only ones constructed of a greater complex destined to the Carioca bourgeoisie, which was supposed to present six multi-storey apartment buildings – the six-storey blocks are

120 A strategy of mediation

Figure 4.8 View of Lucio Costa's Park Hotel São Clemente, Nova Friburgo. From *L'Architecture d'Aujourd'hui*'s special issue on Brazil, September 1947. © *L'Architecture d'Aujourd'hui*.

suspended on top of *pilotis*, and arranged in an amphitheatre layout at the edges of the park (Figure 4.9).

In response to the unfavourable exposure to the west, and to the need of disencumbering the façades overlooking the park, Costa designed a façade in which two solar screening systems – *cobogó* and *brise-soleil* – alternated themselves at irregular intervals. This way, he obtained a surface that has an almost pictorial chromatic quality, hiding the presence and effect of the different depth loggias. While the loggias and apartments, on the park side, are shielded from direct sunlight – nothing further from the conceptual transparency of the Ministry's *brise-soleils* – the penetration of natural light and the view of the park from the inside are filtered through a diaphragm that is sensitive to the climatic and landscape conditions. The loggia presents, at least in its design intentions, a profound connection with Luso-Brazilian tradition. Costa himself explained how the choice of the distributive solutions of the apartments had been guided by the desire

> to bring back [...] a feature of the traditional Brazilian house: the two verandas, the social one and the domestic one; two spaces, one in front to welcome guests, and one in the back, connected to the dining room, bedrooms, and services.[81]

A strategy of mediation 121

Figure 4.9 View of Lucio Costa's Parque Guinle residential complex, Rio de Janeiro. Casa de Lucio Costa.

Costa explained this distribution scheme as a hybridisation of native dwellings (*oca*) with the houses of the first colonisers (*rancho de feitoria*). Although this solution was only partially successful in the Parque Guinle apartments,[82] it is symptomatic of the desire to make contemporary lifestyles compatible with traditional ones.

It is no coincidence that, in *Registro de uma vivência*, the residences of the following years, almost all intended for family or friends – the apartment for his daughter Maria Elisa in Leblon (1963), the three houses for the poet Thiago de Mello in Barreirinha in the Amazonas (1978–1987), the two villas built in Gávea in the 1980s, Costa-Moreira Penna[83] and Duvivier-Byington – are presented in direct sequence with those of the 1940s; despite the years' distance, the same spirit seems to hold together – in a process of gradual emancipation from modernist canons – these domestic architectures, which were studied in relation to the site conditions and to the specific client personality.[84] The house for Edgard Duvivier, concealed from the street by a low white wall, also takes advantage of the natural slope, articulating itself in height, reaching out toward the view of the Corcovado on which look the grand windows of the living room, the horizontal windows of the dining room, and the private verandas of the bedrooms. The route though the social area and the one through the more

Figure 4.10 View of the *muxarabi* in the patio of Lucio Costa's Casa Costa-Moreira Penna, Rio de Janeiro. Casa de Lucio Costa.

intimate family areas follow the natural descent of the slope, starting from the entrance garden and ending with the more informal one at the foot of the climb. Similarly, in the nearby residence for his daughter Helena Costa, the rooms of the house are arranged around an inner patio connected to the dining room, qualifying it with the traditional role of domestic veranda (Figure 4.10); whereas, the winter garden onto which the large living room looks holds the traditional role of public veranda. Revisiting traditional houses was a central theme in Costa's idea of residence, as is the case for these two-faced houses respectively declined in a vertical and horizontal layout. Costa – by now octogenarian – seems to have entrusted the testament of his long research to the Costa-Moreira Penna house. While the main façade – of vague Palladian inspiration – shows a suspended and symmetrical rationalist loggia – and a partially and asymmetrically hollow volume on the ground floor – the secondary façade, well planted in the ground, articulates itself in an informal design of verandas, balconies, loggias, and terraces; grand windows alternate with *janelas de rótula* and vertical embrasures; the white volume is surmounted by a roof in traditional tiles and the interiors present a mix of modern and colonial furnishings, panels of *azulejos*, *treliça* diaphragms, and white-plastered lowered-vault ceilings.[85] As Sérgio Ferro claims, Costa works "like a quality eclectic architect," seeking "what is best"[86] in the colonial style. In a small note commenting on the project in *Registro*, Costa says he believes to have solved the almost 100-year-old conundrum, defining his solution as an "openly contemporary house, but with a sense of *saudade* of our past. A Brazilian house – something the neo-colonial style has failed to obtain."[87]

Notes

1 For more information, see José Pessôa, ed., *Lucio Costa: documentos de trabalho* (Rio de Janeiro: Edições do Patrimônio-IPHAN, 1999), which collects many of the scientific opinions elaborated by Costa over the years, together with other important documents regarding his activity at the Patrimônio; and Gaia Piccarolo, *Un progetto di mediazione. Lucio Costa fra tutela del patrimonio e nuova architettura* (Santarcangelo di Romagna: Maggioli, 2014).
2 Manfredo Tafuri, *Teorie e storia dell'architettura* (Bari: Laterza, 1973; 1st edn 1968), 66.
3 In general, the inclusion of these assets within the heritage was justified in function of their artistic quality, first of all, and, second, for their historical and social relevance; the assets excluded from these categories, and generally defined as mere artistic or architectural "curiosities," were simply worth being inventoried.
4 According to Costa, neo-classical or eclectic buildings generally did not deserve the qualification as works of art, and therefore were also undeserving of any subsequent constraint, although he often opted for their preservation. There were, however, some exceptions, like the house of Antonio Virzi in Rua do Russel or the house in Rua São Clemente in Rio.
5 Costa, "Problema mal posto," in Pessôa, ed., *Documentos de trabalho*, 277 (document of 19 November 1972, in response to the opinion of Paulo Santos).
6 An emblematic case is that of the neo-colonial Solar Monjope, of his former mentor and then opponent José Mariano Filho, defined as "a false testimony, an example of how a Brazilian house has never been." Nonetheless, in a scientific report of 1973 Costa suggested its protection on a federal – not national – level by virtue of its privileged position within the landscape of the side of the Corcovado mountain, and as the result of "a dedicated and generous personal effort." Pessôa, ed., *Documentos de trabalho*, 283–284. Unfortunately this would not prevent its demolition in the same year. See Fernando

Atique, "De 'casa manifesto' a 'espaço de desafetos'; os impactos culturais, políticos e urbanos verificados na trajetória do Solar Monjope (Rio, anos 20 – anos 70)," *Estudos Históricos Rio de Janeiro* 29, no. 57 (January–April 2016): 215–234.
7 Costa often uses the term *desafogo* (outlet) in his opinions, intended – in a hygienist sense – as an intervention aimed at favouring the circulation of light and air; put simply, aimed at favouring "urban salubrity." This is an argument that Costa seems to borrow from the functionalist urbanism of the Athens Charter, rooted in the relation between past and present that it advocates.
8 José Pessôa, "Lucio Costa e o Rio de Janeiro," in Ana Luiza Nobre et al., eds, *Um modo de ser moderno. Lucio Costa e a crítica contemporânea* (São Paulo: Cosac & Naify, 2003), 146–158; 151.
9 For Ouro Preto, in particular, at the end of the 1950s Costa prescribed a series of works whose utopian and anachronistic objective was to harmonise where possible – and otherwise camouflage – any dissonant element with respect to the colonial-era urban fabric.
10 Lia Motta, "A SPHAN em Ouro Preto, uma história de conceitos e critérios," *Revista do Patrimônio Histórico e Artístico Nacional*, no. 22 (1987): 108–122; 110.
11 In this regard, see Cristiane Souza Gonçalves, "Experimentações em Diamantina. Um estudo sobre a atuação do SPHAN no conjunto urbano tombado 1938–1967," PhD dissertation, FAU-USP, 2010.
12 This was an approach that was contrary to the criteria identified in the *Conclusions* of the 1931 Athens Charter, which invited to resist the temptation of leading the monument toward a stylistic unity, respecting its historical stratifications. See Gustavo Giovannoni, "La Conferenza Internazionale di Atene pel restauro dei monumenti," *Bollettino d'Arte* XXV, no. IX (March 1932): 408–419; 416.
13 It is no coincidence that Costa himself proposed the "preventive" protection of the Igreja de São Francisco in Pampulha, which risked being demolished despite the fact that its construction had begun only five years earlier. See Pessôa, ed., *Documentos de trabalho*, 67–68.
14 The following year, in 1948, the same fate of the Pampulha church fell onto the Ministry of Education, officially registered at the request of the architect Alcides da Rocha Miranda in the *Livro do Tombo de Belas Artes* only three years after its inauguration. The constraint was extended to the entire block on which the Ministry insisted, as an emblematic example of the modernist relationship between building and city, as well as a portion of urban public space enhanced by landscape and sculptural works well-integrated in the architectural structure: a sort of privileged *enclave* in which modernist utopia was translated into actual built reality.
15 See paragraph "A new humanism," Chapter 5, this volume.
16 Accurately accounted for in the descriptive report delivered upon Costa's return from the trip, in Pessôa, ed., *Documentos de trabalho*, 21–42.
17 Costa to Le Corbusier, Rio de Janeiro, 14 April 1939. FLC, I3-3-76. In reporting the experience to Le Corbusier, Costa defines the collective residential blocks arranged around a central core as "'radiant' villages." Even in other sites, Costa accurately describes the urban organisation of the missionary villages and highlights their modernity: the "collective housing blocks" composed by the aggregation of residential "cells" were surrounded by a porticoed passageway. Every village was reasonably spaced from the others in order to form an organic whole. Also see Costa, "Os Sete Povos das Missões," *Registro de uma vivência* (São Paulo: Empresa das Artes, 1995), 488–494.
18 That of São Miguel is considered a pioneering example of regional museum, at an international level. Among other references, see Carlos Eduardo Dias Comas, ed., *Lucio Costa e as missões: um museu em São Miguel* (Porto Alegre: PROPAR-UFRGS, 2007).
19 Pessôa, ed., *Documentos de trabalho*, 39.
20 In order to ensure a full understanding of the meaning of the ruins, Costa suggested recalling the original life of the missionary villages through a series of educational panels that explained – "in an appealing and objective form, always keeping in mind a popular use" – the way in which "the social life of the community" took place. Pessôa, ed., *Documentos de trabalho*, 39–40.

21 The *Brazil Builds* exhibition catalogue earned Costa a specific mention: "The architect of SPHAN's various restorations and constructions is Lucio Costa, well known for his work in modern architecture. It is refreshing to find a society of this kind which realizes that only honestly contemporary design is suitable for such a museum. The simple glass-walled building provides a pleasantly non-competitive background for the brilliantly arranged sculpture." Philip Goodwin, *Brazil Builds: Architecture Old and New 1652–1942* (New York: Museum of Modern Art, 1943), 42.
22 On the Hotel de Ouro Preto see in particular Carlos Eduardo Dias Comas, "O passado mora ao lado: Lúcio Costa e o projeto do Grande Hotel de Ouro Preto, 1938/40," *ARQ-texto* 1, no. 2 (January–June 2002b): 18–31; and Lauro Cavalcanti, *Moderno e brasileiro. A história de uma nova linguagem na arquitetura (1930–60)* (Rio de Janeiro: Jorge Zahar, 2006), 109–120.
23 Mello Franco de Andrade to Washington de Araújo Dias, 29 August 1938, cit. in Cavalcanti, *Moderno e brasileiro*, 110.
24 José de Souza Reis's interview by Teresinha Marinho, 7 December 1982, kindly made available to me by the staff of the ACI-RJ.
25 Specifically, the SPHAN came to form two groups, respectively supporting the proposal for the functional conversion of an existing building – put forth by Renato Soreiro – or one of the Niemeyerian variants.
26 José Mariano Filho, one of the most heated opponents of Niemeyer's project, accused Costa of having joined the SPHAN "under the protection of old friends" and of exercising the "modest role of dictator of the architecture department." Mariano Filho, "Um caso de autophagia," *Diário de Notícias*, 14 May 1939.
27 Costa to Mello Franco de Andrade, n.d. [1938], ACI-RJ, "Série Obras, Hotel de Ouro Preto." The draft copy is held at the Casa de Lucio Costa: CLC, VI A 01-02225.
28 As stated by the Athens Charter, "the whole of the past is not, by definition, entitled to last forever; it is advisable to choose wisely that which must be respected"; and "the great lesson of history" is that "never has a return to the past been recorded, never has man retraced his own steps." Le Corbusier, *The Athens Charter* (New York: Grossman Publishers, 1960), 86–88.
29 The *pau a pique*, also called *taipa de mão*, is a traditional construction technique consisting of vertical and horizontal boards made of wood (or other material such as bamboo) and filled with clay; the resulting walls can subsequently be plastered. It is worth noting that Costa used pillars with square cross-sections instead of *pilotis* in some of his houses of the 1940s, whereas the *pilotis* in Niemeyer's original project for the Ouro Preto hotel (the drawings of which are held at the ACI-RJ) have round cross-sections.
30 Costa to Mello Franco de Andrade, n.d. [1938].
31 Note that in the following projects for the historical centre of Diamantina, Niemeyer would no longer resort to an "adapted-modern" style as in the case of the hotel of Ouro Preto.
32 Costa, "Documentação necessária," *Revista do Serviço do Patrimônio Histórico e Artístico Nacional*, no. 1 (1937): 31–39. Henceforth quoted from Alberto Xavier, ed., *Lúcio Costa: sôbre arquitetura* (Porto Alegre: Editora UniRitter, 2007, 1st edn 1962), 86–94.
33 This was a programme that reflected the objectives set by Mello Franco at the beginning of the first issue of the magazine. These objectives consisted in "spreading the knowledge of the artistic and historical values that Brazil possesses, committedly contributing to their study"; and, at the same time, engaging in the training and formation of scholars and specialists. Mello Franco de Andrade, "Programa," *Revista do Serviço do Patrimônio Histórico e Artístico Nacional*, no. 1 (1937): 3–4.
34 Costa, "O Aleijadinho e a arquitetura tradicional", *O Jornal*, 1929 (special issue on Minas Gerais), reported in Xavier, ed., *Sôbre arquitetura*, 12–16.
35 As mentioned by Otávio Leonídio, the three fundamental volumes inaugurating a historiographical tradition aimed at considering the theme of Brazil's formation – a tradition to which Costa's historical and critical writings can also be traced – are *Casa-grande & senzala* by Gilberto Freyre (1933), *Raízes do Brasil* by Sérgio Buarque de Holanda (1936), and *Formação do Brasil contemporâneo* by Caio Prado Jr. (1942).

Leonídio Ribeiro, "Lucio Costa, historiador?" in Ana Luiza Nobre et al., eds, *Um modo de ser moderno*, 181–189.
36 Costa, "Documentação necessária," 86.
37 Costa, "Documentação necessária," 92.
38 Le Corbusier himself, in 1911, noticed windows that were wider than high running across the entire length of the walls in the vernacular architecture of Tarnovo (Bulgaria) during that *Voyage d'Orient* he had undertaken under the influence of William Ritter. See Le Corbusier, *Le Voyage d'Orient* (Paris: Les Éditions Forces Vives, 1966).
39 See Francesco Passanti, "The Vernacular, Modernism, and Le Corbusier," *Journal of the Society of Architectural Historians* 56, no. 4 (December, 1997): 438–451. In the text *Précisions sur un etat présent de l'architecture et de l'urbanisme*, which Costa must have known well, Le Corbusier shows a strong aesthetic propensity for vernacular architecture, as well as a tendency toward assimilating the popular suburb housings of the grand South-American metropolises – as Liernur sharply notes – to modern objects of serial production, striking examples of the "new 'lyricism.'" See Jorge Francisco Liernur, "Un nuovo mondo per lo spirito nuovo: le scoperte dell'America Latina da parte della cultura architettonica del XX secolo," *Zodiac*, no. 8 (1992): 104.
40 Giuseppe Pagano, in Italy, is one of many examples. See Pagano and Guarniero Daniel, *Architettura rurale italiana* (Milano: Hoepli, 1936).
41 Costa, "Notas sobre a evolução do mobiliário luso-brasileiro," *Revista do Serviço do Patrimônio Histórico e Artístico Nacional*, no. 3 (1939): 149–162; 159.
42 Costa, "A arquitetura dos Jesuítas no Brasil," *Revista do Serviço do Patrimônio Histórico e Artístico Nacional*, no. 5 (1941): 9–100.
43 Costa, "A arquitetura dos Jesuítas no Brasil," 54–63.
44 In August 1948, the director of SPHAN requested the minister of Education to finance Costa's first trip to Portugal, "to proceed with studies that have turned out to be necessary in order to elucidate the capital points of Portuguese influence in the formation and evolution of the plastic arts in Brazil." Mello Franco de Andrade to Clemente Mariani Bittencourt, 12 August 1948. ACI-RJ, LC V01(01). In the early 1950s, other trips would follow this first one. For more in-depth information on the relationship with Portugal, see my previous writings on the subject: Gaia Piccarolo, "Lucio Costa's Luso-Brazilian Routes: Recalibrating 'Center' and 'Periphery'," in Patricio Del Real and Helen Gyger, eds, *Latin American Modern Architectures: Ambiguous Territories*, (London/New York: Routledge, 2012), 33–52; "Across the Atlantic Back and Forth. Lucio Costa's Cultural Peregrinations between Brazil and Portugal," in Ana Esteban Maluenda et al., eds, *Rutas ibero-americanas. Contactos e intercambios en la arquitectura del siglo XX/Rotas de intercâmbio na arquitetura do século XX/Exchange Paths in Twentieth Century Architecture* (Madrid: Mairea Libros, 2017), 15–38. See also: Maria Elisa Costa and José Pessôa, eds, *A arquitetura portuguesa no traço de Lucio Costa. Bloquinhos de Portugal* (Rio de Janeiro: Casa de Lucio Costa, 2012).
45 Costa, "O objetivo principal da excurção através das províncias portuguesas ...," ACI-RJ, PLC/V02(01/4). The report would only be published in 1995, in *Registro de uma vivência*.
46 Costa, "A arquitetura brasileira colonial," in *Proceedings of the International Colloquium on Luso-Brazilian Studies* (Nashville, TN: The Vanderbilt University Press, 1953), 121–122.
47 Costa, "A arquitetura de Antônio Francisco Lisboa revelada no risco original da Capela Franciscana de São João del Rei," in Rodrigo José Ferreira Bretas, *Antônio Francisco Lisboa: o Aleijadinho* (Rio de Janeiro: Publicações da DPHAN, 1951), 11–21; the following contribution, entitled "Risco original de Antônio Francisco Lisboa" and issued in the *Revista do Patrimônio Histórico e Artístico Nacional*, was published in 1969.
48 This rediscovery is mainly due to the French art historian Germain Bazin, who published – between 1956 and 1958 – the two volumes *L'architecture religieuse baroque au Brésil*, and – in 1963 – *Aleijadinho et la sculture baroque au Brésil*. Shortly after, several studies on the subject also appeared in the United States.

49 Costa, "Antônio Francisco Lisboa, o Aleijadinho," *Revista do Patrimônio Histórico e Artístico Nacional*, no. 18 (1978): 529 (conceived as a script for a short film on the work of the artist).
50 Costa, *Registro*, 517.
51 Costa, *Registro*, 451–454. The text was conceived as "symmetrical" to another text entitled "Tradição ocidental." In this last text, Costa reviews the architectural styles from the times of ancient Greece to the Baroque period, within which he also includes Brazilian colonial art, thus highlighting its integration in Western art.
52 From the Trás-os-Montes region.
53 Costa, *Registro*, 498–514.
54 Peter Craymer, Walter Gropius, Hiroshi Ohye, Max Bill, and Ernesto Nathan Rogers, "Report on Brazil," *The Architectural Review* 116, no. 694 (October, 1954): 234–250; 240.
55 Already in 1924, Costa spoke in Hegelian terms of "spirit of an individual people," expressing the concept of nation as a spiritual entity (Costa, "A alma dos nossos lares. Porque é erronea a orientação da architectura do Rio: fala-nos um verdadeiro e commovido artista," *A Noite*, 19 March 1924). The same idealistic origin belongs to the idea – repeatedly expressed from the late 1940s – of the existence of a "national personality" (or "national genius," "native artistic genius") seemingly presiding over the evolutionary process of artistic forms.
56 Jorge Francisco Liernur, "*The South American Way*. El 'milagro' brasileño, los Estados Unidos y la Segunda Guerra Mundial (1939–1943)," *Block*, no. 4 (1999): 23–41.
57 Costa, "A arquitetura dos Jesuítas no Brasil," and Hanna Levy, "A propósito de três teorias sobre o barroco," *Revista do Serviço do Patrimônio Histórico e Artístico Nacional*, no. 5 (1941): 9–100, 259–284.
58 While, at this time, Costa limited himself to referring to those "most recent interesting theories that attribute greater capacity to the Baroque phenomenon, defining it as a permanent anti-classic attitude," d'Ors would be explicitly quoted – as we will see in Chapter 5 – in the 1952 essay "Considerações sobre arte contemporânea."
59 Costa, "A arquitetura dos Jesuítas no Brasil," 11.
60 In "Razões da nova arquitetura" (published in 1936), Costa identifies German art with a "not in the least recommendable Baroque emphasis," which was associated to a sense of "ornamental fury," "licentiousness," and even "plastic corruption," barely sparing Brazilian Baroque as it was diluted in its excesses by the sobriety of Latin and Mediterranean tradition.
61 Costa, "A arquitetura dos Jesuítas no Brasil," 66.
62 Costa to Capanema, 3 October 1945. CPDOC, GC b Costa, L., 1-A.
63 Costa, "Carta depoimento," in Xavier, ed., *Sôbre arquitetura*, 123–128; 125.
64 Costa, "Muita construção, alguma arquitetura e um milagre," *Correio da Manhã* (15 June 1951), published as a separate volume with the title *Arquitetura brasileira. Depoimento de um arquiteto carioca* (Rio de Janeiro: Cadernos de Cultura do Serviço de Documentação do Ministério de Educação e Saúde, n. 5, 1952). Reported in Xavier, ed., *Sôbre arquitetura*, 169–201.
65 See Carlos Eduardo Dias Comas, "Brazil Builds e a bossa barroca: notas sobre a singularização da arquitetura moderna brasileira." http://docomomo.org.br/wp-content/uploads/2016/01/Carlos-Eduardo-Comas.pdf.
66 Costa, "Imprévu et importance de la contribution des architectes brésiliens au développement actuel de l'architecture contemporaine," *L'Architecture d'Aujourd'hui*, no. 42–43 (August, 1952): 4–7; 7.
67 Costa, Foreword to Stamo Papadaki, *The Work of Oscar Niemeyer* (New York: Reinhold Publishing Corporation, 1950), 1–3.
68 Costa, "A arquitetura de Antônio Francisco Lisboa …," 540.
69 In 1953, the magazine *Manchete* published an interview to Max Bill – "Max Bill, o inteligente iconoclasta," *Manchete*, no. 60 (13 June 1953) – partially reported in Xavier, ed., *Sôbre arquitetura*, 252–254. Also see the aforementioned "Report on Brazil," *The Architectural Review*, 238–239.
70 Costa, "Oportunidade perdida," *Manchete*, no. 63 (4 July 1953). Reported in Xavier, ed., *Sôbre arquitetura*, 258–259.

128 *A strategy of mediation*

71 In this regard, see Chapter 5, this volume.
72 These are all examples of windows screened by wooden grates, producing a perforated surface that allows light to penetrate while also shielding the view and allowing some privacy. They are typical of Islamic and Iberian architecture. They are also very widespread in Portugal, therefore also characterising the architecture of Brazil. The *muxarabi* differs from the other types of screened windows because it protrudes from the wall surface.
73 These are windows equipped, on the inner side, with two benches placed one in front of the other.
74 Guilherme Wisnik, *Lucio Costa* (São Paulo: Cosac & Naify, 2001), 38.
75 Apart for the Hungria Machado house, which is located in Rio and is based on an introverted layout arranged around a patio, the other residences we are dealing with are immersed in the natural landscape.
76 Costa, "A alma dos nossos lares."
77 Sophia Telles notes how, in Costa, "the apparent identity between colonial constructive logic and that of the modern project fails to sublimate the fragile horizon of a past that does not impose itself if not as an exercise of a more affective character and, precisely for this reason, always within the limits of a certain nostalgia." Sophia da Silva Telles, "Lucio Costa: monumentalidade e intimismo," *Novos Estudos*, no. 25 (October, 1989): 75–94; 88.
78 Both are commissioned by César Guinle, son of the entrepreneur Eduardo Guinle.
79 Despite the significant relations with the slightly older Hotel de Ouro Preto – designed by Niemeyer under Costa's supervision – the two buildings show substantial differences in authorial approaches. The bedroom floor is paradigmatic in this case: Niemeyer treats it as a sculptural volume in which the loggias are carved out, subjecting the traditional elements to a process of abstraction that makes them almost unrecognisable, whereas the Costian poetic seems instead to indulge in the use of vernacular elements. Costa also designed, for the same site, the never-constructed Capela do Cônego, which presented a butterfly roof and a spindly bell tower articulating the rough-stone volume, giving the architecture a modest and rustic tone similar to that of the hotel.
80 On the complex of Parque Guinle, published in various international magazines, see Ana Luiza Nobre, "Guinle Park: a Proto-Superquadra," in FarOs el-Dahdah, ed., *Lucio Costa: Brasilia's Superquadra* (Munich: Prestel, 2005), 33–40.
81 Costa, *Registro*, 212.
82 Costa claims that "the agents failed to sell the idea; this way, the opportunity to recover this still-valid distribution scheme, and re-establish the bond, was lost" (Costa, *Registro*, 212).
83 Designed for his daughter Helena and her husband Luiz Fernando Gabaglia Moreira Penna.
84 This design attitude confirms the already recorded tendency to avoid or shy away from sacrificing – to use Comas's words – "usefulness to rhetorical impulse." This lack of formalism also connotes Costa's work method, as he often entrusted the construction phase of his design solutions to his collaborators already from the early 1940s.
85 Sophia Telles's reaction in front of the house of Helena Costa, "all white and collected with its *muxarabi*," is one of admiration for Costa's freedom in re-proposing the "calm and peaceful lines of the colonial house" and its "severe, robust, and massive character." Sophia da Silva Telles, "Pequena crônica," *AU, arquitetura e urbanismo* VII, no. 38 (October–November 1991): 171.
86 Sérgio Ferro, *Arquitetura e trabalho livre*, ed. Pedro Fiori Arantes (São Paulo: Cosac & Naify, 2006), 313.
87 Costa, *Registro*, 226.

5 Shaping the true Machine Age
Art, city, landscape

Parisian experiences

At the beginning of the 1950s, at the height of the international enthusiasm for the new "phenomenon" of Brazilian architecture, Costa began a new professional phase, marked by the dilemma – to which he was destined to find no solution – between his acquired international notoriety and his tendency to shy away – as he was prone to do – from the consequences that such public visibility necessarily entailed.

As evidenced by various letters and documents dating back to 1950, Costa never missed an opportunity to point out – in response to the numerous tributes that came from the most disparate sources – how his contribution to the unexpected success of Brazilian national architecture was largely "symbolic," and that it was his name that benefited from the international notoriety "of our architects of modern spirit," "whose work advanced the prestige of Brazilian architecture abroad,"[1] and not vice versa. In a letter addressed to André Bloc presumably in the same period, Costa attributed the "limited character" of his participation "in the development of contemporary architecture" to the fact that his professional activity was "practically nil."

> I do not practice in any studio, I do not have an office and I do not accept assignments. Buildings constructed under my direction are very rare and always due to special circumstances. It is therefore to our architects of modern spirit and to Le Corbusier that we must turn to directly.
>
> I am by nature conservative, and I am rather concerned with our ancient buildings. If I approve and participate in the common effort aimed at social and artistic renewal, it is because the sick injustice of our present day weighs on my heart and I passionately desire a return to a normal life, founded, once and for all, on a legitimate social state (intrinsically popular, as a necessary consequence of the new techniques of production and mass distribution), so that the architectural style of the time – following a period of cultural impoverishment, which seems inevitable – may eventually evolve, though varied in intentions, forms, and processes, under an architectural invocation of the same spirit, as in the great artistic cycles of the past.[2]

This passage contains an effective synthesis of many of the thematic issues that will be at the centre of his theoretical reflection in the coming decades. For the moment, however, we will concentrate on the first statement, in which Costa dismisses his professional activity as "practically nil." This was not the case, exactly; Costa did reject more assignments than the ones he accepted – not only related to design projects, but also to education, consultations, participations in conferences, committees, and commendations[3] – but the 1950s represented a moment of intense activity. Although irrevocably marked by the personal tragedy of the loss of his wife Julieta Guimarãens Costa in 1954,[4] the professional results of the decade – which closed with the inauguration of the new capital he designed in the Planalto Central – was that of a prolific period from the viewpoint of design and extremely rich from the perspective of international relationships.

Costa first appeared consistently in the European press from 1948, with his participation in the symposium on "new monumentality," upon the invitation of *The Architectural Review*. From the beginning of the 1950s, he would start to move within an ever-expanding and ever more prestigious network of relationships, fuelled by a series of opportunities for collaboration and exchange that were taking shape at the beginning of the decade. Europe, and Paris in particular, became the centre of his new professional interests. Beginning in the late 1940s, his trip to Portugal conducted on behalf of the SPHAN to study the colonial roots of Brazilian architecture provided an opportunity to strengthen his relations with Europe, destined to have important repercussions later in his career. His second stay in Portugal at the beginning of 1952 coincided, probably not by chance, with a series of family and professional commitments in Europe. Among the various stops between the Portuguese peregrinations were Rome, Marseilles – where he visited the Unité d'Habitation of Le Corbusier – and Paris, where he participated in the meetings of the committee charged with evaluating the project of the UNESCO headquarters, the so-called Panel of Five, also composed of Le Corbusier, Walter Gropius, Sven Markelius, and Ernesto Nathan Rogers.[5] In September 1952, Costa was in Venice to take part in the International Conference of Artists promoted by UNESCO – the first prestigious international showcase for his theories on the relationship between art, architecture, and society – and then again in Paris, where he began to set up the project of the Maison du Brésil, destined to rise in the Cité Universitaire not far from Le Corbusier's Swiss Pavilion. His two important Parisian assignments, which took place a short time apart, are extremely significant to understand the balance between the common struggle in the name of the CIAM principles and the search for personal affirmation – on the part of Le Corbusier, above all. This struggle was in fact at the base of conflicts and negotiations, despite the rhetoric of "'team work' over individual ambition"[6] that, at least in principle, was the supposed foundation of the relationships.

As annotated by sources and accurate reconstructions of the history of the UNESCO headquarters – which we refer to for a deeper understanding of the difficult construction process in its various phases and of the role of the various actors involved[7] – this experience has often been given a "tragic" dimension by its protagonists: Rogers speaks of "drama," Costa of "common martyrdom," "rather trying experience,"[8] Le Corbusier defines it as one of the "saddest adventures of his life."[9] This, however, was not due solely to the difficult relations with the UNESCO officials, but also to subtle divergences within the different working groups. The stakes were indeed of the utmost importance and implied a choice of principle on several fronts. On the one hand, there was the battle for the affirmation of modern values within an extremely delicate context and programme, especially if we consider the previous relationships of Le Corbusier with public institutions in Paris and the failed experiences of the competition for the Geneva Palace of Nations and the design of the United Nations Headquarters in New York. On the other hand, as Barbara E. Shapiro rightly points out, there was a generational clash between the "early pioneers of modernism, embodied in CIAM, and the late modernists of the 1950s, practitioners who exhibited a more inclusive, forgiving, and flexible pragmatism."[10] On the part of the Five – firmly united in the complex task assigned to them, even in the face of the complications given by Le Corbusier's constant attempts to carve himself out a dominant role in the design process – an idealistic tension was much more evident compared to the various other project groups, from the one initially commissioned by UNESCO – made up of Eugène Beaudouin, with Howard Robertson and Eero Saarinen as advisors – to the group that was finally appointed, selected by the same Five, comprising Marcel Breuer, Bernard Zehrfuss, and Pier Luigi Nervi. It was a unique opportunity for the Five to solidify the principles, already widely discussed on the theoretical level,[11] referring to a monumental form capable of expressing "the spiritual requirements of the 20th century,"[12] which was inextricably linked to the fundamental theme of the synthesis of the arts on which Le Corbusier had insisted for several years. This issue in fact should have been managed with the utmost intransigence as well as with an awareness of the sense of moral responsibility in the matters of art and society that the nature of the enterprise entailed. The episode has significant similarities with that of the Ministry of Education in Rio, from the methods of task assignment to the attempt of modifying the site in order to avoid a direct confrontation with its historical Parisian setting,[13] and it was only natural that Costa had tended to reiterate some of the same mechanisms, becoming an energetic defender – as before – of the principle of "architectural ethics" over that of "professional ethics."[14] Following the Five's rejection of the design proposals formulated by Beaudouin, and with the new possibility of entrusting the project to Le Corbusier, Costa did not hesitate to take a stand against the "ethical objections"[15] raised with particular intransigence by Robertson, based on the incompatibility between Le Corbusier's roles of commissioner and designer.

> The precedent of the exclusion of Le Corbusier, and the enormous debt of architects all over the world towards this exceptional personality, force us to recognise, precisely in the name of ethics, that the circumstances of the case in question transcend the strict observance of professional codes. In fact, no one has ever remembered to invoke professional ethics whenever Le Corbusier's ideas were used in Brazil, the USA, Britain, and elsewhere [...]. It is the spirit of the law that must prevail when a text is omitted: Jesus was legally placed on the cross.[16]

The same Rogers, reporting the story on *Casabella continuità* in 1959, agreed that it was "a clear case in which, by falsely interpreting its own nature and ends, to keep up appearances, democracy condemned reality and defended 'mediocracy'."[17] In his report, Rogers emphasised the crucial importance of the Five "in the phase of the critical setting up of the general problem," a concept reiterated by Le

132 *Shaping the true Machine Age*

Corbusier – although with less subdued tones – when he states, in a letter published in the same magazine, that "it is time the public knew that the Comité des Cinq played a leading role in this undertaking although this seems to be a thing that is readily forgotten," also mentioning the numerous "sketches that Lucio Costa and I so often gave to the Comité."[18] Costa's contribution seems in fact to have been crucial – albeit less conspicuous than that of Le Corbusier – in the development of the definitive planivolumetric solution for the building. According to Christopher E.M. Pearson, Zehrfuss later testified that Costa's attitude was extremely open to dialogue and collaboration, "often selecting what turned out to be the most promising sketch," while Rogers later recalled that Costa had been the first to suggest the Y-shaped layout of the Secretariat, despite the fact that it was a formal solution already belonging to Breuer's expressive repertoire. In particular, Pearson argued that, in the last phase of the design, it was Costa "who put the final elements in place." In fact, he attributes him the suggestion of extending one wing of the Secretariat "in a long, flat curve parallel to the Avenue de Suffren, and positioning the Conference Building in the south part of the site, [...] at the corner of the Avenues de Suffren and de Ségur."[19] In a 1959 letter written to Rogers commenting on the experience, Costa explicitly recognises his contributions, apologising "for having made you share in my anguish and my obstinacy."

> For one, I think that with the vehemence of my arguing I probably made a decisive contribution towards getting UNESCO off the one-way street to mediocrity on which they had set out in the beginning.
> Then, I remember that while walking alone along the "*quais*" after the tumultuous dinner with Claudius Petit and other colleagues, I got the idea that instead of keeping the plan rigid by means of uniform curves (statically perfect in the case of a skyscraper), one could adopt a softer arc for the principal façade so as to give great grace and nobility[20] to the group. I also realised that for the Assembly Hall, instead of Breuer's oval and axial form, we could use the normal form situated laterally, so as to create a great approach square with a monumental work of sculpture as counterpoint. I also remember that during the meeting of the following day the atmosphere was dull and uncertainty reigned when I announced to Gropius that, once and for all, I had something useful to propose. The agreement was unanimous; in the afternoon there were no more problems, the waters were calm again.[21]

The letters preserved in Costa's archive, although not very many, testify to his commitment to follow the commission's work from afar, at least until the final design was approved;[22] however, they also testify the relationship of mutual esteem that he maintained with the other components of the Five, and with Gropius above all, with whom the common experience cemented an affectionate friendship destined to continue unaltered in the years to come.[23] Yet, as emerges from an undated note addressed to William Holford,[24] the difficult affair left an indelible mark on Costa, leading him, from that moment on, to reject similar collaborations, even of great prestige, including repeated invitations from the São Paulo Biennial: to the 2nd Biennial of 1953, to take part in the commission in charge of awarding the architectural prizes, together with Le Corbusier, Ernesto Nathan Rogers, Max Bill, Alvar Aalto, and José Luis Sert;[25] and again in 1959, to participate in the 5th

Biennial as a representative of Brazilian architecture, a role for which he had suggested the nomination of his former partner Gregori Warchavchik instead.[26]

The story of the Maison du Brésil also developed with ups and downs for several years, exemplifying the sometimes conflicting nature – despite Costa's unshakable "faith" in the master – of his relationship with Le Corbusier,[27] again focused on the ambiguity of each other's roles within a relationship based on personal connection rather than on regulated rigid professional codes. Charged by the Brazilian minister of Education Péricles Madureira de Pinho – who took advantage of Costa's presence in Paris for the UNESCO commitment – to draw up the preliminary design of the building, which according to government directives had to be entrusted to a Brazilian architect, Costa decided to assign its development and construction to Le Corbusier's atelier. Although the habit of entrusting others with the executive development of his projects while himself maintaining supervision was a normal practice for Costa,[28] in this case the choice acquired the sense of a symbolic repayment to Le Corbusier, who – once their contacts were resumed a few years after the end of the Second World War – had expressed a certain dissatisfaction with the outcome of the collaboration for the Ministry of Education in Rio, which caused a series of unpleasant misunderstandings between the two.[29] Costa was also disappointed in seeing published – on the pages of the September 1947 monographic issue of *L'Architecture d'Aujourd'hui* dedicated to Brazil – a drawing by Le Corbusier based on a model of the final project for the Ministry, presented as a project of his own hand, which Costa defined as "false testimony" on countless occasions. The episode of the Parisian student residence would gradually transform into the "mirror image"[30] of the Ministry's. Predictably, far from adhering faithfully to the preliminary project, Le Corbusier overturned its layout and architectural language with the assistance of a series of bureaucratic manoeuvres, claiming the paternity of the project and denying the Brazilian architect what could have been – if we exclude the Brazilian pavilions for New York and for the Milan Triennale of 1964 – his only work realised outside of Brazil (Figure 5.1).[31] Despite his discontent for the progressive distortion of the project, Costa actively participated in the whole process, also thanks to the constant intermediation of André Wogenscky, commissioned by Le Corbusier to follow its development. Proving his complete autonomy from the master, Costa demanded the power to approve all the phases, including the finishing work, colours, and interior furnishings,[32] worried that the final handover to Le Corbusier could nullify his desire to deliver a comfortable and welcoming residence to Brazilian students in Paris, destined to last over time and displaying a certain national character. It was precisely on this issue – which was most delicate since it implied inalienable language and expressive choices – that the incompatibility became complete, giving rise to a series of polemical exchanges and further recriminations regarding the Ministry. The finished building of the Maison du Brésil, inaugurated in July 1959, came in line with Le Corbusier's brutalist contemporary production, and represented for Costa – who later declared that he did not recognise himself in the project – the most "anti-Brazilian" architectural work possible.

> We like clear and natural solutions, those that are simple and harmonious, as we are sensitive to grace. We do not like what is brutal, unattractive, complicated. Cuts and angular, aggressive forms annoy us.[33]

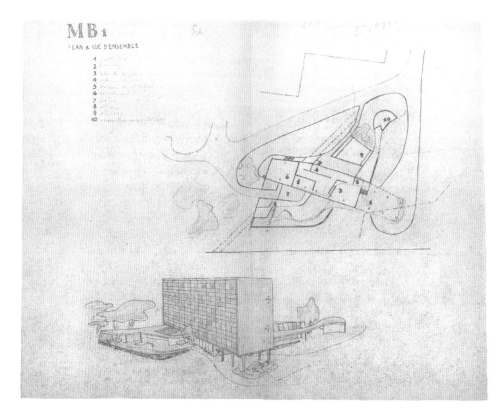

Figure 5.1 Lucio Costa, preliminary project for the Maison du Brésil, Paris. Plan of the ground floor and perspective view, 1952. Casa de Lucio Costa.

Art and the emancipation of the masses

At the beginning of the 1950s, Costa's previous theoretical elaborations on the great themes of the "integration of the arts," the legitimacy of plastic expression, and the role of art in contemporary society found a significant moment of systematisation. The International Conference of Artists promoted by UNESCO – held in Venice from 22 to 28 September 1952 and involving a vast deployment of intellectual energies from around the world – certainly was a fundamental detonator. On this occasion, consecrated to the theme of the *synthèse des arts* in the context of a broader reflection on the role of the artist in contemporary society, and as an expert selected in the field of architecture for the *exposés généraux*, Costa presented an essay entitled "L'architecte et la societé contemporaine,"[34] preceded by an introduction entitled "L'art et l'avènement des masses."[35] Together with the essay "Considerações sôbre arte contemporânea,"[36] published in Brazil the same year – of which the Venice report contained substantial passages – it represents the actual summary of this theoretical period. The three mentioned writings – which must be treated jointly given the numerous thematic overlaps and close time of elaboration – present a convergence of many ideas that had been developed in texts of earlier years, even in the context of practical professional opportunities. In the previous chapters, we tried to reconstruct the complexity of the factors involved in orienting the nature and content of these ideas. This time, however, they appear to be part of a broader theoretical framework, the core of which revolved around the concept of architecture as a plastic art, identified as a keystone for the radical re-foundation of its social role. After a long introduction to the "new concept of housing unit," a clear tribute to Le Corbusier, Costa went on to analyse the architect's role in contemporary society under its various aspects – technical, sociological, and artistic – starting from the fundamental premise that it should:

> delimit and order the constructed space, keeping in mind not only the efficiency of its use, but, above all, the individual well-being of the "users"; a well-being that will not be just limited to physical comfort, but must also include psychological comfort in the extent to which this may depend on the contingencies of the architectural project.[37]

Costa identifies the reasons for the crisis of the social role of architecture in the discrepancy between the rapid technical transformations and the longer social ones. The technicians – artists, architects, and urban planners *in primis* – had the task of educating the masses and the elites in order to inspire new artistic values in them, facilitating the process destined to lead to the affirmation of a new historical cycle where art would again hold its deserved social role. The aspiration to overcome social inequalities, not only on the material level but also on the cultural one, and the consequent re-foundation of art on legitimate "popular roots,"[38] had what Costa called "integration of the arts" as a corollary, distinguishing it from Le Corbusier's formula of "synthesis of the arts."[39]

In order to express this thesis, Costa proceeded as usual through a dialectic discourse, taking up the idealistic theory of a development of civilisation – or of a "history of the spirit" to put it in Hegelian terms – that was determined by art forms. Reprising the topic of the cyclical resurrection of a "national personality," he took the opportunity to highlight the importance of the Brazilian contribution in having placed "due emphasis on the problem of the plastic quality and the lyric and passionate content in a work of architecture." With a prophetic tone, guided by the idealistic substratum of his own cultural formation, he developed an all-encompassing artistic theory,[40] aimed – as already mentioned – at integrating the "formal Baroque excesses" of the national tradition into the "new tradition" of modern architecture.[41] Resuming and expanding the distinction between the "Oriental-Gothic" and "Greek-Latin" spirit he had already outlined in 1936 in the written project report of the University Campus, he argued that the history of world art was governed by two distinct and opposite formal concepts: the "organic-functional" concept, answering needs of a functional nature and according to which the work of art developed similarly to a living organism where each part contributes to the whole; and the "plastic-ideal" concept, which instead proceeded through the imposition of pure geometric shapes *a priori*, to which functional needs are later adapted. Based respectively on dynamic and static compositional principles – exemplified by Gothic and classical architecture or by the naturalistic metaphors of the flower and the crystal – these two formal concepts found their origin and maximum popularity in particular geographical areas, corresponding to the Nordic-Eastern axis for the dynamic conception and to the

Mesopotamian-Mediterranean axis for the static one (Figure 5.2). While maintaining an uninterrupted dialogue throughout the centuries – with overlapping influences running across each other's boundaries – these two plastic concepts maintained their substantial duality until the "advent" of modern architecture. Only this architecture, thanks to the conquests of contemporary building techniques, allowed the total fusion of the two concepts in a new unitary synthesis, capable of opening "virtually unlimited" plastic possibilities through the co-existence of "now open, now contained" forms.[42] According to Costa, the coexistence of these two opposing formal conceptions proved to overcome the cyclical motions of "Classical-Baroque" or "Classical-Romantic" observed "by the intellectual acuteness of Mr. Eugenio D'Ors [sic]," in favour of their coexistence or fusion, which had already been exemplified by the colonial architecture of Ibero-America, participanting in both static and dynamic currents for genetic and chronological reasons. Thus, Costa seemed to substantially liquidate the opposition between rationalism and organicism that had everyone in Europe and the United States picking sides in those years.

Inextricably linked to this theory, and based on the absolutely central role that art played for Costa in the evolution of society, was his answer to the issue of the apparent irreconcilability between the gratuitousness and militancy of the work of art, between art as an end in itself and its social function. This answer was prophetic – given the way Brazilian architecture would be received from the following years – yet it seemed more like the result of a desire to clarify what Costa had long considered the basic misunderstanding of functionalism rather than the result of a need to legitimise the formal freedom of the "carioca group" he represented. Given that art by definition cannot but be an end in itself – as it is germinated by the urgency moving the artist – the fact that it finds substantiation starting from an individual's choice among many different solutions that are all adequate from the functional point of view – a choice guided by a certain "plastic intention"[43] – guarantees its "permanence in time once the factors that have led to its existence stop acting on it, not only as a testimony of a dead civilisation, but as a manifestation that is still alive and current." Therefore, not only was it a contradiction to accuse a work of art – or of architecture – of individualism, since it can only be the result of a creative individuality, but not giving artistic expression its freedom – in the name of an alleged social commitment – can only falter society's arduous journey toward a new and higher understanding of art itself, based on the idea that "there is something transmissible in the individual experience of each person." In this sense, in Costa's vision, art during the Machine Age played a role that was complementary to that of industry, thanks to the emancipating potential of those "legitimate yearnings for free choice and individual or collective imagination of the proletarian mass, oppressed by the harshness and monotony of the mechanised work imposed by modern production techniques." As an instrument to reach the "heart of the masses," and as an "active form of evasion and individual and collective psychological rehabilitation," art was for Costa a key tool for the intellectual emancipation of society as a whole, constituted by individuals capable of thinking and being moved. Combined with the material well-being and living standards "worthy of human conditions" that mass production and distribution would make available to everyone, art would allow the transfer of the "eternal aspiration to social justice from the utopian level to one of inevitable reality."[44]

These formulations resumed again, published and reworked on numerous occasions in the following years, confirming the central role that the theme had for

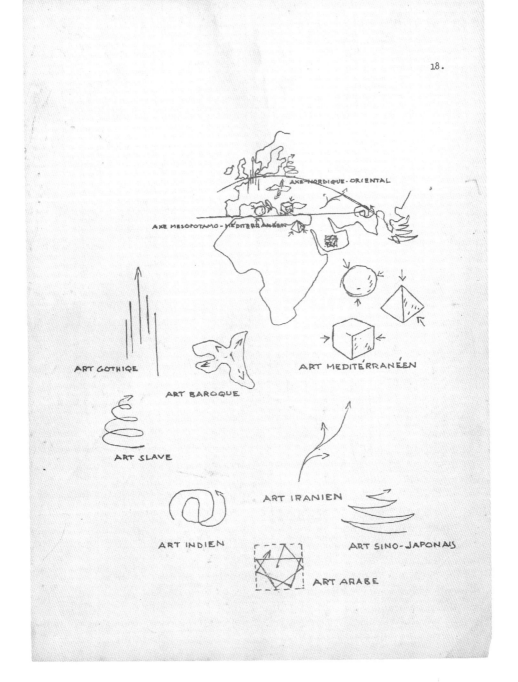

Figure 5.2 Lucio Costa, illustrations for the text "Considerações sobre arte contemporânea," 1952. Casa de Lucio Costa.

138 *Shaping the true Machine Age*

Costa and how much his civilisation and social renewal project depended on it. At the same time, he was well aware of the convergence of some issues that were dear to him with the new concerns affecting the international debate, of which the post-war CIAM meetings – and in particular the lively discussion on the "Heart of the city"[45] addressed by the VIII CIAM in Hoddesdon in 1951 – represented paradigmatic examples. It is worth noting that Costa sent a text entitled "Architecture, art plastique – Considérations à propos de l'art contemporain et du nouveau concept de monumentalité" to James Maude Richards, editor of *The Architectural Review*, saying that he hoped that "the whole thing will not sound already out of date" and asking to hand in afterwards "this French original to the direction of the CIAM as a tardy Brazilian contribution in addition to the reports collected on their last meeting, held in England,"[46] evidently referring to the VI CIAM held at Bridgewater, in 1947.

Despite these convergences, at the culmination of Brazilian architecture's worldwide fame, it was precisely the extreme confidence in progress and in art as a form of redemption – which was understandable in a country that had experienced only a small glimpse of the Second World War – that marked the separation between a Brazil "doomed to modernity"[47] and a Europe in search of alternatives – one that would prove to be unbridgeable only a few years later with the construction of Brasilia. Among the first alarm bells of such incompatibility was the already mentioned criticism directed by Max Bill at the formalism of Brazilian architecture,[48] exempting only the Pedregulho housing complex by Affonso Eduardo Reidy. While Brazilian modernism provided an opportunity to address the issue of free form, opening up new possibilities to modern architecture and granting permanent citizenship to Le Corbusier's Law of the Meander, the curse of formalism and lack of social commitment continued to weigh on the reception of Brazilian architecture – and particularly on Niemeyer's career – even in the following decades. On the eve of the Golden Years,[49] while the old continent exhausted by war saw the modern masters move more cautiously through the rubble of the old ideologies, the Brazilians did not give up the machinist utopia, although they gave it a vaguely hedonistic treatment. Therefore, while Niemeyer continued to explore all the unlimited possibilities of free form – barricading himself behind the utopia of a "democracy of beauty" and enthusiastically adhereing to the communist cause – Costa, meanwhile, tenaciously pursued the implications of a civilising project born under the sign of modernism, pairing – not without some ambiguity – a quietly intimist production with the search for a new monumentality, able to bear the aspirations that were implicit in that project in symbolic terms.

On the occasion of the Extraordinary International Congress of Art Critics held in September 1959 in Brasilia under the aegis of the art critic Mário Pedrosa – in which the programme was aimed at discussing the two main topics of "The New City" and of the "Synthesis of the Arts"[50] – Costa presented the same content he had introduced at the UNESCO conference in Venice – this time, however, with the title "A arte e a educação," and with opening greetings that presented how, in his view, Brasilia constituted a milestone in the process of the country's civilisation.

> The integration of the arts within a new city – this is the beautiful topic that brings us together here today. Considerations of quite another nature – the desire to give this country a solid industrial basis, to provide it with the

communications network necessary for the creation of economic wealth and independence – inspired the overall objectives within which the transfer of the nation's capital might be said to serve as a keystone. And thus we find ourselves today, one thousand kilometres from the coast, on an upland plateau where just over two years ago there was nothing but desert and solitude. This meeting is of great symbolic importance; it demonstrates that this nation's technological, economic, and social development will not occur at the expense of heart and intelligence – as has happened so often in the past, and as still happens. Instead, such development will be predicated upon considerations of art – just as happened with Brasilia itself.[51]

In search of a new monumentality

Costa's first important contribution to the international debate actually took place at the end of the 1940s, and was focused – not by chance – on the theme of "new monumentality." Already known as one of the authors of the Ministry of Education and as the main theorist of Brazilian architecture, he was called to take part in the Symposium "In Search of a New Monumentality,"[52] organised in 1948 by the magazine *The Architectural Review*, alongside important figures such as Gregor Paulsson, Henry-Russell Hitchcock, William Holford,[53] Sigfried Giedion, Walter Gropius, and Alfred Roth.

It was a fundamental opportunity to discuss a theme – already raised in 1943 by Sigfried Giedion, José Luis Sert, and Fernand Léger in the "Nine Points on Monumentality"[54] – that reached the core of one of the most sensitive issues of modernism's critical revision in the post-war years: seeking a way to combine the rejection of monumentalism in the traditional sense – especially since monumentalism was inextricably associated with the architectural expressions of totalitarian regimes – with the widespread need of "satisfying the ordinary man's aspirations towards some visible expression of his collective consciousness," broadening the modern architectural idiom in order to fulfil, in Giedion's words, the people's "aspirations for joy, for luxury, and for excitement."[55] The discussion, no doubt, was carried out with a slight embarrassment in dealing with a theme that, until recently, had been purposely removed from the modern debate and was full of political and ideological implications – the introduction explicitly cites the fear that the initiative could be interpreted as "a retreat from the principles of the modern architectural movement." However, what also emerged from the debate were more than a few ambiguities about the meaning to be attributed to the terms "monument" and "monumentality," which also produced fractures between divergent positions within the broader context of generally shared intentions.

Therefore, when questioned on the possibility of a contemporary and intrinsically democratic monumental expression, Costa states, in agreement with Gropius, that this could only be achieved unconsciously when the architects recognised "the plastic foundations common to all the arts," and:

> becoming imbued (similarly to painters and sculptors in their own sphere) with a passion to conceive, to plan, and to build – from this moment, their wholly functional works will respond to the higher purpose animating them and will express themselves in appropriate plastic terms acquiring, as a result of their symmetry and proportion, a noble and dignified grace.[56]

He returns again to the theme of grace when he tries to define, in more detail, the ways and principles through which this idea of monumentality could be concretised:

> This monumentality is one that is not exclusive of grace, and does not ignore the part played by trees, undergrowth, and fields in the natural setting; what characterises the modern concept of urbanism, stretching from the town to the suburbs and thence into the country, is that it abolishes the picturesque by incorporating the bucolic into the monumental; a monumentality whose effects are not limited only to civic centres, but extend to buildings in which its manifestation is implied by the dimensions and volumes, as well as by the particular plastic forms.

This is a crucial passage, in which Costa's idea of monumentality is contained *in nuce*, presenting a formidable anticipation of the principles that will animate, about ten years later, the plan of the new capital of Brazil. Taking advantage of the opportunity to address an international audience, the text then returns to the theme of the architect's responsibility. He in fact should be called – in Corbusian terms – to take on an eminently pedagogic role toward society as a whole, and toward authority in its various forms in particular, especially when he is to be involved in projects invested with particular symbolic and representative implications.

> The urgent task facing architects, therefore, is not merely to appeal to the authorities to adapt their social legislation and current building regulations to present technical conditions, in order to facilitate the execution of measures such as those sponsored by CIAM; it also involves an appeal to the responsible professional authorities – both in the administrative field and in university training centres – because when the time comes, the public authorities will seek their advice and act accordingly.[57]

Le Corbusier's lesson is finally referred to as the "definite doctrinal foundation of present professional teaching," which will allow the realisation of the utopian ideal – "that clear and distant mirage located far away from the tragic turmoil in which we live, move, and have our being" – of the so-called "true machine age," in which finally "reason will come into its own."

In the following decade, Costa had the opportunity to practically apply these theoretical formulations in a series of planning occasions of very different nature and scale, united by a more or less explicitly monumental and representative programme. Between 1953 and 1955, in addition to his contribution to the UNESCO headquarters in Paris, he developed two projects for religious buildings – of which only one was built – and his first design exercise on the theme of the isolated monument – which remained only on paper. Subsequently, in 1957, he won the competition for the design of the new capital of the country, the ultimate keystone of the synergy between modern architecture and the State in defining the monumental expression of Brazil in the race toward modernisation. Despite the obvious difference in scale and programme, in these projects it is possible to read the continuity of a research path around the theme of monumentality that had already been explored at a theoretical level.

Shaping the true Machine Age 141

The never-constructed Church of Nossa Senhora de Copacabana[58] was based on a layout shaped like a half-violin and consisted of a continuous covering of reinforced concrete similar to a lowered dome that opened like a shell at the entrance, enclosing a warm interior space flooded with natural light on three sides. The sinuous main volume – to which a raised platform acting as a churchyard and a small attached service area were added – was flanked by a soaring bell tower, whose tapered-up volume recalled that of the chapel of São Francisco de Assis in Pampulha. It was an unusual plastic and structural gesture for Costa's poetics – drawn from an incessant formal research, made through successive approximations that greatly distanced it from the formal synthesis of Niemeyer's sketches – denoting the search for a continuous spatiality able to symbolically and physically unite the religious community under one big roof (Figure 5.3).

On the contrary, in the altar for the International Eucharistic Congress – which was realised by Alcides da Rocha Miranda on the basis of Costa's sketch on the Aterro do Flamengo (not yet occupied by the landscape project of Roberto Burle Marx) – Costa dematerialised architecture into the shape of a large sail unfurled toward the Baía de Guanabara, reducing the covered area to a small pavilion, open on all sides, arranged to accommodate the altar, the pulpit, and the seats for prelates and other personalities. The iconicity of this lightweight sail – wide open to atmospheric agents and visible from a distance among the profiles of the coast of Niterói and Pão de Açucar – resolved the need for representativeness of the event with one simple gesture, clearly manifesting its temporary nature[59] (Figure 5.4).

The year 1954 saw the conception of another unrealised but rather important project, since it not only contained the embryonic solution of successive projects for isolated monuments – such as that to João Pinheiro in Belo Horizonte, and that to Estácio de Sá in Rio de Janeiro[60] – but it also had some surprising connections with the subsequent plan for Brasilia. This was the project for the monument to

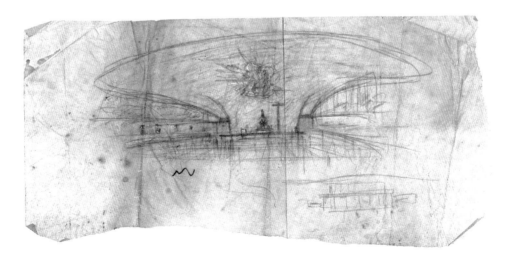

Figure 5.3 Lucio Costa, sketch of the Church of Nossa Senhora de Copacabana, Rio de Janeiro. Perspective view of the interior, 1953. Casa de Lucio Costa.

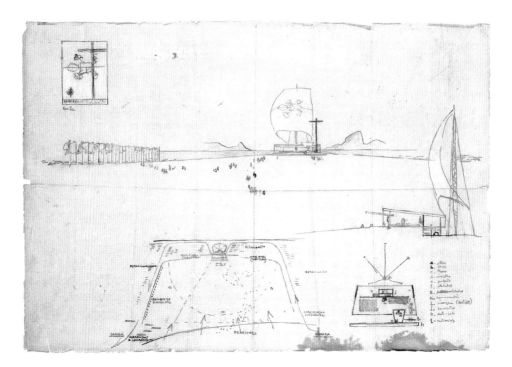

Figure 5.4 Lucio Costa, sketches of the altar for the International Eucharistic Congress, Rio de Janeiro. Plans, section and perspective view, 1954–1955. Casa de Lucio Costa.

Prince Henry the Navigator in Sagres, Portugal, which was prepared for the competition that was announced for the fifth centenary of the death of this hero of the era of maritime discoveries. Costa took advantage of the opportunity to present a personal tribute to both Portuguese culture and landscape, which were a focus of his interests given his recent study trips there on behalf of the SPHAN. In the preamble to the draft report he explains – almost literally anticipating the incipit of the descriptive report of Brasilia's Plano Piloto – that, although he was not willing to participate in the competition, his memory of his visit to Sagres and the study of photographic documentation allowed him "to *feel* the problem and to clearly see the solution." Therefore, his first concern in this case was the nature of the intervention in relation to the site.

> The natural configuration of the promontory discourages the use of "architectural masses" for the vain purpose of competing with it or completing it; it imposes, on the contrary, the adoption of simple and pure forms, detached from the ground as much as possible in order to be discerned as a plastic gesture that is clearly perceivable from a distance, whose noble intention is to spiritualise the bare and rude beauty of the landscape.[61]

The sketches denote a tiring design process in search of an ultimate solution, oscillating between an organic-shaped layout with a vertical element similar to a sail,

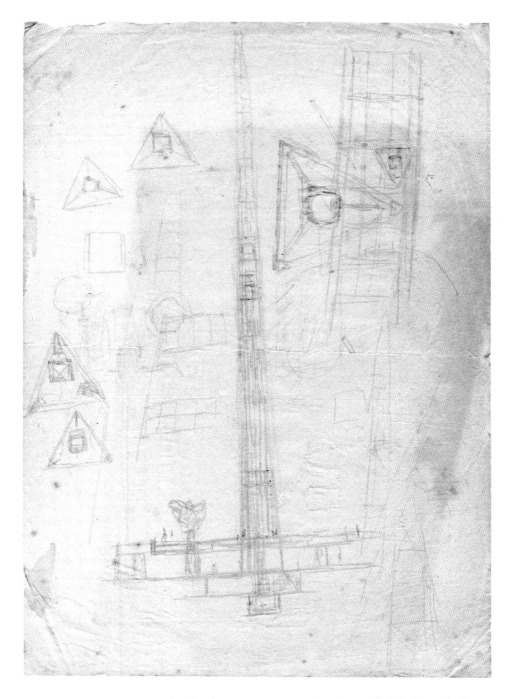

Figure 5.5 Lucio Costa, studies for the monument to Prince Henry the Navigator in Sagres, Portugal, 1954. Arquivo Central do IPHAN – Seção Rio de Janeiro.

and a more rigorously geometrical design, in which a gigantic and more-or-less trapezoidal-based pyramid emerged from a triangular concrete platform suspended above three pillars (Figure 5.5). This pyramidal element – which would become recurrent in Costa's monumental projects henceforth – was conceived as an abstract sculptural form, probably linked to the traditional use of the triangular shape as a symbolic representation of death, but also to the memory of the traditional monumental fountains (*chafariz*) of Mestre Valentim in Rio de Janeiro.[62] The interior space of the monument, which shows several analogies to the future monument to Estácio de Sá, was divided into three levels, each corresponding to one of the stages of the site's ritual path of appropriation: starting from the crypt carved into the rock – where the statue of Prince Henry would have been collocated – moving toward the large covered space of the ground floor – home of the actual tomb and open toward the landscape through large windows – and culminating in a platform overlooking the ocean. This platform, accessible through two ramps, was connected to the tomb below by a small skylight and was marked by the presence of a sculpture that recalled Jacques Lipchitz's *Prometheus* for the Ministry of Education.

A *maquisard* in urban planning

In 1957, the victory in the competition for the new capital of the country – whose presentation was entrusted to a few rather modest drawings and a lucid project report that seems to have particularly impressed the jury[63] – represented the most significant moment of Costa's entire professional career, definitively consolidating his reputation on the international scene. The construction of the new federal capital in the country's inland, strongly supported by President Juscelino Kubitschek, was the opportunity to test the monumental image of the nation that had been elaborated during the years of Vargas in a renewed democratic framework and in a new Brazil born from the ashes of the Estado Novo. It was no coincidence, perhaps, that the design of the capital was entrusted to Costa's plan – since he had always supported the collaboration between architecture and the State in the construction of a modern and civilised country – and to the architecture of Niemeyer – a skilled creator of forms capable of prefiguring what Brazil aspired to become. Aware of not having any previous experience in urban planning[64] nor a technical structure able to actually manage a site of that size – yet determined to contribute to a cause that seemed to somehow represent the natural outcome of the position for which he was unanimously renowned – Costa resorted, as he had done in Sagres, to a rhetorical formula of self-legitimisation, opening the descriptive memory of the Plano Piloto of the new capital with an *excusatio non petita*.

> First of all, I must apologise to the Director of the NOVACAP and to the Jury of this Competition for the summary manner in which this plan for the new capital is suggested; then, also, I must justify myself because it was not my intention to enter the competition and, point of fact, I am not doing so. I am merely passing on a possible solution for the problem issued by the competition notice that took shape almost spontaneously in my head. For this reason, I make this submission not as a duly qualified professional – I don't even have a studio – but simply as a *maquisard* [partisan] of urban planning who has no intention of developing the proposed idea except perhaps as a consultant.[65]

Shaping the true Machine Age 145

Also in this case, the first point regards the relationship that the new urban organism must establish with the site in view of its status as a capital city, whose plan was therefore first called upon to interpret the symbolic and representative nature of the new urban proposal.

> Founding a city in the wilderness is a deliberate act of conquest, a gesture after the manner of the pioneering colonial tradition. [...] Brasilia should not be envisaged merely as an organism capable of fulfilling the vital functions of any modern city adequately and effortlessly; not merely as an "urbs," but as a "civitas," possessing the virtues and attributes inherent in a capital. And, for this to be possible, the planner must be imbued with a certain dignity and nobility of "intent," because that fundamental attitude will give birth to the sense of order, utility, and proportion that alone can confer on the project as a whole the desirable monumental quality.[66]

He therefore reprises the theme of proportion, dignity, and nobility of intentions that he had already theorised in *The Architectural Review* Symposium. His first choice regards the original foundation act, "the elementary gesture of one who marks or takes possession of a place: two axes crossing at right angles; the sign of the cross itself." Subsequently, this basic symbol was adapted to the specific topography of the site, resulting in the particular configuration of the urban layout, with the two ends of the axes "curved in order to contain it within the equilateral triangle limiting the urbanised area." This conception, according to which the monumental character of the urban scheme was expressed primarily in its relationship with the site and the landscape in which it was inserted, found a further conceptualisation in the letter sent in 1960 – date of the inauguration of the new capital – in response to journalist Antônio Callado's critiques on the city.

> The "monument," in the case of a capital city, is not something that could be left for afterwards, as in the modern English towns; the monument here is the whole city, and, contrarily to a garden village [*cidade aldeia*] which should soberly be inscribed within the landscape, the capital city needs to impose itself with full control.[67]

And again, in 1967:

> Normally, urbanisation consists in creating the conditions for the city to happen, because the element of surprise makes its way with time; while in the case of Brasilia it was a matter of taking possession of the location and imposing – in the manner of the conquerors or of Louis XIV – an urban structure capable of allowing, in a short period of time, the installation of a Capital. Unlike the cities that conform and adjust to the landscape, in the empty *cerrado* and under an immense sky, as in the open sea, the city has created the landscape.[68]

As stated in the Symposium, the act of "incorporating the bucolic into the monumental" could produce a new form of urban landscape, able to impose itself on the solitary and wild immensity of the Planalto Central. While in Sagres Costa had opted not to compete with the bare beauty of the landscape, in Brasilia his intent was to tame the landscape through a colonising operation – full of intellectual and symbolic implications – of nature through architecture, which was expressed at best in the radical modification of the topography through the construction of the city on a system of embankments. The idea of resorting to this age-old technique – of which Costa, during the elaboration of his plan, had had the opportunity to view examples of in two photographic volumes on ancient Chinese architecture[69] – came from the practical need to make large soil movements to allow the crossing of the axes at different levels in the Plataforma Rodoviária; however, it actually had the fundamental objective, according to Costa, of guaranteeing, in modern terms, "the cohesion of the project as a whole" and to give the plan "a surprisingly monumental emphasis,"[70] as well as, of course, to establish complex visual and perceptive relationships between the different urban elements (Figure 5.6).

The landscape matrix of the urban structure appears evident in the sketches related to the plan development process, testifying to – as had happened in the sketches of Sagres and in general in Costa's design method – a patient research on

Figure 5.6 Aerial view of Brasilia's monumental axis during the construction. Casa de Lucio Costa.

form and its gradual germination. His pencil willfully lingered on the unsolved issues by saturating the sheet with scattered marks, until – unexpectedly, in a corner of the page – portions of solutions slowly emerge like fragments of reality, in a process in which writing (thought) and drawing (project) feed off of and verify each other respectively. The configuration of the monumental axis, subject of most sketches, progressively emerged from a meticulous study of the flow of circulation, from the contextual assessment in section and in plan, but mostly from a bird's-eye view in which the perspective – always foreshortened and never statically axial – of the new artificial landscape supporting the architecture – the last already fundamentally outlined in its main volumetric elements – appears as an accurate prefiguration of reality (Figure 5.7). In almost all sketches, the Television Tower stands in a raised and dominant position, even more relevant than the Congress's, which was not by chance since it was the only building – together with the Plataforma Rodoviária – that Costa would personally design. Conceived as "a highly plastic element" functioning as a recognisable visual landmark – "a plastic gesture clearly perceivable in the distance," as stated in the draft of the Sagres report[71] – and, in turn, as a privileged observation point, the Tower is configured as a pyramid-shaped steel structure, resting on a monumental triangular-shaped concrete base, which in turn is suspended on three sculptural pillars of cement – a clear evolution of the never-constructed Portuguese monument of Sagres.

However, the sketches of the design process of the plan also reveal a previous solution abandoned in favour of the one presented in the competition (Figure 5.8). Here, the urban layout is structured on two rectilinear axes perpendicular to each other, where the second axis constitutes the side of an equilateral triangle with its own vertex along the main axis.[72] Although this "unused" version of the plan reveals a much more evident reference to Le Corbusier's Ville Radieuse – reprising the articulation of the various urban functions along the linear axis – it also testifies, from its time of inception, how it mainly differed from the model because it was based on the recurring figure of the triangle. This configuration was certainly intended to harmoniously insert the urban layout into the topography and into the territorial and landscape layout of the site, to take advantage of the area included within the bifurcation of the two main branches of Lake Paranoá; however, it was also partly imputable to the symbolic importance that Costa attributed to the equilateral triangle. In addition to defining the geometric figure within which the urban area was inscribed, the triangle gave shape to the Three Powers Square, which symbolised the autonomy and equality of the three fundamental powers of the democratic State and which – standing out from the wild landscape – celebrated the civilising epic of the new capital as the victory of man over the untamed nature of the *cerrado*.[73]

> I am particularly moved by the decision to locate the seats of the three powers of the State not in the centre of the city but at its edge, upon a triangular embankment that opens out like the palm of a hand at the end of the outstretched arm formed by an *esplanada* lined with Ministries. Raised up in this manner and embodied in pure and dignified forms, these seats of power stand in contrast to the surrounding natural landscape and at the same time seem to offer themselves to the people: Vote! The power is yours! The dignity of intention inspiring the urban layout of the city, that so profoundly moved André Malraux,[74] is tangible, and there for all to see. The Three Powers Square is the Versailles of the people.[75]

Figure 5.7 Lucio Costa, study for Brasilia's Plano Piloto. Perspective view of the Three Powers Square, 1957. Back of the envelope with non-identified text draft. Casa de Lucio Costa.

Shaping the true Machine Age 149

Figure 5.8 Lucio Costa, studies for Brasilia's Plano Piloto. Design process, 1957. Casa de Lucio Costa.

In the words he spoke at the 1959 Extraordinary International Congress of Art Critics, Costa left no room for doubt: Brasilia's conception seemed to show that a democratic monumentality was not only possible, but already materialised in the constructed utopia of the Brazilian capital. In the same occasion, Giedion himself praised the new capital as "a symbol of courage and creative spirit." And yet, after Costa's project was unveiled to the public, Giedion had expressed an authentic concern for the rigidity of the Brasilia plan more than once, declaring he was decidedly against the symbolism that in his opinion was inherent in the winning competition project. However, while he voices "reservations about the reasons for the rigidity of the plan of Brasilia" in a letter addressed to Costa in December 1957[76] – also claiming that he had "no fear of axes and symmetries nor of monumental expression," and saying he was ready to discuss his position after gaining more knowledge of the matter – in a letter to Niemeyer of the following year he uses less cautious words, even encouraging him to modify the plan in progress.

> You know how much I admire Lucio Costa and his architecture. But this time neither I nor others can agree with a scheme that is interesting to look at but unfortunately not monumental but decorative.
> Change, change the plan! It is still possible. Make a human city out of an ornament.[77]

150 *Shaping the true Machine Age*

This unexpected reaction of one of the most enthusiastic observers of the Brazilian architectural scene was a clear testimony of how the challenge launched by the Symposium in 1948 – searching for a monumental expression suitable for the new times – was still far from being resolved even after a whole decade. As could be expected, things deteriorated significantly after the coup that, on 31 March 1964, established a military regime in Brazil destined to last about two decades. Bruno Zevi's reaction in this regard was immediate, and emblematic, given that he had kept himself out of the group unanimously praising the capital on the occasion of the 1959 Extraordinary International Congress of Art Critics.

> The facts have gone beyond our fears. [...] In a few hours, the sinister city of officials, artificially dressed in Niemeyer's structuralist decorations, has turned into a prison, blocked on all sides by the virgin forest. Lucio Costa's plan has the shape of an airplane, but the democrats have remained on the ground, without hope of escape. A tragic event, worthy of being considered by urban planners around the world.[78]

Reading Brasilia as a closed, schematic, abstract, inhuman, autocratic, elitist, and classist city was a *leitmotiv* of its reception in the following decades, partly exacerbated by the apparent distance maintained by the author of the plan from the building site.[79] In addition to forsaking the inauguration ceremony – a choice due to the desire of "leaving all the credit for the architectural expression and effective construction of the city to Niemeyer and Pinheiro,"[80] and of "sharing his impediment" with his wife Leleta, who died a few years before the competition – he would simply "follow and approve" the works from afar, from the NOVACAP (Companhia Urbanizadora da Nova Capital) office in Rio de Janeiro, and through a constant exchange of correspondence with the main building managers and with the various involved authorities. However, his involvement and active participation in the vicissitudes of the capital continued well beyond the actual duration of the construction site: Costa intervened in a large number of issues – drawing up projects and providing advice on specific topics for many years to come – but he also defended "his" city whenever he deemed it necessary to clarify his position, often demoralised by what he could only interpret as a total misunderstanding of the real intentions of the plan by part of his detractors. In 1973, he clearly indicates his impatience for the umpteenth demonstration of disapproval, coming this time from Pierre Vago, in a letter addressed to Senator Cattete Pinheiro.

> I got tired of explaining that Brasilia is a special case, a singular one, where the urban planner had to proceed in an opposite way to the usual one. [...] The regularity and order of its layout does not prevent the construction of Brasilia from being an eminently democratic act in the highest sense. The same name attributed to its main square bears witness to this.
> The critic seems to confuse democracy with chaos, with disorder. Now, to those who (like me) live with total disorder, with the institutionalised disorder of our old metropolises, it seemed convenient to instil, from birth, serenity and urban order to the new capital.[81]

And again, at the beginning of his autobiographical book written in the last years of his life, he writes:

> Despite all the criticisms and restrictions, more or less preconceived, I understand that Brasilia was worth it and that over time it will acquire more and more human content and urban consistency, establishing itself as the legitimate democratic capital of the country. It was conceived and born as a democratic capital and the connotation of an autocratic city that has been attributed to it, as a result of the long period of authoritarian rule, will pass.[82]

As in the Estado Novo years, Costa kept a proud distance from the military regime. He did not hesitate to express his dissent, even if on rare occasions or in private circumstances – in a 1964 letter to the Smithsons, he asks them to understand the delay in his reply, reminding them of how "a few peculiar things have happened in this country in between"[83] – and sought for a battle through cultural action rather than through an open political militancy, as instead other Brazilian architects and intellectuals did in the same years. By following his reticent nature, reluctant to occupy "the first line," he was only consistently adhering to his conviction – which was increasingly maturing in an actual evolutionary theory of society, named "teoria das resultantes convergentes" (theory of convergent results)[84] – according to which society is destined to follow a virtuous path, and every symptom of violence and social injustice is destined to leave its place, in due time, to a new historical cycle dominated by reason.

Landscape and urbanism

At the heart of Costa's concept of urban planning was the idea that "urbanising consists in bringing a little city into the countryside and a little bit of the countryside into the city."[85] This was an idea that oversaw the plan of Brasilia, and that, as we have seen, was not the fruit of an impromptu intuition but that had roots in his previous reflection on "new monumentality." Costa had in fact already underlined, on the occasion of the 1948 Symposium, the importance of the role of vegetation and of the "natural setting" in urban planning, arguing that "what characterises the modern concept of urbanism, stretching from the town to the suburbs and thence into the country, is that it abolishes the picturesque by incorporating the bucolic into the monumental."[86] Indeed, a landscape vision permeates every choice regarding the urban project of Brasilia, from the minutest to the most general, structuring the plan itself and overseeing the spatial relationships that defined its urban configuration. It was no coincidence that, to the three scales that were central to the initial Plano Piloto – the collective or monumental one, the daily or residential one, and the social or gregarious one – Costa added a bucolic one from the beginning of the 1960s.[87] This scale referred to the extensive open space surrounding the more densely built-up area, determining the parameters of use and occupation of the terrain in wooded areas or in open recreational spaces, where it was necessary to keep low occupation levels and building heights. As a matter of fact, all the elements that made Brasilia a city capable of "bringing a little city into the countryside and a little bit of the countryside into the city" were already present in the Plano Piloto. The conclusion of the competition report sounds like a real manifesto of this urban conception.

> Thus, while monumental, the city is also comfortable, efficient, welcoming, and homelike. At one and the same time, it is disperse and compact, rural and urban, imaginative and functional. Although vehicular traffic is managed without intersections, the ground is returned, as much as possible, to the pedestrian. [...] We have an efficient highway system on the one hand and, on the other, landscaped parks and gardens.
>
> Brasília, capital of the highways and skyways, *cidade parque*. The century-old dream of the Patriarch.[88]

Following the example of Le Corbusier, as Martino Tattara clearly points out,[89] Costa introduced a series of neologisms in the competition report, destined to become permanently attached to the capital city, including *superquadra, plataforma rodoviária, eixo monumental*, and *cidade parque*. The latter, in particular, identified a new urban model that resembled and at the same time differed – just as the four scales that structured the plan reinterpreted the four functions of the Athens Charter in a less rigid way – from Le Corbusier's Ville Verte.[90] In this sense, the so-called "Memória descritiva do Plano Piloto" can be understood, according to Tattara, as an eminently foundational text in the meaning attributed to this term by Françoise Choay, or a text whose objective is to develop an autonomous conceptual apparatus capable of giving shape to new spatial concepts. Costa attributed a fundamental importance to the use of correct terminology, showing great awareness of the foundational role of words in the text of the Brasilia competition report and their strong significance in orienting the final design, as a set of principles able to guide the construction of the city and its subsequent development, even – or rather, programmatically – without the use of an exhaustive graphic and technical apparatus.

> The expression "avenida" must be banned from the municipal vocabulary. As specified in the Plano Piloto, it is a *cidade parque* – aerial and *rodoviaria*; a city, therefore, where the roadways can directly access its heart, which is the platform at the intersection of the two axes, monumental and residential.[91]

The aspiration to conceive the new capital as a *cidade parque* therefore became clear in all aspects of the plan and even in the apparently most trivial details, often specifying, with great botanical care, the tree and plant species to be placed in the various urban sectors.[92] From the residential scale of the *superquadras* – surrounded by a tree-lined strip that defined their spatial identity and represented a natural permeable limit – to the immense grass expanses of the monumental axis – which Costa claimed to be a legacy of the "immense English lawns" of his childhood – and to the public parks that flanked the monumental axis, constituting the "lungs" of the city; from the cemeteries conceived as "tree-lined gardens," with tombs conceived as "simple stone slabs," to the Forum of Imperial Palms dedicated to Le Corbusier in the Three Powers Square, to the protection of the wild beauty of the shores of the lake, "with woods and fields in a natural and rustic manner so that all the urban population can enjoy its simple pleasures" (Figure 5.9), and finally to the *cinturão verde* (green belt) that Costa provided to maintain around the built area as a buffer zone between the urban centre and the regional development.

Figure 5.9 Aerial view of Brasilia's Plano Piloto from Lake Paranoá, with the Palácio da Alvorada in the foreground. gta Archiv/ETH Zurich, Sigfried Giedion.

The *superquadra* is undoubtedly one of the key inventions of the Plano Piloto, emblematic of a conceptually alien approach to any form of rigid normative prescription, whereas the indications provided in the report exclusively refer to the type of relationship that should take place between open space and built space, aimed at respecting an open and relatively low-density settlement model, in which the terrain was strictly public and could be crossed in all directions.

> For each *quadra*, one particular type of tree would be chosen, the ground would be sown with grass and, on the inner approaches, an additional curtain of bushes and shrubbery [...] would be planted to protect the residential area on all sides from the view of passers-by. This layout has the double advantage of guaranteeing orderly urbanisation even when the density, type, pattern or architectural quality of the buildings vary, and of giving the inhabitants broad shady groves in which to walk or rest, other than the public open spaces foreseen within the *quadras* themselves. Within these *superquadras*, the residential buildings could be arranged in many ways, provided that two general principles are always observed: a maximum uniform height of possibly six stories on

154 *Shaping the true Machine Age*

pilotis, and the separation of vehicular and pedestrian traffic, particularly in the approaches to the primary school and the local community facilities existing in each *quadra*. [...] another strip of land is set aside, equivalent to a third row of *quadras*, for flower and vegetable gardens, and orchards.[93]

A crucial spatial and morphological function was assigned to the vegetative element. The reference to the "passers-by" and the shielding function of the bushes and plants eliminated any remaining idea of a delimiting barrier, in favour of a porous and visually permeable border that was also capable of ensuring the coherence of the whole, even in the eventuality of poor architectural quality of the buildings (Figure 5.10).[94] Attention to perceptive factors – denoting a landscape sensitivity totally unrelated to the established methods of functionalist urbanism – permeates the competition report, based on a "logical-spatial sequence that is articulated as a real 'journey' through the urban organism,"[95] a journey during which the author stopped, now and again, to focus on the relations between the parts, and especially on the "visual impressions" according to which the various urban solutions were conceived: from the uninterrupted view of the monumental axis – which was required to remain unbuilt upon for this purpose precisely – to the opportunity provided by the outgoing traffic system to "say *goodbye* to the capital," to the opening of different views toward the park and monumental axis from the entertainment centre's restaurants and tea rooms.

As has been rightly pointed out often, the photographs of the early years of the capital – in which vast black-and-white lunar landscapes highlight the skeletons of large public buildings against the background of an inhospitable desert – contributed to a distorted reception of the city, designed instead to be founded on the "blunt predominance of the greenery on the white of the built mass."[96] Costa did not fail to record this perceptive distortion, recognising its origins in the construction delays and in the recurring discrepancies with the original plan's intentions.[97]

> What is still missing – and what exasperates me – are the green curtains of the tall trees, designed to provide relief and spatially define each *quadra*. It is easy to imagine how the appearance of the city would be different if such frameworks already existed, juxtaposed in extension and in depth along the entire residential axis.[98]

Or again:

> The environmental-landscape issue of the *quadras* has been badly set up from the beginning. I always wanted them to be treated naturally, like English parks: access avenues to buildings, and large trees, grouped together, emerging from the green lawn where the inhabitants could open their deck chairs and children could play freely; no rigid "embellishment," only large patches of flowers – tibouchine, jasmine, acacia, oleander, etc.[99]

In this last passage, taken from a letter aimed at denouncing the excessive asphalted surface present in the *superquadras*, what emerges – besides the reference to English parks – is a taste for a treatment of open spaces that is as light and "un-designed" as possible, so as to provide a place where inhabitants could enjoy the simplicity of human relationships and the secluded intimacy with nature that is typical of the

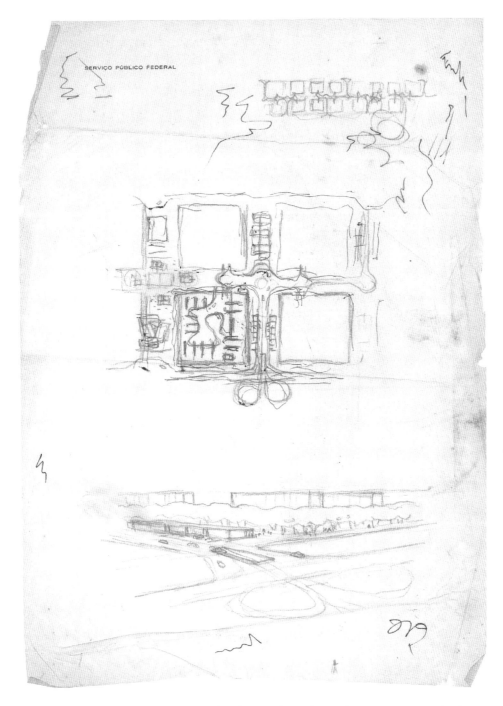

Figure 5.10 Lucio Costa, original sketches for Brasilia's Plano Piloto competition. Plan layout and perspective view of the *superquadra* conception, 1957. Casa de Lucio Costa.

rural condition. Costa therefore imagined introducing a "human scale closer to our traditional domestic and family life" in the heart of the residential sector of the capital,[100] but also endowing the city with natural attractions able to compensate for the uniform landscape of the Planalto Central. Interesting in this regard is a letter in which Costa prompts Niemeyer for Roberto Burle Marx's involvement in the design of open spaces and green areas of the capital.

> Since these are immense areas, we cannot reason by single orders, as we would end up in an impasse yet again. All the more so as our intention is to give the city a natural and unpretentious landscape appearance, limiting the "elaborate" areas to certain well-defined sectors. But the meadows, the flowered fields, the arboretums, and the woods demand a responsible management and one we can live up to.[101]

The idea of a co-presence of the rural and the urban (emphasising the contrast), implied – in addition to a careful study of the relationship between open and built-up areas within the urban fabric – a certain relationship between the city and its territory, which involved the delicate issue of the satellite cities and the so-called Núcleo Bandeirante, the first settlement of the *candangos* located within the metropolitan area of the Plano Piloto. Opposing the occupation of the areas adjacent to the Plano Piloto, Costa unreservedly defended the principle, also of clear Anglo-Saxon origin, of the neat separation between the main urban nucleus and the satellite settlements, prescribing that the empty areas surrounding the capital be turned into a buffer area – the so-called "green belt" – intended for agriculture and pasture farming. As happened with the stark transition from the embankment of the Three Powers Square to the bare vegetation of the *cerrado*, the vivid contrast between the urban centre – monumental, political, and administrative – and the rural scenario – of grazing flocks, vegetable gardens, orchards, and cultivated fields – would have been able to evoke the taking over of the site, with the same strength of the initial gesture, as an act of civilisation in a universal perspective – *sub specie aeternitatis*[102] (Figure 5.11).

Figure 5.11 View of Brasilia's system of embankments. gta Archiv/ETH Zurich, Sigfried Giedion.

This concern would continue to preoccupy Costa in the decades following the inauguration; in addition to some urban furniture projects – such as the pedestrian plaza in the Plataforma Rodoviária, the Municipal Plaza and the fountain of the Television Tower – he developed, in collaboration with his daughter Maria Elisa and his son-in-law Eduardo Sobral, a system of Quadras Econômicas and projects of densification and urban expansion aimed at regulating the occupation of the territory surrounding the Plano Piloto, in order to prevent the territorial model of the original proposal from being distorted by careless interventions.[103]

In 1987, in regards to UNESCO's initiative to register the city – as "fait majeur dans l'histoire de l'urbanisme"[104] – in the list of World Heritage Sites, Costa drew attention to the diversity and the uniqueness of Brasilia as an "elected" city, whose identity must be maintained and preserved. To justify its inclusion, he relied on his "original urban planning proposal" and in particular on the necessity to comply with the four scales lying at the foundation of its urban structure: "the symbolic and collective one, or monumental; the domestic one, or residential; the social one, or gregarious; and the recreational one, or bucolic."[105] In the important text "Brasília revisitada," annexed to the 1987 decree, he also gives detailed provisions for the proper protection of each of the four aforementioned scales and indicates the strategies for the future expansion of the city, jointly addressing the two issues at hand: "on the one hand, how to allow [Brasilia] to grow, ensuring the permanence of the testimony of the original proposal; on the other, how to preserve it without suppressing the vital impulse inherent in such a young city."[106] In the same way, in the letter sent by Costa to Ítalo Campofiorito in 1990 and intended to regulate the protection of the plan of Brasilia at a national level – which was issued a few years after its registration in the list of UNESCO World Heritage Sites – emphasis was placed on the need to preserve the particular relationship between the built and open spaces that characterised it – that is to say, its peculiar urban form rather than the architectural image of the individual buildings, except of course for the more representative ones.

> Reasoning in the rigorous and fundamental terms of design – of *urban composition* – the time has come to define and limit the future spatial volumetry of the city; that is to say the relationship between the green areas to be maintained *in natura* (or cultivated as fields, orchards, and woods), and the white areas to be built upon. The time has come; or rather, the last chance in which it is still possible to revitalise this confrontation and therefore preserve, forever, the original character of Brasilia as a *cidade parque* – the *facies* that differentiates the capital from the other Brazilian cities. For many reasons, this restriction alone will be able to ensure that future generations have the opportunity and the right to know Brasilia as it was originally conceived.[107]

The unprecedented and experimental approach to protection that was adopted for the Brasilia plan – explicitly disengaged from the authenticity of the material of which the city was composed, and referring solely to the parameters of land occupation that identified the settlement model – projected it into a utopian, universal, and timeless dimension, which perhaps is the area it more appropriately belonged to. What this approach meant to preserve was the civilising effort of a nation, and the utopia pursued by a specific architectural and urban culture under the aegis of an economic progress that also aimed at becoming the engine of social progress, above all. The permanence of the plan guaranteed the permanence of its condition of utopia, confidently built on the *tabula rasa* of the Planalto Central and whose mode of protection could only reflect the non-conventionality of its urban conception.

After Brasilia, Costa began to systematically extend his professional activity to urban planning, receiving various assignments both in Brazil and abroad, constantly accompanying his already intense commitment to Brazilian cities within the SPHAN with several original design contributions. As expected, special attention was dedicated to the city of Rio, the subject of a number of urban proposals at different scales – some of which were completely or partially developed – based on the attempt to reconcile the dizzying real-estate development of the city with the need to protect the coherence and quality of the "urban landscape" as much as possible. The lesson of Brasilia, by analogy or by contrast, is evident in all these projects: from the proposed extension of the Avenida Atlântica and from the Plano Piloto for the Baixada de Jacarepaguá to the proposals of the 1970s for the improvement of the vehicle and pedestrian circulation flows; from the various urban arrangements to the proposals formulated in 1974 to "contain and regulate, within a certain limit, the disorderly expansion and excessive densification."[108] Here, Costa importantly suggested the reduction of the lot building areas, the regulation of the allowed maximum heights according to the occupancy rates in certain areas, and above all a massive and systematic planting of new trees, seen as the only possible solution to "cushion the ostentatious ugliness of anti-architecture that was spreading not only in the suburbs of Rio but throughout the country."

The access to Glória hill, and to the 18th-century church located on its top, was a paradigmatic case of the indissoluble link between urbanism and landscaping. Costa had already urged the SPHAN – in a scientific opinion of 1943 – to provide for the "progressive liberation" of the hill from the existing buildings and to prevent the construction of any new tall buildings, so as not to jeopardise the view toward the Outeiro de Glória church – its "*mise-en-scène*" – and to incorporate the hill into the system of existing parks. For Costa, this operation was "strictly landscape related" and was part of the broader demolition operation of the Santo Antônio hill and the construction operation of the Aterro do Flamengo, rendering a service to the "'urban landscape' in one of its most characteristic areas, seeped with tradition." Aware of the delicate operation, he also recommended avoiding – in planning the access to the church – any monumentality, decoration, and "counterfeiting" of the authentic style of the building.[109] Faithful to this idea, he rejected the project elaborated by Roberto Burle Marx, which he believed to be lacking the "desirable unity and simplicity" and to be too fragmented to coexist with the architectural purity of the chapel, preferring a previous project by José de Souza Reis.[110] Finally, dissatisfied with both proposals, Costa elaborated a new project for the church access, developing a zigzag path that was sensitive to the site and that was realised with stone material obtained from the demolitions of the *cais* of Flamengo, of which he personally followed the construction, choosing the exact location for each of the recovered stones.

While in this case the challenge was to develop corrective measures capable of re-establishing a possible order in the already congested urban fabric of the site, in the case of the Plano Piloto for the Baixada de Jacarepaguá region – which included the entire coastal stretch of the Barra da Tijuca[111] – the goal was the opposite, since it was a matter of regulating and encouraging the future urbanisation of a vast region[112] characterised by a landscape and natural condition of enormous value and still substantially intact. Costa himself recorded the contradictory nature of the endeavor, expressing regret for the "thankless task of violating ecology," while also becoming aware of the need to give the entire urban population an "outlet" (*desafogo*) to the sea, lakes, and mountains.

> What is most attractive in the region is its light and rustic air, the scale – the beaches and dunes seem endless – and that unusual feeling of being in an untouched, primordial world.
>
> Thus, the first instinctive impulse is always to prevent it from changing in any way. But on the other hand, it seems clear that a space of such proportions and so open and accessible will not be able to continue to remain untouched forever; sooner or later it will have to be urbanised. The intense occupation of the area is already irreversible.
>
> It is therefore natural to look at the embankments, the scaffolding, the structures, the dwellings that are multiplying, and all this anticipated progressive visual pollution of the landscape, with a certain amount of embarrassment and regret – not to mention guilt – in the hope that the future definition of the duly separated nuclei, the free areas, and the intense arborisation might help confer an urban and environmental coherence to the whole, capable of compensating, at least in part, for the lost naturalness.[113]

This consideration is at the heart of Costa's urban conception: the urban planner has the difficult task of reconciling the vital impulse of the private initiative with the respect for the site's vocation; he has the task of combining a lifestyle adapted to the expectations of a rapidly growing modern metropolis with the atavistic aspiration of man to be in contact with natural elements. The attitude that Costa chose to adopt was of extreme lucidity, and was based on trusting progress and reason as instruments capable of positively steering human action in the process. For Costa, modern cities were "living organisms in a permanent process of transformation,"[114] and thus it would make no sense to pretend to limit their growth in the name of preserving the status quo. In the name of this principle, and based on conditions very different from that of Brasilia – since the public administration had the responsibility, in addition to providing basic road infrastructure, to establish the criteria for land use that private initiatives would then be required to follow[115] – Costa placed the planning of the area within a broader reading of its role within the whole urban organism. Therefore, as happened for Brasilia, he prefigured the scenario of a blunt confrontation between urban and rural, installing the nucleus of a new metropolitan centre in a position that was properly distant from the coast, specifying the use of the different areas according to their strategic location with respect to the city and the main landscape features. He also identified – showcasing an evident update with respect to the most innovative urban planning practices in the international field – the principle of step-by-step occupation, able to support the onset of new needs and to allow the gradual consolidation of the new settlement methods.[116] Even with the necessary gradual transition from a more compact fabric to a more and more rarefied one, the plan denoted a clear preference for a building pattern consisting of towers

160 Shaping the true Machine Age

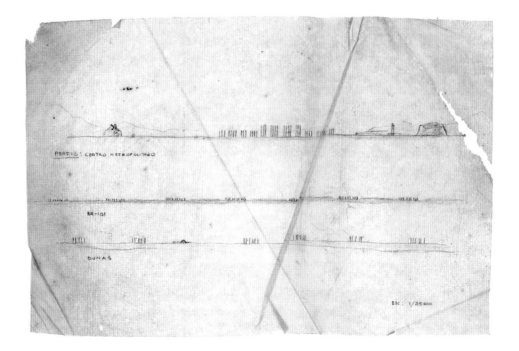

Figure 5.12 Lucio Costa, sketches of the "Plano Piloto para a urbanização da baixada compreendida entre a Barra da Tijuca, o Pontal de Sernambetiba e Jacarepaguá." Territorial sections, 1969. Casa de Lucio Costa.

appropriately distanced from each other, with the intention of making the most of the views and "defining and giving spatial rhythm to the landscape, thus compensating for the limited remnants of wild land"[117] (Figure 5.12). In the design indications for the future Metropolitan Centre, Costa used a particular urban system for the first time, the so-called Green Arcades (*Arcadas verdes*). These were open commercial galleries, with a vaulted roof, arranged on both sides of a tree-lined garden, sometimes divided into four symmetrical lawns. This solution, although never realised, was reintroduced in many of his subsequent urban planning proposals, including the competition for the new capital of Nigeria,[118] the proposal of a new urban centre in São Luis do Maranhão, the project for the Casablanca Corniche, and finally the project for the Setor Hoteleiro Norte in Brasilia. Costa attributed this solution the crucial role of mediator between the scale of the built environment and that of the street, creating a sort of multi-functioned urban "animation centre" for the exclusive use of pedestrians and introducing a significant corrective measure to the threat of urban alienation.

A new humanism

At the margins of an article on the Barra da Tijuca project, Costa noted that in his urbanistic approach "the user, the sociologist, and the psychologist are always

Shaping the true Machine Age 161

present," adding that he did not place himself under any "school" but considered himself fundamentally "by nature and education, a humanist," and this condition was reflected in what he conceived.[119] This is a crucial claim, full of implications to help fully understand how to place his work with respect to the new themes that were emerging in international architectural and urban culture starting from the post-war period and throughout the following decades.

Contrary to what has often been said, in the Plano Piloto of Brasilia the strain toward supporting the values of a more human urbanism – in which the individual and his needs acquired an important central stance – found ample space. The social or gregarious scale – from the collective facilities of the *superquadras* defining the neighbourhood unit to the actual civic centre – was given the task of constructing the community fabric that, together with the grandeur of the monumental scale, allowed the capital to recognise itself as being *civitas* instead of *urbs*; or rather, as an inclusive urban organism, in which citizens could identify and find adequate spaces to express the necessary collective dimension of urban life. Costa imagined the cultural and entertainment centre located near the Plataforma Rodoviária as a vital connective area for socialisation. His concept of the centre drew on the most disparate urban models, significantly drawing inspiration from the immense storehouse of tradition rather than from the repertoire of functionalist urbanism. With its concentration of cultural and leisure attractions (cinemas, theatres, cafes) arranged in "a harmonious and continuous architectural whole," this modern urban centre – located at the intersection of the two axes – aspired to blend the atmosphere of the pulsating centres of the main European and American cities – a "mixture of Piccadilly Circus, Times Square, and the Champs-Elysées"[120] – with the human scale of traditional historical centres, like the Rua do Ouvidor in Rio de Janeiro and the Venetian *calli* (streets between two continuous rows of buildings). Despite the elusiveness of the drawings, the text of the report lingers on descriptions of spatial articulations, sequences of pedestrian walkways and porticoed connections, perceptive gradations between small courts with cafes, systems of loggias overlooking the park, and on the visual impact of the iconic urban front entirely covered by luminous advertising signs. The trivialisation of this conception in the constructed reality of Brasilia distressed and frustrated Costa for many years.[121] In fact, in the numerous cases in which he found himself having to defend the capital, he relied on the incompleteness of what he often called the *coração da cidade* (the heart of the city) or simply *core* – as he wrote in 1985, "it is necessary to properly develop the urban centre, the 'heart' of the city, its still unfinished 'core'"[122] – giving the term an evocative power that revealed his in-depth knowledge of the debate held at the VIII CIAM in Hoddesdon in 1951.

> I must remind you – he wrote in *Jornal do Brasil* in 1976 – that the large Plataforma Rodoviária with an open view on the beautiful esplanade, which is the *traix d'union* of the so-called Plano Piloto with the so-called satellite cities, has always been understood, precisely, as a point of articulation of the four main sectors [*quarteirões*] that constitute the urban centre, that is, the "core" of the city.[123]

And yet, in one of his few visits to Brasilia in the 1980s, Costa was struck more than anything else by the evening vitality of the Rodoviária, when the entire metropolitan population animated the nodal point of public transport, transforming it into a flowing crossroads endowed with a strong popular connotation that the "true Brazilians who built the city" have legitimately made their own,[124] far from the "sophisticated and cosmopolitan" centre he had imagined. The idea of a *Brasil verdadeiro* (real Brazil) imposing itself on the abstraction of the plan – of a "reality that has overcome the dream" – was a leitmotif of Costa's *a posteriori* evaluation of the Brasilia plan, often vacillating between enthusiastic approval and resigned acceptance. The aspiration for a "definitive Brasil,"[125] one that was civilised – in contrast with the actual country that was still underdeveloped – emerged where Brasilia showed its weakest side, that of social segregation.

> It is natural that Brasilia has its problems, which are in reality nothing more than the contradictions and problems of the developing and non-integrated country itself, where the recent tradition of an agrarian and slave economy and late unplanned industrialisation have left the tenacious mark of pauperism. The simple transfer of the capital cannot resolve these fundamental contradictions, especially since powerful interests have benefitted from this status of "chronic anomaly" which, on the outskirts of the city, has regained its rights.[126]

The aspects Costa complained about were basically two. First, the formation of satellite cities even before the complete occupation of the Plano Piloto had taken place, which he considered an "irrational anticipation"[127] that was contrary to the intentions of the plan; instead, he rather supported an "architecturally contained occupation destined for economic dwellings" in contrast with the "policy of decentralisation and premature peripheral dispersion" implemented by the various administrations.[128] His second concern was the failure to realise the main "social" measure envisaged by the plan, that is to say the coexistence of different social strata in the residential urban sector. This would have been achieved thanks to the neighbourhood units of four *superquadras* destined for inhabitants of different social status, which would have avoided "the establishment of unwanted processes of spatial and social segregation"[129] and the "stratification of the city in rigidly differentiated economic areas [...] offering an adequate solution to the problem of urban coexistence of social classes in the capitalist regime."[130] In his opinion, this measure failed because of the "false realism" of the real-estate market and the "utopian abstraction" of conceiving "a single standard of apartments, as if society were already without classes."[131] It is evident that for Costa the still unbridgeable distance between the "negative Brazil" and the "definitive Brazil" was not a sufficient reason to delegitimise a plan conceived for a more advanced stage of civilisation, thus proving its true utopian nature, a foretaste – at the organisational/settlement level – of the "universal tendency" according to which "the whole world is destined to belong to the middle class."[132]

The particular articulation between the individual sphere and the collective one that was at the centre of the Brasilia plan was indeed destined to become, for all the following decades, the real knot around which Costa's commitment to urban planning and constant exercise of thought inextricably intertwined, which, from a certain point on, he was able to express in disparate occasions, from essays – usually written in the context of his rare participation in international conferences – to consultancies, testimonies, letters, scattered notes, and, later, interviews.[133] In

1976, invited by the Italians Carlo Lotti and Mario Nervi[134] to participate in the international competition for the plan of the new capital of Nigeria, Costa opened the competition report with an enlightening programmatic declaration:

> The town is the palpable expression of the human need for contact, communication, organisation, and exchange – under a peculiar physico-social circumstance, in a historical context.
>
> In the tasks of the engineer, man is mostly envisaged as a *collective* being, as a "number," and therefore a *quantity* criterion prevails; albeit [whereas], in the eyes of the architect, man is foremost considered as an *individual*, as a "person," prevailing therefore the criterion of *quality*.
>
> On the other hand, the interests of man as an individual don't necessarily coincide with the interests of the same man as a collective being; it is up to the urban designer to try to solve, within the limits of possibility, this fundamental contradiction.[135]

This declaration – surprisingly aligned with the international urban debate that since the end of the 1950s was increasingly settling on a new opening to the social and psychological needs of the individual capable of overcoming a mechanistic conception of society – sheds a new light on the simplistic assimilation of Costa's vision to the CIAM's functionalist orthodoxy. It is therefore not surprising that Peter Smithson included Costa among the first contacts, albeit still at an informal spoken level, in view of the formalisation of the so-called "new CIAM." A contact that preceded by less than a year the same Congress of Otterlo, which would decree the dissolution of CIAM in September 1959, marking the end of the formative phase of Team X.[136] The content of Smithson's letter suggests that the recipients had been carefully selected as "'like minds' known to be working on similar problems," with which "vital contacts" had occurred and with which the respective "chance meetings have been fruitful to the exchange of ideas."[137] As a matter of fact, the year before, Costa had had the chance to personally meet Peter Smithson in Bern, Switzerland, together with Denys Lasdun[138] and Arthur Korn, on occasion of the discussion promoted by the magazine *Architectural Design* in its issue on "Capital Cities," where the problem of "creating a city from scratch" was tackled through the cases of Brasilia, "a new city," and of the Smithson's plan for Berlin, "a new core." If in this case some discrepancies emerged in particular with Korn,[139] Smithson was evidently inclined to underline the similarities between his plan and Costa's, both considered, significantly, as not hierarchical urban conceptions, driven by a "constellation of principles, of which not one is the absolute generator." The end of the discussion focuses exactly on the role of the urban center as a generator of collective gathering opportunities for the enhancement of civic life, as the same Smithson claims:

> In doing this plan we were working, as Mr. Costa was, to a programme. It is not an ideal plan, but it fits the given statistical material of areas, functions, and so on. But the thing one should bring out is that at the heart of this pleasurable human intercourse is some sort of symbol of the meeting of like minds at an intense level, and we made one gesture towards this here; we did the same thing as Mr. Costa – we accentuated the east-west, north-south crossing,

and at this point we have placed the "Techological Centre" as a sort of boat over the top of the crossing and you pass underneath [...] we selected this "Technology" as being, as it were, the "cathedral of the mind" in this instance.[140]

It is therefore evident that the "new CIAM" saw in Costa – whose ideas seem to have circulated since his participation in the UNESCO Conference in Venice in 1952[141] and whose reputation grew intensily after Brasilia's competition – a potential partner, by virtue of an affinity of ideas, or – to use the words of Peter Smithson – of "some common ideological basis." Yet, as had happened with the CIAM, the various invitations to attend the meetings were not honoured by the Brazilian architect, who simply maintained sporadic correspondence with some of the exponents of the new group.[142] The relationship with the Smithsons intensified in 1964 as a result of their assignment for the British embassy in Brasilia; but it was at the International Town Planning Congress held in Florence in October 1967 that Costa had another crucial opportunity to meet some of the main members of Team X and share his ideas in urban planning. The Congress – organised by Anthony Krafft, director of the magazine *Architecture, Formes + Fonctions* and already in contact with Costa for some time,[143] and by the Municipality of Florence – saw the participation of Costa alongside Jacob B. Bakema, Georges Candilis, Peter Smithson, and Heikki Siren, who had all been called to devise an answer to the alarming 1966 flood of the Arno River. On this occasion, the different approach of Costa and Smithson on an apparently marginal – but actually substantial – issue like that that of the presence of cars in the historical centre, revealed symptomatic differences that bring us to reflect on which aspects their visions were destined to diverge on. While Smithson condemned the effect of the cars on the monuments in the name of an idea of Florence as a sort of "living" museum, Costa defended the coexistence of cars and pedestrians in the name of an idea of the historic centre as a living and pulsating heart, where "the lively movement of cars represents the blood that maintains their contemporaneity," suggesting the creation of new tree-lined parking areas around the centre to be meant as a landscaped "buffer zone" between the historical core and the more recent urban developments.[144] Furthermore, both in his contribution to the debate and in his final appeal to the Florentine people, Costa envisaged the planning of a Second Florence, a new city confidently built in the future – able to control the uncontainable growth of the city and to contribute to the harmonic development of the suburban areas – representing the union, invoked in various occasions starting from 1961, of a trust in progress and in the birth of a new humanism[145] worthy of the Renaissance. And it is precisely from this vision of the future – founded on an unshakable faith in progress and in a positive evolutionary movement – that we can measure his distance from the other speakers, more than from any other aspects.

With extreme fidelity to the modernist lesson, Costa placed himself "above" history, to some extent; and from this privileged position he set out to find in history an intrinsic *ratio*, which would manifest itself in the cyclical alternation of formal constants, in the occurrence of unexpected convergences, in the concatenation between apparently unrelated events, and, finally, in the tension leading toward an inevitable progress. The deterministic optimism inherent in this approach forcefully emerged in the above-mentioned "theory of convergent results," formulated in

Figure 5.13 Portrait of Lucio Costa in Brasilia during the construction, 1957. Casa de Lucio Costa.

166 *Shaping the true Machine Age*

1952 in "L'architecte et la societé contemporaine," according to which a new propulsive thrust would follow each moment of stagnancy in the evolutionary process, until reaching an "unprecedented historical cycle, more fruitful and, this time, truly human."[146] According to Costa, it was the scientific and technological development – expression of human intelligence and therefore of nature itself – that in this process had the task of guiding society on a virtuous and rational path. This idea – developed in an essay elaborated in 1961 on the occasion of the centenary of the Massachusetts Institute of Technology,[147] and at the centre of Costa's proposal for a Museum of Science and Technology elaborated in the 1970s – found numerous formulations in texts on disparate subjects, often of political nature, and with an increasingly prophetic tone.[148]

In Costa's view, the commitment to peace during the years of cold war[149] could not be separated from the commitment to improve the environment of human life, namely through architecture and urban planning. In 1962, when invited by Richard Neutra to participate in the Californian Convention of Architects of Monterrey, Costa as usual declined the invitation, but suggested that attendees at the Congress discuss the theme of "Architecture and coexistence."

> As you probably know I am a pacifist. I believe we should establish bridges between the two halves of the world instead of deliberately destroying them. Architects are the same everywhere. They are concerned with life, usefulness, decency, and beauty. A few years ago, the Russians were copying American planes, now they have conquered space. Very soon they will be doing creative and significant architecture. Coexistence is not a matter of choice but of fact. Historical fact: the means of destruction being what they are, war on a world scale is not feasible anymore. So let's begin coexistence through architecture.[150]

At the beginning of his eightieth decade, in a letter addressed to the Argentine architect and intellectual Alberto Petrina, Costa again insisted on the great misunderstanding of functionalism. In this regard, he remembered how Le Corbusier's lesson was, despite the many misunderstandings and interpretations that were in his opinion distorted, fundamentally aimed at the "integral man"[151] – that is, the possibility of "giving men – to all men – equal material conditions of life and of time availability, to allow them, individually, a multiform development according to the character, vocation, and capacity of each one." And, while attributing to an ending era the conviction that "the new architecture and social transformations were part of the same general process of ethical renewal of the world," he did not abandon trust "in a more human and more just world," where the balance and integration between "the collective on the grand scale and the irreducibility of the individual" would finally be possible.

Notes

1. Costa to an unidentified editor, Rio de Janeiro, 18 November 1950. CLC, VI A 01-03290.
2. Costa to André Bloc, n.d. CLC, VI A 01-01814. Bloc was the director of the magazine *L'Architecture d'Aujourd'hui*, which in 1952 would publish Costa's essay "Imprévu et importance de la contribution des architectes brésiliens au développement actuel de l'architecture contemporaine." Maria Elisa Costa dates the letter around 1950.

3 The correspondence held in his private archive allows us to reconstruct the many commitments that Costa declined, the prizes he did not personally collect, and the many publication proposals that had no outcome.
4 The death of his wife in a tragic car accident, in which Costa himself was the driver, was destined to profoundly change the architect's approach to life and to his profession. In a letter to his friend Rodrigo Mello Franco de Andrade, he writes:

> Although I love New York, coming to Paris is always a pleasure. This city is at the same time monumental and active, bohemian and familiar. But it brings me a mortal nostalgia. Leleta has always loved being here and her memory continues to live in my heart, more and more. As you may have sensed, I only travel for the girls [...]. Motherless because of me, my first commitment is toward them. The other professional commitments – public or private – will be honoured when God wishes.

Costa to Mello Franco de Andrade, n.d. CLC, VI A 01-01002.
5 It is not clear who was responsible for Costa's involvement, although we can assume that Paulo Carneiro's presence as Brazilian delegate of UNESCO did have a relevant role, since – according to Barbara Shapiro – he was also the one who had recommended Le Corbusier for the commission. Christopher E.M. Pearson claims that the names of the committee candidates were submitted by the CIAM to the Director-General of UNESCO, Jaime Torres Bodet; Pearson also reports a letter in which Le Corbusier informs Costa that Gropius, Markelius, and Rogers had already accepted and that he "would be pleased if you would join us in making up a homogeneous committee." Le Corbusier to Costa, 6 March 1952. FLC I3(4)52-53, 284. See Christopher E.M. Pearson, *Designing UNESCO: Art, Architecture and International Politics at Mid-Century* (London: Routledge, 2016, 1st edn Ashgate Publishing, 2010), 124, 137.
6 Barbara E. Shapiro, "'Tout ça est foutaise, foutaise et demi!' Le Corbusier and UNESCO," *RACAR: Revue d'Art Canadienne/Canadian Art Review* XVI, no. 2 (1989): 171–179, 298–307; 172.
7 See, in particular, the already-mentioned publications by Barbara E. Shapiro and Christopher E.M. Pearson.
8 Costa, "L'idea della curva," *Casabella continuità*, no. 226 (April 1959): 7–8.
9 See Pearson, *Designing UNESCO*, 193.
10 Shapiro, "'Tout ça est foutaise...'" 173.
11 See paragraph "In search of a new monumentality."
12 Walter Gropius, "Cronaca di un lungo lavoro," *Casabella continuità*, no. 226 (April 1959): 5–7.
13 The attempt by part of the Five to replace the site of Place de Fontenoy with one in the Bois de Boulogne – which Shapiro rightly traces back to the modernist idea according to which a direct confrontation with the historical urban fabric would have hindered full creative freedom – recalls Le Corbusier's attempt to move the site of the Ministry from the established lot in Esplanada do Castelo to a vacant lot on Baía de Guanabara (as well as Costa's attempt to move the site for the Rio University Campus in the Lagôa Rodrigo de Freitas).
14 In a letter of 1972 (perhaps addressed to the President of the Instituto de Arquitetos do Brasil), Costa states:

> It is the architectural ethics that count. As for the so-called "professional ethics" – the ones that allow the patient to die while searching for a breach capable of justifying a possible saving intervention – I only used them once, twenty years ago, in a commemorative article for C da M [*Correio da Manhã*] and for the sole purpose of explaining why, in the case of the Ministry of Education, the responsible architects did not take them into account.

CLC, VI A 01-00767.

168 Shaping the true Machine Age

15 The documents held in the Casa de Lucio Costa attest the commitment by part of Costa and Gropius in joining forces so as to deal with the controversy raised in the press regarding the alleged "ethical objections" underlying the exclusion of Le Corbusier as designer.
16 Costa to Mr. Thomson (non-identified, regarding a previous communication by Howard Robertson), n.d. CLC, VI A 01-02355.
17 Ernersto Nathan Rogers, "Il dramma del Palazzo dell'UNESCO," *Casabella continuità*, no. 226 (April 1959): 2–25.
18 Le Corbusier, "Due metodi di lavoro," *Casabella continuità*, no. 226 (April 1959): 8.
19 Pearson, *Designing UNESCO*, 151, 183.
20 Note that these are the same fundamental qualities attributed by Costa to the idea of monumentality (see paragraph "In search of a new monumentality").
21 Costa, "L'idea della curva," *Casabella continuità*, no. 226 (April 1959): 7–8.
22 When, in October 1953, Gropius proposed that only three of the Five (himself, Le Corbusier, and Rogers) should continue the work – because of Costa's remote distance and because of an accident suffered by Markelius – Costa writes: "As for me you may always count Le Corbusier's vote twice, I will stand with him under any circumstances." Costa to Gropius, n.d. CLC, VI A 01-00286.
23 In 1958, congratulating Costa for winning the Brasilia competition, Gropius would show complete confidence in the lucidity and intelligence of the plan: "I am excited and elated that this great venture for once fell into the right hands. Your plan is superb, simple and convincing. All power to you that it may pilot the execution of the City all the way through!" Gropius to Costa, 29 January 1958. CLC, VI A 02-01823.
24 Costa to Holford, CLC, VI A 01-01840.
25 See the correspondence between Le Corbusier and Paulo Carneiro, in Cecília Rodrigues dos Santos et al., *Le Corbusier e o Brasil* (São Paulo: Tessela-Projeto, 1987), and Carneiro's letter to Costa, 17 February 1953. CLC, VI A 02-00735. The prize, dedicated to the work of a great contemporary architect, would be awarded to Walter Gropius.
26 See Costa to Lourival Gomes Machado, 12 January 1959. CLC, VI A 01-00707; and Costa to Sérgio Buarque de Holanda, Paulo Mendes de Almeida and Lourival Gomes Macahdo, 12 February 1959. CLC, VI A 01-03230.
27 For more information on the relations between Costa and Le Corbusier (and, more in general, between Le Corbusier and Brazil), the obligatory reference is to the aforementioned volume *Le Corbusier e o Brasil*.
28 Costa applied this work method to most of his built work. This is the case, for example, in the first half of the 1950s, of the headquarters of the Banco Aliança and of the Sede Social do Jockey Club Brasileiro, the constructions of which were followed by Augusto Guimarães Filho and Jorge Hue respectively.
29 See the correspondence reported in *Le Corbusier e o Brasil*.
30 *Le Corbusier e o Brasil*, 245.
31 Apart from the New York and the Milan pavilions, all projects elaborated by Costa outside of Brazil were in fact destined to remain only on paper.
32 In 1958, Le Corbusier entrusted the development of the interiors to Charlotte Perriand, who from this moment on would hold an affectionate relationship with Costa and with his daughter Maria Elisa.
33 Costa to Le Corbusier, 5 February 1956. *Le Corbusier e o Brasil*, 274.
34 Costa, "L'architecte et la societé contemporaine," *L'artiste dans la société contemporaine (conférence internationale des artistes, Venise, 22–28 Septembre 1952). Témoignages recueillis par l'UNESCO* (Paris: UNESCO 1954), 88–99, republished in *Arquitectura* XXV, no. 47 (June 1953): 7–23, with the title "O arquiteto e a sociedade contemporânea." Reported in Alberto Xavier, ed., *Lúcio Costa: sôbre arquitetura* (Porto Alegre: Editora UniRitter, 2007, 1st edn 1962), 230– 251.
35 Costa, *Registro de uma vivência* (São Paulo: Empresa das Artes, 1995), 262– 267. Also published in *Architecture, formes + fonctions* XV (1969): 67– 69.
36 Costa, "Considerações sobre arte contemporânea" (Rio de Janeiro: Cadernos de Cultura do Serviço de Documentação do Ministério de Educação e Saúde, 1952). Henceforth quoted from Xavier, ed., *Sôbre arquitetura*, 202–229. In addition to presenting great

overlaps with contemporary texts – like "Imprévu et importance de la contribution des architectes brésiliens au développement actuel de l'architecture contemporaine," "O arquiteto e a sociedade contemporânea," "L'art et l'avènement des masses" – "Considerações" also presents passages taken from previous texts, like "Muita construção, alguma arquitetura e um milagre," "In Search of a New Monumentality," some excerpts from the already-mentioned Universidade do Brasil campus project report, and from "Sobre o ensino da arquitetura." Finally, it also presents substantial overlaps with a text that remained unpublished until 2002 – issued in the *Mais!* supplement of the newspaper *Folha de São Paulo*, on 24 February 2002, 12–13, entitled "Arte moderna e socialismo" (CLC, V B 05-00575).

37 Costa, "O arquiteto e a sociedade contemporanea," in Xavier, ed., *Sôbre arquitetura*, 230.
38 Costa, "Considerações sobre arte contemporânea," in Xavier, ed., *Sôbre arquitetura*, 221.
39 Costa points out that we should speak of integration and not synthesis of the arts, as it does not consist in a fusion but in a co-existence, one in which each discipline maintains its autonomy while also enriching itself through the shared mutual contribution.
40 Theoretically imbued with formalist theories on history of art, like Heinrich Wölfflin's "Principles of Art History" and the explicitly mentioned theories on Baroque by Eugeni d'Ors.
41 Jorge Francisco Liernur, "*The South American Way*. El 'milagro' brasileño, los Estados Unidos y la Segunda Guerra Mundial (1939–1943)," *Block*, no. 4 (1999): 23–41; 33.
42 Costa, "Considerações sobre arte contemporânea," 202–229.
43 In the text "Formes et Fonctions" – first published in 1967 in the magazine *Architecture, formes + fonctions* XIII (1967): 26–27 – in addition to reprising the dichotomy between static formal conceptions and dynamic ones, as formulated in "Considerações sobre arte contemporânea," Costa returns to the issue of the misunderstanding of functionalism, showing how the inalienable contribution of the "intention that drives the process of formal integration" was at the base of all formal and expressive results, through examples of Luso-Brazilian colonial architecture.
44 Costa, "Considerações sobre arte contemporânea," 202–229.
45 See Jaqueline Tyrwhitt, José Luis Sert, and Ernesto Nathan Rogers, *The Heart of the City: Towards the Humanisation of Urban Life* (London: Lund Humphries, 1952).
46 Costa to Maude Richards, n.d. CLC, VI A 01-01812.
47 See Guilherme Wisnik, Adrian Forty and Elisabetta Andreoli, eds, *Doomed to Modernity*, in *Brazil's Modern Architecture* (London/New York: Phaidon, 2004), 22–55.
48 See paragraph "Baroque and national personality."
49 In Brazil, the 1950s represent a phase of great optimism corresponding to the economic boom and to the democratic transition to the presidency of Juscelino Kubitschek, which followed the turbulent conclusion of the so-called "Vargas Era" that took place around the middle of the decade. See Fernando Luiz Lara, *The Rise of Popular Modernist Architecture in Brazil* (Gainesville, FL: University Press of Florida, 2008).
50 The Congress was organised by AICA (Association Internationale des Critiques d'Art) and was held on 17–25 September 1959 in Brasilia, Rio, and São Paulo, a few months before the inauguration of Brasilia.
51 Costa, "Saudação aos críticos de arte," *Registro*, 298–299. English translation in Alessandro Balducci et al., eds, *Brasilia. A Utopia Come True/Un'utopia realizzata 1960–2010* (Milano: Triennale Electa, 2010), 142–144.
52 "In Search of a New Monumentality: a Symposium by Gregor Paulsson, Henry-Russell Hitchcock, William Holford, Sigfried Giedion, Walter Gropius, Lucio Costa and Alfred Roth," *The Architectural Review* 104, no. 621 (September 1948): 117–128. The indication of Costa's name was due to Agnes Claudius, who nominated him when questioned by her editor on who in Brazil "is considered the best writer on the theory and philosophy of architecture today." Agnes Claudius to Costa, 24 January 1947. CLC, VI A 02-01601.
53 Holford would later be part of the Brasilia competition committee.
54 Sigfried Giedion, *Architecture You and Me. The Diary of a Development* (Cambridge, MA: Harvard University Press, 1958), 48–51.

55 "In Search of a New Monumentality," 118, 120. Note that Giedion mentions the Ministry of Education in Rio as an emblematic example of a modern building capable of expressing a new monumentality.
56 This quote and the following ones are taken from Costa, "In Search of a New Monumentality," 127.
57 Here, the implicit reference is clearly the Ministry, the definitive project of which had to place itself in direct opposition to the municipal regulations in force and to the same professional ethics. See Costa, "Relato pessoal," *Modulo* X, no. 40 (September 1975): 23–24 (reported in *Registro*, 135–138).
58 Costa elaborated the project at the request of Carmen Saavedra (who commissioned the Casa Saavedra in Petrópolis) and of Father Barbosa Lemos.
59 The final solution would, however, greatly differ from the original sketch, as it changed the balance between the built volume and the sail element and it partly distorted the lightness of the original proposed design.
60 They were both developed respectively in the early and late 1960s, and both were actually constructed. For more information on these monumental projects and their shared qualities, see José Pessôa, "A persistência de uma ideia. Sagres e os riscos dos monumentos modernos de Lúcio Costa," *Arquitextos* 15, no. 175.01 (December 2014). www.vitruvius.com.br/revistas/read/arquitextos/15.175/5374; Gaia Piccarolo, "Lucio Costa's Luso-Brazilian Routes: Recalibrating 'Center' and 'Periphery'," in Patricio Del Real and Helen Gyger, eds, *Latin American Modern Architectures: Ambiguous Territories* (London/New York: Routledge, 2012), 33–52.
61 Costa, "Conquanto não pretendesse competir...," n.d. ACI-RJ, LC-CE05.
62 And perhaps also to the Trylon and Perisphere of the 1939 New York World's Fair, which Costa knew well. Note that the same element would be used by Oscar Niemeyer in different monumental projects, like the Ermida Dom Bosco, erected in 1957 near Lake Paranoá to celebrate the future construction of the new capital in Planalto Central.
63 The jury included Israel Pinheiro (president), Oscar Niemeyer, Paulo Antunes Ribeiro, Luis Hildebrando Horta Barbosa, André Sive, Stamo Papadaki, and William Holford. Sources agree that William Holford – whom at the time was involved in the planning of Canberra – played a key role in the selection of Costa's plan. See William Holford, "Brasília: a New Capital City for Brazil," *Architectural Review*, no. 122 (1957a): 394–402. For more information on the Brasilia competition, see Milton Braga, *O concurso de Brasilia: sete projetos para uma capital* (São Paulo: Cosac & Naify, 2010).
64 The largest-scale projects up to this time were limited to the scale of small settlements, and none had actually been implemented: from the 1934 proposal for the workers' village in Monlevade to that for a popular residential neighbourhood in Quinta do Rouxinol (Portugal), where, in 1953, Costa developed a lozenge-shaped layout for the first time, which he then re-proposed for the region of Alagados in Salvador de Bahía, for the São José do Cajuru residential neighbourhood in São José dos Campos, and for the Quadras Econômicas in Brasilia.
65 Costa, "Memória descritiva do Plano Piloto," reported in *Registro*, 283–295. The original version of "Memória" – including both the written manuscript and the typed copy that was delivered during the competition – is held at the Casa de Lucio Costa. The English translation within this chapter is quoted, with some adjustments, from *Brasília. A Utopia Come True*, 32–49; 32.
66 Costa, "Memória descritiva do Plano Piloto," 32.
67 Costa to Antônio Callado, 21 February 1960. FCRB, Carlos Drummond de Andrade collection (published in *Correio da Manhã*, on 28 February 1960, and reported in Xavier, ed., *Sôbre arquitetura*, 305–307).
68 Costa, "O urbanista defende sua cidade," 1967. CLC, III B 13-02953. Reported in *Registro*, 301–303; 303. In answering the Smithsons on their plans for their visit to Brasilia, Costa writes:

> April, May, June, July are considered better because it succeeds [*sic*, they follow] the rainy season: the air is not so dry, grass is still green, the blue sky is inhabited by

beautiful white clouds that gather silently [...] (clouds are very important in the aerial perspective of the "cerrado" – savannah).

CLC, VI A 02-00712.
69 See Costa, *Registro*, 304.
70 Costa, "Memória descritiva do Plano Piloto," 36.
71 Costa, "Conquanto não pretendesse competir..."
72 See Costa, sketches of the Plano Piloto design process, n.d. CLC, III B 02-00578.
73 The *cerrado* is a tropical savannah that covers a vast semi-arid eco-region of Brazil, called the *sertão*. In Brazilian imagination, the *sertão* is the physical and the symbolic territory that best represents alterity to civilisation. The geographic and climatic inhospitality of the region has fueled a rich literary tradition inspiring this image, from which stand out *Os Sertões* by Euclides da Cunha and *Grande sertão: veredas* by João Guimarães Rosa.
74 During the Extraordinary International Congress of Art Critics André Malraux proved to be one of the most enthusiastic supporters of the enterprise of the new capital. In 1959, Costa was assigned the Comanderie des Arts et des Lettres of the French government upon Malraux's initiative.
75 Costa, "Saudação aos críticos de arte," 144.
76 Giedion to Costa, 4 December 1957. GTA, 43-K-1957-12-04(G).
77 Giedion to Niemeyer, 8 October 1958. GTA, 43-K-1958-10-08(G).
78 Bruno Zevi, "Brasilia: le forme denunciano i contenuti tremendi," *L'architettura cronache e storia* X, no. 104 (June 1964): 77. Also see Bruno Zevi, "Brasilia troppo in fretta. Capitale di plastici ingranditi," *L'Espresso*, no. 246 (January 1959). Note that Costa would not contribute to the issue dedicated to Brasilia by the Italian *Zodiac* magazine, which contacted him various times with no success.
79 During the construction, Costa visited Brasilia only once, at the beginning of the works in 1957 (see Figure 5.13). In a letter to Israel Pinheiro Filho (son of Israel Pinheiro, first director of the NOVACAP, main political authority responsible for the construction of Brasilia, and first mayor of the Distrito Federal), Costa admits he never participated in any of the meetings of the Conselho de Arquitetura e Urbanismo. Costa to Pinheiro Filho, n.d. CLC, VI A 01-02646.
80 Letter to the editors of *Time* magazine, clipping in CLC, VI A 01-03227.
81 Costa to Cattete Pineiro, 27 July 1973. CLC, VI A 01-00060.
82 Costa, *Registro*, 18. In this regard, also see the text "O urbanista defende sua cidade" (p. 301):

> It [Brasilia] was built in such a short time precisely to ensure irreversibility despite the changes in governments and administrations. And, in fact, it has already resisted, in the seven years of its existence, to four new presidents and various mayors, and to unexpected events of political and military nature, proving its good constitution.

83 Costa to Alison and Peter Smithson, n.d. CLC, VI A 02-00712. The object of this exchange was the assignment to the two English architects of the project for the embassy of Brasilia. The Casa de Lucio Costa holds the documented request to Costa, by William Holford, to take part in the jury – an invitation that Costa declined.
84 See paragraph "A new humanism."
85 Costa, *Registro*, 277.
86 Costa, "In Search of a New Monumentality," 127.
87 See José Pessôa, "Brasília e o tombamento de uma idéia," in *Anais do 5° Seminário DOCOMOMO-Brasil*, (São Carlos: SAP-EESC-USP, 2003).
88 Costa, "Memória descritiva do Plano Piloto", 48.
89 Martino Tattara, ed., *Lucio Costa. Brasilia Plano Piloto* (Venezia: Università IUAV di Venezia-Associação Casa de Lucio Costa, 2010).

90 Ítalo Campofiorito reports – after having accompanied Le Corbusier on his first tour of the new capital – that the Swiss-French architect claimed that Brasilia was the first Ville Verte ever realised. See the handwritten notes in CLC, III B 13-02781.
91 Costa to Israel Pinheiro, n.d. CLC, VI A 01-03020.
92 The placement of the Imperial Palms is an emblematic case, as Costa would unreservedly fight for their removal from the wrong arrangement along the residential axis for years, in the fear that "this interminable weak row of spaced palms could be maintained in the landscape of the city; interfering, with its insistent verticality, with the predominant serene horizontal character of the residential quadras, already marked by the dense tree population defining it." Costa to Carlos Magalhães, n.d. CLC, VI A 01-02629.
93 Costa, "Memória descritiva do Plano Piloto," 42.
94 In 1958, in a debate on *Architectural Design* on "Capital Cities," Costa writes:

> I want to see the minimum of houses. I want to forget [them] – they are six storeys – not very high. There are houses, but they are a background, the second temple. The main view is simply road with trees all around. The buildings are higher than the trees, but they are still apart and so it doesn't count very much – you feel only architectural intensity in the central part. That is why I say it is not so large. Even if the residential area extends 6 kilometers, it is almost as if you are out of town when you leave the centre.
> "Capital Cities. Lucio Costa, Arthur Korn, Denys Lasdun, Peter Smithson discuss."
> *Architecural Design* XXVIII no. 11 (November 1958): 439–440.

In the same debate, to Arthur Korn's provocation on the "escapism" of Costa's attitude of running "away from the fact that there are 500.000 people living," and to suggest "the trees as the key to the housing problem," Costa answers: "You can't pretend that all the buildings going to be built in those different cuadras [sic] are going to be worthwhile. We must prepare to have buildings that have no significance and place them in the background."
On the relation between built form and vegetation in Brasilia, see also Martino Tattara, "Brasilia, *cidade parque*. Il progetto della città come pratica del limite." PhD dissertation, Università IUAV di Venezia, 2008; Guilherme Wisnik, "Brasília: tábula rasa e memória." *L'ADC L'architettura delle città. The Journal of the Scientific Society Ludovico Quaroni 5*, no. 8 (31 July 2016): 81–92.
95 Tattara, ed., *Brasilia Plano Piloto*, 20. Costa had already experimented with this approach in his report of the University Campus.
96 Costa, "Brasília. Lei do predomínio verde...," n.d. CLC, III B 13-00093.
97 A series of letters from Niemeyer to Costa clearly attest how, during construction, the main concern was that of correctly interpreting and maintaining the relation between built and non-built environment, as prefigured by Costa's plan. See Niemeyer to Costa, 8 February 1960 (CLC, VI A 02-00686), and 22 September 1975 (CLC, VI A 02-00975).
98 Costa to Cattete Pineiro, 27 July 1973.
99 Costa to José Carlos Mello, 27 October 1983. CLC, VI A 01-01008.
100 Costa, "Brasília revisitada 1985/1987. Complementação, preservação, adensamento e expansão urbana," *Projeto* no. 100 (June 1987): 115–122; 118.
101 Costa to Niemeyer, n.d. CLC, VI A 01-02172.
102 See Costa to José Galbinski, n.d. CLC, VI A 01-01854.
103 In 1987, the firm C&S planejamento urbano ltda. (Costa and Sobral) would create some Quadras Econômicas in Guará and Taguatinga, based on Costa's project.
104 ICOMOS report on the proposal to include Brasilia in the list of World Heritage assets, drawn up by Léon Pressouyre and addressed to the Prefect of the Distrito Federal José Aparecido de Oliveira. CLC, III B 13-00914.
105 See Costa to José Aparecido, 4 October 1987. ACI-RJ, PLC/BR19 (09), and Costa, "Patrimônio da Humanidade," 21 September 1987. CLC, V C 05-00226.
106 Costa, "Brasília revisitada 1985/1987..." The text is accompanied by a 1:25,000-scale masterplan.

107 "Processo n. 1305-T-90," 14 March 1990, IPHAN, and Costa to Campofiorito, n.d. [1990]. CLC, VI A 01-01994. The letter is transcribed almost entirely in *Registro*, as a synthesis of Costa's own conception of protection of the capital. The full version is reported in José Pessôa, ed., *Lucio Costa: documentos de trabalho* (Rio de Janeiro: Edições do Patrimônio-IPHAN, 1999), 291–294.
108 Costa, *Registro*, 378.
109 Pessôa, ed., *Documentos de trabalho*, 47–52.
110 Costa, "A solução apresentada por R.B.M....," n.d. CLC, III D 01-03259.
111 The plan was commissioned to Costa in 1969 and would involve him in his capacity of consultant of the SUDEBAR (Superintendência para o Desenvolvimento da Barra da Tijuca) until the end of the 1970s, when he would leave his post due to the gradual increasing changes to the original proposed plan.
112 Within the area of which can be inscribed the entire Plano Piloto of Brasilia.
113 Costa, "Registro pessoal," 30 July 1977. CLC, III B 01-02132.
114 Costa, "Processo no. 02/001941/78," n.d. CLC, III B 01-02170.
115 Costa, "PP da Baixada de Jacarepaguá. Avaliação," n.d. CLC, III B 01-02986.
116 In the documents related to the plan, Costa insists on the fact that these are simple "normative instructions" to be verified and applied with a certain tolerance margin, if not reformulated on the basis of new elements in subsequent stages.
117 Costa, "Plano Piloto para a urbanização da baixada compreendida entre a Barra da Tijuca, o Pontal de Sernambetiba e Jacarepaguá," in *Registro*, 344–354; 349.
118 In which Costa participated in 1976–1977, in collaboration with the Italians Carlo Lotti and Mario Nervi.
119 Costa, handwritten notes on the margin of an unidentified document on the Barra da Tijuca, n.d. CLC, III B 01-02359.
120 Costa, "Memória descritiva do Plano Piloto," 32–49.
121 In many texts, letters, and messages addressed to the most diverse recipients, Costa would insist – up until the last years of his life – on the need to complete the construction according to the guidelines of the Plano Piloto. Again, in 1994, he would write the governor asking him to give the owners of the façades along the Plataforma Rodoviária a deadline for the completion of the luminous advertisements on both sides, in order to not compromise the symmetry of the whole.
122 Costa, "Brasília, 85" [to José Aparecido de Oliveira], n.d. CLC, III B 10-00826.
123 Costa, article published in *Jornal do Brasil* in 1976 and reported in *Registro*, 320–321.
124 Costa, *Registro*, 311 (text taken from an interview of 1984).
125 Costa to Campofiorito, n.d. [1990].
126 Costa, "O urbanista defende sua cidade," 301.
127 An anticipation that came from NOVACAP's decision to donate lots of land outside the metropolitan area, in order to replace the *candangos* that populated the various informal settlements that had developed near the construction site. See Costa to Senador... [unidentified], n.d. CLC, VI A 01-04312.
128 Costa, "Brasília, 85."
129 Costa, "Memória descritiva do Plano Piloto."
130 Costa to Senador... [unidentified], n.d.
131 Costa, "O urbanista defende sua cidade," 302.
132 As Costa wrote to Ítalo Campofiorito in 1990:

> It would have been a foolish thing – a crime – to plan the city according to the measure of the still partially undeveloped current scale. And since – capitalism or socialism – the universal tendency is that the world should become, at least, middle class, the so-called Plano Piloto can be considered an anticipation.

> (Pessôa, ed., *Documentos de trabalho*, 291)

133 The themes that are addressed in these contributions greatly exceed the disciplinary boundaries of architecture and art, leading to the fields of economics, politics, science, technology, religion, etc.
134 Son of the famous Italian engineer Pier Luigi Nervi.

135 Costa, "Theoretical urban conception and regional grid scheme for the new capital city of the Federal Republic of Nigeria," 1976. CLC, III B 15-00321 (partly reported in *Registro*, 358–362).
136 See Eric Mumford, *The CIAM Discourse on Urbanism, 1928–1960* (Cambridge, MA/London: The MIT Press, 2000).
137 Peter Smithson to Costa, 6 January 1959. CLC, VI A 02-03674. The letter is also addressed to Eames, Johnson, Kahn, Rudolph, Scharoun, and Whyte.
138 See Lasdun to Costa, 18 July 1958. CLC, VI A 02-03119.
139 See n. 100.
140 "Capital Cities. Lucio Costa, Arthur Korn, Denys Lasdun, Peter Smithson discuss," 441.
141 Giancarlo De Carlo mentions the theory of convergent results, which suggests that the text "L'architecte et la societé contemporaine" had circulated among the members of Team X. See Ismé Gimdalcha [Giancarlo De Carlo], *Il progetto Kalhesa* (Ragusa: Edizioni di Storia e Studi Sociali, 2014, 1st edn Marsilio, 1995), 157.
142 With the Smithsons and Georges Candilis in particular. In Costa's archive, we find traces of at least two invitations to Team X meetings: the one held in 1962 at the Abbaye de Royaumont, near Paris, and the one held in Toulouse in 1971. See Candilis to Costa, 3 July 1962 (CLC, VI A 02-04346) and 2 February 1971 (CLC, VI A 02-01411); Alison and Peter Smithson to Costa, 17 November 1970. CLC, VI A 02-01566.
143 As can be inferred from a draft of a letter held in the Casa de Lucio Costa, it was Anthony Krafft who proposed including Costa among those invited to Florence. Costa to Krafft, n.d. CLC, VI A 01-04543.
144 "Extraits de l'intervention de Lucio Costa, arch. Rio de Janeiro," *Proposte per Firenze*, supplement of *Architecture, formes + fonctions*, no. 14 (1967–1968): 10–11.
145 In a final appeal to the Florentine people, made on the occasion of the Congress, Costa cites his theory according to which scientific and technological development will open the door to a new concept of humanism. "Un appel de Lucio Costa," *Proposte per Firenze*, 14–15.
146 Costa, "O arquiteto e a sociedade contemporânea," 251.
147 Costa, "O novo humanismo científico e tecnológico" ("A New Scientific and Technological Humanism"), *Registro*, 392–395.
148 See the pages of *Registro* in which these texts are reported (379–404). The project for a Museum of Science and Technology, in which an immersive installation – perhaps reminiscent of the opening section of the 1964 Triennale, to which Costa had contributed with the project for the Brazilian pavilion – aimed at transporting the visitor inside the Costian conception of the central role of man in the universe.
149 See, above all, Costa, "Letter to the Americans," *Registro*, 383–385. In 1962, Costa was in Moscow for the World Congress for Peace and Disarmament.
150 Costa to Neutra, 31 March 1962. CLC, VI A 02-03223.
151 Costa to Petrina, published on *Summa* magazine in 1982 and quoted in *Registro*, 322.

Bibliography

Archives and libraries

Arquivo Central do IPHAN (Instituto do Patrimônio Histórico e Artístico Nacional), Seção Rio de Janeiro
Arquivo da Biblioteca Paulo Santos, Rio de Janeiro
Arquivo Gregori Warchavchik, São Paulo
Arquivo Histórico, Museu Nacional de Belas Artes, Rio de Janeiro
Avery Library, Columbia University, New York
Biblioteca centrale di Architettura, Politecnico di Milano, Milan
Biblioteca centrale di Architettura "Roberto Gabetti," Politecnico di Torino, Turin
Biblioteca do Instituto dos Arquitetos do Brasil, Rio de Janeiro
Biblioteca e arquivo da Faculdade de Arquitetura da Universidade de São Paulo
Biblioteca Lucio Costa, Universidade Federal de Rio de Janeiro
Biblioteca Nacional, Rio de Janeiro
Biblioteca Paulo Santos, Rio de Janeiro
Casa de Lucio Costa, Rio de Janeiro
Centro de Pesquisa, Biblioteca e Centro de Documentação, Museu de Arte de São Paulo
Centro de Pesquisa e Documentação de História Contemporânea do Brasil, Fundação Getúlio Vargas, Rio de Janeiro
Fondation Le Corbusier, Paris
Fundação Casa de Rui Barbosa, Rio de Janeiro
Fundação Oscar Niemeyer, Rio de Janeiro
gta Archiv, Institut für Geschichte und Theorie der Architektur, Eidgenössischen Technischen Hochschule, Zürich
Library of the Collegi d'Arquitectes de Catalunya, Barcelona
Library of the Fondazione Giangiacomo Feltrinelli, Milan
Library of the Fondazione Luigi Einaudi, Turin
Museu Dom João VI, Escola de Belas Artes, Universidade Federal do Rio de Janeiro
Núcleo de Pesquisa e Documentação, Faculdade de Arquitetura, Universidade Federal do Rio de Janeiro

Magazines and journals

A & V
A Casa
A Noite
A Notícia
A.C.

Bibliography

AA Files
Acrópole
Ademi
Annali della Scuola Normale Superiore di Pisa
Architectura no Brasil
Architectural Design
Architecture, formes + fonctions
Architekt
Architettura
ARQ
ARQtexto
Arquine
Arquitectura, Arquitetura
Arquitectura Viva
Arquitetura e Construção
Arquitetura e Engenharia
Arquitetura e Urbanismo
Arquitetura Revista
Arquitextos (Portal Vitruvius)
Arte e Decoração
Artes & Ensaios
AU, arquitetura e urbanismo
Barroco
Base, revista de arte, técnica e pensamento
Block
Boletim de Ariel
Bollettino d'Arte
Brasil. Arquitetura contemporânea
Cadernos de Arquitetura e Urbanismo
Cadernos de Arquitetura Ritter dos Reis
Cadernos PROARQ
Caramelo
Casabella, Casabella continuità
CJ Arquitetura
Comunità
Correio da Manhã
Cultura
Debates sobre Estética e Urbanismo
Design Interiores
Desígnio, Revista de História da Arquitetura e do Urbanismo
Diário da Noite
Diário de Notícias
Diário de São Paulo
Diário Nacional
Docomomo Journal
Docomomo Newsletter
Domus
ENBA, Revista de Arte
Espaço e Debates
Estudos Históricos Rio de Janeiro
Folha de São Paulo
Forum Educacional

Future Anterior: Journal of Historic Preservation History, Theory and Criticism
Gávea
Gazeta
Goya
Habitat
Hunch
IBPC Patrimônio Cultural
Ilustração Brasileira
Itinerários, Araraquara
Jornal de Letras
Jornal do Brasil
Jornal do Commercio
JornAU
Journal of Architectural Education
Journal of Latin American Studies
Journal of the Society of Architectural Historians
L'ADC L'architettura delle città. The Journal of the Scientific Society Ludovico Quaroni
L'Architecture d'Aujourd'hui
L'Architettura: cronache e storia
L'Espresso
L'homme et l'architecture
Le culture della tecnica
Lotus International
Manchete
Módulo
National Identities
Novos Estudos
O Cruzeiro
O Dia
O Estado de São Paulo
O Globo
O Jornal
O Lápis
O Paíz
Óculum
On Site Review
Para Todos
Piracema
PÓS – Revista do Programa de Pós-Graduação em Arquitetura e Urbanismo da FAUUSP
Projeto, Projeto/Design
Pro Arte
RACAR: Revue d'Art Canadienne/Canadian Art Review
Rassegna
Revista Brasileira de Ciências Sociais
Revista da Directoria de Engenharia – PDF
Revista da Semana
Revista de história da arte e arqueologia
Revista do Club de Engenharia
Revista do Instituto de Estudos Brasileiros
Revista do Serviço do Patrimônio Histórico e Artístico Nacional
Revista USP
Rio Artes

Sinopses
Summa
Techniques et Architecture
The Architectural Forum
The Architectural Review
The Atlantic Monthly
Visão
Zodiac

Collections of writings by Lucio Costa

Lúcio Costa: obras completas. Edited by Roberto Sussmann. Belo Horizonte: Escola de Arquitetura/UMG, 1961.
Lúcio Costa: sôbre arquitetura. Edited by Alberto Xavier. Porto Alegre: Centro dos Estudantes Universitários de Arquitetura, 1962 (anastatic edition by Ana Paula Canez. Porto Alegre: UniRitter, 2007).
Lucio Costa: obra escrita. Edited by Alberto Xavier. Universidade de Brasília, Instituto de Artes e Arquitetura, Departamento de arquitetura e urbanismo, typewritten, Biblioteca FAU-USP, 1966–1970.
Razones de la nueva arquitectura 1934 y otros ensayos. Edited by Arnaldo Carrilho. Barcelona: Embajada del Brasil, 1986.
Registro de uma vivência. São Paulo: Empresa das Artes, 1995.
Lucio Costa: documentos de trabalho. Edited by José Pessôa. Rio de Janeiro: Edições do Patrimônio-IPHAN, 1999.
Com a palavra: Lucio Costa. Edited by Maria Elisa Costa. Rio de Janeiro: Aeroplano, 2000.
Lucio Costa, XXe siècle brésilien: témoin et acteur. Edited by Jean-Loup Herbert. Saint-Etienne: Université de Saint-Etienne, 2001.
Arquitetura. Rio de Janeiro: José Olympio, 2002.
Lucio Costa. Edited by Ana Luiza Nobre. Rio de Janeiro: Beco do Azougue, 2010.

Selected writings and statements by Lucio Costa

For references to Costa's texts, the date of publication is used (and not the date of elaboration). For reasons of space, individual contributions within the text collections cited above are not listed, except for the cases in which the original publication source was found. The following list is given in chronological order.

"A alma dos nossos lares. Porque é erronea a orientação da architectura do Rio: fala-nos um verdadeiro e commovido artista." *A Noite*, 19 March 1924.
"Um architecto de sentimento nacional. Lucio Costa e a sua excursão artistica pelas velhas cidade de Minas. Considerações sobre nosso gôsto e estilo." *A Noite*, 18 June 1924.
"O palácio da Eimbaxada Argentina. Fala a O Jornal o sr. Lucio Costa, vencedor do concurso de projectos estabelecido pelo governo argentino." *O Jornal*, 28 April 1928.
"O arranha-céo e o Rio de Janeiro. 'O Paiz,' em proseguimento da sua 'enquête,' ouve os architectos constructores Preston & Curtis e Lucio Costa." *O Paíz*, 1 July 1928.
"O Aleijadinho e a arquitetura tradicional." *O Jornal*, special issue on Minas Gerais, 1929.
"O novo director da Escola de Bellas Artes e as directrizes de uma reforma. Um programa em breve entrevista com o architecto Lucio Costa. O estylo 'colonial' e o 'Salon'." *O Globo*, 29 December 1930.
"Uma Escola viva de Belas Artes." *O Jornal*, 31 July 1931.
"Impotência espalhafatosa." *Diário da Noite*, 9 September 1931.
"A direção da Escola de Belas Artes." *Correio da Manhã*, 19 September 1931.

"Razões da nova arquitectura." *Revista da Directoria de Engenharia – PDF* III no. 1 (January 1936): 3–9.
"Ante-projecto para a Villa de Monlevade. Memorial descriptivo." *Revista da Directoria de Engenharia – PDF* III, no. 3 (May 1936): 114–128.
"Documentação necessária." *Revista do Serviço do Patrimônio Histórico e Artístico Nacional*, no. 1 (1937): 31–39.
"Uma questão de oportunidade." *Revista da Directoria de Engenharia – PDF* IV, no. 3 (May 1937): 120–139.
"Universidade do Brasil." *Revista da Directoria de Engenharia – PDF* IV, no. 3 (May 1937): 120–135.
"Notas sobre a evolução do mobiliário luso-brasileiro." *Revista do Serviço do Patrimônio Histórico e Artístico Nacional*, no. 3 (1939): 149–162.
"A arquitetura dos Jesuítas no Brasil." *Revista do Serviço do Patrimônio Histórico e Artístico Nacional*, no. 5 (1941): 9–100.
"Considerações sobre o ensino da arquitetura." *ENBA, Revista de Arte*, no. 3 (September 1945).
"Depoimento do arquiteto Lucio Costa sobre a arquitetura moderna brasileira. A margem do livro 'Arquitetura contemporanea no Brasil,' editora Gersum Carneiro, 1947 – Rio." *O Jornal*, March 14, 1948 (known as "Carta depoimento").
"In Search of a New Monumentality: a Symposium by Gregor Paulsson Henry-Russell Hitchcock, William Holford, Sigfried Giedion, Walter Gropius, Lucio Costa and Alfred Roth." *The Architectural Review* 104, no. 621 (September 1948): 117–128.
"Ensino do desenho." *Cultura* I, no. 1 (September–December 1948): 47–68.
Foreword to *The Work of Oscar Niemeyer*, by Stamo Papadaki. 1–3. New York: Reinhold Publishing Corporation, 1950.
"Preface to *Frei Bernando de São Bento, o arquiteto seiscentista do Rio de Janeiro*." In *Três artistas beneditinos*. Edited by Dom Clemente Maria Da Silva Nigra, 11–13. Rio de Janeiro: Ministério da Educação e Cultura, 1950.
"A arquitetura de Antônio Francisco Lisboa revelada no risco original da Capela Franciscana de São João del Rei." In *Antônio Francisco Lisboa: o Aleijadinho*. Edited by Rodrigo José Ferreira Bretas, 11–21. Rio de Janeiro: Publicações da Diretoria do Patrimônio Histórico e Artístico Nacional, Ministério da Educação e Cultura, 1951.
"Muita construção, alguma arquitetura e um milagre." *Correio da Manhã*, 15 June 1951.
"Não, motorista. Conselhos do arquiteto Lúcio Costa em prol da redução dos acidentes de trafego." *Diário de Notícias*, 23 November 1951.
Arquitetura brasileira. Rio de Janeiro: Cadernos de cultura do Serviço de Documentação do Ministério de Educação e Saúde, 1952.
"Considerações sobre arte contemporânea." Rio de Janeiro: Cadernos de Cultura do Serviço de Documentação do Ministério de Educação e Saúde, 1952.
"Imprévu et importance de la contribution des architectes brésiliens au développement actuel de l'architecture contemporaine." *L'Architecture d'Aujourd'hui*, no. 42–43 (August 1952): 4–7.
"A arquitetura brasileira colonial." In *Proceedings of the International Colloquium on Luso-Brazilian Studies* (Washington, DC, 15–20 October 1950), 121–122. Nashville, TN: The Vanderbilt University Press, 1953.
"O arquiteto e a sociedade contemporânea." *Arquitectura* XXV, no. 47 (June 1953): 7–21.
"Lúcio Costa defende a nossa arquitetura moderna. Oportunidade perdida." *Manchete*, no. 63 (4 July 1953): 49.
"A crise da arte contemporânea." *Brasil. Arquitetura contemporânea*, no. 1 (August–September 1953): 2–3.
"L'architecte et la societé contemporaine." In *L'artiste dans la société contemporaine (conférence internationale des artistes, Venise, 22–28 septembre 1952). Témoignages recueillis par l'UNESCO*, 88–99. Paris: UNESCO 1954.

"Em difesa do ideal de comunhão das artes. Apêlo de Lúcio Costa aos estudantes de Arquitetura." *Módulo*, no. 2 (August 1955).
"Testimony of a Carioca Architect. Concrete, Sun, and Vegetation." *The Atlantic Monthly* (February 1956): 137–139.
"Relatório do Plano Piloto de Brasília." *Módulo* III, no. 8 (July 1957): 33–48.
"Meio século de Oscar Niemeyer." *Correio da Manhã*, 14 September 1957.
"Niemeyer acumula vida." *Para Todos*, no. 38–39 (December 1957).
"Capital Cities. Lucio Costa, Arthur Korn, Denys Lasdun, Peter Smithson discuss." *Architectural Design* XXVIII, no. 11 (November 1958): 437–441.
"L'idea della curva." *Casabella continuità*, no. 226 (April 1959): 7–8.
"Lúcio Costa retifica: não é meu o projeto, é de Le Corbusier." *Correio da Manhã*, 3 May 1959.
"A arte e a educação." *Arquitetura e Engenharia* IX, no. 55 (September–October 1959): 12–13; *Módulo* 3, no. 16 (December 1959): 26–28.
"L'art et l'éducation." *Architecture, formes + fonctions* VII (1960): 81–83.
"Lúcio Costa (pesaroso e irritado) sintetiza Brasília para Callado." *Correio da Manhã*, 28 February 1960.
"Prospeto arquitetônico." In *Tricentenário de Parati. Notícias Históricas*. Edited by José de Souza Azevedo Pizarro e Araújo, 80. Rio de Janeiro: Publicações da Diretoria do Patrimônio Histórico e Artístico Nacional, Ministério da Educação e Cultura, 1960.
"O novo humanismo scientifico e tecnológico." *Módulo* 5, no. 23 (June 1961): 2–7.
"Le Corbusier no Brasil. Depoimentos de Lúcio Costa, Heráclio Sales, Gustavo Capanema, Geraldo Ferraz e Miranda Netto; destaques dos jornais." *Arquitetura*, no. 8 (February 1963): 7–18.
"Arquitetura contemporânea." In *Rio de Janeiro em seus quatrocentos anos. Formação e desenvolvimento da cidade*. Edited by Fernando Nascimento Silva, 242–257. Rio de Janeiro-São Paulo: Distribuidora Record, 1965.
"Témoignage sur Le Corbusier et son oeuvre." *L'Architecture d'Aujourd'hui*, no. 119 (March 1965): 112–113.
"Formes et fonctions." *Architecture, formes + fonctions* XIII (1967): 26–27.
"Extraits de l'intervention de Lucio Costa, arch. Rio de Janeiro." *Proposte per Firenze*, supplement of *Architecture, formes + fonctions*, no. 14 (1967–1968): 10–11.
"Un appel de Lucio Costa." *Proposte per Firenze*, supplement of *Architecture, formes + fonctions*, no. 14 (1967–1968): 14–15.
"Interpretação de Brasília." *Arquitetura*, no. 76 (October 1968): 17–18.
"L'urbaniste défend sa capitale." *Architecture, formes + fonctions* XIV (1968): 18–21.
"L'art et l'avènement des masses." *Architecture, formes + fonctions* XV (1969): 67–69.
Plano-pilôto para a urbanização da baixada compreendida entre a Barra da Tijuca, pontal de Sernambetiba e Jacarepaguá. Rio de Janeiro: Agência Jornalística Image, 1969.
"Risco original de Antônio Francisco Lisboa." *Revista do Serviço do Patrimônio Histórico e Artístico Nacional*, no. 17 (1969): 239–246.
"Brasília dez anos depois segundo Lúcio Costa." *Revista do Club de Engenharia*, no. 386 (March–April 1970): 6–12.
"Urbanista não quer rever Brasília." *Acrópole*, no. 385 (June 1971): 35–36.
"Carta dirigida ao senador Cattete Pinheiro reafirmando pontos fundamentais do Plano-Piloto de Brasília." In *Brasília – Uma realidade urbanística e administrativa do País. I Seminário de Estudos dos Problemas Urbanos de Brasília*, 279–281. Brasília: Senado Federal – Comissão do Distrito Federal, 1974.
"Considerações em torno do Plano Piloto de Brasília." In *Brasília – Uma realidade urbanística e administrativa do País. I Seminário de Estudos dos Problemas Urbanos de Brasília*, 21–28. Brasília: Senado Federal – Comissão do Distrito Federal, 1974.

"Primeira carta dirigida ao senador Cattete Pinheiro." In *Brasília – Uma realidade urbanística e administrativa do País. I Seminário de Estudos dos Problemas Urbanos de Brasília*, 289–292. Brasília: Senado Federal – Comissão do Distrito Federal, 1974.
"Ronchamp." *Jornal do Brasil*, 23 August 1975.
"Roquebrune." *Jornal do Brasil*, 23 August 1975.
"Relato pessoal." *Módulo* X, no. 40 (September 1975): 23–24.
"Antônio Francisco Lisboa, o Aleijadinho." *Revista do Patrimônio Histórico e Artístico Nacional*, no. 18 (1978): 75–82.
"Lúcio Costa, 80 anos: penso em termos do próximo." Interview by Ruy Portilho. *O Estado de São Paulo*, 27 February 1982.
"Lúcio Costa, 80 anos: sou apenas um franco-atirador em urbanismo." Interview by Frederico Morais. *O Globo*, 27 February 1982.
"Lúcio Costa por ele mesmo. Na festa dos 80 anos, as lembranças boas e más de uma vida." Interview by Roberto Marinho de Azevedo. *Jornal do Brasil*, 27 February 1982.
"Lúcio Costa pergunta." [Carlos Drummond de Andrade] *Jornal do Brasil*, 11 March 1982.
"Le Corbusier: a arquitetura e as belas-artes." *Revista do Patrimônio Histórico e Artístico Nacional*, no. 19 (1984): 53.
Preface to *Salão de 1931: Marco da revelação da arte moderna em nivél nacional*, by Lucia Gouvêa Vieira. Rio de Janeiro: Funarte-Instituto Nacional de Artes Plásticas, 1984.
"A beleza de um trabalho precursor, síntese da tradição e da modernidade." Interview by Haifa Y. Sabbag. *AU, arquitetura e urbanismo* I, no. 1 (January 1985): 14–19.
"Lúcio Costa, O sonho foi menor...." Interview by Haifa Y. Sabbag. *AU, arquitetura e urbanismo* I, no. 2 (April 1985): 36–40.
Preface to *Rodrigo e seus tempos* by Rodrigo Mello Franco de Andrade, 5–10. Rio de Janeiro: Fundação Nacional Pró-Memória, 1985.
"Destruí algo que existía." Interview by Haifa Y. Sabbag. *AU, arquitetura e urbanismo* II, no. 5 (April 1986): 18–21.
"Entrevista: Lúcio Costa sobre Aleijadinho." Interview by Carlos Zílio, Jorge Czaikowski, and Ronaldo Brito. *Gávea*, no. 3 (June 1986): 32–59.
"Brasília revisitada 1985/1987. Complementação, preservação, adensamento e expansão urbana." *Projeto*, no. 100 (June 1987): 115–122.
"Ministério, da participação de Baumgart à revelação de Niemeyer." Interview by Hugo Segawa. *Projeto*, no. 102 (August 1987): 158–160.
"Um problema malposto." *Projeto*, no. 103 (September 1987): 95.
"Lúcio Costa: a vanguarda permeada com a tradição." Interview by Hugo Segawa. *Projeto*, no. 104 (October 1987): 145–154.
"Revolução corbusiana na arquitetura ainda não foi superada." *O Globo*, 14 October 1987.
"O projeto para o Ministério da Educação e Saúde Pública. Relato de Lúcio Costa." *Módulo*, no. 96 (November 1987): 23–27.
"Presença de Le Corbusier, entrevista com Lúcio Costa." Interview by Maria Cristina Burlamaqui, Ronaldo Brito, and Jorge Czajkowski. *Arquitetura Revista*, no. 5 (1987): 2–15.
"Brasília é uma síntese do Brasil." Interview by Beatriz Marinho. *O Estado de São Paulo*, 13 February 1988.
"Lúcio Costa declara guerra à inflação." *Jornal do Brasil*, 13 August 1988.
"Interessa ao estudante." *Arquitetura Revista*, no. 8 (1990): 6–7.
"Arquiteto de saudades." Interview by Isabel Cristina Mauad. *O Globo*, 29 December 1991.
Brasília, cidade que inventei. Relatório do Plano Piloto de Brasília. Brasília: Governo do Distrito Federal, 1991.
"Cidades estão desarticuladas." diz Lúcio Costa. *Folha de São Paulo*, 8 September 1991.
"Lucio Costa: homenagem aos seus 90 anos de vida." Interview by Lauro Cavalcanti and Claudia Coutinho. *IBPC Patrimônio Cultural*, 27 February 1992.

"Um guia para a defesa do patrimônio." *Jornal do Brasil*, supplement *Idéias Ensaios*, no. 139 (1 March 1992): 4–7.
"Explicando as novas quadras." Interview by Hugo Segawa. *Projeto*, no. 162 (April 1993): 62–65.
"A concepção das superquadras de Brasília." Interview by Juan Antonio Zapatel. *Sinopses*, no. 20 (December 1993): 42–44.
"Lúcio Costa: revelações de 90 anos." Interview by Alfredo Britto and Ítalo Campofiorito. *Piracema* I, no. 1 (1993): 69–81.
"Lei das resultantes convergentes." *Revista do Patrimônio Histórico e Artístico Nacional*, no. 23 (1994): 92–93.
"O risco moderno." Interview by Mario Cesar Carvalho. *Folha de São Paulo*, supplement *Mais!*, no. 5 (23 July 1995): 4–6.
"Je suis comme je suis." Interview by Ana Luiza Nobre. *AU, arquitetura e urbanismo*, no. 74 (October–November 1997): 71–73.
"Arte moderna e socialismo (Carta aos meus amigos comunistas)." *Folha de São Paulo*, supplement *Mais!* (24 February 2002): 12–13.
"Interview by Matheus Gorovitz." *JornAU* I, no. 6 (December 2002–January 2003): 19–24.
"Como fotografar Brasília." *Folha de São Paulo*, 21 February 2007.
"Entrevista com Lúcio Costa, 23.2.1992." In *Tantas vezes paisagem*. Edited by Ana Rosa de Oliveira, 33–45. Rio de Janeiro: FAPERJ, 2007.

Selected writings on Lucio Costa and his works

For reasons of space, the individual contributions within volumes or magazine issues entirely dedicated to the figure of Costa are not cited separately, even if these have been cited separately in the endnotes. The following list is given in alphabetical order.

"A arte no 'Palácio da Educação.' Detalhes de um dos mais belos edificios do mundo." *O Jornal*, 10 June 1945.
"A força da genialidade paradoxal e sutil do mestre do modernismo brasileiro." *Projeto Design*, no. 265 (March 2002).
"A nomeação para professores da Escola Nacional de Bellas Artes, de dois artistas modernos." *Diário da Noite*, 22 April 1931.
"A reforma da Escola de Bellas Artes e o Salão official deste anno." *Diário da Noite*, 26 August 1931.
"A sede do MEC: onde a arte começou a mudar. Gustavo Capanema, Carlos Drummond de Andrade, Lucio Costa." *Módulo* X, no. 40 (September 1975): 4–24.
"Academia francesa de arquitetura premia Niemeyer, Burle Marx e Lúcio Costa." *O Globo*, 23 June 1982.
"Apartamentos economicos Gambôa." *Revista da Directoria de Engenharia – PDF* I, no. 1 (July 1932): 6.
"Architectura colonial. O concurso José Mariano Filho." *Ilustração Brasileira*, March 1923.
"Architectura tradicional. Um attraente concurso de arte colonial." *Revista da Semana*, 7 April 1923.
"As residências do Dr. Daut de Oliveira e Ex. Senhora D. Adelaide Daut de Oliveira." *Arquitetura e Urbanismo* III (September–October 1938): 227–247.
"Bellas-Artes. Instituto Brasileiro de Architectos – O concurso de architectura tradicional." *O Jornal*, 10 February 1924.
"Brazil, Lucio Costa and Niemeyer Soares, architects." *The Architectural Review* 86, no. 513 (August 1939): 72–73.
"Brésil, Park-Hotel São Clemente." *Techniques et Architecture*, no. 1–2 (1947): 72–74.
"Casa na Gávea." *Projeto*, no. 134 (August 1990): 46–48.
"Começa a viver a Brasília de Lúcio Costa." *Visão* (27 June 1958).

"Concurso de ante-projectos do novo edifício do Club de Engenharia." *Revista do Club de Engenharia* II, no. 20 (September 1936): 1098–1101.

"Concurso de ante-projectos para o Ministério de Educação e Saúde Pública." *Revista da Directoria de Engenharia – PDF* IV, no. 18 (September 1935): 510–519.

"Concurso de ante-projectos para o pavilhão do Brasil na Exposição de Philadelphia." *Architectura no Brasil* V, no. 28 (April–May 1926): 117–128.

"Dossiêr Lucio Costa." *Artes & Ensaios*, no. 9 (2002): 118–129.

"Edifício do Ministério da Educação e Saúde, Arquitetos – Lucio Costa – Oscar Niemeyer Filho – Afonso E. Reidy – Jorge M. Moreira – Carlos Leão – Ernani M. Vasconcellos." *Arquitetura e Urbanismo* IV (July–August 1939): 17–25.

"Especial Lucio Costa." *AU, arquitetura e urbanismo* VII, no. 38 (October–November 1991): 46–117.

"Facciate secondo l'orientamento." *Domus*, no. 210 (June 1946): 31.

"Falta alguém para tombar o monumento que é Lúcio Costa." *O Globo*, 14 April 1975.

"Flats at Rio de Janeiro. Lucio Costa: Architect." *The Architectural Review* 108, no. 644 (August 1950): 88–94.

"Habitações para operários no bairro da Gambôa Rio de Janeiro." *Base, revista de arte, técnica e pensamento*, no. 1 (August 1933): 13.

"Inauguração, ontem, do novo edifício do Ministério da Educação." *O Jornal*, 4 October 1945.

"Lagôa-Barra no risco de Lúcio Costa." *Jornal do Brasil*, 24 January 1980.

"Living." *The Architectural Forum* 87, no. 5 (November 1947): 92–98.

"Lucio Costa 1902–1998: arquitectura moderna y clima." *ARQ*, no. 41 (April 1999): 52–53.

"Lúcio Costa afirma nos EUA que a ciência vai impor no mundo todo a justiça social." *O Jornal*, 9 April 1961.

"Lúcio Costa dá adeus a Brasília." *Jornal do Brasil*, 9 August 1988.

"Lúcio Costa denuncia desvio em seu plano para a Barra e pede reexame." *O Globo*, 24 June 1986.

"Lúcio Costa faz da Barra a capital do Rio." *Jornal do Brasil*, 25 April 1969.

"Lúcio Costa foi agraciado pela França." *O Dia*, 1 July 1971.

"Lúcio Costa muda seus hábitos." *Acrópole* XXXII, no. 373 (May 1970): 11, 36.

"Lúcio Costa teme que emancipação prejudique a Barra." *Jornal do Brasil*, 8 May 1988.

"Lucio Costa, projeto para uma residência." *Revista da Directoria de Engenharia – PDF* III, no. 12 (September 1934): 88.

"Lúcio Costa: Brasília é um exemplo de como não se deve fazer uma cidade." *O Globo*, 23 May 1963.

"Lucio Costa: homenagem aos seus 90 anos de vida." *IBPC Patrimônio Cultural*, 27 February 1992.

"Lúcio Costa: nada pode deter o crescimento de Brasília." *Correio da Manhã*, 14 April 1961.

"Lucio Costa. Cem anos." *Projeto Design*, no. 265 (March 2002): 21–31.

"Lúcio revisita Brasília." *AU, arquitetura e urbanismo*, no. 17 (April–May 1988): 20.

"Mania de grandeza." *A Notícia*, 29 June 1942.

"Ministère de l'Education et de la Santé Publique, Rio de Janeiro: Lucio Costa, Oscar Niemeyer, Alfred [sic] Reidy, Carlos Leao, Jorge Moreira, architects." *L'Architecture d'Aujourd'hui* XVIII, no. 13–14 (September 1947): 13–19.

"Ministério da Educação. Lançamento da pedra fundamental do edifício para sua sêde." *Jornal do Commercio*, 25 April 1937.

"Móveis de Lúcio Costa na OCA." *Correio da Manhã*, 12 December 1963.

"O arquiteto que deixou o Brasil mais moderno." *Folha de São Paulo*, supplement *Mais!*, 23 July 1995.

"O estudo de Lucio Costa permitiu o 'amadurecimento' do problema e originou a nova Copacabana." *Módulo* X, no. 41 (December 1975): 62.

"O Instituto de Arquitetos do Brasil e o nosso Pavilhão na Feira de Nova York." *Arquitetura e Urbanismo* IV (May–June 1939): 470.

"O nosso salão de 1924. É modesta a secção de architectura; os estudos coloniaes e seus derivados." *A Noite*, 4 September 1924.

"O novo Palácio da Embaixada Argentina. Julgamento dos projectos dos architectos brasileiros." *Jornal do Brasil*, 14 April 1928.

"O Palácio da Embaixada Argentina no Rio de Janeiro. O Jury deu o premio ao projecto Lucio Costa." *Gazeta*, 15 April 1928.

"O pavilhão brasileiro na feira mundial de Nova York." *Arquitetura e Urbanismo* IV (May–June 1939): 471–480.

"O pavilhão do Brasil na Exposição de Philadelphia. Um ante-projecto discutido." *O Globo*, 23 December 1925.

"O revolucionário tranquilo." *Folha de São Paulo*, supplement *Mais!*, 24 February 2002.

"O Salão de MCMXXIV." *Ilustração Brasileira*, August 1924.

"Parabéns, dr. Lúcio. Um mestre da cultura brasileira." *Jornal do Brasil*, supplement *Idéias Ensaios*, no. 139, 1 March 1992.

"Park Hotel São Clemente: Lucio Costa, architecte." *L'Architecture d'Aujourd'hui* XVIII, no. 13–14 (September 1947): 50–52.

"Park Hotel São Clemente." *L'homme et l'architecture* 7, no. 1–2 (1947): 72–78.

"Pavillon du Brésil, Exposition internationale de New-York 1939: Lucio Costa, Oscar Niemeyer, Paul L. Wiener, architects." *L'Architecture d'Aujourd'hui* XVIII, no. 13–14 (November 1947): 20–21.

"Projecto de Solar em estylo tradicional brasileiro. Lucio Costa architecto." *O Lápis* (September 1931): 31.

"Projeto de Lúcio Costa (Brasília)." *Arquitetura e Engenharia* VII, no. 44 (March–April 1957): 7–13.

"Quadras econômicas, projeto de Lúcio Costa." *Módulo*, no. 89–90 (January–April 1986): 138–139.

"Reportaje a Lúcio Costa." *Pro Arte*, no. 181, 25 January 1956.

"Residência moderna." *Arte e Decoração* I, no. 1 (August 1977): 22–23.

"Residência na Gávea." *Projeto*, no. 117, December 1988.

"Salão de 1931. A guerrilha de Lúcio Costa." *Rio Artes* (March 1993): 23.

"Salvador: preservação e renovação do centro urbano." *CJ Arquitetura*, no. 2 (August 1973): 60–70.

"São Miguel. O ponto de partida." *Jornal do Commercio*, 17 November 1968.

"Tanzânia quer Lúcio Costa para planejar sua capital." *O Globo*, 3 July 1979.

"Um marco das relações de Le Corbusier com o Brasil." *Projeto*, no. 102 (August 1987): 105–108.

"Un nouveau quartier résidentiel. Parc Edouardo Guinle." *L'Architecture d'Aujourd'hui* XIX (December 1947): 32–35.

"Unidade de turismo, veraneio e week-end, Cabo Frio, consultor Lúcio Costa." *CJ Arquitetura*, no. 1 (May–July 1973): 20–28.

Alberto, Klaus Chaves. "Três projetos para uma Universidade do Brasil." Master thesis, Universidade Federal do Rio de Janeiro, 2003.

Alcântara, Antônio Pedro Gomes de. "Sobre Lucio Costa." In *Ideólogos do patrimônio cultural*, 35–61. Rio de Janeiro: Instituto Brasileiro do Patrimônio Cultural, 1991.

Aliata, Fernando and Claudia Shmidt. "Otras referencias. Lúcio Costa, el episodio Monlevade y Auguste Perret." *Block*, no. 4 (December 1999): 54–61.

Andrade, Antonio Luiz Dias de. "O nariz torcido de Lúcio Costa." *Sinopses*, no. 18 (December 1992): 5–17.

Andrade, Carlos Drummond de. "Lembranças de um papel." *Rio Artes* (March 1993): 25.

———. "Lúcio Costa e o papel mágico." *Jornal do Brasil*, 3 March 1982a.

———. "Lúcio Costa na repartição." *Jornal do Brasil*, 4 March 1982b.
Andrade, Mário de. "Escola de Belas Artes." *Diário Nacional*, 4 October 1931.
Andrade, Rodrigo Mello Franco de. "Apontamentos para a História da Arte no Brasil. Classificação do acervo da nossa arquitetura civil." *O Estado de São Paulo*, 26 August 1947.
———. "O caso da Escola de Belas Artes." *O Jornal*, 18 September 1931.
Arantes, Otília Beatriz Fiori. "Esquema de Lúcio Costa." *Block*, no. 4 (December 1999): 42–53.
———. "Lúcio Costa e a 'boa causa' da arquitetura moderna." In *Sentido da formação: Três estudos sobre Antonio Candido, Gilda de Mello e Souza e Lúcio Costa*. Edited by Otília Beatriz Fiori Arantes and Paulo Eduardo Arantes, 115–133. Rio de Janeiro: Paz e Terra, 1997.
———. "Resumo de Lucio Costa." *Folha de São Paulo*, supplement *Mais!*, 24 February 2002.
Ávila, Cristina. "Brasília: Lúcio Costa, o espaço urbano e as ressonâncias barrocas." *Barroco*, no. 17 (1996): 291–297.
Azevedo, Eliane. "O baú dos 100 anos. Exposição sobre a vida e a obra do arquiteto Lucio Costa marca a comemoração do seu centenário." *Jornal do Brasil*, 27 February 2002.
Balducci, Alessandro, Antonella Bruzzese, Remo Dorigati, and Luigi Spinelli, eds. *Brasilia. A Utopia Come True/Un'utopia realizzata 1960–2010*. Milano: Triennale Electa, 2010.
Bandeira, Manuel. "A Revolução e as Belas Artes." *Para Todos*, 26 September 1931a.
———. "O 'Salão dos tenentes'." *Diário Nacional*, 5 September 1931b.
Barata, Mário. "Lúcio Costa, jovem octagenário." *Jornal do Commercio*, 25 February 1982.
Barbosa, Elmer Corrêa. "Lúcio Costa. A revolução nas artes plásticas." *Jornal do Brasil*, 6 January 1981.
Barki, José. "A invenção de Brasília: o 'risco' de Lúcio Costa." In *Arquitetura e movimento moderno*. Edited by Cêça Guimaraens, 147–170. Rio de Janeiro: FAU-UFRJ, 2006.
Braga, Milton. *O concurso de Brasilia: sete projetos para uma capital*. São Paulo: Cosac & Naify, 2010.
Braga, Rubem. "Lúcio Costa urbanista." *Manchete*, 13 March 1954.
Buchmann, Armando. *Lúcio Costa. O inventor da cidade de Brasília: Centenário de nascimento*. Brasília: Thesaurus Editora, 2002.
Buzzar, Miguel Antonio. "Lúcio Costa, a ENBA e a arquitetura moderna brasileira." In *180 anos de Escola de Belas Artes*, 397–405. Rio de Janeiro: Universidade Federal do Rio de Janeiro, 1998.
Campofiorito, Ítalo. "Brasília Revisitada." *Revista do Patrimônio Histórico e Artístico Nacional*, special issue (1990): 171–176.
Canez, Anna Paula and Hugo Segawa. "Brasília: utopia que Lúcio Costa inventou." *Architextos* 11, no. 125.00 (October 2010).
Cardoso, Lucio Adauto. "Construindo a utopia: Lúcio Costa e o pensamento urbanístico no Brasil." *Espaço e Debates*, no. 27 (1989): 76–91.
———. "O urbanismo de Lucio Costa: uma contribuição brasileira ao concerto das nações." In *Cidade, povo e nação: Gênese do urbanismo moderno*. Edited by Luiz Cesar de Queiroz Ribeiro and Robert Pechman, 95–122. Rio de Janeiro: Civilização Brasileira, 1996.
Carlucci, Marcelo. "As casas de Lucio Costa." Master thesis, Universidade de São Paulo, 2005.
Carrilho, Arnaldo. "Lúcio Costa e o episódio brasileiro." *Módulo*, no. 93 (January–February 1987): 18–23.
Carrilho, Marcos José. "Lúcio Costa, patrimônio histórico e arquitetura moderna." PhD dissertation, Universidade de São Paulo, 2002.
Cerqueira, Carlos Gutierrez. "Considerações acerca d'O nariz torcido de Lucio Costa." *Architextos* 15, no. 180.04 (May 2015).
Coelho, Carla Maria Teixeira. "Conjunto residencial Parque Guinle e a preservação de edifícios residenciais modernos." Master thesis, Universidade Federal do Rio de Janeiro, 2006.

Comas, Carlos Eduardo Dias. "A feira mundial de Nova York de 1939: o pavilhão brasileiro/ New York World's Fair of 1939 and the Brazilian pavilion." *ARQtexto*, no. 16 (2010a): 56–97.

———. "Arquitetura moderna, estilo campestre. Hotel, Parque São Clemente." *Arquitextos* 11, no. 123.00 (August 2010b).

———. "Arquitetura moderna, estilo Corbu, pavilhão brasileiro." *AU, arquitetura e urbanismo*, no. 26 (October–November 1989): 92–101.

———, ed. *Lucio Costa e as missões: um museu em São Miguel*. Porto Alegre: PROPAR-UFRGS, 2007.

———. "Lucio Costa e a revolução na arquitetura brasileira 30/39. De lenda(s e) Le Corbusier." *Architextos* 2, no. 022.01 (March 2002a).

———. "O passado mora ao lado: Lúcio Costa e o projeto do Grande Hotel de Ouro Preto, 1938/40." *ARQtexto* 1, no. 2 (January–June 2002b): 18–31.

———. "Protótipo e monumento, um Ministério, o Ministério." *Projeto*, no. 102 (August 1987): 136–149.

——— and Marcos Leite Almeida, "Brasília cinquentenária: a paixão de uma monumentalidade nova." *Architextos* 10, no. 119.01 (April 2010c).

Cordeiro, Caio Nogueira Hosannah. "A reforma Lucio Costa e o ensino da arquitetura e do urbanismo da ENBA à FNA (1931–1946)." In *IX Seminário nacional de estudos e pesquisas "História, sociedade e educação no Brasil"*, Universidade Federal da Paraíba, João Pessoa, 31 July–3 August 2012, https://histedbrnovo.fe.unicamp.br/pf-histedbr/seminario/seminario9/PDFs/2.19.pdf.

Corona, Eduardo. "Mestre Lúcio." *Acrópole* XXXII, no. 373 (May 1970): 10.

Correia, Telma de Barros. "O modernismo e o núcleo fabril: o anteprojeto de Lúcio Costa para Monlevade." *PÓS – Revista do Programa de Pós-Graduação em Arquitetura e Urbanismo da FAUUSP*, no. 14 (December 2003): 80–93.

Costa, Maria Elisa, ed. *Acervo Lucio Costa (achados)*. Rio de Janeiro: Casa de Lucio Costa, 2009.

———, ed. *Lucio Costa 1902–2002*. Brasilia-Rio de Janeiro: Centro Cultural do Banco do Brasil-Paço Imperial, 2002.

———. *Lucio Costa, inventor de Brasília*. Rio de Janeiro: Casa de Lucio Costa-Escola da Cidade, 2014.

——— and José Pessôa. *A arquitetura portuguesa no traço de Lucio Costa. Bloquinhos de Portugal*. Rio de Janeiro: Casa de Lucio Costa, 2012.

Coutinho, Sylvia Ribeiro. "A Escola de Belas Artes em *Registro de uma vivência*: uma análise das memórias de Lucio Costa." In *Edição 190 anos EBA*. Edited by Carlos Gonçalves Terra, 171–193. Rio de Janeiro: EBA-UFRJ, 2006.

el-Dahdah, Farés. "Brasília, um objetivo certa vez adiado." *Architextos* 10, no. 119.02 (April 2010a).

———, ed. *Lucio Costa Arquiteto*. Rio de Janeiro: Casa de Lucio Costa, 2010b.

———, ed. *Lucio Costa: Brasilia's Superquadra*. Munich: Prestel, 2005.

———. "Lucio Costa Preservationist." *Future Anterior: Journal of Historic Preservation History, Theory and Criticism* III, no. 1 (2006): 58–67.

Epstein, David G. Brasilia. *Plan and Reality: a Study of Planned and Spontaneous Urban Development*. Berkeley, CA: University of California Press, 1973.

Evenson, Norma. *Two Brazilian Capitals: Architecture and Urbanism in Rio de Janeiro and Brasilia*. New Haven, CT; London: Yale University Press, 1973.

Falbel, Anat. "As vicissitudes de dois arquitetos modernos." *Projeto Design*, no. 346 (December 2008): 112–115.

Ferraz, Geraldo, "Falta o depoimento de Lucio Costa." *Diário de São Paulo*, 1 February 1948.

———. "Individualidades na história da atual arquitetura no Brasil. V – Lúcio Costa." *Habitat* VI, no. 35 (October 1956b): 28–43.

Ficher, Sylvia. "Lucio Costa (1902–1998): Modernism and Brazilian Tradition." *Docomomo Journal*, no. 23 (2000): 16–22.
——— and Ricardo Trevisan. "Brasília Cidade nova." *Architextos* 10, no. 119.04 (April 2010).
Galvão, Anna and Beatriz Ayrosa. "A monumentalidade em Lúcio Costa: projeto de arquitetura e cidade moderna." PhD dissertation, Universidade de São Paulo, 2005.
Gazaneo, Jorge O. and Mabel M. Scarone. *Lucio Costa*. Buenos Aires: Instituto de Arte Americano e Investigaciones Estéticas, 1959.
Geoffroy, Nora Guimarães. "O brilho do equívoco em Lucio Costa." In *Edição 190 anos EBA*. Edited by Carlos Gonçalves Terra, 151–170. Rio de Janeiro: EBA-UFRJ, 2006.
Gorovitz, Matheus. *Brasília: uma questão de escala*. São Paulo: Projeto, 1985.
———. "Os riscos da modernidade: um estudo dos projetos de Le Corbusier e Lúcio Costa para o campus da Universidade do Brasil." *Projeto Design*, no. 264 (February 2002): 22–25.
———. *Os riscos do projeto: contribuição à análise do juízo estético na arquitetura*. Brasília-São Paulo: Edunb-Studio Nobel, 1993.
Guerra, Abílio. "Lúcio Costa, Gregori Warchavchik e Roberto Burle Marx: síntese entre arquitetura e natureza tropical." *Revista USP*, no. 53 (March–May 2002a): 18–31.
———. "Lúcio Costa, modernidade e tradição. Montagem discursiva da arquitetura moderna Brasileira." PhD dissertation, Universidade Estadual de Campinas, 2002b.
Guimarãens, Cêça de. *Um certo arquiteto em incerto e secular roteiro*. Rio de Janeiro: Relume Dumará, 1996.
Habitat, no. 40–41 (March–April 1957). Special issue on Brasilia.
Holford, William. "Brasília: a New Capital City for Brazil." *Architectural Review*, no. 122 (1957a): 394–402.
———. "O concurso para o plano piloto de Brasília: declarações de membros do júri." *Módulo*, no. 8 (July 1957b): 22–28.
Holston, James. *The Modernist City: an Anthropological Critique of Brasilia*. Chicago, IL: Chicago University Press, 1989.
JornAU I, no. 6 (December 2002–January 2003). Special issue on Lucio Costa.
Katinsky, Júlio Roberto. "Lucio Costa." *Revista do Instituto de Estudos Brasileiros* (1972): 33–55.
Krieger, Peter. "Lucio Costa, der Planer von Brasilia ist gestorben." *Architekt*, no. 8 (August 1998): 435.
Kubitschek, Juscelino. *Por que construí Brasília*. Brasília: Senado Federal, Conselho Editorial, 2000.
Lissovsky, Maurício and Paulo Sérgio Moraes de Sá. *Colunas da educação: a construção do Ministério da Educação e Saúde (1935–1945)*. Rio de Janeiro: Edições do Patrimônio, 1996.
Lobo, Maria da Silveira and Roberto Segre, eds. *Cidade nova: síntese das artes/Congresso Internacional Extraordinário de Crítica de Arte*. Rio de Janeiro: FAU-UFRJ, 2009.
Luccas, Luís Henrique Haas. "Arquitetura moderna e brasileira: o constructo de Lucio Costa como sustentação." *Architextos* 6, no. 063.07 (September 2005).
Luz, Maturino. "Lucio Costa no Sul: o Museu das Missões." *Cadernos de Arquitetura Ritter dos Reis*, no. 2 (October 2000): 25–45.
Machado, Maísa Tude. "A contribuição de Lúcio Costa para a estética do modernismo." Master thesis, Universidade Federal do Rio de Janeiro, 1999.
Marianno (Filho), José. "A desnacionalização da Escola de Belas Artes." *O Jornal*, 1 August 1931a.
———. "Escola nacional de arte futurista." *O Jornal*, 22 July 1931b.

———. "Mas, que capadócio." *Diário da Noite*, 11 September 1931c.
———. "O incrível edifício do Ministério da Educação." In *Debates sobre Estética e Urbanismo*. Edited by José Marianno (Filho). Rio de Janeiro: Gráf. C. Mendes Junior, 1943.
———. "Uma a Deus, outra ao diabo." *Diário da Noite*, 8 September 1931d.
———. "Um caso de autophagia." *Diário de Notícias*, 14 May 1939.
Martins, Carlos Alberto Ferreira. "Arquitetura e Estado no Brasil. Elementos para uma investigação sobre a constituição do discurso moderno no Brasil: a obra de Lucio Costa, 1924–1952." Master thesis, Universidade de São Paulo, 1987.
———. "Estado, cultura e natureza na origem da arquitetura moderna brasileira: Le Corbusier e Lúcio Costa, 1929–1936." *Caramelo*, no. 6 (1993): 129–136.
Martins, Fernando. "O bom gosto agradece. A história também." *Ademi* (August 1980): 27–29.
Martins, Maria Clara Amado. "Barra da Tijuca. Uma arquitetura entre a ética e a estética." PhD dissertation, Universidade Federal do Rio de Janeiro, 2007.
Maurício, Jayme. "Lúcio Costa o homem." *Correio da Manhã*, 17 January 1970.
———. "O 'tempo livre' brasileiro na Trienal." *Módulo* IX, no. 38 (December 1964): 38–44.
Mello, Donato, Jr. "Um campus universitário para a cidade do Rio de Janeiro." *Arquitetura Revista*, no. 2 (1985): 52–72.
Mello, Thiago de. "As casas amazônicas de Lúcio Costa." *Design Interiores*, no. 17 (December 1989): 107–111.
Menéres, Antonio. "Lúcio Costa. A lição do arquitecto." *Jornal de Letras*, 1 July 1998.
Módulo, no. 8 (June 1957). Special issue on Brasilia.
Monnier, Gérard, ed. *Brasilia: L'épanouissement d'une capitale*. Paris: Éditions A. et J. Picard, 2006.
Moraes, Nana. "Obra de mestre." *Arquitetura e Construção* 14, no. 8 (August 1998): 78–85.
Morais, Frederico. "Lúcio Costa: 'Como arquitetura brasileira, nada se distingue'." *O Globo*, 13 Feburary 1980.
Moreira, Fernando Diniz. "A Surface for Breathing. Lucio Costa and Parque Guinle, Brazil." *On site review*, no. 9 (2003): 30–32.
———. "Lucio Costa: Tradition in the Architecture of Modern Brazil." *National Identities* 8, no. 3 (September 2006): 259–275.
Name, Daniela. "Maestro das pranchetas. Exposição marca o centenário de Lucio Costa." *O Globo*, 5 March 2002.
Niemeyer, Oscar. *Minha experiência em Brasília*. Rio de Janeiro: Editora Revan, 1961.
Nobre, Ana Luisa. "A razão e as razões de Lucio Costa." *AU, arquitetura e urbanismo* XVII, no. 100 (February–March 2002): 100–103.
———. "Autobiografia da arquitetura brasileira." *AU, arquitetura e urbanismo*, no. 62 (October–November 1995): 28.
———. "O novo mundo de Lúcio Costa." *Projeto Design*, no. 222 (July 1998): 12.
———, João Masao Kamita, Otavio Leonídio Ribeiro, and Roberto Conduru, eds. *Um modo de ser moderno. Lucio Costa e a crítica contemporânea*. São Paulo: Cosac & Naify, 2003.
Noto, Felipe de Souza. "Paralelos entre Brasil e Portugal: a obra de Lucio Costa e Fernando Távora." Master thesis, Universidade de São Paulo, 2007.
Oliveira, Márcia David de. "O lugar da arte: o caso do projeto do Ministério da Educação e Saúde Pública, Rio de Janeiro, 1935–1945." Master thesis, Universidade de São Paulo, 2005.
Oliveira, Rogério de Castro. "As modernidades eletivas de Le Corbusier e Lucio Costa: Rio de Janeiro, 1936." *ARQtexto* 1, no. 2 (January–June 2002): 152–167.
Ouriveis, Maria Amélia Corrêa. "Lições de um arquiteto." *Arquitetura e Construção* 11, no. 6 (June 1995): 66–73.
Pavilhão do Brasil. Feira Mundial de Nova York de 1939. New York: H. K. Publishing, 1939.
Peregrino (Junior), João. "O Salão nº 38." *O Cruzeiro* III, no. 45, 12 September 1931.

Pereira, Margaret da Silva. "Lúcio Costa (1902–1998): Master Planner of Brasília." *Docomomo Journal*, no. 20 (1999): 6–7.

——— et al. "1931 Arte e Revolução: Lúcio Costa e a reforma da Escola de Belas Artes." UFRJ, Programa de Pós-graduação em Urbanismo (CD), 2010.

Pessôa, José Simões de Belmont. "A persistência de uma ideia. Sagres e os riscos dos monumentos modernos de Lúcio Costa." *Arquitextos* 15, no. 175.01 (December 2014).

———. "Brasília e o tombamento de uma idéia." In *Anais do 5º Seminário DOCOMOMO-Brasil*. São Carlos: SAP-EESC-USP, 2003.

———. "Introdução: o que convêm preservar." In *Lucio Costa: documentos de trabalho*. Edited by José Simões de Belmont Pessôa, 11–19. Rio de Janeiro: Edições do Patrimônio-Iphan, 1999.

——— and Maria Silvia Muylaert de Araújo. "Vila Operária de Gambôa." *Módulo*, no. 76 (1983): 52–55.

Petrina, Alberto. "Lúcio Costa: apuntes para una biografía revolucionaria." *Summa*, no. 186 (April 1983): 18–22.

Piccarolo, Gaia. "Across the Atlantic Back and Forth. Lucio Costa's Cultural Peregrinations between Brazil and Portugal." In *Rutas ibero-americanas. Contactos e intercambios en la arquitectura del siglo XX/Rotas de intercâmbio na arquitetura do século XX/Exchange Paths in the Twentieth Century Architecture*. Edited by Ana Esteban Maluenda et al., 15–38. Madrid: Mairea Libros, 2017.

———. "Encontros e desencontros. Lucio Costa e Gustavo Capanema." In *Lucio Costa Arquiteto*. Edited by Farés El-Dahdah, 149–177. Rio de Janeiro: Casa de Lucio Costa, 2010a.

———. "L'architettura come impegno civile. Lucio Costa nel Brasile di Vargas (1930–1945)." PhD dissertation, Politecnico di Torino, 2010b.

———. "Un dibattito: il grattacielo e Rio de Janeiro. Intervista a Lucio Costa." *Le culture della tecnica*, no. 20 (2010c): 75–99.

———. "Lucio Costa's Luso-Brazilian Routes: Recalibrating 'Center and 'Periphery'." In *Latin American Modern Architectures: Ambiguous Territories*. Edited by Patrício Del Real and Helen Gyger, 33–52. London; New York: Routledge, 2012.

———. *Un progetto di mediazione. Lucio Costa fra tutela del patrimonio e nuova architettura*. Santarcangelo di Romagna: Maggioli, 2014.

Pinheiro, Maria Lucia Bressan. "Lucio Costa e a Escola Nacional de Belas Artes." In *Livro de resumos e anais do 6º Seminário Docomomo Brasil*. Niterói: UFF, 2005. http://docomomo.org.br/wp-content/uploads/2016/01/Maria-Lucia-Bressan-Pinheiro.pdf.

Puppi, Marcelo. "Modernidade e academia em Lúcio Costa: ensaio de historiografia." *Revista de história da arte e arqueologia*, no. 1 (1994): 123–142.

Quintanilha, Aline Cristina Silveira. "O encontro da memória com o novo nas casas de Lucio Costa." Specialization thesis, Pontifícia Universidade Católica do Rio de Janeiro, 2003.

Rezende, Luiz Eduardo. "Rio ainda provoca paixão em Lúcio Costa." *Jornal do Brasil*, 18 October 1991.

Ribeiro, Otavio Leonídio. "Crítica e crise: Lucio Costa e os limites do moderno." *Cadernos de Arquitetura e Urbanismo* 13, no. 14 (December 2006): 147–158.

———. *Carradas de razões. Lucio Costa e a arquitetura moderna brasileira*. Rio de Janeiro: PUC-Rio-Loyola, 2007a.

———. "Em busca da palavra do mestre." *Novos Estudos*, no. 79 (November 2007b).

Rossetti, Eduardo Pierrotti. "Brasília, 1959: a cidade em obras e o Congresso Internacional Extraordinário dos Críticos de Arte." *Architextos* 10, no. 111.03 (August 2009).

———. "Riposatevi, a Tropicália de Lúcio Costa na XIII Trienal de Milão." *Desígnio, Revista de História da Arquitetura e do Urbanismo*, no. 4 (September 2005): 81–89.

Rubino, Silvana Barbosa. "Gilberto Freyre e Lúcio Costa, ou a boa tradição – O patrimônio intelectual do Sphan." *Óculum*, no. 2 (September 1992): 77–80.

———. "Lúcio Costa e o patrimônio histórico e artístico nacional." *Revista USP*, no. 53 (March–May 2002): 6–17.
Rudofsky, Bernard. "Cantieri di Rio de Janeiro." *Casabella* (April 1939): 12–17.
Saboia, Patricia. "Estudos de vida." *Jornal do Brasil*, 9 May 1994.
Santos, Cecília Rodrigues dos. "Lucio Costa: problema mal posto, problema reposto." *Architextos* 10, no. 115.01 (December 2009).
Santos, Paulo. "Presença de Lucio Costa na arquitetura contemporânea do Brasil, Conferência." Rio de Janeiro, 1960. Typescript, Biblioteca Paulo Santos.
Segawa, Hugo. "Do mestre, com carinho: memórias afetivas de Lúcio Costa, cidadão do mundo." *Projeto*, no. 192 (December 1995): 79–81.
———. "Dispensando retórica." *Projeto*, no. 134 (August 1990): 48.
———. "El invisible Lucio Costa (1908–1998)." *Arquine*, no. 20 (summer 2002): 13.
———. "La invención de Brasil: Lucio Costa, 1902–1998." *Arquitectura Viva*, no. 61 (July–August 1998): 74–75.
———. "Três casas para Thiago de Mello." *Projeto*, no. 125 (September 1989): 78–85.
———. "Una vanguardia impregnada de tradición: Lucio Costa y la herencia brasileña." *A & V*, no. 13 (1988): 24–27.
Segre, Roberto. "Humanismo, técnica e estética: Lucio Costa pensador." *Projeto Design*, no. 265 (March 2002b).
———. *Ministério da Educação e Saúde. Ícone urbano da modernidade brasileira (1935–1945)*. São Paulo: Romano Guerra, 2013.
———. "O edifício do Ministério da Educação e Saúde (1936–1945): Museu 'vivo' da arte moderna brasileira." *Architextos* 6, no. 069.02 (February 2006).
———. "O pêndulo de Lucio Costa." *Projeto Design*, no. 265 (March 2002c).
———. José Barki, José Kós, and Naylor Vilas Boas. "É hora de reconhecer o pai do modernismo. Contribuição dada por Lucio Costa foi muito além de Brasília." *Jornal do Brasil*, 27 February 2002a.
Silva, Maria Angélica da. "Formas e as palavras na obra de Lucio Costa." Master thesis, Pontifícia Universidade Católica do Rio de Janeiro, 1991.
Slade, Ana. "Arquitetura moderna brasileira e as experiências de Lucio Costa na década de 1920." Master thesis, Universidade Federal Rio de Janeiro, 2007.
Sombra, Fausto. "Luís Saia e Lúcio Costa. A parceria no Sítio Santo Antônio." *Architextos* 14, no. 161.03 (October 2013).
Souza, Tude de. "O Palacio de Educação." *O Jornal*, 2 October 1945.
Suzuki, Marcelo. "Lina e Lucio." PhD dissertation, a Universidade de São Paulo, 2010.
Tattara, Martino. "Brasilia, *cidade parque*. Il progetto della città come pratica del limite." PhD dissertation, Università IUAV di Venezia, 2008.
———, ed. *Lucio Costa. Brasilia Plano Piloto*. Venezia: Università IUAV di Venezia-Associação Casa de Lucio Costa, 2010.
———. "(Re)Writing the City: an Assessment of Brasilia's Legacy." *Hunch*, no. 12 (2009): 112–121.
Tavares, André. "Ideologia de uma arquitetura brasileira." In *Novela bufa do ufanismo em concreto. Episódios avulsos das crises conjugais da arquitectura moderna no Brasil (1914–1943)*. Edited by André Tavares, 96–107. Porto: Dafne editora, 2009a.
———. "O verdadeiro espírito da razão." In *Novela bufa do ufanismo em concreto. Episódios avulsos das crises conjugais da arquitectura moderna no Brasil (1914–1943)*. Edited by André Tavares, 108–119. Porto: Dafne editora, 2009b.
Telles, Sophia da Silva. "Lucio Costa: monumentalidade e intimismo." *Novos Estudos*, no. 25 (October 1989): 75–94.
Vasconcellos, Eduardo Mendes de. "Le Corbusier e Lucio Costa, 'le Maître' e o Mestre, ou o intercâmbio de saberes." Rio de Janeiro: Mímeo Prourb-UFRJ, 1998. http://docomomo.org.br/wp-content/uploads/2016/01/Eduardo-Vasconcellos.pdf.

Vidal, J. D., ed. *Lucio Costa: desenhos de juventude*. Belo Horizonte: Companhia Brasileira de Metalurgia e Mineração, 2001.
Vidal, Laurent. *De Nova Lisboa à Brasilia. L'invention d'une capitale, XIXe–XXe siècle*. Paris: IHEAL éditions, 2002.
Vieira, Lucia Gouvêa. *Salão de 1931: marco da revelação da arte moderna em nivél nacional*. Rio de Janeiro: Funarte-Instituto Nacional de Artes Plásticas, 1984.
Wisnik, Guilherme. "Brasília: tábula rasa e memória." *L'ADC L'architettura delle città. The Journal of the Scientific Society Ludovico Quaroni* 5, no. 8 (31 July 2016): 81–92.
———. *Lucio Costa*, São Paulo: Cosac & Naify, 2001.
———, ed. *O risco: Lucio Costa e a utopia moderna, depoimentos do filme de Geraldo Motta Filho*. Rio de Janeiro: Bang Bang Filmes Produções, 2003.
———. "Plástica e anonimato: modernidade e tradição em Lucio Costa e Mário de Andrade." *Novos Estudos*, no. 79 (November 2007).
Xavier, Alberto. "Trajetória de um 'maquis'." *AU, arquitetura e urbanismo*, no. 1 (January 1985): 20–21.
Zevi, Bruno. "Brasilia: le forme denunciano i contenuti tremendi." *L'architettura cronache e storia* X, no. 104 (June 1964): 77.
———. "Brasilia troppo in fretta. Capitale di plastici ingranditi." *L'Espresso*, no. 246 (January 1959).
———. "Un piano per Brasília. La nuova capitale volerà." In *Cronache di Architettura 5*. Edited by Bruno Zevi. Bari: Laterza, 1978.

General reference

"A architectura moderna na cidade de São Paulo. Dois aspectos da residencia Warchavchik recentemente construida." *Para Todos* X, no. 501 (21 July 1928): 35.
"A estréa de Marinetti no Brasil. Sua primeira conferencia, hontem, no lyrico, entre vaias e palmas prolongadas." *O Jornal*, 16 May 1926.
"A Exposição Internacional do Centenario." *Architectura no Brasil* II, vol. IV, no. 24 (September 1923): 143–157.
"Cidade Universitaria do Rio de Janeiro. Le Corbusier e P. Jeanneret." *Revista da Directoria de Engenharia – PDF* (March 1937): 185–186.
"IV Congresso Pan-Americano de arquitetos, Rio de Janeiro 1930." *Arquitetura e Urbanismo* V, no. 2 (1940).
"La cité nouvelle" (contributions by Mario Pedrosa, William Holford, Richard Neutra, Bruno Zevi, Alberto Sartoris, Lucio Costa, André Bloc, Meyer Shapiro, Raymond Lopez, Giulio Carlo Argan, Gillo Dorlfes, Jean Prouvé, Herbert Read, François Le Lionnais). *Architecture, formes + fonctions* VII (1960): 71–88.
"Max Bill, o inteligente iconoclasta." *Manchete*, no. 60 (13 June 1953).
"Noticiario technico, artistico e social. Commendador Dr. Raphael Rebecchi engenheiro-architecto." *Architectura no Brasil* I, no. 4 (January 1922): 151–152.
"O renascimento da architectura no Brasil (a Exposição Internacional do Centenario)." *Architectura no Brasil* I, no. 3 (December 1921): 93–116.
"Origem e finalidade dos Congressos Pan-Americanos de arquitetos." *Arquitetura e Urbanismo* V, no. 2 (1940): 66–96.
"Progetto per l'Università del Brasile a Rio de Janeiro: arch. Marcello Piacentini, arch. Vittorio Morpurgo." *Architettura*, no. 17 (September 1938): 521–550.
"Projeto do Ministério da Educação e Saude, Le Corbusier e P. Jeanneret." *Revista da Directoria de Engenharia – PDF* (March 1937): 182–183.
"Rapporto Brasile." *Zodiac*, no. 6 (1960): 56–139.
"Report on Brazil" (contributions by Peter Craymer, Walter Gropius, Hiroshi Ohye, Max Bill, Ernesto Nathan Rogers). *The Architectural Review* 116, no. 694 (October 1954): 234–250.

"Testimonianze dei protagonisti sul Palazzo dell'UNESCO" (contributions by Walter Gropius, Lucio Costa, Le Corbusier, Sven Markelius, Pier Luigi Nervi, and Bernard Zehrfuss). *Casabella continuità*, no. 226 (April 1959): 5–10.

180 anos de Escola de Belas Artes. Rio de Janeiro: Universidade Federal do Rio de Janeiro, 1998.

Agache, Alfred. *La remodelation d'une capitale. Aménagement – Extension – Embellissement.* Paris: Société Coopérative d'Architectes, 1932.

Al Sayyad, Nezar, ed. *Forms of Dominance. On the Architecture and Urbanism of the Colonial Enterprise.* Aldershot: Avebury, 1992.

Albuquerque, Roberto Cavalcanti de. *Gilberto Freyre e a invenção do Brasil*. Rio de Janeiro: José Olympio, 2000.

Altberg, Alexandre, ed. *1º Salão de arquitetura tropical inaugurado a 17 de abril de 1933 pelo Exmo. Sr. Ministro Washington Pires*. Exhibition catalogue, n.p., n.d.

Amaral, Aracy A., ed. *Arquitetura neocolonial: América Latina, Caribe, Estados Unidos*. São Paulo: Fundação Memorial da América Latina, 1994.

———. *Artes plásticas na Semana de 22*. São Paulo: Perspectiva, 1970a.

———. *Blaise Cendrars no Brasil e os modernistas*. São Paulo: Martins Fontes, 1970b.

———, ed. *Modernidade, art brésilien du 20e siècle*. Paris: Ministère des affaires étrangeres, Association francaise d'action artistique, 1987.

Anderson, Stanford. "Memory Without Monuments: Vernacular Architecture." *Traditional Dwellings and Settlements Review* XI, no. 1 (fall 1999): 13–22.

Andrade, Antônio Luiz Dias de. "Um estado completo que pode jamais ter existido." PhD dissertation, Universidade e São Paulo, 1993.

Andrade, Carlos Drummond de. "O Ministro que desprezou a rotina." *Módulo* X, no. 40 (September 1975): 21–22.

Andrade, Mário de. *A lição do amigo. Cartas de Mário de Andrade a Carlos Drummond de Andrade*. Rio de Janeiro: José Olimpio, 1982.

Andrade, Rodrigo Mello Franco de. "Contribuição para o estudo da obra do Aleijadinho." *Revista do Serviço do Patrimônio Histórico e Artístico Nacional*, no. 2 (1938): 255–297.

———. "Os arquitetos no congresso de museus." *Módulo* II, no. 6 (December 1956): 4–7.

———. "Programa." *Revista do Serviço do Patrimônio Histórico e Artístico Nacional*, no. 1 (1937): 3–4.

Andreoli, Elisabetta and Adrian Forty, eds. *Brazil's Modern Architecture*. London: Phaidon, 2004.

Architettura e società: l'America Latina nel XX secolo. Milano: Jaca Book, 1996.

Argan, Giulio Carlo. "Architettura moderna in Brasile." *Comunità*, no. 24 (1954): 48–52.

Atique, Fernando. "De 'casa manifesto' a 'espaço de desafetos;' os impactos culturais, políticos e urbanos verificados na trajetória do Solar Monjope (Rio, anos 20 – anos 70)." *Estudos Históricos Rio de Janeiro* 29, no. 57 (January–April 2016): 215–234.

Arquitectura popular em Portugal. Lisboa: Sindicato Nacional dos Arquitectos, 1961.

Arquitetura civil (textos escolhidos da Revista do Instituto do Patrimônio Histórico e Artístico Nacional). 3 vols. São Paulo: MEC-IPHAN, 1975.

Arquitetura contemporânea no Brasil. 2 vols. Rio de Janeiro: Editora Gersum Carneiro, 1947–1948.

Badaró, Murilo. *Gustavo Capanema: a revolução na cultura*. Rio de Janeiro: Nova Fronteira, 2000.

Banham, Reyner. *Age of the Masters: a Personal View of Modern Architecture*. Guildford: Architectural Press, 1975.

Barbalho, Alexandre. *Relações entre Estado e Cultura no Brasil*. Ijuí: Editora Unijuí, 1998.

Bardi, Lina Bo. "Lettera dal Brasile." *L'Architettura: cronache e storia* 2, no. 9 (July 1956): 182–187.

Bardi, Pietro Maria. *Lembrança de Le Corbusier: Atenas, Italia, Brasil*. São Paulo: Nobel, 1984.

———. *O modernismo no Brasil*. São Paulo: Sudameris-Banco Frances e Italiano para a America do Sul, 1978.

Batista, Eduardo Luis Araújo de Oliveira. "Blaise Cendrars – The Third Element in the Pau Brasil Movement." *Itinerários*, Araraquara, no. 33 (July–December 2011): 139–156.

Bazin, Germain. *Aleijadinho et la sculpture baroque au Brésil*. Paris: Le Temps, 1963.

———. *L'architecture religieuse baroque au Brésil*. 2 vols. Paris: Librairie Plon, 1956, 1958.

Benevolo, Leonardo. *History of Modern Architecture*. vol. 2. Cambridge, MA: The MIT Press, 1977. 1st edn 1971.

Bergdoll, Barry, Carlos Eduardo Dias Comas, Jorge Francisco Liernur, and Patricio Del Real, eds. *Latin America in Construction: Architecture 1955–1980*. New York: The Museum of Modern Art, 2015.

Blackmore, Lisa. *Spectacular Modernity: Dictatorship, Space, and Visuality in Venezuela, 1948–1958*, 1st edn. Pittsburgh, PA: University of Pittsburgh Press, 2018.

Bomeny, Helena, ed. *Constelação Capanema: intelectuais e políticas*. Rio de Janeiro: Editora Fundação Getúlio Vargas, 2001.

———. "Três decretos e um Ministério: a propósito da educação no Estado Novo." In *Repensando o Estado Novo*. Edited by Dulce Pandolfi, 137–166. Rio de Janeiro: Editora Fundação Getúlio Vargas, 1999.

Bonduki, Nabil, ed. *Affonso Eduardo Reidy*. Lisboa-São Paulo: Editorial Blau-Instituto Lina Bo and P.M. Bardi, 2000.

Bracco, Sergio. *L'architettura moderna in Brasile*. Rocca San Casciano: Cappelli, 1967.

Brillembourg, Carlos, ed. *Latin American Architecture 1929–1960. Contemporary Reflections*. New York: Monacelli Press, 2004.

Brito, Ronaldo. "A Semana de 22: o trauma do moderno." In *Sete ensaios sobre modernismo*. Edited by Sérgio Tolipana et al., 13–18. Rio de Janeiro: Funarte, 1983.

Bruand, Yves. *Arquitetura contemporânea no Brasil*. São Paulo: Perspectiva, 1997. 1st edn 1982.

Bullrich, Francisco. *Arquitectura latinoamericana 1930/1970*. Barcelona: Gili, 1969.

Burns, Edward Bradford. *Nationalism in Brazil. A Historical Survey*. New York: Frederick A. Praeger, 1968.

Campofiorito, Ítalo. "A arquitetura brasileira até hoje." *Módulo* XI, no. 42 (March 1946): 16–27.

———. "As primeiras árvores." *Revista do Patrimônio Histórico e Artístico Nacional*, no. 26 (1997): 10–21.

Cândido, Antônio. "A Revolução de 1930 e a cultura." *Novos Estudos*, no. 4 (April 1984): 27–36.

Canizaro, Vincent B., ed. *Architectural Regionalism. Collected Writings on Place, Identity, Modernity and Tradition*. New York: Princeton Architectural Press, 2007.

Capanema, Gustavo. "Depoimentos." *Módulo*, no. 85 (May 1985): 27–32.

Cardoso, Joaquim. "Um tipo de casa rural do Distrito Federal e Estado do Rio." *Revista do Serviço do Patrimônio Histórico e Artístico Nacional*, no. 7 (1943): 209–256.

Cardoso, Luiz, Antonio Fernandes, and Olívia Fernandes de Oliveira, eds. *(Re)Discutindo o modernismo: universalidade e diversidade do movimento moderno em arquitetura e urbanismo no Brasil*. Salvador: Mestrado em Arquitetura e Urbanismo da UFBa, 1977.

Carone, Edgard. *A primeira republica (1889–1930): texto e contexto*. Rio de Janeiro: Difel, 1976.

———. *A republica nova (1930–1937)*. São Paulo: Difusão Europeia do Livro, 1974.

Carranza, Luis E. and Fernando Luiz Lara. *Modern Architecture in Latin America: Art, Technology, and Utopia*. Austin, TX: University of Texas Press, 2014.

Carvalho, José Murilo de. "Brazil 1870–1914. The Force of Tradition." *Journal of Latin American Studies* 24 (1992): 145–162.
Casciato, Maristella, and Stanislaus von Moos, eds. *Twilight of the Plan: Chandigarh and Brasilia.* Mendrisio: Mendrisio Academy Press, 2007.
Catalogo da XXXI Exposição Geral de Bellas Artes. Rio de Janeiro: Typ. Revista dos Tribunaes, 1924.
Cavalcanti, Lauro, ed. *Modernistas na repartição.* Rio de Janeiro: Editora UFRJ/Paço Imperial/ Tempo Brasileiro, 1993.
———. *As preocupações do belo. Arquitetura moderna brasileira dos anos 30/40.* Rio de Janeiro: Taurus, 1995.
———. "Architecture, Urbanism, and the Good Neighbor Policy: Brazil and the United States." In *Latin American Architecture 1929–1960. Contemporary Reflections.* Edited by Carlos Brillembourg, 50–59. New York: Monacelli Press, 2004.
———. *Moderno e brasileiro. A história de uma nova linguagem na arquitetura (1930–60).* Rio de Janeiro: Jorge Zahar Editor, 2006.
———. *When Brazil was Modern: Guide to Architecture 1928–1960.* New York: Princeton Architectural Press, 2003.
———, Farés el-Dahdah, and Francis Rambert, eds. *Roberto Burle Marx: the Modernity of Landscape.* Barcelona: Actar, 2011.
Cavalcanti, Roberto. "Le Corbusier, la France et le Brésil; influences réciproques." In *Le Corbusier. Europe et la Modernité*, 106–109. Budapest: Editions Corvina, 1991.
Cerávolo, Ana Lúcia. "Interpretações do Patrimônio: arquitetura e urbanismo moderno na constituição de uma cultura de intervenção no Brasil, anos 1930–60." PhD dissertation, Universidade de São Paulo, 2010.
Chaslin, François. *Un Corbusier.* Paris: Seuil, 2015.
Chuva, Márcia Regina Romero. "Os arquitetos da memória: a construção do patrimônio histórico e artístico nacional no Brasil (anos 30 e 40)." PhD dissertation, Universidade Federal Fluminense, 1998.
———. *A invenção do patrimônio: continuidade e ruptura na constituição de uma política oficial de preservação no Brasil.* Rio de Janeiro: MinC-IPHAN-Departamento de Promoção, 1995.
Ciucci, Giorgio. "A Roma con Bottai." *Rassegna* II, no. 3 (July 1980): 66–71.
———. *Gli architetti e il fascismo: architettura e città 1922–1944.* Torino: Einaudi, 1989.
Cohen, Jean-Louis. *Le Corbusier (1887–1965): un lyrisme pour l'architecture de l'ère mécaniste.* Colon: Taschen, 2004.
———, ed. *Le Corbusier: an Atlas of Modern Landscapes.* New York: MoMA, 2013.
Comas, Carlos Eduardo Dias. "Brazil Builds e a bossa barroca: notas sobre a singularização da arquitetura moderna brasileira." http://docomomo.org.br/wp-content/uploads/2016/01/Carlos-Eduardo-Comas.pdf.
———. "Le Corbusier: os riscos brasileiros de 1936." In *Le Corbusier Rio de Janeiro 1929, 1936.* Edited by Yannis Tsiomis, 26–31. Rio de Janeiro: Centro de Arquitetura e Urbanismo do Rio de Janeiro, 1998a.
———. "Modern Architecture, Brazilian Corollary." *AA Files* (summer 1998b): 3–13.
———. "Precisões brasileiras. Sobre um estado passado da arquitetura e urbanismo modernos." PhD dissertation, Paris VIII Université Vincennes-Saint Denis, 2002.
———. "Uma certa arquitetura moderna brasileira: experiência a re-conhecer." *Arquitetura Revista*, no. 5 (1987): 22–27.
Compagnon, Olivier and Diogo Cunha, eds. *Les intellectuels et le politique au Brésil (XIXe – XXe siècles).* Limoges: Lambert-Lucas, 2016.
Costa, Angyone. *A inquietação das abelhas.* Rio de Janeiro: Pimenta de Mello & Cia, 1927.
Cunha, Cláudia dos Reis e. "Restauração: diálogos entre teoria e prática no Brasil nas experiências do IPHAN." PhD dissertation, Universidade de São Paulo, 2010.
Cunha, Euclides da. *Os Sertões.* Rio de Janeiro: Laemmert, 1903.

Curtis, William J.R. *Le Corbusier: Ideas and Forms*. Phaidon: London, 1995.
——. *Modern Architecture since 1900*. 3rd edn. London: Phaidon, 1996.
Czajkowski, Jorge. "Carlos Leão. Mestre da justa medida." *AU, arquitetura e urbanismo* IX, no. 48 (June–July 1993): XX.
——, ed. *Jorge Machado Moreira*, Rio de Janeiro: Centro de Arquitectura e Urbanismo do Rio de Janeiro, Prefeitura da Cidade do Rio de Janeiro, 1999.
—— and Fernando Sendik, eds. *Guia da arquitetura moderna no Rio de Janeiro*. Rio de Janeiro: Editora Casa da Palavra, Prefeitura da Cidade do Rio de Janeiro, 2000.
d'Ors, Eugeni. *Lo barroco*. Madrid: Alianza-Tecnos, 2002.
Daher, Luiz Carlos. *Flávio de Carvalho: arquitetura e expressionismo*. São Paulo: Projeto, 1982.
Dal Co, Francesco and Marco Mulazzani. "Stato e regime: una nuova committenza." In *Storia dell'architettura italiana. Il primo Novecento*. Edited by Giorgio Ciucci and Giorgio Muratore, 234–259. Milano: Electa, 2004.
Damatz, Paul F. *Art in Latin American Architecture*. New York: Reinhold Publishing Corporation, 1963.
De Vincenzi, Lectícia Josephina Braga. "A fundação da Universidade do Distrito Federal e seu significado para a educação no Brasil." *Forum Educacional* 10, no. 3 (July–September 1986): 16–60.
Deckker, Zilah Quezado. *Brazil Built. The Architecture of the Modern Movement in Brazil*. London-New York: Spon Press, 2001.
Del Brenna, Giovanna Rosso. "Aspetti dell'eclettismo in Brasile." In *Architettura dell'eclettismo: la dimensione mondiale*. Edited by Loretta Mozzoni and Stefano Santini, 475–501. Napoli: Liguori, 2006.
Dennison, Stephanie. *Joaquim Nabuco. Monarchism, Panamericanism and Nation-Building in the Brazilian Belle Epoque*. Oxford: Peter Lang, 2006.
Dos Passos, John. *Brazil on the Move*. London: Sidgwick and Jackson, 1963.
Durand, José Carlos. "Negociação política e renovação arquitetônica: Le Corbusier no Brasil." *Revista Brasileira de Ciências Sociais* 6, no. 16 (July 1991): 5–26.
Fabris, Annateresa, ed. *Ecletísmo na arquitetura brasileira*. São Paulo: Nobel-Edusp, 1987.
Fernandes, José Manuel, ed. *Português suave: arquitecturas do Estado Novo*. Lisboa: IPPAR, 2003.
Ferraz, Geraldo. "Individualidades na história da atual arquitetura no Brasil (I) Gregori Warchavchik." *Habitat* VI, no. 28 (March 1956a): 40–49.
——. *Warchavchik e a introdução da nova arquitetura no Brasil: 1925 a 1940*, São Paulo: Museo de Arte de São Paulo, 1965.
Ferro, Sérgio. *Arquitetura e trabalho livre*. Edited by Pedro Fiori Arantes. São Paulo: Cosac & Naify, 2006.
Ficher, Sylvia and Marlene Milan Acayaba. *Arquitetura moderna brasileira*. São Paulo: Projeto, 1982.
Fonseca, Maria Cecília Londres. *O patrimônio em processo: trajetória da política federal de preservação no Brasil*. Rio de Janeiro: UFRJ-IPHAN, 1997.
Frampton, Kenneth. *Modern Architecture: a Critical History*. 4th edn. London: Thames & Hudson, 2007.
Franco, Luis Fernando. "Warchavchik e a arquitetura." *Gávea*, no. 3 (June 1986): 2–13.
Fraser, Valerie. *Building the New World: Studies in the Modern Architecture of Latin America, 1930–1960*. New York: Verso, 2000.
Freyre, Gilberto. *Aventura e rotina: sugestões de uma viagem a procura das constantes portuguêsas de caráter e ação*. Rio de Janeiro: José Olympio, 1953a.
——. *Casa grande e senzala: formação da família brasileira sob o regime da economia patriarcal*. 16th edn. Rio de Janeiro: José Olympio, 1973. 1st edn. 1933.
——. "Casas de residência no Brasil – Introdução." *Revista do Serviço do Patrimônio Histórico e Artístico Nacional*, no. 7 (1943): 99–127.

———. *Interpretação do Brasil*. Rio de Janeiro: José Olympio, 1947.

———. *O mundo que o português criou: aspectos das relações sociaes e de cultura do Brasil com Portugal e as colônias portuguesas*. Rio de Janeiro: José Olympio, 1940.

———. *Região e tradição*. Rio de Janeiro: José Olympio, 1941.

———. *Sobrados e mucambos: decadência do patriarcado rural e desenvolvimento do urbano*. São Paulo: Companhia Editora Nacional, 1936.

———. "Sugestões para o estudo da arte brasileira em relação com a de Portugal e das colonias." *Revista do Serviço do Patrimônio Histórico e Artístico Nacional*, no. 1 (1937): 41–44.

———. *Um brasileiro em terras portuguesas: introdução a uma possível luso-tropicologia acompanhada de conferências e discursos proferidos em Portugal e em terras lusitanas e ex-lusitanas da Ásia, da África e do Atlântico*. Rio de Janeiro: José Olympio, 1953b.

Gabetti, Roberto and Carlo Olmo. *Le Corbusier e "L'Esprit Nouveau"*. Torino: Einaudi, 1988.

Galvão, Anna Beatriz, "Warchavchik and Modern Movement Architecture in Brazil." *Docomomo Newsletter*, no. 6 (1991): 42–43.

Giedion, Sigfried. *A Decade of Contemporary Architecture*. New York: George Wittenborn, 1951.

———. *Architecture You and Me. The Diary of a Development*. Cambridge, MA: Harvard University Press, 1958.

———. *Space, Time and Architecture: the Growth of a New Tradition*. Cambridge, MA: Harvard University Press, 1941.

Gimdalcha, Ismé [Giancarlo De Carlo]. *Il progetto Kalhesa*. Ragusa: Edizioni di Storia e Studi Sociali, 2014. 1st edn. Marsilio, 1995.

Giovannoni, Gustavo. "La Conferenza Internazionale di Atene pel restauro dei monumenti." *Bollettino d'Arte* XXV, no. IX (March 1932): 408–419.

Gonçalves, Cristiane Souza. "Experimentações em Diamantina. Um estudo sobre a atuação do SPHAN no conjunto urbano tombado 1938–1967." PhD dissertation, Universidade de São Paulo, 2010.

Gonçalves, José Reginaldo dos Santos. *A retórica da perda. Os discursos do patrimônio cultural no Brasil*. Rio de Janeiro: UFRJ-IPHAN, 1996.

Goodwin, Philip. *Brazil Builds: Architecture Old and New 1652–1942*. New York: Museum of Modern Art, 1943.

Gorelik, Adrián. "¿Cien años de soledad? Identidad y modernidad en la cultura arquitectónica latinoamericana." *ARQ*, no. 15 (August 1990): 32–39.

———. "Brasília: Museo della modernità." *Casabella*, no. 753 (2007): 13–20.

———. *Das vanguardas a Brasília. Cultura urbana e arquitetura na América Latina*. Belo Horizonte: Editora UFMG, 2005.

Gubler, Jacques. "Architettura e colonialismo. Un safari storiografico." *Lotus International*, no. 26 (1980): 5–19.

Guimaraens, Cêça, ed. *Arquitetura e movimento moderno*. Rio de Janeiro: FAU-UFRJ, 2006.

Gutiérrez, Ramon and Jorge Moscato. *Architettura latinoamericana del Novecento*. Milano: Jaca Book, 1995.

Harris, Elizabeth D. *Le Corbusier: riscos brasileiros*. São Paulo: Nobel, 1988.

Henriques, Affonso. *Vargas e o Estado Novo*. São Paulo: Editora Record, 1964.

Hitchcock, Henry-Russell and Philip Johnson. *Latin American Architecture since 1945*. New York: Museum of Modern Art, 1955.

———. *The International Style: Architecture since 1922*. New York: W. W. Norton & Company, 1932.

Hobsbawm, Eric. *Nations and Nationalism Since 1780: Programme, Myth, Reality*. Cambridge: Cambridge University Press, 1992.

——— and Terence Ranger, eds. *The Invention of Tradition*. Cambridge: Cambridge University Press, 1983.

Holanda, Sérgio Buarque de. *Raízes do Brasil*. Rio de Janeiro: José Olympio, 1936.

Ideólogos do patrimônio cultural. Rio de Janeiro: Instituto Brasileiro do Patrimônio Cultural, 1991.

Jarcy, Xavier de. *Le Corbusier, un fascisme français*. Paris: Albin Michel, 2015.

Kessel, Carlos. *Arquitetura neocolonial no Brasil. Entre o pastiche e a modernidade*. Rio de Janeiro: Java Editora, 2008.

Korngold, Lucian. "Brasile incerto ed eclettico." *L'Architettura: cronache e storia* 2, no. 17 (March 1957): 806–807.

Lamberti, Mimita. "Le Corbusier e l'Italia." *Annali della Scuola Normale Superiore di Pisa* II, no. 2 (1972): 817–871.

Lara, Fernando Luiz. *The Rise of Popular Modernist Architecture in Brazil*. Gainesville, FL: University Press of Florida, 2008.

Le Corbusier. "L'Autorité devant les taches contemporaines." *L'Architecture d'Aujourd'hui* V, no. 9 (September 1935): 22–23.

———. *La ville radieuse. Éléments d'une doctrine d'urbanisme pour l'équipement de la civilisation machiniste*. Paris: Freal, 1964. 1st edn 1933.

———. *Le Voyage d'Orient*. Paris: Les Éditions Forces Vives, 1966.

———. *Précisions sur un état présent de l'architecture et de l'urbanisme avec un prologue américain un corollaire brésilien suivi d'une température parisienne et d'une atmosphère moscovite*. Paris: Éditions G. Crès et C.ie, 1930.

———. *The Athens Charter*. New York: Grossman Publishers, 1960.

———. *Urbanisme*. Paris: Éditions G. Crès et C.ie, 1925.

———. *Vers une architecture*. Paris: Éditions Crès, 1923.

——— and Pierre Jeanneret. *Oeuvre complète 1910–1929*. Zurich: Les éditions d'architecture, 1965.

——— and Pierre Jeanneret. *Oeuvre complète 1929–1934*. Zurich: Editions Girsberger, 1935.

——— and Pierre Jeanneret. *Oeuvre complète 1934–1938*. Zurich: Editions Girsberger, 1951.

——— and Pierre Jeanneret. *Oeuvre complète 1938–1946*. Zurich: Les éditions d'architecture, 1986.

Lefaivre, Liane and Alexander Tzonis. *Critical Regionalism: Architecture and Identity in a Globalized World*. Munich: Prestel, 2003.

Lefaivre, Liane, Bruno Stagno and Alexander Tzonis, eds. *Tropical Architecture: Critical Regionalism in the Age of Globalization*. Chichester: Wiley-Academy, 2001.

Lejeune, Jean-François and Michelangelo Sabatino, eds. *Modern Architecture and the Mediterranean: Vernacular Dialogues and Contested Identities*. London-New York: Routledge, 2009.

Lemos, Carlos A.C. *Arquitetura brasileira*. São Paulo: Melhoramentos Edusp, 1979.

———. "Arquitetura Contemporânea." In *História da Arte no Brasil*. Edited by Walter Zanini, vol. 2, 825–865. São Paulo: Instituto Moreira Salles, 1983.

Lemos, Cipriano. "Regionalismo o internacionalismo?" *Arquitetura e Urbanismo*, no. 4 (July–August 1938): 171–175.

Lemos, Fernando and Rui Moreira Leite, eds. *Missão portuguesa – Rotas entrecruzadas*. São Paulo: Editora da UNESP, 2003.

Lévi-Strauss, Claude. *The View from Afar*. Chicago, IL: University of Chicago Press, 1985.

———. *Tristes Tropiques*. Paris: Plon, 1955, 1957.

Levy, Hanna. "A propósito de três teorias sobre o barroco." *Revista do Serviço do Patrimônio Histórico e Artístico Nacional*, no. 5 (1941): 259–284.

Liernur, Jorge Francisco. *America Latina*. Milano: Electa, 1990.

———. "Nacionalismo y universalidad en la arquitectura latinoamericana." In *Modernidad y postmodernidad en America Latina. Estado del debate*. Edited by Cristian Fernández Cox, Enrique Browne, Carlos Eduardo Comas, Rodolfo Santa María, Jorge Francisco Liernur, Ada Dewes, and Marina Waisman. Bogotá: Escala, 1991.

Bibliography

———. "*The South American Way*. El 'milagro' brasilenho, los Estados Unidôs y la Segunda Guerra Mundial (1939–1943)." *Block*, no. 4 (December 1999): 23–41.

———. "Un nuovo mondo per lo spirito nuovo: le scoperte dell'America Latina da parte della cultura architettonica del XX secolo." *Zodiac*, no. 8 (1992): 84–121.

Lino, Raul. *Auriverde jornada. Recordações de uma viagem ao Brasil*. Lisboa: Edição de Valentim de Carvalho, 1937.

Lira, José Tavares Correia de. "Ruptura e construção: Gregori Warchavchik, 1917–1927." *Novos Estudos*, no. 78 (July 2007).

———. *Warchavchik. Fraturas da vanguarda*. São Paulo: Cosac & Naify, 2011.

Loomba, Ania. *Colonialism/Postcolonialism*. London; New York: Routledge, 1998.

López-Durán, Fabiola. *Eugenics in the Garden: Transatlantic Architecture and the Crafting of Modernity*. Austin, TX: University of Texas Press, 2018.

Macedo, Danilo Matoso. *Da matéria à invenção. As obras de Oscar Niemeyer em Minas Gerais, 1938–1955*. Brasilia: Camara dos Deputados, 2008.

Machado, Lourival Gomes. *Barroco mineiro*. São Paulo: Perspectiva, 1991.

Magalhães, José Calvet de. *Breve história das relações diplomáticas entre Brasil e Portugal*. São Paulo: Paz e Terra, 1999.

Malhano, Clara Emília Sanches Monteiro de Barros. *Da materialização à legitimação do passado: a monumentalidade como metáfora do Estado 1920–1945*. Rio de Janeiro: FAPERJ-Editora Lucerna, 2002.

Mariano (Filho), José. *À margem do problema arquitetônico nacional*. Rio de Janeiro: Artes Gráficas C. Mendes Junior, 1943a.

———. *Debates sobre estética e urbanismo*. Rio de Janeiro: Artes Gráficas C. Mendes Junior, 1943b.

———. *Estudos de arte brasileira*. Rio de Janeiro: Artes Gráficas C. Mendes Junior, 1942.

———. "Os dez mandamentos do estilo neo-colonial. Aos jovens architectos." *Architectura no Brasil* II, vol. IV, no. 24 (September 1923): 161.

Mário de Andrade: cartas de trabalho. Correspondência com Rodrigo Mello Franco de Andrade (1936–1945). Brasilia: Fundação Nacional Pró-Memória, 1981.

Martins, Carlos Alberto Ferreira. "Hay algo de irracional." *Block*, no. 4 (December 1999): 8–22.

———. "Identidade nacional e estado no projeto modernista. Modernidade, Estado e Tradição. O surgimento, a partir da década de 20, de uma nova visão sobre o Brasil no campo da produção cultural, plástica e musical." *Óculum*, no. 2 (September 1992): 71–76.

Martins, Luciano. *La genèse d'une intelligentsia (Les intellectuelles et la politique au Brésil, 1920–1940)*. Paris: Centre d'étude des mouvements sociaux, 1986.

Mello, Joana. *Ricardo Severo: da arqueologia portuguesa à arquitetura brasileira*. São Paulo: Annablume Editora, 2007.

Miceli, Sergio, ed. *Estado e cultura no Brasil*. São Paulo: Difel, 1984.

———, ed. *Intelectuais e classe dirigente no Brasil (1920–1945)*. São Paulo: Difel, 1979.

———, ed. "SPHAN: refrigério da cultura oficial." *Revista do Patrimônio Histórico e Artístico Nacional*, no. 22 (1987): 44–47.

Mignolo, Walter D. and Arturo Escobar, eds. *Globalization and the Decolonial Option*, 1st edn. London: Routledge, 2013.

Milheiro, Ana Vaz. *A Construção do Brasil. Relações com a cultura arquitectónica portuguesa*. Porto: FAUP, 2005.

Mindlin, Henrique. *Modern Architecture in Brazil*. New York: Reinhold, 1956.

Miranda, Wander de Melo, ed. *Anos JK: margens da modernidade*. São Paulo-Rio de Janeiro: Imprensa Oficial do Estado-Casa de Lucio Costa, 2002.

Mocchetti, Ettore, ed. *Oscar Niemeyer*. Milano: Mondadori, 1975.

Monographic issue on Brazil. *Block*, no. 4 (December 1999).

Monographic issue on Brazil. *L'Architecture d'Aujourd'hui*, no. 13–14 (September 1947).

Monographic issue on Brazil. *L'Architecture d'Aujourd'hui*, no. 42–43 (August 1952).

Monographic issue on Brazil. *The Architectural Forum* 87, no. 5 (November 1947).
Monogaphic issue on *Patrimônio. Arquitextos* 13, no. 149 (October 2012).
Monographic issue on the New York World's Fair. *The Architectural Review* 86, no. 513 (August 1939).
Montaner, Josep Maria. *Después del Movimiento Moderno*. Barcelona: Gustavo Gili, 1993.
Morshed, Adnan. "The Cultural Politics of Aerial Vision: Le Corbusier in Brazil (1929)." *Journal of Architectural Education* 55, no. 4 (May 2002): 201–210.
Motta, Lia. "A SPHAN em Ouro Preto, uma história de conceitos e critérios." *Revista do Patrimônio Histórico e Artístico Nacional*, no. 22 (1987): 108–122.
Mumford, Eric. *The CIAM Discourse on Urbanism, 1928–1960*. Cambridge, MA; London: The MIT Press, 2000.
Nascimento, Flávia Brito do. "Preservando a arquitetura do século XX: o IPHAN entre práticas e conceitos/Preserving Architecture of the 20th Century: the IPHAN between Practices and Concepts." *Cadernos PROARQ*, no. 19 (December 2012): 171–193.
Neto, Napoleão Ferreira da Silva. *O Palácio da Cultura. Poder e Arquitetura*. Fortaleza: Expressão, 1999.
Niemeyer, Oscar. "Hotel de Ouro Preto." *Revista da Directoria de Engenharia – PDF* IX, no. 2 (March 1942): 82–87.
———. *The Curves of Time: the Memoirs of Oscar Niemeyer*. London: Phaidon, 2007.
Nieto, José Ramírez. *El discurso Vargas Capanema y la arquitectura moderna en Brasil*. Bogotá: Universidad Nacional de Colombia, Facultad de Artes, 2000.
Nobre, Ana Luiza. *Carmen Portinho. O moderno em construção*. Rio de Janeiro: Relume-Dumará, 1999.
Nordenson, Catherine Seavitt. *Depositions: Roberto Burle Marx and Public Landscapes under Dictatorship*. Austin, TX: University of Texas Press, 2018.
O ingresso de professores futuristas na Escola Nacional de Bellas Artes. Officio dirigido ao Snr. Ministro da Educação e Saúde Publica pelo Instituto Paulista de Architectos. São Paulo: Typographia Camargo, 1931.
Oliveira, Lúcia Lippi. *A questão nacional na Primeira República*. São Paulo: Editora Brasiliense, 1990.
Ortiz, Renato. *Cultura brasileira e identidade nacional*. São Paulo: Editora Brasiliense, 1985.
Oyarzun, Fernando Perez. *Le Corbusier y Sudamerica: viajes y proyectos*. Santiago: Eds. ARQ, 1991.
Pagano, Giuseppe. *Architettura e cittá durante il fascismo*. Edited by Cesare de Seta. Bari: Laterza, 1990.
———. "Documenti di architettura rurale." *Casabella* VIII, no. 95 (November 1935): 18–19.
——— and Guarniero Daniel. *Architettura rurale italiana*. Milano: Hoepli, 1936.
Paim, Antônio. "Por uma Universidade no Rio de Janeiro." In *Universidades e Instituições Científicas no Rio de Janeiro*. Edited by Simon Schwartzman, 17–96. Brasília: CNPq, 1982.
Papadaki, Stamo. *Oscar Niemeyer*. New York: George Braziller, 1960.
———. *Oscar Niemeyer: Works in Progress*. New York: Rheinhold, 1956.
———. *The Work of Oscar Niemeyer*. New York: Reinhold Publishing Corporation, 1950.
Passanti, Francesco. "The Vernacular, Modernism, and Le Corbusier." *Journal of the Society of Architectural Historians* 56, no. 4 (December, 1997): 438–451.
Pearson, Christopher E.M. *Designing UNESCO: Art, Architecture and International Politics at Mid-Century*. London: Routledge, 2016. 1st edn Ashgate Publishing, 2010.
Pedrosa, Mário. *Dos murais de Portinari aos espaços de Brasília*. São Paulo: Editora Perspectiva, 1981.
Pereira, Margareth da Silva. "A participação do Brasil nas exposições universais. Uma arqueologia da modernidade brasileira." *Projeto*, no. 139 (March 1991): 83–90.
Pessôa, José, Simões de Belmont, Eduardo Vasconcellos, Elisabete Reis, and Maria Lobo, eds. *Moderno e nacional*. Niterói: EdUFF, 2006.

Pinheiro, Gerson Pompeu. "O estado e a arquitetura." *Arquitetura e Urbanismo*, no. 4 (July–August 1938a): 169–170.

———. "Rumo à casa brasileira." *Arquitetura e Urbanismo*, no. 3 (May–June 1938b): 113–115.

Pinheiro, Maria Lucia Bressan. "Mário de Andrade e o Neocolonial." *Desígnio, Revista de História da Arquitetura e do Urbanismo*, no. 4 (September 2005): 97–104.

———. "Origens da noção de preservação do patrimônio cultural no Brasil." *Revista de pesquisa em arquitetura e urbanismo*, no. 3 (February 2006): 4–14.

Prado, Caio, Jr. *Evolução politica do Brasil e outros estudos*, São Paulo: Editora Brasiliense, 1980. 1st edn 1933.

———. *Formação do Brasil contemporâneo*. São Paulo: Brasiliense, 1994. 1st edn 1942.

Proposte per Firenze (contributions by Luciano Bausi, Georges Candilis, Peter Smithson, Jacob B. Bakema, Lucio Costa, Heikki Siren). Supplement of *Architecture, formes + fonctions*, no. 14 (1967–1968).

Puppi, Lionello. *Guida a Niemeyer*. Milano: Mondadori, 1987.

Puppi, Marcelo. *Por uma história não moderna da arquitetura brasileira. Questões de historiografia*. Campinas: Pontes Editores, 1998.

Serra, Raspi, Francoise Joselita, Astorg Bollack, and Tom Killian. *Everyday Masterpieces: Memory & Modernity. A Study of an International Vernacular Architecture between the Two World Wars*. Modena: Panini, 1988.

Reis (Filho), Nestor Goulart. *Quadro da arquitetura no Brasil*. São Paulo: Perspectiva, 2004. 1st edn 1970.

Rodrigo e o SPHAN; coletâneas de textos sobre o patrimônio cultural. Rio de Janeiro: Fundação Nacional Pró-Memória, 1987.

Rodrigo e seus tempos. Rodrigo Mello Franco de Andrade. Rio de Janeiro: Fundação Nacional Pró-Memória, 1985.

Rodrigues, José Wasth. *As Artes Plásticas no Brasil. Mobiliário*. Rio de Janeiro: Edições de Ouro, 1968.

———. *Documentário arquitetônico relativo à antigua construção civil no Brasil*. São Paulo: Livraria Martins Editora, 1944.

Rogers, Ernesto Nathan. "Il dramma del Palazzo dell'UNESCO." *Casabella continuità*, no. 226 (April 1959): 2–25.

Rosa, João Guimarães. *Grande sertão: veredas*. Rio de Janeiro: José Olympio, 1956.

Rovira, Josep M. *José Luis Sert 1901–1983*. Milano: Electa, 2000.

Rubino, Silvana. "As fachadas da história: os antecedentes, a criação e os trabalhos do Serviço do Patrimônio Histórico e Artístico Nacional, 1937–1968." Master thesis, Universidade de Campinas, 1991.

———. "O mapa do Brasil passado." *Revista do Patrimônio Histórico e Artístico Nacional*, no. 24 (1996): 97–105.

Rudofsky, Bernard. *Architecture without Architects: a Short Introduction to Non-Pedigreed Architecture*. New York: Doubleday, 1964.

Sabatino, Michelangelo. *Pride in Modesty. Modernist Architecture and the Vernacular Tradition in Italy*. Toronto-Buffalo, NY; London: University of Toronto Press, 2010.

Sanches, Maria Ligia Fortes. "Construções de Paulo Ferreira Santos: a fundação de uma historiografia da arquitetura e do urbanismo no Brasil." PhD dissertation, Pontifícia Universidade Católica do Rio de Janeiro, 2005.

Sant'Anna, Márcia Genésia. *Da cidade-monumento à cidade-documento. A norma de preservação de áreas urbanas no Brasil, 1937–1990*. Salvador: IPHAN-Ministério da Cultura, 2015.

Santos, Cecília Rodrigues dos. "Mapeando os lugares do esquecimento: idéias e práticas na origem da preservação do patrimônio no Brasil." PhD dissertation, Universidade de São Paulo, 2007.

——, Margareth Campos Reis da Silva Pereira, Romão Veriano da Silva Pereira, and Vasco Caldeira da Silva. *Le Corbusier e o Brasil*. São Paulo: Tessela-Projeto Editora, 1987.
Santos, Mariza Veloso Motta. "Nasce a academia SPHAN." *Revista do Patrimônio Histórico e Artístico Nacional*, no. 24 (1996): 77–95.
——. *O tecido do tempo: a ideia de patrimônio cultural no Brasil 1920–1970*. Brasilia: UNB, Departamento de Antropologia, 1992.
Santos, Paulo. *Quátro séculos de arquitetura*. Barra do Piraí: Fundação Educacional Rosemar Pimentel, 1977.
Sartoris, Alberto. *Encyclopédie de l'architecture nouvelle. Ordre et climat américains*. Milano: Hoepli, 1954.
——. *Gli elementi dell'architettura funzionale*. Milano: Hoepli, 1931.
Scarrocchia, Sandro. *Albert Speer e Marcello Piacentini: l'architettura del totalitarismo negli anni trenta*. Milano: Skira, 1999.
Schwartz, Jorge, ed. *Brasil: de la antropofagia a Brasilia, 1920–1950*. Valencia: Generalidad Valenciana, 2000.
Schwartzman, Simon, ed. *Estado Novo, um auto-retrato (Arquivo Gustavo Capanema)*. Brasília: Editora Universidade de Brasília, 1983.
——, Helena Bomeny, and Vanda Ribeiro Costa. *Tempos de Capanema*. Rio de Janeiro-São Paulo: Paz e Terra-Edusp, 1984.
Segawa, Hugo. "Arquitetura na Era Vargas: o avesso da unidade pretendida." In *Moderno e nacional*. Edited by José Pessôa, Eduardo Vasconcellos, Elisabete Reis, and Maria Lobo, 83–99. Niterói: EdUFF, 2006.
——. *Arquiteturas no Brasil – 1900–1990*. São Paulo: Edusp, 1998a.
——. "Gustavo Capanema e a moderna arquitetura brasileira." *Projeto*, no. 73 (March 1985): 34.
Segre, Roberto and Rafael Lopez Rangel. *Architettura e territorio nell'America Latina*. Milano: Electa, 1982.
Sert, José Luis. "Raíces mediterráneas de la arquitectura moderna." *A.C.*, no. 18 (April–June 1935): 31–36.
Shapiro, Barbara E. "'Tout ça est foutaise, foutaise et demi!': Le Corbusier and UNESCO." *RACAR: Revue d'Art Canadienne/Canadian Art Review* XVI, no. 2 (1989): 171–179, 298–307.
Souza, Abelardo de. "A ENBA, antes e depois de 1930." In *Depoimento de uma geração: arquitetura moderna brasileira*. Edited by Alberto Xavier, 63–70. São Paulo: Cosac & Naify, 2003.
Souza, Wladimir Alves de. "La restauration des monuments au Brésil." *Le monument pour l'homme. Actes du II Congrès International de la Restauration*. Venezia: ICOMOS, 1964.
Tafuri, Manfredo. "'Machine et mémoire.' La città nell'opera di Le Corbusier." *Casabella*, no. 502, 503 (April–May, June–July 1984).
——. *Teorie e storia dell'architettura*. Bari: Laterza, 1973; 1st edn, 1968.
—— and Francesco Dal Co. *Architettura contemporanea*. Milano: Electa, 1976.
Tavares, André. *Novela bufa do ufanismo em concreto. Episódios avulsos das crises conjugais da arquitectura moderna no Brasil (1914–1943)*. Porto: Dafne editora, 2009.
Tentori, Francesco. *Vita e opere di Le Corbusier*. Bari: Laterza, 2007.
Tinem, Nelci. *O alvo do olhar estrangeiro: o Brasil na historiografia da arquitetura moderna*. João Pessoa: Manufatura, 2002.
Tognon, Marcos. "Arquitetura fascista e Estado Novo: Marcello Piacentini e a tradição monumental no Rio de Janeiro." In *Cidade, povo e nação: gênese do urbanismo moderno*. Edited by Luiz Cesar de Queiroz Ribeiro and Robert Pechman, 157–164. Rio de Janeiro: Civilização Brasileira, 1996.
Torres, Alberto. *O problema nacional brasileiro*. Brasília: Editora da UnB, 1982. 1st edn 1914.

Tostões, Ana Cristina. "Moderno e nacional na arquitetura portuguesa. A descoberta da modernidade brasileira." In *Moderno e nacional*. Edited by José Pessôa, Eduardo Vasconcellos, Elisabete Reis, and Maria Lobo, 101–124. Niterói: EdUFF, 2006.

Tota, Antonio Pedro. *O amigo americano: Nelson Rockefeller e o Brasil*. São Paulo: Companhia das Letras, 2014.

Trento, Angelo. *Le origini dello Stato populista. Società e politica in Brasile 1920–1945*. Milano: Franco Angeli, 1986.

Tsiomis, Yannis, ed. *Conférences de Rio: Le Corbusier au Brésil*. Paris: Flammarion, 2006.

———, ed. *Le Corbusier Rio de Janeiro 1929, 1936*. Rio de Janeiro: Centro de Arquitetura e Urbanismo do Rio de Janeiro, 1998.

Tyrwhitt, Jaqueline, José Luis Sert, and Ernesto Nathan Rogers, eds. *The Heart of the City: Towards the Humanisation of Urban Life*, London: Lund Humphries, 1952.

Umbach, Maiken and Bernd Huppauf, eds. *Vernacular Modernism: Heimat, Globalization, and the Built Environment*. Stanford, CA: Stanford University Press, 2005.

Underwood, David. *Oscar Niemeyer and the Architecture of Brazil*. New York: Rizzoli, 1994a.

———. *Oscar Niemeyer and the Brazilian Free-Form Modernism*. New York: George Braziller, 1994b.

Uzeda, Helena Cunha de. "A Academia de Belas Artes de Río de Janeiro y su influencia en el desarrollo de la arquitectura moderna brasileña." *Goya*, no. 289–290 (October 2002): 293–302.

———. "Ensino acadêmico e modernidade. O curso de arquitetura da Escola Nacional de Belas Artes 1890–1930." PhD dissertation, Universidade Federal do Rio de Janeiro, 2006.

Vaudagna, Maurizio, ed. *L'estetica della politica. Europa e America negli anni Trenta*. Bari: Laterza, 1989.

Warchavchik e as origens da arquitetura moderna no Brasil. São Paulo: MASP, 1971.

Warchavchik, Gregori. "Acerca da arquitetura moderna." *Correio da Manhã*, 1 November 1925.

———. *Arquitetura do século XX e outros escritos*. Edited by Carlos Alberto Ferreira Martins. São Paulo: Cosac & Naify, 2006.

Weimer, Günter. *Arquitetura popular brasileira*. São Paulo: Martins Fontes, 2005.

Williams, Daryle. *Culture Wars in Brazil. The First Vargas Regime, 1930–1945*. Durham, NC-London: Duke University Press, 2001.

Wisnik, Guilherme. "Formalismo e tradição: a arquitetura moderna brasileira e sua recepção crítica." Master thesis, Universidade de São Paulo, 2003.

Wölfflin, Heinrich. *Principles of Art History. The Problem of the Development of Style in Later Art*. New York: Dover, 1950. 1st edn 1932.

———. *Renaissance and Baroque*. Ithaca, NY: Cornell University Press, 1966.

Wright, Frank Lloyd. *An Autobiography*. London: Faber and Faber Limited, 1965.

Xavier, Alberto, ed. *Depoimento de uma geração: arquitetura moderna brasileira*. São Paulo: Cosac & Naify, 2003. 1st edn 1987.

——— Alfredo Britto, and Ana Luiza Nobre. *Arquitetura moderna no Rio de Janeiro*. São Paulo: Rioarte-Fundação Vilanova Artigas-Editora Pini, 1991.

XVIII Exposição Geral de Bellas Artes 1931. Escola Nacional de Bellas Artes, n.p., n.d. Printed catalogue.

Zanini, Walter. *História geral da Arte no Brasil*. vol. 2. São Paulo: Instituto Moreira Salles-Fundação Djalma Guimarães, 1983.

Zevi, Bruno. *Storia dell'architettura moderna*. Torino: Einaudi, 1950.

Index

A Noite 9
Aalto, Alvar 132
academicism, academic 8, 9, 11–17, 19–23, 26, 28, 45, 54, 56, 72, 77, 85, 86, 98, 106, 114
Africa 51, 109
Agache, Donat Alfred 11, 40
Aleijadinho (Antônio Francisco Lisboa) 6, 11, 12, 89, 96, 97, 106, 107, 109–111, 113–115
Allies, the 70
Altberg, Alexandre 35
Amaral, Inácio Azevedo do 47, 49, 51
anonymous architecture 106, 107
antropophagy 57
Architectural Design 163
The Architectural Forum 80, 105
The Architectural Review 110, 130, 138, 139, 145
Architecture, Formes + Fonctions 164
Arno River 164
Arquitetura e Urbanismo 72
Art Nouveau 10
art of the State 3, 100
Aterro do Flamengo 100, 141, 158
Athens Charter on restoration (1931) 98
Athens Charter *see* CIAM (1933) 98, 152
authority 2, 49, 52, 68, 78, 140
Avenida Atlântica 158
Avenida Central 37
Axis Powers 70
azulejos 54, 55, 57, 114, 115, 118, 123

Bahiana, Gastão 16, 23, 24
Baía de Guanabara 52, 141
Baixada de Jacarepaguá 158
Bakema, Jacob B. 164
Bandeira, Manuel 11, 12, 19, 20, 23, 25, 39, 40, 42, 82, 89
Baroque 6, 77, 89, 107, 109–113, 115, 116, 135, 136
Barra da Tijuca 159, 160, *160*

barro armado com madeira 37, 107
Baumgart, Emílio Henrique 35, 59, 78
Beaudouin, Eugène 131
Berlin-Dahlem Botanical Garden 72
Bern 163
Bienal de São Paulo 132
Bill, Max 115, 132, 138
Bittencourt, Paulo 35
Bloc, André 129
Brasilia 1, 6, 7, 54, 57, 69, 100, 138, 139, 141, 142, 145, *146*, *148*, *149*, 149–152, *153*, *155*, *156*, 157–164, *165*; Alvorada Palace *153*; Catetinho 100; cathedral 100; *cidade parque* 152, 157; *cidades-satélites* (satellite cities) 156, 161, 162; *cinturão verde* 152; Congress 147; Esplanada dos Ministérios 147; fountain of the Television Tower 157; Lake Paranoá 147, *153*; monumental axis 147, 152, 154; Municipal Plaza 157; Núcleo Bandeirante 156; pedestrian plaza in the Plataforma Rodoviária 157; Plano Piloto 100, 142, 144, *148*, *149*, 151-153, *153*, *155*, 156-158, *160*, 161, 162; Plataforma Rodoviária 146, 147, 152, 157, 161; Quadras Econômicas 157; Setor Hoteleiro Norte 160; *superquadra* 152–154, *155*, 161, 162; Television Tower 147, 157; Three Powers Square 147, *148*, 152, 156
brasilidade (Brazilianness) 72
Brazil Builds exhibition, New York (1943) 78, 88, 111
Brazilian flag 21, 72, 73
Brazilian Golden Years 138
Brazilian pavilion, New York World's Fair (1939) *see* Costa, Lucio, projects
Brecheret, Victor 20
Breuer, Marcel 131, 132
brise-soleils 47, 54, 72, 75, 120
Brunhs, Angelo 42
Buarque de Holanda, Sérgio 38, 89

Index

Buddeus, Alexandre 17, 26
Burle Marx, Roberto 19, 54, 72, 83, 100, 114, 141, 156, 158

Cais of Flamengo 158
Callado, Antônio 145
Campofiorito, Ítalo 111, 157
Campos, Ernesto de Souza 47, 49, 51
Campos, Francisco 11–13, 15, 16, 19, 22, 23, 25, 26, 40
candangos 156
Candilis, Georges 4, 164
Capanema, Gustavo 5, 34, 38, 39, 41–43, 45, 47, 49–52, 55, 57–60, 66, 69–71, 78, 79, 81, *81*, 82, 85–89, 113, 116
Cardoso, Joaquim 89
Carmo (Igreja do), Ouro Preto 103
Casa dos Contos, Ouro Preto 103
Casa Modernista Exhibit 17, 26, 27
Casabella continuità 132
Cattete Pinheiro, Edward 150
cerrado 145, 147, 156
chafariz 144
Chambelland, Rodolfo 9, 23–25
Champs-Elysées 161
Choay, Françoise 152
Church of Nossa Senhora do Rosário, Ouro Preto *112*
Church of Outeiro da Glória, Rio de Janeiro 158
Church of São Francisco de Assis, Ouro Preto *98*, 113
Church of São Francisco de Assis, Pampulha *see* Niemeyer, Oscar
CIAM (Congrès Internationaux d'Architecture Moderne) 4, 6, 29, 35, 68, 69, 76, 96, 98, 102, 104, 130, 131, 138, 140, 161, 163, 164
Cinelândia 98
CIRPAC (Comité International pour la Résolution des Problèmes de l'Architecture Contemporaine) 29
Cité Universitaire, Paris 130
Club de Engenharia 37, 42
cobogó 75, 120
Coelho Duarte, Cesário 22
cold war 166
colonial Baroque 77, 111
colonisation 98
Columbus Memorial Lighthouse Competition 26
Comissão do Plano da Universidade 47
congresses: Extraordinary International Congress of Art Critics (1959) 138, 149, 150; Californian Convention of Architects of Monterrey (1962) 166; International Conference of Artists, Venice (1952) 6, 69, 130, 134; International Congress of Luso-Brazilian Studies, Washington (1950) 109; International Town Planning Congress, Florence (1967) 164; IV Pan-American Congress of Architects, Rio de Janeiro (1930) 13, 17, 20
Conselho Nacional de Belas Artes 19
Conselho Regional de Engenheiros e Arquitetos (CREA) 42
Constitution of 1934 66; of 1937 (or Polaca) 89
Constitutionalist Revolution (1932) 35
Corcovado 121
Corrêa Lima, Attilio 100
Corrêa Lima, José 16
Correias 22, 25
Correio da Manhã 25, 26, 43, 113
Costa, Helena 123
Costa, Lucio, exhibition pavilions: Brazilian Pavilion at the Exposition of Philadelphia 10; Brazilian pavilion for the Milan Triennale (1964) 133; Brazilian pavilion, New York World's Fair (1939) 6, 54, 57, 70–73, *73*, 74–76, *76*, 77, 82, 101, 111–114, 133
Costa, Lucio, institutional projects: competition for the Argentine embassy 10; *see also* Ministry of Education and Public Health
Costa, Lucio isolated monuments: monument to Estácio de Sá, Rio de Janeiro 141, 144; monument to João Pinheiro 141; monument to Prince Henry the Navigator 142, *143*, 144–147
Costa, Lucio, museum projects: Museu das Missões 100, 101, *102*, 103, 104; Museum of Science and Technology 166
Costa, Lucio, projects with Carlos Leão: headquarters of the Club de Engenharia 37
Costa, Lucio, religious projects: Altar for the International Eucharistic Congress 141, *142*; Church of Nossa Senhora de Copacabana 141, *141*
Costa, Lucio, residential projects: Casas sem dono 37, 116; castle for Baron Smith de Vasconcellos 9; Costa-Moreira Penna house 121, *122*, 123; cottage for Arnaldo Guinle 9; Duvivier-Byington house 121; Ernesto Gomes Fontes house 22, *22*, 116; home-atelier for Rodolfo Chambelland 9; house for Modesto Guimarães 22; Hungria Machado house 117; Maria Elisa Costa house 121; Marinho de Azevedo house 117; Parque Guinle residential complex 100, 119, 121, *121*; Pedro Paulo Paes de Carvalho house 117; renovation

of a colonial residence for João Baptista da Costa 9; Saavedra house 117, *117*, 118, *118*; São Clemente Park Hotel 100, 119, *120*; Solar Brasileiro 9; Thiago de Mello houses 121; *see also* Maison du Brésil

Costa, Lucio, urban and landscape projects: access to Outerio da Glória hill 158; capital of Nigeria 160, 163; Cidade Operária de Monlevade 37; Green Arcades (Arcadas Verdes) 160; Plano Piloto para a urbanização da baixada compreendida entre a Barra da Tijuca, o Pontal de Sernambetiba e Jacarepaguá 158, *160*; project for the Casablanca Corniche 160; University Campus, Rio de Janeiro *see* University Campus; urban centre in São Luis do Maranhão 160; *see also* Brasilia

Costa, Lucio, Warchavchik & Lucio Costa construction company projects: Marimbás nautical club 35; renovation of Paulo Bittencourt's residence 35; residential building for Maria Gallo 35; Schwartz house 35, *36*; Vila Operária da Gambôa 35

Costa, Maria Elisa 121, 157
coup d'état of 1937 66, 89
Cuchet, Francisque 9

d'Ors, Eugeni 111, 116, 136
da Costa, João Baptista 9
da Rocha Miranda, Alcides 19, 35, 89, 141
da Silva Cunha, Domingos 47, *48*
da Silva, João Lourenço 35
da Veiga Guignard, Alberto 83
de Andrade, Mário 19, 21, 38, 89, 106
de Andrade, Oswald 10
de Carvalho, Flávio 13, 22
de Mello, Heitor 9
de Mello, Thiago 121
de Menezes, Celso Antônio 17, 19, 26, 38, 72, *81*
de Morais Neto, Prudente 38
de Morais, Vinícius 89
de Oliveira Filho, Candido 25
de Sá Pereira, Lino 15
de Sá, Estácio 141, 144
de Souza Reis, José 51, 58, 89, 158
de Souza, Luíz Nunes 23
democracy, democratic 3, 7, 38, 66, 81, 131, 138, 139, 144, 147, 149–151
Departamento de Administração do Serviço Público 78
Departamento Municipal de Educação 39
Departamento Nacional da Educação 87
dépose (anastylosis) 100

desafogo urbano 98, 159
Di Cavalcanti (Emiliano Augusto Cavalcanti de Albuquerque Melo) 21
Diamantina 9, 10, 106
Diretório Academico 23, 42
Divisão de Conservação e Restauração (SPHAN) 99
Divisão de Estudos e Tombamentos (SPHAN) 90
do Amaral, Tarsila 10, 15
dogmatism, dogmatic 4, 91
Dorner, Alexander 96
Drummond de Andrade, Carlos 5, 39, 40, 42–44, 58, 60, 66, 82, 89
Duvivier, Edgard 121

eclecticism, eclectic 8, 9, 90, 98, 106, 123
Empire 98
Escola Politécnica 39
Escriptorio Technico Heitor de Mello 9
Escritório do Plano 47
Esplanada do Castelo 39, 47, 52–54, 70
Estado Novo 2, 5, 35, 38, 59, 66, 70, *71*, 85, 86, 89, 144, 151
Estremadura 111
Europe 4, 8, 10, 15, 82, 98, 115, 130, 136, 138
European 4, 6, 15, 36, 52, 66, 83, 90, 107, 109, 130, 161
evolutionary line of Brazilian architecture 3, 96, 98, 99
Exposição do Estado Novo, Rio de Janeiro (1938) 70, *71*
Exposição Geral of the School of Fine Arts (1924) 9

Faculdade Nacional de Arquitetura, Faculty of Architecture 39, 83, 87, 88
Fazenda Columbandê 110
fenêtre en longueur 106
Fernandes Saldanha, Firmino 42
Ferraz, Geraldo 19
Ferreira Bretas, Rodrigo José 109, 114
Ferro, Sérgio 123
Fertin, Mário 40, 41
Florence 164
Flushing Meadows, New York 71
Fragoso, Paulo 42
French Artistic Mission 90
Freyre, Gilberto 38, 89
functionalism 88, 136, 166

Galvão, Rafael 40, 41
Gelosías 118
Giedion, Sigfried 4, 28, 68, 69, 139, 149
Glória hill 158
Gobbis, Vittorio 20
Gomes, Gastão 25

Gonzaga, Leonel 25
Good Neighbour Policy 70
Grande Hotel de Ouro Preto 6, 101–103, *105*
grands travaux 34
Gropius, Walter 4, 35, 130, 132, 139
Guimarãens Costa, Julieta (Leleta) 130, 150
Guimarães, Modesto 22

Haussmann, Georges Eugène 52
heart of the city / core of the city 138, 139, 152, 161, 163, 164
heritage 2–4, 6, 9, 10, 17, 69, 88–91, 96, 98, 99, 103, 106, 157
Heuberger, Theodor 15, 20
Hitchcock, Henry-Russell 139
Holford, William 132, 139

identity (Brazilian cultural and artistic) 3, 6, 54, 69, 77, 89, 96, 115
identity building 4, 88, 96
Imperial Palms (*Palmeiras Imperiais*) 56, 152
Inconfidência Mineira 89
Independence Centenary International Exposition of Brazil, Rio de Janeiro (1922) 9
Instituto Brasileiro de Arquitetos 9
Instituto Central de Arquitetos 39, 42
Instituto de Arte, Universidade do Distrito Federal 37, 38
Instituto Nacional de Música 51
Instituto Paulista de Architectos *18*
Intentona Comunista 39
International Style 35, 76, 88
IPHAN (Instituto do Patrimônio Histórico e Artístico Nacional) 12
Itacolomy stone 103
Itamaraty Palace 11
Itararé 23

janelas de rótula 118, 123
janelas-conversadeiras 118
Jeanneret, Pierre 36
Jesuit architecture 100, 107, *108*, 111
Jornal do Brasil 161

Kelly, Celso 20, 38
Korn, Arthur 163
Krafft, Anthony 164
Kubitschek, Juscelino 7, 144
Kunstwollen 38, 111

L'Architecture d'Aujourd'hui 55, 88, *112*, 114, *120*, 133
Lagôa Rodrigo de Freitas 47, 49
landscape 4, 16, 17, 57, 72, 75, 83, 98, 99, 101, 102, 114, 119, 120, 129, 141, 142, 144, 145, 146, 147, 151, 152, 154, 156, 158–160, 164
Lasdun, Denys 163
Latin America 9, 69, 70
Law of the Meander 78, 138
Le Corbusier (Charles-Édouard Jeanneret) 4, 5, 11, 12, 15, 28, 29, 36–38, 42, 45, 47, 49–59, *56*, 66, 67, 68, 72, 77, 78, 81–83, 88, 100, 107, 111, 113, 114, 117, 129–133, 135, 138, 140, 147, 152, 166; Centrosoyuz 45; Maison Loucheur 37; Museum of Knowledge of Brazil 56; Museum of Unlimited Growth 56, 57; Palace of Nations 131; Palace of the Soviets 56; Plan Voisin 104; Swiss Pavilion 130; United Nations Headquarters 131; Ville Radieuse 49, 147; Ville Verte 98, 152; *see also* Maison du Brésil
Leão, Carlos de Azevedo 5, 35–39, 43, 50, 89, 101; *see also* Costa, Lucio, projects
Léger, Fernand 139
Lévi-Strauss, Claude 1
Levy, Hanna 111
Lipchitz, Jacques 72, 83, 144
Livro do Tombo de Belas Artes 101
Lotti, Carlo 163
Louis XIV 52, 145
Lourenço Filho, Manoel Bergström 87
Luso-Brazilian architecture 77, 104, 106, 109, 117
Luso-Brazilian tradition 77, 88, 90, 120

Machine Age 129, 136, 140
machine civilisation 66, 68
Madureira de Pinho, Péricles 133
Maison du Brésil 6, 130, 133, *134*
Malfatti, Anita 19, 20
Malraux, André 147
Marajoara style 40
Mariana 10
Mariano Filho, José 9, 10, *10*, 12, 17, 21; Solar Monjope 9
Markelius, Sven 130
Marseilles 130
Massachusetts Institute of Technology 166
Maude Richards, James 138
Mayerhofer, Lucas 101
Mello Franco de Andrade, Rodrigo 11, 12, 23, 25, 39–42, 69, 82, 85, 89, 90, 101, 102, 105
Memória, Archimedes 9, 25, 26, 40, 41, 43, 44
Mestre Ataíde (Manuel da Costa Ataíde) 109, 111
Mestre Valentim (Valentim da Fonseca e Silva) 109, 111, 144
mestres de obra 38, 106

Minas Gerais 9, 10, 37, 89, 109, 113, 115
Minho 110
Ministry of Education and Public Health: new seat 5, 6, 34, 39, 41–45, *45*, *46*, 47, 51–54, *54*, *55*, 59, 60, 66, 68, 70–72, *71*, 78–79, *80*, 81–83, *81*, *84*, 86, 88, 100, 102, 113, 114, 120, 131, 133, 139, 144; institution 11, 12, 42, 58, 59, 70, 71, 79, 89
Ministry of Foreign Affairs 11
Misericórdia de Parati 110
modern movement 6, 88
modernisation, modernisation process 2, 3, 5, 6, 70, 71, 105, 140
modernism, Brazilian 1–4, 6, 8, 13, 29, 36, 52, 54, 71, 77, 78, 82, 88, 90, 100, 114, 116, 131, 138, 139
modernity 1, 6, 13, 15, 78, 114, 117, 138
MoMA (Museum of Modern Art) 88
Monteiro de Carvalho, Alberto 42, 50
monumentality 6, 54, 72, 75, 130, 138–140, 149, 151, 158
Morales de los Rios, Adolfo 39
Moreira, Jorge Machado 5, 19, 23, 40, 41, 43, 45, 50, 51, 53
Morpurgo, Vittorio 56, 60
Moses, Herbert 26
Mussolini, Benito 51
Muxarabi 118, *122*

Napoleon 52
nation building, process, project 2, 3, 68, 85, 89
national personality 83, 110, 114, 135
National School of Fine Arts (Escola Nacional de Belas Artes), Rio de Janeiro 39, 42, 90; Caminhoã award 19; Congregação 11, 16, 23–26; Costa directorship 5, 8, 11, 12, *14*, 15, 16, *18*, 25, 28, 34, 35, 40, 43, 44, 83, 89; Costa formation 8, 9; Le Corbusier's conferences 11, 15, 50; Salão de 31 (Salão Lucio Costa, Salão dos tenentes, 38a Exhibition of the National School of Fine Arts) 19–21, 23; Technical and Administrative Board 16, 23, 24
nationalist 66, 69
neo-colonial architecture, movement, style 9, 10, 71, 101, 103, 114, 119, 123
Nervi, Mario 163
Nervi, Pier Luigi 131
Neutra, Richard 166
new architecture 3, 5, 6, 34, 44, 47, 52, 68, 78, 83, 96, 103, 117, 166
New Republic (Nova República) 5
New York 6, 54, 57, 70, 71, 72, *73–75*, 76, 76, 82, 86, 88, 101, 111, 113, 114, 131

New York World's Fair (1939) 6, 70, 71, *73–75*, 76, 76, 82
Niemeyer, Oscar 1, 3, 5, 6, 19, 37, 43, 45, 50, 51, 53, 54, 57, 58, 60–78, *74–76*, 82, 83, 89, 96, 100, 101–105, *105*, 111–117, *112*, 138, 141, 144, 149, 150, 156; Church of São Francisco de Assis, Pampulha *112*, 115, 141; Pampulha complex 57, 76, 82, 100, *112*, 113, 114, 115, 141; *see also* Grande Hotel de Ouro Preto
Nine Points on Monumentality 139
Niterói 141
NOVACAP (Companhia Urbanizadora da Nova Capital) 144, 150
Nova Friburgo 100, 119, *120*

O Globo 13, *14*, 15, 26
O País 10
Oca 121
Ofaire, Charles 66
Old Republic (República Velha) 15
Ouro Preto, Villa Rica 6, 10, *97*, 99, 101–104, *105*, *112*, 113, 114

Paes de Carvalho, Pedro Paulo 22
Pampulha complex *see* Niemeyer, Oscar
Panel of Five, the Five, Comité des Cinq 6, 69, 130–132
Pão de Açucar 141
Papadaki, Stamo 114
Paris 6, 68, 69, 129–131, 133, *134*, 140
Passeio Público 98
Patio 35, 56, 57, 72, 73, *74*, 75, 101, 116–118, *122*, 123
pau a pique 104, 117
Paulsson, Gregor 139
Pavilhão das Grandes Indústrias 9
Pavilhão dos Estados 98
Pavilhão Monroe 98
Pederneiras, Raul 24
Pedregulho housing complex *see* Reidy, Affonso Eduardo
Pedrosa, Mário 139
Penteado, Olívia Guedes 19
Pereira Passos, Francisco Franco 52
Perret, Auguste 37
Perriand, Charlotte 36, 107
Petit, Claudius 132
Petrina, Alberto 166
Petrópolis *117*, *118*
Piacentini, Marcello 41, 42, 49–51, 56, 60
Piccadilly Circus 161
Pinheiro, Gerson Pompeu 15, 22, 40, 41
Pinheiro, Israel 150
Plan Agache *see* Agache, Donat Alfred
Planalto Central 7, 130, 145, 156, 158

Index

plastic intention 76, 77, 87, 88, 136
Portinari, Cândido 19, 23, 38, *55*, 83, 114, 118
Portugal 106, 107, 109, 110, 130, 142, *143*
Portugal, Ademar 35
Portuguese architecture 106, 109, 110
post-war 4, 138, 139, 161
Prado, Paulo 19
Praia de Santa Luzia 52
preservation 9, 69, 88–90
Price, Thomas 72
Putz, Leo 17

Quinta da Bôa Vista 47

rancho de feitoria 121
Rebecchi architecture firm 9
redes 116
regime 19, 70, 86, 87, 162; dictatorial 35; military 7, 150, 151; totalitarian 66, 139; Vargas 68
regionalism 117
Reidy, Affonso Eduardo 5, 19, 22, 40–43, 45, 50, 100, 138; Pedregulho housing complex 138
restoration 4, 90, 96, 98, 99
Revista da Directoria de Engenharia – PDF 38, 41, 47, 59
Revista do Serviço do Patrimônio Histórico e Artístico Nacional 105, 111
Revolution of 1930 11
Rio de Janeiro 4, 5, 8–10, 13, 15, 16, *22*, 26, 27, 28, 34, 35, *36*, 37, 39, 42, *45*, 46, 51, 52, *54*, *56*, 57, *57*, 69, 75, 98–100, 102, 104, 113, 117, 119, *121*, 122, 131, 133, 141, *141*–*143*, 144, 150, 158, 161
Roberto, Marcelo 22
Roberto, Milton 19
Robertson, Howard 131
Rogers, Ernesto Nathan 4, 110, 111, 113, 130–132
Rome 41, 70, 130
Roth, Alfred 139
rue corridor 40, 47

Saarinen, Eero 131
Sabará 10
Sagres 142, *143*, 144–147
Salão de Arquitetura Tropical, Rio de Janeiro (1933) 35
Salão dos Artistas Brasileiros, Rio de Janeiro (1929) 20
Santo Alexandre in Belem do Pará, altarpieces 111
Santo Antônio hill 158
Santos Dumont airport 78, 100; Estação de Hidroaviões 100
Santos, Paulo 12, 39, 98

São Miguel, Sete Povos das Missões, Rio Grande do Sul 100, *102*, 103, 105, 113
São Paulo 12, 15, 17, 19, 20, 35, 68, 132
saudade 123
Second World War 70, 81, 133, 138
Semana de Arte Moderna (Modern Art Week), São Paulo (1931) 15, 19
Sert, José Luis 4, 69, 132, 139
Serviço de Obras 39, 47, 59, 60, 78
Serviço do Patrimônio Histórico e Artístico Nacional (SPHAN) 6, 38, 68, 69, 85–90, 96, 98–102, 104, 107, 110, 111, 116, 117, 130, 142, 158
Siren, Heikki 164
skyscraper 10, 132
Smithson, Alison and Peter 4, 151, 163, 164
Sobral, Eduardo 157
Sociedade Brasileira de Belas Artes 9
Soeiro, Renato 89
Solar Monjope *see* Mariano Filho, José
Souza Aguiar, Eduardo 39–41, 59, 78
St. Louis Exposition (1904) 98
Syndicato Nacional de Engenheiros 42
synthesis of the arts, synthèse des arts, integration of the arts 77, 131, 134, 135, 138

tabula rasa 15
Tafuri, Manfredo 96
Team X 163, 164
Teixeira, Anísio 37, 39theory of convergent results 4, 151, 164
Times Square 161
Tiradentes (Joaquim José da Silva Xavier) 89
Toulon 4
tradition 3, 6, 13, 38, 47, 54, 77, 78, 82, 88, 89, 90, 96, 98, 106, 107, 110, 111, 117, 119, 120, 135, 145, 158, 161, 162
traditionalism, traditionalist 8–10, 13, 28
treliça panels 72, 75, 104, 118, 123

Uchoa, Hélio 19
UNESCO headquarters 6, 69, 130–133, 140; organization 6, 69, 130, 131, 134, 138, 157, 164
Unité d'Habitation 130
United States 70, 77, 81, 82, 136
Universidade do Brasil 5, 34, 38, 39, 47, 49, 86
Universidade do Distrito Federal 5, 28, 34, 37–39, 50, 86
University Board 16, 24, 25
University Campus: Rio de Janeiro 34, 41–43, 47, 49–52, 55, *56*, 57, 58, 59, 61, 68, 76, 135; Rome 41

University of Rio de Janeiro 16
USA *see* United States

Vago, Pierre 150
Valentim, Fernando 9, 10
van der Rohe, Mies 37, 107, 113
Vargas Era 6
Vargas, Getúlio 2, 5–7, 11, 22, 23, 38, 43, 44, 50, 59, 66, 68–71, 79, *81*, 82, 86–89, 144
Vasconcellos, Ernani 19, 40, 41, 43, 45, 50
Venice 6, 69, 130, 134, 138, 164
Veranda 110, 116–121, 123

vernacular architecture 6, 107
Versailles 3, 147
Victoria Regia 72, 75

Warchavchik, Gregori 5, 13, 17, 19–22, 26, 27, 28, 35, 36, *36*, 38, 44, 69, 113, 133; House in Rua da Bahia 35; House in Rua Itápolis 35; *see also* Costa, Lucio, projects
Wiener, Paul Lester 72
Wogenscky, André 133
Wright, Frank Lloyd 26, 27, 35

Zehrfuss, Bernard 131, 132
Zevi, Bruno 150